DISABILITY MEDIA STUDIES

Disability Media Studies

Edited by
Elizabeth Ellcessor *and* Bill Kirkpatrick

NEW YORK UNIVERSITY PRESS
New York

NEW YORK UNIVERSITY PRESS
New York
www.nyupress.org

© 2017 by New York University

References to Internet websites (URLs) were accurate at the time of writing. Neither the author nor New York University Press is responsible for URLs that may have expired or changed since the manuscript was prepared.

ISBN: 978-1-4798-6782-0 (hardback)
ISBN: 978-1-4798-4938-3 (paperback)

For Library of Congress Cataloging-in-Publication data, please contact the Library of Congress.

New York University Press books are printed on acid-free paper, and their binding materials are chosen for strength and durability. We strive to use environmentally responsible suppliers and materials to the greatest extent possible in publishing our books.

Manufactured in the United States of America

10 9 8 7 6 5 4 3 2 1

Also available as an ebook

CONTENTS

CHAPTERS BY TOPIC (MEDIUM)

Introduction

Toward a Disability Media Studies

ELIZABETH ELLCESSOR, MACK HAGOOD, AND
BILL KIRKPATRICK

In a crowded mall, a flash mob dances to the 1983 synth-pop hit "Safety Dance," led by a slightly nerdy guy in a red sweater-vest (fig. I.1). He kicks, he gyrates, and for the grand finale he strides through the air, held up by other dancers as crowds of shoppers cheer. Then the music stops, he is dropped unceremoniously back into his wheelchair, and Artie's dream of able-bodiedness ends in dejection at the reality of his disabled existence.

Figure I.1. A group of young men, with Artie front and center, doing a hip-hop-inspired dance in a shopping mall.

This scene from *Glee* (Fox, 2009–2015)[1] met with sweeping critical praise: the *A. V. Club*'s Todd VanDerWerff said it "might be THE best" episode of *Glee* ever, while *Time*'s James Poniewozik called it "entertaining, arresting and moving in an unqualified sense."[2] But the representation of disability is complicated. The admirable politics of visibility that led *Glee* to include a wheelchair user as a central character are undermined by the industrially convenient casting of an able-bodied actor (Kevin McHale) in the part. Mainstream critics praised McHale's supposedly realistic performance, but persons with disabilities[3] pointed out that, in fact, his acting was all wrong, his contorted posture an "inaccurate portrayal of the way an average paraplegic sits."[4] Even when the show had Artie dancing in his wheelchair, his moves were a pale imitation of the strength and artistry of dance troupes like AXIS that incorporate wheelchairs.[5] The storyline itself—in which Artie dreams (not for the last time) of a better existence as an able-bodied person—reinforced the dominant but problematic idea that people with disabilities are inevitably miserable and want nothing more than to be "fixed."[6] Clearly, many disagreed that the show's depictions were an "unqualified" success.

Not only is the representation of disability complicated, but the issue is becoming more urgent. As medical science achieves new breakthroughs in the "repair" of impairments, media representations of disability are proliferating as never before. In the early 21st century, television shows from *House* (Fox, 2004–2012) to *Breaking Bad* (AMC, 2008–2013) to *Switched at Birth* (ABC Family, 2011–2017) to *Friday Night Lights* (NBC, 2006–2011) prominently featured characters with disabilities. Major films like *Avatar* (James Cameron, 2009), *The King's Speech* (Tom Hooper, 2010), and *The Theory of Everything* (James Marsh, 2014), among countless others, make disability central. Indeed, the full gamut of popular culture—from athletes racing on carbon-fiber legs to viral videos of Deaf persons switching on their new cochlear implants—is awash in representations of disability. Beyond representation, disability is at the center of important technological innovations and political debates regarding a range of media technologies, such as the Digital Rights Management on e-books that ostensibly protects copyrights but has the side effect of preventing blind people from activating needed speech-to-text features.

Given all this, the question for researchers and students becomes: how do we make sense of the relationships between disability and media? We need perspectives and methodological tools to analyze how disability shapes media texts, technologies, and industries—and how our media, in turn, shape what it means to be "disabled" or "able-bodied" in contemporary society. We require ways of understanding disability and media in terms of political and economic forces; epistemology (how we come to know the world) and phenomenology (how we experience it); the stories we tell about it and the goals and constraints of the media industries that circulate those stories; material technologies and official policies; and audiences' understandings of themselves and the world. We need theories and strategies that help us grasp the interplay of disability and popular culture, account for the slippery constructedness of "disability" and "able-bodiedness," incorporate the knowledges and lived experiences of people marked as "disabled," and analyze struggles over meaning, inclusion, and power.

Two main academic disciplines currently offer many of the theories and methods we need: disability studies and critical-cultural media studies. The rich history of disability studies provides a wealth of insights into disability as narrative trope, cultural identity, lived experience, socioeconomic status, and political category. Media studies is a humanities-centered, mostly qualitative field that explores how the media work as cultural, political, and economic institutions, as sites of meaning-making and ideological contestation, and as resources for social and individual identity formation and expression.

Importantly, however, neither disability studies nor media studies, on its own, has adequately grappled with the complexities of disability and media *together*. Scholars in each field are generating useful insights and approaches, but they are far from integrating the insights or building on the approaches of the other. In fact, often they are not even talking to each other: each has its own conferences, journals, Facebook groups, etc., and still rare is the crossover scholar who feels equally at home in both fields. Our claim is that these fields need to learn from each other—have an interdisciplinary conversation, share insights and perspectives, and adapt the most useful theories and methodologies from each other—in order to advance our understanding of media and disability. This book stages one such conversation and begins to demonstrate the power of *disability media studies* (DMS), a scholarly orientation and research agenda that reflects awareness of—and then builds on—the strengths of these two areas. There is excellent work being done on *both* sides, and our purpose in this anthology is to help each understand the value and contributions of the other so that, in concert, they may develop this emerging field.

What is the nature of this conversation? We get into details below, but three overarching hopes form our vision. First, through this dialog, we hope that more disability scholars will move beyond textual analysis of media representations to consider more fully the role of media within economic and ideological circuits of production and reception. Second, we hope that media scholars will become aware of a broader range of embodiments that shape and are shaped by our encounters with media. In other words, the field needs to recognize dis/ability as central to the study of media. Third, and above all, we hope that *all* scholars will recognize themselves in the critically oriented, humanities-centered concern with social, cultural, and economic justice that unites both disability studies and media studies, energizing their scholarship and helping develop disability media studies on theoretical, methodological, and political common ground.

This collection brings together these scholarly traditions in the belief that their proximity and cross-pollination will prove useful to readers and generative to scholars. We do not wish for this volume, and the interventions it offers, to constrain disability media studies by naming it: in staging a deliberately cross-disciplinary conversation between chapters, we leave open powerful possibilities for ongoing innovation and theoretical germination. In this introduction, then, we will outline the foundations and current state of disability studies and media studies before staking out the common ground upon which disability media studies can be built.

Disability Studies

Disability studies is a relatively new field whose scholarship has emerged within a range of traditions, primarily rhetoric, English, ethics, art history, gender and queer studies, and the social sciences (including education and developmental psychology). Although disability studies is gaining a structural foothold in universities thanks to an ever-increasing number of dedicated programs, this interdisciplinary legacy—as well as its widespread, even fundamental orientation toward accessibility and activism beyond the academy—is responsible for many of the core strengths and achievements of disability studies scholarship.

By interrogating the social, physical, economic, and ideological conditions of disability and able-bodiedness, disability studies in both its scholarly and activist modes has challenged the subaltern status of persons with disabilities and opened new areas of inquiry across the political, cultural, and academic spectrum. It has given us new tools with which to study narrative and representation, led the study of embodiment in new directions, and been at the forefront of research on norms and normalization. For media scholars and students new to disability studies, we would highlight three core contributions as a way into the field: its articulation of *disability as socially constructed*, the *identification of and challenges to the "normate" subject position*, and the *emphasis upon lived experience as an epistemological basis* for making claims.

First, disability studies has challenged the medicalization and pathologization of disability, widely known as the *"medical model" of disability*. The medical model understands disability as an ontological "fact" in the world rather than a constructed social and political position. People with bodily differences "have something wrong with them" and are regarded as medical problems to be solved. This is still the dominant, "common sense" way of thinking about disability. But pathologization inevitably leads to social and political marginalization; for persons with disabilities, it can lead to existential threats, such as involuntary sterilization, selective abortion, or euthanasia, while leaving unaltered the structures and ideologies that privilege able-bodiedness and devalue alternative embodiments.

In the 1970s, disability activists in the UK challenged the medical model and argued instead for the *"social model" of disability*,[7] which has also been taken up by disability scholars. The social model draws a distinction between "impairment" and "disability"; it posits that while bodies may have *impairments*, those impairments become *disabilities* only in the context of specific physical and social environments. In that sense, disability is not (as in the medical model) a "fact" about a person, but a status imposed by society: needing a wheelchair, for example, only becomes a "disability" given the absence of ramps and elevators—or given the attitudes, beliefs, and power structures encountered in a discriminatory ableist society.

The social model has enormous political implications, since it suggests that disability is not a physical or mental "defect" that inevitably locates certain individuals outside the bounds of "normal" society, but a socially constructed, oppressed, minority identity imposed on certain individuals because of their *perceived* difference.[8] From this position, it becomes possible to advocate for rights and resources and to use the legal and justice systems to fight discrimination. So powerful is the social model in making civil-rights arguments that activists successfully used it to advocate for the Americans with Disabilities Act (1990), and its logic informs that act's language and provisions. While it can be problematic to lump together individuals with wildly varying experiences, identities, and challenges under the homogenizing category "disabled," there can be, depending on context, strategic advantage in constructing an essentialized "disabled" identity in organizing for social change.[9]

Aside from the social model's political utility, derived from its rejection of the ontology of disability, it helps to understand how the model has shaped the study of media within disability studies, which is through what Mack Hagood calls the "sociotextual approach": the pairing of the social model and textual analysis. This research has been heavily invested in critiquing stereotypical representations of persons with disabilities, arguing that these depictions contribute to ableist attitudes, which in turn inform and justify practices and policies that reproduce the social and material conditions of disability. For instance, Colin Barnes has argued that harmful "disabling stereotypes" abound in books, films, and television, while Martin Norden identifies and critiques problematic disability tropes such as "the innocent" and "the cyborg villain."[10] Some scholars have extended such analyses to consider representational patterns; an influential example referenced several times in this volume is Rosemarie Garland-Thomson's taxonomy of representational strategies for depicting persons with disabilities: the sentimental mode, the wondrous mode, and so forth.[11] Through such analyses, disability studies has demonstrated how people with impairments may be disabled by the prejudice and othering that is modeled, legitimated, and recirculated by media depictions.[12]

While the social model and sociotextual approach remain useful in destabilizing assumptions about disability and the stereotypes that support those assumptions, they have come under critique for oversimplifying the complex relationships among bodies, experiences, institutions, technologies, ideologies, and representations that constitute "disability" in any given society. For example, Robert McRuer acknowledges how generative Garland-Thomson's taxonomy has been, but he argues that it is less a universal framework than a reflection of contemporary ideas about disability.[13] Furthermore, media analyses informed by the sociotextual approach tend toward the moral evaluation of "positive" or "negative" depictions of disability, rather than considering representation in a broader context of media production, consumption, interpretation, and cultural impact.

The impairment/disability dichotomy at the heart of the social model has also been critiqued from a poststructuralist perspective, especially the work of philosopher Michel Foucault and feminist theorist Judith Butler, which says that impairment and disability *both* are socially constructed.[14] In other words, if the social model maintains that "disability" is not a "fact" about a person, then poststructuralists add that neither is "impairment" a fact, certainly no more so than race and gender are "facts" about people. In this view, discursive power informs our perception and valuation of bodily non-normativity, making "impairment" an unstable category that only has meaning when measured against ever-shifting and contextually dependent bodily norms.[15] For example, vision that would count as "impaired" in contemporary Western society, given automobiles, the centrality of literacy, and other vision-dependent phenomena, likely would often have been considered within the range of the "normal" in the agrarian contexts of earlier centuries.

This strong social constructionism has also influenced a second important contribution of disability studies: the identification of the *"normate" subject position* as constructed and reproduced via a range of material, social, and cultural institutions. In short, not only are the categories of "impaired" and "disabled" socially constructed, but so are the categories of "normal" and "able-bodied." Lennard Davis's foundational essay on "constructing normalcy" traces the transition from the social valorization of ideal (and thus unattainable) forms of embodiment to the moral ascendency of normal (and thus ostensibly possible) bodies.[16] The pursuit of normalcy becomes an imperative: the supposed attainability and desirability of normalcy translate into a rejection of all that is outside the norm and encourage—even compel—individuals to mold themselves into a hegemonically dominant form of embodiment.[17] Davis traces the emergence of prescriptive "normality" in the nineteenth century, its creation of the disabled person as a "problem," and its subsequent destabilization by the proliferation of scientific and medical markers of abnormality (which have, in the meantime, become so numerous that "normal" may now be losing its meaning).[18]

Garland-Thomson extended the theorization of norms in her coinage of the term "normate" to refer to a privileged body, without stigma, that functions as a universal type in a given society.[19] The critical potential of the normate stems from its descriptive power, as the recognition of the normate subject position makes it possible to identify how such positions are upheld by built environments, social institutions, and cultural discourses including media texts. Furthermore, by naming the usually invisible or unmarked norm (as "cis" does in gender theory), the normate also enables theorization without recourse to a possibly essentialized category of "disability" that, as mentioned above, invites difficulties of definition and scope. Returning to the introductory example of *Glee*'s Artie, we can see how even an ostensibly "pro-disability" text reinforces the fundamental desirability of the normate and, in its ableist implication that non-able-bodied persons can never be truly happy, works to enforce bodily normalcy.

Given the emphasis on social construction in the social model and the normate, it is important to note that many disability scholars have argued that some embodied phenomena are, in fact, irreducible to social constructions. Susan Wendell, for instance, highlights the experience of pain as a component of many disabled people's lives that is inherently subjective, rather than social.[20] This leads to the third major contribution of disability studies (and disability activism): the insistence upon *lived experiences* as a basis for critique and analysis. Traced back to activists' calls for "nothing about us, without us," this is an epistemology that refutes the medical model of disability by treating the voices and marginalized perspectives of people with disabilities as valid sources of knowledge.[21]

This valuation of lived experience has two major implications. First, it means that people with disabilities are welcomed as creators of knowledge in a range of scholarship. For instance, many scholars working within disability studies "claim disability"[22] or otherwise choose to articulate their "relationship to disability."[23] Additionally, academic works may include disabled voices through various forms of direct quotation and may offer credit to participants or collaborators beyond standard academic practice.[24] Second, this epistemological stance entails taking subjective forms of knowledge seriously, including experiences of pain, specific narratives of oppression, and phenomenologies of everyday life. Disability is never a single experience or a generalizable phenomenon; it is always multiple, always contains contradictions, and is, at best, a political category used to group shared experiences without erasing the differences that persist.

Several disability theorists attempt to bring together the above threads—the political and critical advantages of social constructionist perspectives, including the social model and the normate, and the significant insights offered by the valuation of subjective disability experiences—in new ways. For instance, Tobin Siebers critiques the poststructuralist perspective associated with Foucault and Butler for its inability to grapple with "the difficult physical realities faced by people with disabilities" and its tendency to present their bodies "in ways that are conventional, conformist, and unrecognizable" to people living with disability.[25] Siebers instead proposes the concept of "complex embodiment," which "raises awareness of the effects of disabling environments on people's lived experience of the body" (recalling the social model) but which also emphasizes that "some factors affecting disability, such as chronic pain, secondary health effects, and aging, derive from the body" (incorporating material contexts, phenomenology, and medicalization).[26] Similarly, Alison Kafer offers a "political/relational model" of disability in which disability arises from the variable relationships of bodies, minds, and social and physical environments.[27] In this model, neither disability, ability, nor impairment is self-evident. Kafer agrees that impairment and disability are both socially constructed in context but argues that the social model may ignore lived experiences of impairment and politically marginalize disabled people who are interested in medical interventions or cure.[28] In terming her model "political/relational," Kafer attends to the dynamics of power that shape particular relationships among people, institutions, culture, and material structures and that produce disability as a meaningful category of analysis.

Siebers and Kafer also suggest different ways of complicating the category of disability by situating it in relation to other identities. Siebers offers complex embodiment as an expansion of intersectionality,[29] a feminist theory by which analysis of social oppression must consider multiple axes of identity, including race, gender, class, and sexuality. Kafer draws upon Jasbir Puar's theory of "assemblage," which challenges the essentialism that can inhere in identity categories; disability (like race, gender, and sexuality) is thus considered "as events, actions, and encounters between bodies."[30] Such theoretical complications pave the way for more nuanced analyses of media and culture that go beyond the sociotextual and that invite more direct engagement with the subjective knowledges of persons with disabilities.

While calling attention to these specific contributions and scholars, we also recognize that there are too many important concepts and studies emerging from disability studies—including recent intersectional work on media—to highlight them all here, although many are referenced and explained in the chapters that follow.[31] Nonetheless, as a primer on core concepts for those new to disability studies, we hope that the above already begins to illustrate what disability studies can offer to other disciplines.

Media Studies

There are many varieties of media studies, with varying methods, underlying assumptions, and names. Schools and scholars dedicated to the study of media may be affiliated with journalism, mass communications, rhetoric, film, telecommunications, information science, or many other nomenclatures. This plethora of names sits atop a variety of approaches: some work, termed "communication science" or "media effects," draws upon psychological or other social scientific methods to study the effects of engagement with media on our thoughts and behaviors;[32] "mass communications" tends to focus on the economic and institutional aspects of media systems, content, and audiences, often with an emphasis on persuasion, public relations, and propaganda;[33] film studies is often indebted to art history and formal or aesthetic analysis of texts, to traditions of literary interpretation, or to a range of theories of reception from (most prominently) Freudian and cognitive psychology to analyze film-audience relationships;[34] and we're just scratching the surface. There is much excellent work in all of these traditions—some of it related to disability—yet they are not the focus of this volume.

Instead, this collection foregrounds—and posits as a productive foundation for DMS—a strand of media studies based in the critical humanities and in which media are analyzed first and foremost for their role in struggles over social, political, and economic *power*. In this approach, media texts, audiences, industries, and technologies are inseparable from their specific social contexts, i.e., their attendant political, material, and economic conditions, since it is within specific contexts that particular meanings have particular consequences for social relations and power. Since these struggles are often expressed in relationships between media and race, gender, class, sexuality, and other categories of difference, media studies is radically interdisciplinary at its core, borrowing from feminist theory and queer studies to analyze gender and the media, from Marxist traditions to study class and socioeconomic status and the media, and so on. Indeed, many within disability studies might draw on similar groundings in British cultural studies, poststructuralism, and feminist, queer, and critical race scholarship.

To help orient scholars coming from disability studies who wish to engage with new ways of studying media, we will highlight two key theoretical approaches and methods that set media studies apart from other humanities-based approaches: the valuation of *popular culture in everyday life* and an *integrated approach* to the study of media that uses diverse methodologies to consider the production, circulation, and reception of mediated culture in specific social and industrial contexts.

First, the study of *popular culture* means taking seriously the elements of everyday life, including the pleasures available in media texts. In contrast to aesthetic approaches that seek to separate "good/high" art from "bad/low" art, or effects-based approaches that try to identify causal relationships between media consumption and one's thoughts and behaviors, media studies is interested in how people actually make sense of media artifacts—even socially stigmatized media forms—and what they do with them as they go about their lives. Again, power is central: drawing on Michel de Certeau's conception of the practice of everyday life as a space in which individuals and social formations may exercise agency and "poach" at the margins of powerful social structures and ideologies, media studies has sought to highlight the politics of commonplace activities, pleasures, and cultural artifacts.[35] A well-known example is Janice Radway's study of romance novels, a genre widely considered "trashy" but in which (mostly women) readers often find empowerment, not to mention valuable pleasures.[36] Popular culture, in this view, is a site of continual struggle, a space in which the relationships of power and oppression in a society can be exposed, challenged, reinforced, and rearticulated by those who find power and pleasure within cultural artifacts. It can also provide resources for identity formation, coalition and capacity building, and collective political action.[37]

Popular culture is not synonymous with "mass" or mainstream culture; instead, it is "popular" precisely because it is taken up by individuals who recognize in it something that enables them to make sense of their everyday lives and relationships, and that helps them navigate their social and material world.[38] Of course, often the texts that offer such opportunities are those mass-produced by corporate media industries, so it is easy to dismiss them as unimportant at best and nefarious at worst: we are all familiar with complaints that "tawdry" reality shows like *Jersey Shore* (MTV, 2009–2012) "dumb down" our society. But media studies instead analyzes how individuals and groups encounter and use such cultural products in a variety of ways through a process of *negotiation*.

Negotiation refers to how readers selectively attend to and interpret texts to form their own meanings from them.[39] As advanced by Stuart Hall, the theory of negotiation recognizes that every complex text contains a wealth of possible meanings, and which ones you privilege will depend on your ideological position, social location, cultural context, and beliefs and values. The text will "prefer" some of its possible meanings by making them more obvious, appealing, or commonsensical within a given context, but it can never fully shut down or erase alternatives. Audiences might resist the text's dominant meanings, attend more to those ineradicable alternatives for their own pleasure or empowerment, or make "perverse" sense of the text to fit their own context. As readers (viewers, listeners, etc.), we "negotiate" with the text, situationally adapting our reading to our specific contexts, needs, or pleasures. Unlike certain influential approaches in the field of English that privilege the meanings "within" the text as the ones of greatest interest to the analyst, media studies seeks to identify meanings that *could* be activated

Figure I.2. Artie, sitting in his wheelchair, alone and looking wistful in the shopping mall.

and subject positions that *could* be adopted when "reading" (making sense of) a given text in a given context.

For example, returning to *Glee* (fig. I.2), we may adopt the preferred reading of the text by endorsing the inclusion of Artie and enjoying the show's validation of his importance and humanity. In doing so, we would also accede to a dominant cultural ableism, taking for granted that someone with a mobility impairment would dream of, and aspire to, able-bodiedness. Alternatively, we may adopt a more negotiated or even oppositional reading that works against such ideologies. We might bristle as the text suggests that Artie is incomplete or unfulfilled because of his disability, and despite our pleasures in the text, we may never forget that, on an industrial level, the producers hired an able-bodied actor for the role. In other words, rather than simply adopting the meanings put before us (much less the messages that the creators may consciously *want* us to adopt), our response to *Glee* may be complicated and ambivalent, marked by both pleasure and aggravation, endorsement and rejection. One task of the scholar, in this view, is to move beyond a text's "preferred" reading in order to discover how audiences are *actually* negotiating textual meanings in specific settings, or how those negotiations shift depending on the social context or audiences' own experiences.

There is controversy within media studies about how significant this struggle might be in any given case: in the face of pervasive and systemic inequality and discrimination, what are the potential political roles of a popular culture that (according to some critiques) functions primarily to reproduce dominant ideologies of consumer capitalism?[40] We cannot explore such questions at length here, but we do find extraordinary value in an approach that takes audience agency and popular culture— even "bad" culture—seriously, even in the face of structural oppression. Thus one of the contributions of media studies is to interrogate the politics of popular culture and the processes of negotiation.

A second contribution of media studies to a disability media studies is methodological; how, after all, can we possibly account for the diversity of meanings, interests, and contexts that are relevant to understanding the place of popular media in everyday life? Media studies approaches are less about interpreting texts than tracing the ideological struggles that surround media artifacts using mixed methodologies. In other words, while many scholars in English embrace the negotiated nature of meaning, they tend to limit themselves methodologically to textual analysis, thus missing out on a lot of contextual information offered by the study of text, audience, industry, social context, and technology together. While textual analysis remains important to media studies, it is just one part of an *integrated approach* to media.

Taking such an approach means studying media texts not in relative isolation, but together with their industrial conditions of production, the social, political, and material contexts of their reception, and the active participation of audiences in producing meanings—all as interrelated phenomena.[41] What makes this approach useful is its insistence on the circulation of artifacts, meanings, and power among various sites, texts, institutions, and individuals. In other words, an integrated approach to the study of media and culture rejects the limitations of a purely textual (or representational) analysis as well as the simplistic explanations of an industrial, top-down analysis that ascribes *too* much power to authors, cultural producers, or the economic system itself. Mediated culture is, instead, the complicated result of interactions among industries, audiences, economics, and broader social and political contexts, none of which completely control the meaning-making process.

Media studies scholarship might be loosely grouped into studies of texts, audiences, industries, and social contexts, though scholars often articulate linkages among these domains. Methodologically, textual studies include aesthetic, discursive, and representational analyses.[42] Studies of audiences, often referred to as reception studies, incorporate ethnographic and interview methods, as well as theories of phenomenology and affect.[43] One strand of this scholarship, fan studies, has been particularly attentive to the ways in which audiences go "beyond" a text to create new cultural artifacts and practices out of existing cultural material and produce new ways of interacting with media.[44] Critical industry studies brings together cultural studies and political economy approaches, often using discursive analysis and interviews or other ethnographic methods to illuminate the dynamics of media production and distribution;[45] critical policy studies similarly unpack the meanings embedded in media regulations.[46] Studies that prioritize media's social context often employ critical historiography and ideological analyses, connecting media texts to larger sociohistorical struggles.[47] There are many media scholars who articulate texts, audiences, industries, and social contexts, particularly with respect to identity; a paradigmatic example is Julie D'Acci's *Defining Women*, which included detailed audience and industrial analysis and linked *Cagney and Lacey* (CBS, 1982–1988) to a larger context of U.S. televisual representations of women and gender politics in the 1980s.[48] More recently, *How to Watch Television*—a collection of many scholars' work—offers snapshots of many of these methodological approaches and demonstrates how they might inform one another and foster more complex understandings of media, their producers, their audiences, and their situatedness in time and space.[49]

A final point in this regard is that, although media studies is concerned with the production of meanings in these multiple interactions and contexts, such meanings do not remain at the level of ideas. Instead, they exist in the material sense of discursive and economic practices that involve physical bodies doing things, physical places that are constructed in particular ways, and subjective feeling or affect that is generated when audiences encounter texts.[50] In other words, meaning and materiality are inseparable: ideas are embodied in and shaped by material conditions and human practice, made meaningful by the discourses that inform them and that they in turn inflect. Media technologies themselves raise further issues of materiality and embodiment: how we interact with buttons, dials, or gaming consoles; how we plug in earbuds or position ourselves to view screens; how manufacturers imagine the bodies that will engage with their creations; and in countless other ways.

As the above suggests, this approach to media studies makes media analysis exponentially more complex than textual analysis alone. This is why the methodologies and perspectives of media studies can be so powerful, and why we hope more disability scholars will embrace them: in the negotiation of culture, situated within large and small struggles over meaning and power, we see opportunities for agency and self-expression, for political change, and for reimaginings of the "common-sense" (hegemonic) ways of being in the world.

Toward a Disability Media Studies

From the preceding reviews of disability studies and media studies, it is apparent that there is common ground to be found in the goals, methods, and values of each. Disability studies' validation of the epistemology of lived experience, for instance, is complemented by media studies' valorization of everyday life. More basically, as both fields are invested in the identification of relations of power and oppression, and the transformation of those relations via critique and activism aimed at both representations and structures, we see a unity of purpose that indicates a powerful collaborative potential. In this section we identify the most notable benefits of a disability media studies fusion, then offer a brief summary of how each chapter speaks to this shared project of formulating a richly contextual and politically engaged field.

First, we believe that the theories and methods of media studies can expand and enhance the ways that disability scholars analyze media texts, technologies, and cultures. Due to the rich attention that media studies gives to the politics of popular culture, its pervasive interest in negotiation as foundational to the production and reception of media artifacts, and its integrated approach to the study of media, it can help disability studies not just move (even further) beyond the sociotextual approach when studying mediated cultures, but also do a better job of meeting the specific theoretical and methodological challenges of studying electronic media in context and with appropriate complexity. Such an approach would consider more thoroughly how media representations are connected to systems of structure and agency, better accounting for economic and material institutions and forces, social and political contexts of media production and reception, technological limitations and affordances, and the ways that audiences negotiate meanings. In practice, this suggests the need for more ethnographic and reception research from disability scholars of media, a more thorough understanding and appreciation of the political economy of media production, and the industrial strategies, cultures, and practices that inform the creation and distribution of media representations.

Second, media studies could clearly benefit from more interaction with disability studies. Most urgently, media scholars need to elevate disability to greater significance among their categories of analysis. Despite emerging from an interest in social and cultural power, the field has been slow to address issues of disability on anything like the scale seen in analyses of race, class, gender, and sexuality. With questions of normativity and marginality so crucial to the discipline, it is not entirely clear why media studies is still far from incorporating disability into its working knowledges, standard curricula, and professional routines. Nonetheless, as the contributions to this volume demonstrate, disability is not just "another Other"[51] but in fact raises profound issues of theory, epistemology, and methodology that enrich the study of media and society.

Beyond that, we hope that more media scholars will engage with concepts such as the social model (and its successors) and the "normate." We suspect, following Gerard Goggin and Christopher Newell,[52] that many of our media studies colleagues, even though they have moved past essentialist understandings of race and gender, still have an implicit understanding of disability rooted in the medical model. This explanation, however, is no justification. An encounter with theories from disability studies will help more media scholars see the constructedness of disability and able-bodiedness, the ideological power of ableism and bodily normativity, and the role of media technologies, institutions, and representations in producing and upholding—as well as potentially challenging—these constructions and ideologies. Such insights would align well with media studies work on hegemonic representation and the ways in which texts, audiences, and institutions interact.

Additionally, media studies would benefit from greater appreciation of an epistemology that trusts lived and physical experiences as a basis for critique and analysis. We recognize that this raises significant theoretical questions that we are not able to delve into here—such as how to think about the discursive construction of subjectivity—but we welcome scholarship that continues to explore such issues and believe the encounter will be productive. For example, media studies (with notable exceptions)[53] has tended to neglect the physical experiences and technological interactions that structure media use at a material level, often silently assuming normative forms of spectatorship or sensory engagement. As Mara Mills and Jonathan Sterne have shown, however, we need to understand the ways that media and information technologies are intertwined with the standardization and regulation of the human body.[54] This gap could be addressed in part through increased attention to the normate in conjunction with media studies methodologies for studying reception and its valuation of the practices of everyday life. By studying the lived experiences of people with disabilities—who often use media quite differently and, in doing so, reveal unnoticed limitations and unexpected possibilities of media technologies, structures, and texts—disability media studies can better address media's materiality and a wider range of practices of reception.

We also want to emphasize the many areas of overlap between disability studies and media studies. For example, both fields are radically open to useful ideas across the humanities and borrow freely from feminist cultural theory, critical race theory, queer studies, and others. Even at the level of specific theories, the stage for dialog is set; one example invoked by multiple authors in this book, coming from both disciplines, is Michel Foucault's notions of biopower and biopolitics.[55] These concern the ways that modern states use scientific discourses, techniques of normalization and standardization, and surveillance of their populations' health and biological functioning (from birth rates to body mass index to sexual behavior) to regulate conduct and manage society. Media studies has taken up these concepts in work on everything from makeover shows to data mining,[56] while disability studies has found biopolitics especially generative in analyzing how some bodily differences are set apart as particularly threatening for the state.[57] By already sharing some theoretical vocabularies, then, the two fields are primed to meet on a disability media studies common ground.

Finally, we firmly believe that the political impulses of these fields are complimentary and would be strengthened through cross-pollination. In the words of Rosemarie Garland-Thomson, "The aim of much disability studies is to reimagine disability, to reveal how the storied quality of disability invents and reinvents the world we share."[58] In short, she calls for attention to discourse as a cultural and material force that structures our experiences, which clearly aligns with the political imperatives of media studies: the fundamental political commitments of both fields are tied to questions of normativity, marginality, unjust distributions of power, and the role of ideology in maintaining systems of inequality. By working in concert, a disability media studies might produce scholarship that radically rethinks received knowledges about the workings of culture, society, and identity. What we seek is not simply a sharing but a fundamental reorientation toward interdisciplinarity that results in new questions about how, where, and with what consequences media and bodies are co-constitutive within specific social contexts, material conditions, political realms, policy frameworks, and economic and historical landscapes.

We are encouraged that these fusions are beginning to occur in scholarship across several continents, within a variety of publications, and at a range of disciplinary locations. Ever more journals, special issues, monographs, and other collections of research focus on media and disability, bringing together work on accessibility, translation, representation, health, gender, race, and other thematics with studies of television, digital media, film, medical imaging, visual culture, and other forms of mediation.[59] Furthermore, in a demonstration of how vibrant and productive a disability media studies can be, scholars across the disciplines are bringing media studies and disability studies into fruitful dialog with queer theory, postcolonialism, fat studies, gender studies, and more.[60]

The present collection joins this work by providing an accessible collection of essays in which scholars grapple with the ways in which disability studies and media studies may inform and enrich one another. To help expand and deepen the scholarly interchange between these fields, we have brought together a wide range of scholarship that addresses disability in relation to texts, industries, technologies, and audiences. We asked our authors to analyze their objects of study with an awareness of speaking beyond their normal disciplinary audience—in the sense of both making their work accessible beyond their disciplinary colleagues and striving to chip away at those disciplinary walls in the process. Each is addressing certain fundamental questions: How does your study engage and extend questions of media representations beyond the textual? How does it expand existing media scholarship by incorporating an appreciation of normalization, ableism, and alternative epistemologies? How does it contribute to the interdisciplinary dialog between disability studies and media studies?

The resulting essays do not represent a perfect synthesis of disability and media studies, whereby the scholars from each tradition have suddenly adopted the theories, methods, and perspectives of the other; we are not presenting a "third way" or demonstration of "how it should be done." Instead, we see this volume as part of an ongoing dialog about the interdisciplinary study of disability and media. We believe such conversation is the most productive way forward for better understanding the intersections of media and disability. No reader will find equal value in all chapters, but we believe all readers can find something of value in each.

Our aim is academic, to be sure, but it is also political: as representations of disability proliferate across an ever-wider range of media, and as new technologies give rise to new questions of access and open new possibilities for—but also new barriers to—cultural participation, it becomes an increasingly urgent social issue to understand the countless ways in which ability and disability drive our cultural narratives and frame our public discourse. The essays that follow begin to develop that understanding and, more importantly, point the way for other scholars, students, producers, and consumers of media to grapple productively with media, popular culture, and the meanings of disability.

How to Use this Book

In order to stage an interdisciplinary conversation and exchange of ideas, this book is organized thematically. Scholars are not grouped by background or approach, but are placed according to the themes and topics that they address (production, gender, technology, etc.). Such an arrangement may be particularly attractive in teaching this text, as students can be guided through points of commonality and difference, extending these interdisciplinary conversations into the classroom. In less structured contexts, this arrangement may similarly prompt reflection and suggest means for further developing disability media studies in our readers' own scholarship, public engagement, or experiences of popular culture. As an alternative to the thematic organization, we have provided a table of contents that lists chapters by medium (see Chapters by Topic [Medium]). Such groupings may prove more resonant for particular teaching needs and may suggest a starting point for scholars coming to this text with a background specifically in film or television studies.

In addition, we have provided short abstracts at the beginning of each chapter, summarizing the topic and enabling readers to quickly recognize the tradition from which an author is coming to this conversation. Each abstract also highlights the chapter's primary contributions to those from outside of that field, indicating what it might offer to a larger DMS approach. Though we cannot predict or direct the cross-pollinations that this collection may inspire, we hope these abstracts will help readers understand the rationale for each chapter's inclusion and its value beyond its home discipline and core readership. These abstracts may also be useful in making decisions about teaching; often, those chapters stemming from the disciplinary home of the course or instructor might be more easily taught first, building on recognizable ideas, while those that offer less familiar approaches may require additional time or supplementary activities in the classroom.

In short, though readers are certainly invited to read this collection in its entirety, there is no expectation that they read linearly. Nomadic ventures across and among the chapters and afterwords are encouraged, and alternative imaginings of structure are welcome. In these different arrangements of chapters or sections, different issues may rise to the forefront of thought and discussion, and such diversity of use and interpretation will only foster the growth of disability media studies as a more robust and dynamic field.

Chapter Breakdown

The first thematic section focuses on Access and Media Production. It begins with "Kickstarting Community," in which Elizabeth

Ellcessor considers how crowdfunding and online community for the web series *My Gimpy Life* (2013–2014) illuminate what she calls "cultural accessibility"—the ability to access culturally relevant, collaborative, and inclusive media. Next, in "*After School Special* Education," Julie Passanante Elman shows how disability media studies can illuminate the workings of traditional media industries, demonstrating how ABC's *After School Specials* (1972–1995) consistently linked heterosexuality with able-bodiedness and represented adolescence as a process of "overcoming disability."

The second section focuses on Disability and Race. Alex Porco's chapter, "Throw Yo' Voice Out," exemplifies how disability media studies can reveal unexpected dimensions of texts by showing how non-normative voices (including lisps, slurs, and other markers of vocal disability) intersect with race to become signifiers of authenticity and originality in hip-hop. Lori Kido Lopez's chapter, "How to Stare at Your Television," considers how "freak shows" and their reality TV successors implicate viewers in the witnessing of racialized dynamics of ability.

In the next section, Disability and Gender, Ellen Samuels's "Prosthetic Heroes," situates *Iron Man 3* (Shane Black, 2013) in relation to the reintegration of disabled veterans and the broader War on Terror. Her focus on masculinity is complemented by a focus on femininity in D. Travers Scott and Meagan Bates's analysis of advertisements for anxiety medications. They argue that these commercials do not merely feminize mental impairments like anxiety and depression, but in fact produce them as constitutive of "normal" contemporary femininity.

The three chapters in the next section offer very different approaches to the study of Disability and Celebrity Culture. First, Krystal Cleary draws upon queer and disability theory, audience research, and celebrity studies to analyze Lady Gaga's performances of disability, arguing that the mainstreaming of disability culture that some see in Gaga's jewel-encrusted wheelchairs and neck braces may equally be read as an appropriation that minimizes lived experiences of disability. Next, Katie Ellis and Gerard Goggin use South African sprinter Oscar Pistorius's fatal shooting of girlfriend Reeva Steenkamp to explore how disability is implicated in the governing of race, gender, sexuality, and normalcy. Finally, Tasha Oren demonstrates how three films about engineer and well-known Autist Temple Grandin reveal changing understandings of autism, as well as the possibilities inherent in film style to represent non-neurotypical individuals.

Reflections on Disability and Temporality ground the next two chapters. First, Shoshana Magnet and Amanda Watson investigate how comics and graphic novels allow for non-linear representations of time, making it possible to depict the ways that people with disabilities are made to suffer under modern temporalities. Then, Robert McRuer analyzes the film *Any Day Now* (Travis Fine, 2012), demonstrating how "homonormativity," or the mainstreaming of queer life narratives into dominant social frameworks such as marriage, fails to incorporate disability, leaving room for radical challenges to this social order.

The last section, Disability and Technology, explores contexts in which mediation may rely upon or produce disability. First, Toby Miller examines the physical, economic, and environmental consequences of media technologies on the people who assemble and disassemble them, showing how disablement is intrinsic to the social inequalities upon which we build our media systems. Mack Hagood's chapter, "Disability and Biomediation," uses the case of tinnitus—a condition marked by a ringing in the ears—and its attendant diagnostic and therapeutic media to propose a framework for the study of biotechnological mediation. Finally, Bill Kirkpatrick demonstrates how popular conceptions of disability, through the rhetorical figure of the disabled "shut-in," shaped media policy in the 1920s while, as part of the same process, the emergence of radio changed the social and cultural meanings of disability.

The book also includes two afterwords, by leading scholars in disability and media studies, staging an initial conversation of the sort this volume aims to provoke. First, disability scholar Rachel Adams uses the case of eighteenth-century artist Matthias Buchinger as a starting point for her reflections on disability media studies, appreciating the ways that the contributions to this volume offer multiple frameworks for analyzing the layers of mediation and the complexities of disability that Buchinger represents, but also calling for more historical and international work. Then, from a media studies perspective, Mara Mills and Jonathan Sterne propose "dismediation," a method by which we seek out the media in disability, and the disability in media. Critiquing media studies canons and looking forward to new questions and strategies, this afterword offers a provocative future for disability media studies.

NOTES

1 *Glee*, "Dream On," directed by Joss Whedon, written by Brad Falchuk, Fox, May 18, 2010.

2 Todd VanDerWerff, "Glee: 'Dream On,'" *A.V. Club*, May 18, 2010, www.avclub. com; James Poniewozik, "Glee Watch: Dream until Your Dream Comes True," *Time*, May 19, 2010, http://entertainment.time.com.

3 Appropriate terminology has been a long-standing debate among disability scholars and activists. Many prominent disability organizations and policies, particularly in North America, favor the term *people with disabilities* as "person-first" language that foregrounds the core humanity of the individual. The problem with *people with disabilities* is that it seems to imply that disability and impairment are innate rather than constructed. In other contexts, *disabled people* is preferred because it avoids conflating impairment with disability and communicates the ways that people are "disabled" by society rather than by the "impairment" that constitutes their difference. The question of terminology is further complicated by the issue of those who are widely regarded as "disabled" but who themselves reject that construction; the best example is Deaf persons who understand themselves as belonging to a linguistic and cultural minority group, not as "impaired" or "disabled."

These debates are far from settled, and one can raise valid theoretical and political objections to all of the currently acceptable labels. In this volume, we have tended to prefer *persons with disabilities* (which highlights the diversity and citizenship of individuals, rather than the flattening of "people") as the term most frequently endorsed by prominent disability activists at the time we are writing; however, several authors have used other formulations in their chapters, a choice that we have respected. Furthermore, where it is most important we have privileged more theoretically precise—if perhaps somewhat jargony—language such as "bodily non-normativity." We encourage readers to remember that *no* term would be neutral or value-free and that our choices of language in this volume—almost certain to appear dated all too soon—are driven by fundamental respect and a commitment to social justice for "persons with disabilities."

4 Bob Vogel, "Irony of the Best-Known Wheelchair User," *Roho*, January 4, 2012, https://roho.com.

5 Kociemba, "'This Isn't Something I Can Fake.'"

6 Or, if all else fails, killed: the 2016 film *Me before You* (Thea Sharrock), for example, features a quadriplegic—again played by an able-bodied actor (Sam Claflin)—who chooses euthanasia over being a "burden" to the woman he loves.

7 Union of the Physically Impaired against Segregation and the Disability Alliance, "Fundamental Principles of Disability," *Centre for Disability Studies*, November 22, 1975, http://disability-studies.leeds.ac.uk.

8 Shakespeare, "The Social Model of Disability," 214–15; Corker and Shakespeare, *Disability/Postmodernity*.

9 For more on strategic essentialism, see Gayatri Chakravorty Spivak, "Subaltern Studies: Deconstructing Historiography," in Ranajit Guha and Gayatri Chakravorty Spivak, eds., *In Other Worlds: Essays in Cultural Politics* (Oxford: Oxford University Press, 1988): 197–221.

10 Barnes, "Disabling Imagery," 39; Norden, *The Cinema of Isolation*.

11 Garland-Thomson, "Seeing the Disabled."

12 Shakespeare, "Cultural Representation of Disabled People," 283.

13 McRuer, *Crip Theory*, 171–198.

14 Poststructuralism argues that what things are and what they mean are the result of discourse and discursive practices—from the language we use, to how we arrange ourselves in physical space, to how we imagine ourselves in relation to other people and the world. Because discourse is unstable and always changeable, that means that the world and our sense of it is also unstable: we might imagine some things to be natural and unalterable, but in fact they are the result of power struggles over meaning. French theorist Michel Foucault developed many of these ideas, while American philosopher Judith Butler has extended Foucault's theories to analyze, most influentially, gender and sexuality.

15 Tremain, "Foucault, Governmentality," 10–11.

16 Davis, "Constructing Normalcy."

17 See also work on "compulsory able-bodiedness," such as McRuer, "Compulsory Able-Bodiedness."

18 Lennard Davis, *The End of Normal: Identity in a Biocultural Era* (Ann Arbor, MI: University of Michigan Press, 2008).

19 Garland-Thomson, *Extraordinary Bodies*.

20 Susan Wendell, *The Rejected Body: Feminist Philosophical Reflections on Disability* (New York: Routledge, 1996).

21 Charlton, *Nothing about Us without Us*.

22 Linton, *Claiming Disability*.

23 O'Toole, "Disclosing Our Relationships to Disabilities."

24 Kuppers, *Disability Culture*.

25 Siebers, *Disability Theory*, 57.

26 Ibid. "Complex embodiment" draws on and extends two important strands of feminist scholarship: standpoint theory (different social identities and experiences produce different knowledges) and intersectionality.

27 Kafer, *Feminist, Queer, Crip*.

28 Ibid., 7.

29 Kimberlé Crenshaw, "Mapping the Margins: Intersectionality, Identity Politics, and Violence against Women of Color," *Stanford Law Review* 43 (1991): 1241–99.

30 "Q&A with Jasbir Puar" [interview], *Darkmatter Journal*, May 2, 2008, www.darkmatter101.org.

31 See, for example, Alaniz, *Death, Disability, and the Superhero*; Sarah Heiss, "Locating the Bodies of Women and Disability in Definitions of Beauty," *Disability Studies Quarterly* 31, no. 1 (2011), http://dsq-sds.org; Amy Holdsworth, "Something Special: Care, Pre-school Television and the Dis/abled Child," *Journal of Popular Television* 3, no. 2 (2015): 163–78; Sami Schalk, "Reevaluating the Supercrip," *Journal of Literary & Cultural Disability Studies* 10, no. 1 (2016): 71–86.

32 See, for example, Jennings Bryant and Mary Beth Oliver, *Media Effects: Advances in Theory and Research* (New York: Routledge, 2009); Robin L. Nabi and Mary Beth Oliver, *The Sage Handbook of Media Processes and Effects* (Thousand Oaks, CA: Sage, 2009).

33 John Durham Peters and Peter Simonson, *Mass Communication and American Social Thought: Key Texts, 1919–1968* (New York: Rowman & Littlefield, 2004); Stanley J. Baran and Dennis K. Davis, *Mass Communication Theory: Foundations, Ferment, and Future* (Boston: Cengage Learning, 2014); Bruce D. Williams and Michael X. Delli Carpini, *After Broadcast News: Media Regimes, Democracy, and the New Information Environment* (Cambridge, UK: Cambridge University Press, 2011).

34 Christian Metz, *The Imaginary Signifier: Psychoanalysis and the Cinema* (Bloomington: Indiana University Press, 1986); David Bordwell, *Making Meaning: Inference and Rhetoric in the Interpretation of Cinema* (Cambridge, MA: Harvard University Press, 1989)

35 Certeau, *The Practice of Everyday Life*.

36 Janice A. Radway, *Reading the Romance: Women, Patriarchy, and Popular Literature* (Chapel Hill: University of North Carolina Press, 1984).

37 See, for example, Jenkins, *Textual Poachers*; Henry Jenkins, *Convergence Culture: Where Old and New Media Collide* (New York: New York University Press, 2008).

38 For more on this approach to popular culture, see John Fiske, *Reading the Popular* (London: Routledge, 1989).

39 Hall, "Encoding/Decoding."

40 Theodor W. Adorno and Max Horkheimer, *Dialectic of Enlightenment* (Stanford, CA: Stanford University Press, 2002).

41 D'Acci, "Cultural Studies, Television Studies"; du Gay et al., *Doing Cultural Studies*; Johnson, "What Is Cultural Studies Anyway?"

42 Gray, *Watching Race*; Gledhill, *Stardom*; Douglas, *Listening In*; Shawn VanCour, *Making Radio: Early Radio Production and the Rise of Modern Sound Culture, 1920–1930* (Oxford: Oxford University Press, forthcoming). See also Mack Hagood's chapter, this volume, on approaches to technologies that might fit within this set of analyses.

43 Morley, *Family Television*; Ien Ang, *Living Room Wars: Rethinking Media Audiences* (London: Routledge, 1995); Hollis Griffin, *Feeling Normal: Sexuality & Media Criticism in the Digital Age* (Bloomington: Indiana University Press, 2017).

44 Jenkins, *Textual Poachers* and *Convergence Culture*; Gray, Sandvoss, and Harrington, *Fandom*; Hills, *Fan Cultures*.

45 Caldwell, *Production Culture*; Havens, Lotz, and Tinic, "Critical Media Industry Studies"; Holt and Perren, *Media Industries*.

46 Lewis and Miller, *Critical Cultural Policy Studies*; Streeter, *Selling the Air*; Perlman, *Public Interests*.

47 Hilmes, *Radio Voices*; Spigel, *Make Room for TV*; Allen, *Horrible Prettiness*, Bodroghkozy, *Groove Tube*.

48 D'Acci, *Defining Women*; See also du Gay et al., *Doing Cultural Studies*.

49 Ethan Thompson and Jason Mittell, *How to Watch Television* (New York: New York University Press, 2013). For an outstanding introduction to media studies methodologies, see also Michael Kackman and Mary Celeste Kearney, eds., *The Craft of Criticism: Critical Media Studies in Practice* (New York: Routledge, forthcoming).

50 D'Acci, "Cultural Studies, Television Studies," 436.

51 Kudlick, "Disability History."

52 Goggin and Newell, *Digital Disability*.

53 See, for example, Roger Silverstone, *Television and Everyday Life* (London: Routledge, 1994); Toby Miller and Alec McHoul, *Popular Culture and Everyday Life* (London: Sage: 1998); Anna McCarthy, *Ambient Television: Visual Culture and Public Space* (Durham, NC: Duke University Press, 2001); Jussi Parikka, "New Materialism as Media Theory: Medianatures and Dirty Matter," *Communication & Critical/Cultural Studies* 9, no. 1 (March 2012): 95–100.

Recent work on video games and the Internet has begun to lead more media scholars toward questions of materiality; we contend, however, that a disability perspective will both accelerate this necessary exploration and, more importantly, provide resources for questioning the bodily normativity that can all too easily inform such studies.

54 Mills, "Deafening"; Sterne, *MP3*.

55 Foucault, *The History of Sexuality, Volume 1*.

56 Ouellette and Hay, *Better Living through Reality TV*; Kenneth C. Werbin, "Spookipedia: Intelligence, Social Media and Biopolitics," *Media, Culture & Society* 33, no. 8 (November 2011): 1254–65.

57 Mitchell and Snyder, *The Biopolitics of Disability*.

58 Garland-Thomson, "Representing Disability," *PMLA* 120, no. 2 (March 2005): 523.

59 The recent collection *Different Bodies: Essays on Disability in Film and Television* is broadly international, and its authors use disability studies to perform accessible critical analyses of fictional representations, documentaries, and audience reception in relation to film and television texts (Mogk, *Different Bodies*).

Additional works that participate in an emerging disability media studies include: Alper, *Digital Youth with Disabilities*; Ellcessor, *Restricted Access*; Ellis and Goggin, *Disability and the Media*; Ellis and Kent, *Disability and New Media*; Katie Ellis and Mike Kent, eds., "Special Issue: Disability and the Internet," *First Monday* 20, no. 9 (September 2015), http://firstmonday.org; Julie Passanante Elman, *Chronic Youth: Disability, Sexuality, and U.S. Media Cultures of Rehabilitation* (New York: New York University Press, 2014); Fuqua, *Prescription TV*; Haller, *Representing Disability*.

60 See, for example, Jasbir Puar, "The Cost of Getting Better: Ability and Debility," in Lennard Davis, ed., *The Disability Studies Reader*, 4th ed. (New York: Routledge, 2013): 177–84; Rebecca Wanzo, *The Suffering Will Not Be Televised: African American Women and Sentimental Political Storytelling* (Albany: State University of New York Press, 2009); McRuer, *Crip Theory*; Sami Schalk, "Coming to Claim Crip: Disidentification with/in Disability Studies," *Disability Studies Quarterly* 33, no. 2 (2013), http://dsq-sds.org; Mel Y. Chen, *Animacies: Biopolitics, Racial Mattering, and Queer Affect* (Durham, NC: Duke University Press, 2012).

PART I

Access and Media Production

1

Kickstarting Community

Disability, Access, and Participation in My Gimpy Life

ELIZABETH ELLCESSOR

"Access" is a crucial concept in both media studies and disability studies, but the word has very different histories in the two fields. Ellcessor puts the range of meanings of access into dialog through the notion of "cultural accessibility," a term that captures the interrelationships among technological and economic access, access to representation and production, and access to the public sphere. Through her analysis of the Kickstarter-funded web series *My Gimpy Life*, Ellcessor shows how new technologies and funding models allow new forms of access and participation at multiple levels, blurring distinctions between media production and reception in ways that have particular relevance for the study of disability.

"You probably noticed I use a wheelchair. But I never let my disability define me."[1] With this casual aside, *My Gimpy Life* (*MGL*) began its first episode, released on YouTube in the summer of 2012. It was a five-episode web series, created by and starring Teal Sherer, based loosely on her real-life "awkward adventures as a disabled actress trying to navigate Hollywood in a wheelchair."[2] The short series attracted significant attention, winning two 2012 International Academy of Web Television Awards, one for comedy series and one for Sherer's acting.

In spring 2013, Scherer launched a Kickstarter campaign, attempting to raise $50,000 to produce a second season of *MGL*.[3] Kickstarter.com is a crowdfunding site focused on raising money for creative projects. Ultimately, the *MGL* campaign raised over $59,000, which was used to produce four additional episodes, released in spring 2014.

The case of *MGL* brings together a new media form, an emerging funding model, and an intervention in the politics of disability representation and access. Media access and participation have long been part of "the debates on, and practices of, alternative and community media" as well as popular media,[4] particularly as these concepts relate to democracy and civic engagement. This chapter considers how the incorporation of disability into emerging types and institutions of popular media is not only important in terms of representation, but also in terms of how it directs our attention to media technologies, access, and complex relations between media producers and audiences. *MGL* demonstrates that new models of production and new opportunities for interaction with media may support cultural and civic engagement with society through media texts. Such processes also demonstrate the value of cultural accessibility, or the ability to access usable, culturally relevant, collaborative, and inclusive media. Cultural accessibility supports the formation of new forms of disability identity and can be used to further develop civic identities and act within the public sphere.

To organize this chapter, I borrow Nico Carpentier's triad of media participation: media production, interaction with media content, and participation in society *through* media.[5] The first entails access to and activity within organizations involved in producing media content. The second is explicitly about audiences' abilities to interact with media content through various forms of feedback. The third refers to ways in which producers and audiences may use media to intervene in society, inform themselves, or otherwise serve participatory (and even democratic) aims.

Throughout, I conceive of viewers and funders of *MGL* neither as a passive audience nor as necessarily active individual participants. Instead, it is productive to think about the formation of a community centered around *MGL*, comprised of overlapping social groups, forms of interaction, interests, shared goals, or common ideologies. In this way, the media text becomes a kind of hub for the formation of an "affinity space." Importantly, this may also be understood as a kind of celebrity-based affinity space, as Sherer comes to represent the full creative team and is the embodied ambassador of the program through her roles as creator, star, and marketer.[6] Those who are included within the *MGL* community may form connections primarily to her, or the project, and secondarily with one another. These connections form the basis upon which interaction with *MGL* may be transformed to participation in the media, interaction with a media text and community, and participation in society through a media text that is invested in transforming ideologies of disability.

Disability, Media Access, and Independent Television

Before analyzing media production, interaction, and participation in society through media, I will briefly introduce the issues surrounding disability and media access, while also providing a quick overview of web series, or "independent television." The features of independent television may be particularly conducive to promoting various forms of media access for people with disabilities, and *MGL* is one of the few disability-themed web series to rise to popular attention.

There has been a recent rise in disability representation on mainstream U.S. television. Reality programs and documentaries are scattered across cable channels, network television includes characters with physical and psychological disabilities, and cable dramas have incorporated characters with conditions ranging from dwarfism to cerebral palsy, d/Deafness to obsessive-compulsive disorder.[7] This increase in visibility may be cause for celebration: the more media images available, the more likely that they will move beyond stereotype, connect with audiences, and present nuanced portraits of the lives of people with disabilities. As Rosemarie Garland-Thomson argues, "[T]he way we imagine disability through images and narratives determines the shape of the material world, the distribution of resources, our relationships with one another, and our sense of ourselves."[8]

Such celebration, however, may be premature. One of the major criticisms of current disability representation on television has centered on the casting of able-bodied actors in disabled roles. This, along with the dearth of writers, directors, and other production personnel with disabilities, may result in representations that draw more upon stereotypes or assumptions about disabilities than they do upon lived experiences. Furthermore, many representations of disability are located in supporting characters and are formally structured so as to marginalize and isolate these characters from their (normative) social surroundings.[9] This focalization constructs a culturally dominant able point of view through which disability is understood as defect, deficit, or tragedy.[10] Focalization extends to the presumed audience for these programs, which is not typically assumed to include viewers with disabilities. Finally, rarely is any sort of disability community seen; characters struggle with their impairments, societal barriers, and cultural derision in relative isolation, seemingly without support, and sometimes entirely in secret. This reinforces their positioning as a foil or lesson for able-bodied characters, not as the heroes of their own stories.

Thus, it seems that mainstream media representation is not sufficient for incorporating disability into popular culture. Access to images of disability is undeniably important as it allows people with disabilities to form identifications and take up identities within mediated democracies, while exposing able-bodied audiences to different forms of embodied identity. However, when considering access to media—and its cultural and political benefits—it is crucial to move beyond representation to consider *accessibility* as well as *access to production.*

Accessibility refers to the means by which people with disabilities can use media, often entailing specialized features or assistive devices. Well-known examples of accessible media include closed-captioned television, enlarged or simplified remote controls, or Braille books and newspapers. Less well-known features include captions on online video, screenreaders that translate the content of a computer screen to audio, and code that enables computer and internet services to be controlled by input devices other than a mouse or keyboard. In the absence of accessibility, access to media content and representations is dramatically constrained. Though often described technologically, accessibility may also be *cultural*, referring to the active inclusion of culturally relevant disabled perspectives. Cultural accessibility entails reimagining disability and the norms of media production and representation; coalitional, collaborative, and participatory forms of production, reception, and interaction are key to creating culturally accessible media.

Access to production has long been considered important in creating media equity for minority populations. Public television, public access channels, and independent film and video projects have long attempted to encourage access to production for otherwise excluded groups, including women, racial minorities, and members of cultural, religious, or ethnic communities. In order to produce media content, one must have access to appropriate technologies, access to skills development, and often access to funding that can support production. Beyond the simple creation of media texts, access to production should also be inclusive of access to modes of promotion, distribution, and exhibition. That is to say, people must be able to share the media they produce. Historically, this has been difficult, given the high barriers to entry to commercial media industries. For people with disabilities, a lack of accessible tools, discrimination, and passive neglect are possible causes for a pervasive underrepresentation in all capacities related to media production. Recent surveys from the production guilds in Hollywood demonstrate a continued dominance of white men in the industries and do not even include disability as a measured category.[11]

In contrast, online media has offered new opportunities for the creation of media outside of traditional institutions and without historical barriers to financing, production tools, or distribution. For people with disabilities, this has meant increased access to a range of media texts, tools, and communities. Blogs, Twitter, and other social networking sites provide a necessary antidote to stereotypical media representations of disability by allowing individuals with disability to have a public voice with which to "tell the world about their own stories and life experiences."[12] Online media have also increased access to public spaces for people with disabilities, enabling greater participation in all components of everyday life, from shopping to voting.[13] According to Stephen Kuusisto, those who produce web media "will inevitably agree and disagree about the traditional issues that are discussed in the town square but they will also bring to their discussion a further awareness and commitment to disability advocacy. When we consider the long history of social isolation that has surrounded the experience of disability we can sense the remarkable opportunity that is at hand."[14]

Simultaneously, the possibility of media creation outside of traditional industrial structures has allowed for the rise of what have variously been termed web series, webisodes, web media, or independent television programs. What they typically share is an episodic structure, short episodes, a multimedia televisual aesthetic legacy, and distribution via videosharing sites such as YouTube or dedicated websites. Furthermore, they are often venues for independent producers and creative personnel who are interested in both gaining experience and addressing what they see as flaws within the mainstream industry.[15] By intervening in representational politics via series "aimed at underserved niches, primarily people of color, women, and gay people" (and, I would add, people with disabilities), these texts and productions open spaces in which to consider not merely cultural desires but emerging industrial practices.[16] As Alyssa Rosenberg wrote in the *New York Times*, "It's truly independent television, aired not by networks or their streaming competitors, that is telling new stories and expanding subject matter. Web-distributed series, including Jane Espenson and Brad Bell's gay romcom 'Husbands,' Teal Sherer's 'My Gimpy Life,' about an actress who uses a wheelchair, and Issa Rae's 'The Misadventures of Awkward Black Girl' all focus on the kinds of characters who haven't made it to network television—or to streaming alternatives either."[17] Such representational innovation is obviously worthy of attention, but it is only a first step. This chapter asks how media production, interaction with media, and participation in society via media may be enabled and supported in the interest of creating popular media that is not merely technologically but *culturally* accessible to people with disabilities.

Media Production

As described above, access to the means of media production has historically been of concern to advocates for media literacy and those concerned with minority representation. Because mainstream commercial media in the U.S. has often excluded the voices of minority groups, various organizations have developed their own media outlets. Often termed "minority media," these magazines, public access programs, websites, and other ventures have enabled individuals "to speak for oneself, to create narratives and images that counter the accepted, oppressive, or inaccurate ones."[18]

   MGL could be considered under the rubric of minority media. Inclusive representations, and a broad audience, were important to Sherer, who "always wanted to share what it's like being a girl on wheels, and do it with comedy. I don't think people with disabilities are seen enough in the media."[19] *MGL* and its Kickstarter campaign were also covered by *Able*, a long-running magazine aimed at wheelchair users and others with disabilities. The show incorporated several other actors with disabilities, including Teale Sperling, Geri Jewell, and Russell Winkelaar.

The result is the representation not of one actress with a disability, but of a community of disabled actors. The inclusion of actors with disabilities works with the narrative to produce multiple, different representations of disability, contesting stereotypes by refusing to generalize. Furthermore, in *MGL*, experiences of disability are interwoven with storylines about trying to make it in Hollywood, dating, roommate drama, and other recognizable comedic tropes. This enables an appeal to a broad audience and normalizes disability and difference.

In addition to offering viewers access to powerful new representations of disability, *MGL* has prioritized accessibility. The very first episode, "Accessible," addressed the barriers that the main character, Teal,[20] encountered in going on acting auditions, such as the stairs and lack of elevator at a location that resulted in her (unsuccessful) audition in a back alley. Beyond the thematic level, all episodes are closed captioned, and captioner Alex Lotz is prominently credited. Sherer told *PUSH Living* that she is "very passionate about inclusion and equal rights for people with disabilities, and accessibility. It's crazy to me that so many places still aren't physically accessible for people with disabilities and that media isn't always closed captioned so that it is accessible for people that are hearing impaired. I could go on."[21] In addressing accessibility on- and offscreen, *MGL* highlights the ways in which media access is not merely a matter of representational equity, affordability, availability, or choice. Access requires the active construction of material, technological, and cultural options that fulfill the needs of a wide variety of human bodies.

In order to expand access, one must first *have* access to entertainment industries and cultures of production. Carpentier suggests that participation in media production is supported by access to, interaction with, and participation in media organizations. It is not enough to have creative or technical skills; historically, access to production has meant the ability to enter the industry, gain experience, and attract funding. This has not been easy for minorities, as cronyism is embraced, affirmative action is rebuffed, and paths to success are often invisible to those who are not culturally, racially, and otherwise similar to those in power.[22] Because of these structural elements, "advocacy group pressure is not and never will be sufficient to the task of effecting comprehensive change."[23] Thus, as Christian argues, the production of independent television offers to intervene in representations and potentially to transform the industry by operating outside of oppressive structures and reaching a broader audience than was possible in the past, while increasing diversity both behind and in front of the camera.[24]

One instance of a simultaneous intervention in production culture and representations of disability came in the final episode of season two of *MGL*. The season had followed Teal as a commercial she appeared in went viral. During the episode, she has a meeting with an agent. Sitting at a conference table, this smarmy, fast-talking young white man declares that "Hollywood hasn't represented the handicapped"—here, Teal interjects "disabled"—"we want to fix that. . . . They're not too crazy about putting a guy in a wheelchair like that kid on *Glee*." In this exchange, the insensitivity of mainstream production culture is pilloried; the language is corrected, people with disabilities are discussed dismissively, and immediately afterward Teal is offered a role as the (male) lead on the cringingly titled *Cripple Cops*. After this segment, Teal discusses the offer with friends, who are other actors with various disabilities. It later becomes clear that one of her friends—a man in a wheelchair—had been in line for the part and had been discarded when the producers found a better-known disabled person for the role. The callousness of the industry is set against the friendships among characters with disabilities, highlighting the representational politics that are made more possible when operating outside of mainstream structures.

To participate in media and intervene in representations, series such as *MGL* require viable financial backing. Minority media such as magazines have often operated within precarious financial conditions, sustained through either a for-profit subscription model or a non-profit, public-service, or charity model. Uncertainty regarding financing has spelled the end, or change, of any number of such publications. Internet media has opened doors by reducing costs and barriers to entry for would-be producers, but it requires a high degree of entrepreneurship to secure funding for web series projects. This entrepreneurship is similar to that seen in the tech industry, as it rests upon the ability of individuals or groups to create a visible identity (or brand) that aligns with expectations.[25] Many web series, specifically, do this by blurring the line between the creators in their capacity as authors and in their capacity as individuals, creating what might be called microcelebrities, who support the project by speaking for it in public and in social media.

The entrepreneurial self of web series is clearly seen in the example of Felicia Day and has been taken up by Sherer in promoting *MGL*. Day has produced several web series, most notably *The Guild* (2007–2013), and routinely engaged in promotion via social media, television, and various fan communities.[26] Sherer was a regular on two seasons of *The Guild*, playing Venom, a queer woman who was also an aggressive gamer. Connections to *The Guild* are evident in *MGL*: director Sean Becker worked on both series, several actors from the former appear in season two of *MGL*, and Day appears in both seasons, playing a version of herself ("Felicia"). Certainly, access to production is facilitated through such connections. As important, however, is Sherer's adoption of a form of microcelebrity that relies upon slippage between her persona and her acting work, facilitating audience identification and encouraging an auteurist reading of *MGL* as a realist text, drawn from real experiences.

Such auteurism and entrepreneurship are well suited for crowdfunding, which has emerged as an important means of supporting independent television. Crowdfunding involves "the online request for resources from a distributed audience often in exchange for a reward."[27] It is often framed in terms of direct appeals, with creative personnel approaching potential audience members for financial support; this cuts out the middlemen who have functioned as gatekeepers in the past. Games journalist Leigh Alexander explains that "crowdfunding, patronage and similar social media-driven avenues let audiences directly fund the kind of content they want," but adds that this introduces the complication of ongoing interactions with audiences who may come to see themselves as investors.[28] The forms of auteurist entrepreneurship described above, which issue a personal appeal via microcelebrity, are particularly powerful in this environment as they facilitate the ongoing interactions that funders have come to expect from crowdfunded projects.

Importantly, as Tama Leaver indicates, web media require not just production money, but funding for marketing and advertising.[29] In order to save money, many independent television producers "act as their own publicist,"[30] doing interviews, using social media, and otherwise promoting the project. This promotional work, particularly when driven by a microcelebrity, can also form the beginnings of an affective relationship with audiences that may develop into a feeling of community.

This community involvement is particularly notable in the case of marginalized groups such as people with disabilities. One argument in favor of crowdfunding has been that it "radically changes what and how new ideas are brought into the world. The biggest opportunity for crowdfunding is to recruit, train, and retain novice entrepreneurs who traditionally have lacked access through resources due to lack of equity or established track record."[31] In short, with alternate funds come additional opportunities to participate in media production and take risks that would not be supported in traditional production spaces. Projects such as *MGL* can go beyond commercial transactions to support the formation of a persistent community that may, ultimately, produce societal changes on some level.

Interaction with Media Content and Communities

Interaction with media content is never an isolated activity. As many have argued, reading a book, watching a film, viewing television, and surfing the net are all activities located within rich social contexts. These contexts form interpretive communities through which individuals may negotiate a text according to dominant or resistant ideologies.[32] This results in varied interpretations, which audiences have long shared with others, as in the legendary water-cooler discussions of television programming. Carpentier describes interaction with media content as the domain of the audience and demonstrates that such audiences are routinely conceptualized as communities. Such aggregates may be looked upon as markets or as fan communities; Kickstarter campaigns, including that for *MGL*, rely upon a version of community that draws on both registers and offers new, direct forms of interaction with media content.

The dominant discourse around Kickstarter has referred to funders as the "audience" or as "backers," all roughly synonymous with "market." The basic structure of a Kickstarter campaign involves a creator video, a plan, and designated reward levels for contributions of specific dollar amounts. Funders are charged only when a project's financial goals are met; unfunded projects receive no money. This makes it crucial for creators to meet their entire goal, which they often do by offering rewards to incentivize higher contributions. These reward tiers set Kickstarter apart from a preorder, as soliciting different levels of donations is generally non-controversial. Instead, it can be argued that backers are paying for a degree of access to and interaction with the project.

Whether due to fandom, producerly ambitions, or other interests, many individuals seek access to "behind-the-scenes" material. In the interest of full disclosure, I pledged $25 to receive "Access to Production Diaries Website, where Teal will be posting videos, pictures, and blog posts updating you on the entire Season Two production process. Plus Desktop Wallpaper, Special Thanks on the MGL website."[33] In my case, this access was required for better research (though all this material has since been made public). For other backers, higher reward tiers offered greater levels of access to and interaction with the production as it was in progress. In addition to the basic rewards, the highest tier offered backers the opportunity to receive a credit on the final series, meet Sherer, and receive a signed shooting script. These rewards bolster funders' sense of involvement and oversight in Kickstarter projects.

Following the successful crowdfunding of a project, it has been said that "your audience is now your boss"[34] because funders "are deeply affected by the idea that your opportunity would not be possible without them. They want—perhaps fairly—the full right to assess, even in public, whether you delivered on their expectations, whether you rewarded their material faith."[35] This can result in a demanding audience, calling for business plans, prototypes, or the opportunity to do user testing. As Bertha Chin asked, "Would fans now feel entitled to the project now that they've invested money in it?" and would creators "now be obligated to create a piece of work that they think fans want, and would that affect forms of artistic integrity?"[36] Even as the absence of gatekeepers removes one level of oversight from media production, it may be replaced by oversight via the ongoing interactivity of funders in their role as a customer base.

In interacting with funders as a kind of market, creators increasingly take on the roles of public relations, customer service, and user testing to various degrees. Public relations entails "addressing questions and posting regular updates"[37] on the project, whether formally (as in the *MGL* Production Diaries for backers) or informally through social media and other promotional channels, as was done around web series pioneer *Dr. Horrible's Sing-Along Blog* (Josh Whedon, 2008).[38] This ongoing involvement by the creator(s) with the community upholds a reputation for trustworthiness among fans and funders, as does on-time delivery of rewards and products (or regular communication about delays). However, such work requires between two and eleven hours a day during a typical Kickstarter campaign, and substantial investments of time following up on updates, rewards, and so on.[39] Customer service comes up in the delivery of rewards and final projects, which creators often find to be overwhelming in its logistics and sheer material demands.[40] Bertha Chin observes that "if you're already strapped for cash for a project, imagine having to spend even more on printing T-shirts, DVDs, and shipping."[41] Beyond financial burdens, the blurring of "perk" and "purchase" here often results in mistakes, complaints, help requests, and all of the other trials associated with creating and distributing goods. Finally, creators may also find themselves suddenly involved in user testing, either through solicited feedback or through unsolicited advice from funders.

The activities required of a successful crowdfunding campaign are time- and labor-intensive, particularly as they are often forms of social, affective labor that may be unrewarded and quite personal. For instance, Sherer used a personal email address to correspond with over eight hundred backers of *MGL* and engaged directly with those (like me) who needed to correct their names or otherwise ensure receipt of rewards. By using ongoing interactions, microcelebrity, and other forms of community building, creators monetize their affective labor by using it as a means to gain supporters and financial aid. Marc Andrejevic suggests that this "affective" or "immaterial" labor is "becoming generalized—at least in the realms of consumption," meaning that it is increasingly common and constitutive of media experiences.[42] Yet, as crowdfunding is *not* simply consumption, it is through this work that "collective subjectivities are produced and sociality is produced."[43] That is to say, a community may be formed from this work, inclusive of creators and funders, and that may allow creators "to create a following that lasts throughout their campaign and possibly for future projects."[44] Though inextricable from capital, the communication with others and interaction with media that characterize crowdfunding remain significant.

Many creators have used fan communities and other niche groups to develop support for crowdfunding projects by targeting a built-in audience. This may involve reaching out to existing online communities as well as directly addressing fans. The *Inspector Spacetime* (2012) web series took the latter approach, with actor Travis Richey, who first played the character on NBC's *Community* (2009–2014), directly appealing to fans for support in extending the story.[45] Notably, Richey attempted to integrate his roles as fan and producer, claiming a unique authority in the overlapping identities. Felicia Day has done similar work around her web series for the BioWare video game *Dragon Age*, appearing at once as fan and author.[46] Day has also built her own fan community, connected to her acting work with Joss Whedon, *The Guild*, and her YouTube channel, Geek & Sundry.

Sherer, via her role in *The Guild*, benefited from Day's network of fan communities and a broader association with "geek culture."[47] In addition to the overlapping production personnel, Sherer drew upon the "Guild of Extras," a group of *Guild* fans who were extras in season five, to round out her cast.[48] *MGL* was promoted on Geek & Sundry's community forum and also received coverage from outlets such as *The Mary Sue*, an online publication dedicated to women's geek culture. Though *MGL* itself is not necessarily "geeky" in the sense that video games or sci-fi might be, it marketed itself as part of that larger network of industrial and personal connections.

MGL also developed its own fan base during its first season. This community drew from related fandoms but also added new fans, many of whom were people with disabilities. Looking back on season one, Sherer recalled that "even though we didn't find a mass audience, we had a really supportive and loyal group of core fans, and the show got mentioned by NPR, the *New York Times*, lots of great blogs . . . and it even got used as part of disability and media curriculums at colleges."[49] The series, and Kickstarter campaign, were also promoted via disability information and support sites such as paralysis.org and apparelyzed. com. The comments on the Kickstarter page reflect an engaged disability community, with backers posting about their love of the show and its portrayals of disability.

When funders are considered as fans, their contributions seem less like transactions and more like means of signaling the depth of their affective engagement and the cultural capital that may accrue from being visibly "first" or otherwise "leading" a fan community.[50] Sherer described the *MGL* Kickstarter as a means of "putting it into the hands of the fans and saying, 'Do you want this?' And the fans choose if they want it or not."[51] In the process of raising money, engaging with her audience, and posting updates, she observed "how much stronger our community has become. . . . Fans have gotten really excited about it and become very vocal about their love for the show."[52] The "we" here is notable, as it indicates that Sherer positions herself alongside fans and backers as another member of the community.[53] By contributing, spreading the word, and commenting on Kickstarter, fans interact with the conditions of possibility for *MGL*. They take part in a process that may "consolidat[e] a feeling of community between fans who have contributed."[54]

Importantly, Sherer is a member of the Kickstarter community, as well as the *MGL* community. Her profile at the time indicated that she had funded 21 projects (mostly web series), only some of which were successful. This is important because there appears to be an ethos of reciprocation and sharing among would-be creators and those who have crowdfunded successfully. Creators rely on communities of other creators to get advice, design their campaigns, get feedback and publicity, and ship rewards.[55] Sherer's experience as a backer on Kickstarter thus lent her further credibility as a creator.

Interaction with a crowdfunding campaign or fan community opens up possibilities for audiences, consumers, fans—*communities*—to access media production via processes of collaboration. Elizabeth Gerber suggests that what sets crowdfunding apart from other forms of entrepreneurship in a digital age are the "collaborative and community aspects . . . as a group of supporters gathers not only to fund a proposal, but to promote the proposal and to join in the work of making it real."[56] This further extends the accessibility of such projects, as funding is not the only way for those who are financially disadvantaged to participate. In some cases, collaboration is direct, as when creators poll supporters or host discussion boards for conversation.[57] For *MGL*, opportunities for collaboration were somewhat more constrained. Though some reward levels conveyed production titles, and all backers received online recognition,[58] there was no public discussion of possible storylines, casting decisions, or other elements of production. Instead, fans and funders were asked to continuously spread the word about the series. Though this may seem a crass means of building publicity for the Kickstarter and the release of season two, it may equally be reflective of the politics of contemporary popular culture. Choices about media circulation are an important means of participation in media and may enable participation in society via media texts and communities.

Participation in Society through Media

Once communities have formed around media content, particularly content produced with the intent of social change, it is a short step to politicizing those communities and enabling the audience to alter their relations with society at large. Certainly, this is not a direct effect. Yet the power of representation is such that producing images and stories that challenge conventional norms, especially doing so with underrepresented groups involved in production, constitute potentially radical acts in that they expose audiences to a different vision of what media industries could be or do. The task of disability studies is sometimes described in terms of reimagining the way the world is categorized, and the way the world could be in the future.[59] Creating and circulating alternative media content such as *MGL* is not merely a response to the shortcomings of mainstream media but is a proactive attempt to win hearts and minds to what Sherer describes as her mission: "inclusion and access."[60]

First, it should be noted that Sherer embraces a disabled identity and is active in communities of people with disabilities. She describes herself as proud of her disability, participates in physically integrated modern dance companies, and cofounded a theater company, Blue Zone, with two other actors with disabilities.[61] Thus, it is perhaps not surprising that Sherer criticizes inaccessible physical spaces, unfair treatment, pity, and other pitfalls of life with a disability and states that these criticisms are "one of the reasons I created *My Gimpy Life*—deep down I hope that it will somehow help change these things."[62] She views representation as powerful because "society takes a lot of cues from what they see in the media" and has indicated that she would also "like to see more disabled directors, producers, writers" involved offscreen.[63]

The progressive intent of *MGL* is most evident in the third episode of the first season, "Inspirational." The episode contains two storylines; in the main plot, Teal and Felicia audition for *The Vagina Monologues*, while the episode is bookended by Teal's encounters with men who may be interested in her. The first man asks outright if "everything works down there"; a flummoxed Teal says yes, and he asks her out. In the following scene, Teal tells Felicia about this encounter and laments that it happens often, despite being obviously inappropriate. At the end of the episode, a man stops Teal, saying, "Can I ask you a question?" She immediately, and acerbically, affirms that she can be sexual—only to have him respond that he was only going to ask her to coffee. This humorous reversal picks up on the frustrations of encounters with insensitive people and the complex reactions people with disabilities have to these experiences. The main plot is even more explicitly a lesson for nondisabled viewers. Teal's audition goes poorly, but she is highly praised throughout, with the director of the theater company talking about how "inspirational" she is. Teal explains to Felicia that this is insulting, because she wants to be evaluated as an actress, not patronized for being "brave" or "inspirational" by those who don't understand her impairment, her personality, or her life.

This episode critiques common understandings of disability as asexual, as well as involving an inspirational, brave, or heroic struggle against an impoverished life. In doing so, it likely provides an education for some viewers and an opportunity for identification for those who have had similar experiences. This progressive intent may foster the politicization of the audience community, enabling them to unify not only around media content, but around a shared civic culture that may extend to participation in society through media.

Ashley Hinck proposes the notion of a "public engagement keystone as a touch point, worldview, or philosophy that makes other people, actions, and institutions intelligible."[64] She argues that in the case of the Harry Potter Alliance, the stories of the *Harry Potter* universe provide a reference point from which fans can develop public subjectivities and increase their civic engagement. *MGL* can act as a similar "public engagement keystone." It provides what I refer to as "cultural accessibility," in which media are not only technically accessible to people with disabilities, but culturally relevant to their experiences or identities, actively inclusive, and ultimately collaborative in some way. Such content enables audience members to take up or develop identities and make them legible to others via media. This cultural access, then, can enable access to citizen identities. Cultural texts and practices can provide a kind of map for this process of finding footholds and ways of engaging in the public sphere.

The development of cultural identities that can become civic identities may occur through many different actions within a given cultural community or context. For Sherer, producing *MGL* is a kind of activism in society. For backers, funding this series may be understood as a means of using media as a channel for societal or civic participation. For viewers and community members, the transition from cultural to civic identities may be subtle, as civic engagement increasingly uses the forms and content of popular media.[65]

In such a context, the sharing of media content such as *MGL* can be understood as a form of civic engagement. Jenkins, Ford, and Green use "spreadability" to refer to the possibility "for audiences to share content for their own purposes."[66] By recirculating media content, users place it in new contexts and can use it to impart new values, highlight specific meanings, or intervene in dominant discourses. Jean Burgess argues that videos that spread in this way are "mediating mechanisms via which cultural practices are originated, adopted and (sometimes) retained within social networks."[67] In other words, videos are a means of communication not merely due to their content, but because of how they are (or are not) selected, circulated, commented upon, and otherwise made meaningful.

Collaboration between producers and consumers is a defining feature of a culture of spreadability. This may entail the forms of direct collaboration discussed above in relation to crowdfunding, or it may be an indirect and multifaceted collaboration in which many users take up content and share it with their communities for their own purposes. The latter is more representative of the collaboration enabled by the cultural accessibility of *MGL*. For instance, leading up to the release of season two, Sherer posted a Production Diaries video announcing that filming was complete. Accessible only to backers, the video concluded with a request that "since October is Disability Awareness Month, share with a friend!" This followed extensive outreach requests during the Kickstarter campaign, which at one point looked unlikely to succeed. By circulating content, praising the program, highlighting its representational politics, or asking others to contribute, fans and backers were able to take an active role in spreading content, making it meaningful, and potentially altering others' views on disability. Such actions are indicative of the ways in which "our public sphere has been enriched through the diversification of who has the means to create and share culture."[68]

Conclusion

This chapter has used the example of *My Gimpy Life* and Carpentier's tripartite framework of media participation to demonstrate the ways in which independent television crowdfunding can support new representations, production cultures and communities, and civic engagement around disability. There is great promise in these venues to challenge the practices and products of traditional media industries through the production and circulation of alternatives.

However, there is an emerging risk to these possible cultural and political interventions. With the success of crowdfunding platforms have come more established professionals, such as game design studio DoubleFine, television showrunner Rob Thomas of *Veronica Mars* (UPN, 2004–2006), and actor and filmmaker Zach Braff. As those with access to more traditional forms of financing come to crowdfunding—and set records when they do—there is a very real possibility that the opportunities for underrepresented groups will shrink as "expert entrepreneurs become the predominant models of success."[69] It seems likely that such an expert model would mirror traditional industrial structures in "reproducing the aesthetic and values of white, straight, middle-class" and able-bodied men.[70] As those seeking funding might increasingly model themselves and their campaigns on these successes, they may move away from the features of independent media and crowdfunding that enable the production of risky, culturally accessible media content and foster civic engagement.

Such an outcome is by no means inevitable. However, recognizing threats to these conditions of independent media production returns us to the question of media access. Meaningful access to media entails the ability to find, view, interact with, share, respond to, and make media. Too often, people with disabilities are denied access at multiple levels. Projects such as *MGL* offer a form of redress, as they consciously create culturally accessible content that exists in collaboration with a community and offers opportunities for audiences deploy it in their own cultural and civic lives and identities.

This extension of access is, on its own, a significant and positive development. Yet, we could push even further, reconceptualizing access as a flexible relationship among individuals, communities, cultures, technologies, and institutions.[71] Access is not only of concern to people with disabilities, but remains a pressing concern for poor, urban, and rural communities, non-English speakers, and members of minority groups in the United States. The lessons from *MGL* and the study of disability and new media may be productively applied to other forms of access, as well. By doing so, the possibilities for transforming media content and production can only increase. And finally, though much has been learned from centering disability and a lack of access, this essay simultaneously suggests the necessity of thinking through the conditions and experiences of those who do not identify as disabled, and who believe themselves to "have" access to media participation. What are the default conditions, what forms of participation do they support, and how might they exclude alternate perspectives? The study of media access provides important new perspectives on identities, institutions, technologies, and texts, a particularly crucial endeavor in an era of rapid change in the media environment.

NOTES

1 "Accessible." *My Gimpy Life*, June 30, 2012, http://mygimpylife.com.
2 Ibid.
3 The first season was funded by investment company Dracogen.
4 Carpentier, *Media and Participation*, Kindle location 7534.
5 Ibid., Kindle location 1428.
6 Ellcessor and Duncan, "Forming The Guild."
7 See introduction and Lopez, this volume; Carlson, "Wired for Interdependency"; Ellis, "Cripples, Bastards and Broken Things."
8 Garland-Thomson, "Disability and Representation," 523.
9 Norden, *The Cinema of Isolation*.
10 Shohat and Stam, *Unthinking Eurocentrism*.
11 Darnell M. Hunt, "Whose Stories Are We Telling? The 2007 Hollywood Writers Report," Writers Guild of America, West, May 2007, www.wga.org.
12 Haller, *Representing Disability*, 20.
13 Coopman, "Disability on the Net."
14 Kuusisto, "A Roundtable on Disability Blogging."
15 Christian, "Fandom as Industrial Response."
16 Ibid.
17 Alyssa Rosenberg, "Let's Revolutionize Television Content, Too," *New York Times*, September 28, 2013, www.nytimes.com.
18 Gross, *Up from Invisibility*, 19.
19 Greg Gilman, "Kickstarted Web Series 'My Gimpy Life' Kicks Off Season 2 (Video)," *TheWrap*, March 5, 2014, www.thewrap.com.

20 For the sake of clarity, I use "Sherer" to refer to Teal Sherer in her capacity as creator, actor, and semi-public individual and "Teal" to refer to her *My Gimpy Life* character.

21 Deborah Davis, "An Interview with Teal Sherer," *PUSH Living*, November 18, 2014, http://pushliving.com.

22 Beltrán et al., "Pressurizing the Media Industry."

23 Ibid., 163.

24 Christian, "Fandom as Industrial Response."

25 Marwick, *Status Update*.

26 Ellcessor, "Tweeting @feliciaday."

27 Hui, Greenberg, and Gerber, "Understanding the Role of Community," 62.

28 Leigh Alexander, "Six Most Important Lessons from Kickstarter so Far," *Gamasutra*, November 30, 2012, www.gamasutra.com.

29 Leaver, "Joss Whedon, *Dr. Horrible*."

30 Hui, Greenberg, and Gerber, "Understanding the Role of Community," 67.

31 Gerber et al., "Crowdfunding," 1096.

32 Fish, *Is There a Text in This Class?*; Hall, "Encoding/Decoding."

33 "My Gimpy Life Season Two," *Kickstarter*, www.kickstarter.com.

34 Ibid.

35 Leigh Alexander, "Now We Own You: Another Caution for Crowdfunded Content," *Gamasutra*, January 15, 2014, www.gamasutra.com.

36 Chin et al., "Dialogue: *Veronica Mars* Kickstarter."

37 Hui, Greenberg, and Gerber, "Understanding the Role of Community," 67.

38 Leaver, "Joss Whedon, *Dr. Horrible*."

39 Hui, Greenberg, and Gerber, "Understanding the Role of Community," 67.

40 Ibid., 68.

41 Chin et al., "Dialogue: *Veronica Mars* Kickstarter."

42 Andrejevic, "Exploiting YouTube," 411.

43 Ibid., 417.

44 Hui, Greenberg, and Gerber, "Understanding the Role of Community," 68.

45 Booth, "Reifying the Fan."

46 Ellcessor, "Constructing Social Media's Indie Auteurs."

47 Ellcessor, "Tweeting @feliciaday."

48 Bill Wasik, "Extras From The Guild Webseries Make Annual Pilgrimage to Reunite Their Online Tribe," *Wired*, July 22, 2013, www.wired.com.

49 Jill Pantozzi, "Exclusive Premiere & Interview: Teal Sherer's *My Gimpy Life* Season 2!" January 31, 2014. www.themarysue.com.

50 Chin et al., "Dialogue: *Veronica Mars* Kickstarter"; Alexander, "Six Most Important Lessons."

51 Sam Gutelle, "Teal Sherer Seeks $50,000 on Kickstarter for 'My Gimpy Life' Season 2," *TubeFilter*, May 15, 2013, www.tubefilter.com.

52 Ibid.

53 See Booth, "Reifying the Fan," for discussion of the use of "we" in web media productions.

54 Chin et al., "Dialogue: *Veronica Mars* Kickstarter."

55 Hui, Greenberg, and Gerber, "Understanding the Role of Community."

56 Gerber et al., "Crowdfunding," 1096.

57 Hui, Greenberg, and Gerber, "Understanding the Role of Community," 67.

58 The list of backers, author included, is available at http://mygimpylife.com/backers.

59 Garland-Thomson, "Disability and Representation"; Kafer, *Feminist, Queer, Crip*; Titchkosky, *The Question of Access.*

60 Autumn Reeser, "Girl Friday: Teal Sherer," *Move LifeStyle*, December 7, 2012, www.movelifestyle.com.

61 Susan Hawkins, "A Wheelchair in Hollywood: Teal Sherer on Acting, Love, and Life," *Wheelchair Accessibility Blog and Disability News from AMS Vans, Inc.*, September 27, 2013, http://blog.amsvans.com.

62 Reeser, "Girl Friday."

63 Ibid.

64 Hinck, "Theorizing a Public Engagement Keystone."

65 Jenkins, "'Cultural Acupuncture.'"

66 Jenkins, Ford, and Green, *Spreadable Media*, 3.

67 Burgess, "All Your Chocolate Rain Are Belong To Us?," 2.

68 Jenkins, Ford, and Green, *Spreadable Media*, 193.

69 Gerber et al., "Crowdfunding," 1096.

70 Brabham, "Crowdsourcing as a Model," 87.

71 Titchkosky, *The Question of Access.*

2

After School Special Education

Sex, Tolerance, and Rehabilitative Television

JULIE PASSANANTE ELMAN

In her analysis of ABC's *After School Specials* (1972–1995), Elman argues that disability was central to television's "turn toward relevance" and its construction of the "teen viewer." The *Specials* represented coming of age by consistently linking heterosexuality with able-bodiedness and meta-phorically representing adolescence as a process of "overcoming disabil-ity." Simultaneously, they redefined both teen television viewing and teen sexuality as productive rather than damaging. Articulating insights from disability studies to television studies, Elman demonstrates how the *Spe-cials'* disability narratives negotiated the complex terrain of teen sexual-ity, representations of disability, and assertions of commercial television's educational value.

I got to thinkin' about what you were sayin' about handicaps. . . . Well, I was thinkin' I don't have to be a good talker
to be able to skate.
—Tucker "Tuck" Faraday (Stewart Peterson), in "The Skating Rink," ABC's *After School Specials* (1975)

In an era when ABC's *Happy Days* (1974–1984) and its nostalgic vision of 1950s life reigned supreme on prime time, there was little television programming that acknowledged the not-so-happy elements of teen existence. Although young adult "problem novels," such as *The Out-siders* (1967), had become a thriving market by the 1970s, the bulk of the era's network programming seldom "acknowledged that there was more to adolescence than sock hops."[1] The ABC *After School Specials* (1972–1995)[2] were a significant exception. Engaging difficult topics such as teen and adult alcoholism, homosexuality, teen pregnancy, racism, drug abuse, domestic violence, sexually transmitted diseases, teen suicide, and child molestation, the *Specials* advised adolescents, without the imperative of parental intervention or oversight, on how they might begin to cope with such dilemmas.[3] In so doing, this series reaffirmed a broader discourse of adolescence-as-problem—as a developmental "stage" defined by exposure to and weathering of dysfunction. Many people remember watching episodes in health or driver's education classes as educators began incorporating television into the classroom. However, in spite of the series' wide viewership and cult classic status, very little scholarly attention has been paid to the *Specials*.

As adolescence routinely became conceptualized as problem-filled—as a "crisis"—it also increasingly became portrayed in made-for-TV movies like the *Specials* through the metaphoric vehicle of overcoming disability. As a "disease-of-the-week formula" began populating primetime offerings, the *Specials* also featured a preponderance of storylines about physical and cognitive disabilities. Functioning as a form of rehabilitative citizenship training or "*Special* education" for teenagers, the *Specials*' enforcement of disability in the teen body perpetually offered the promise of eventual normalcy through endless rehabilitation and packaged it as "coming of age." The *Specials*, as rehabilitative "edutainment," culturally transmitted medical knowledge and narratives of disability for public consumption, entertainment, and education. In episodes ranging from "It's a Mile from Here to Glory" (1978), about a temporarily disabled teen track star, to "The Kid Who Wouldn't Quit: The Brad Silverman Story" (1987), a semi-biographical story about a mainstreamed student with Down syndrome, the *Specials* transformed stories of disability into stories of growing up, overcoming disability, and getting the girl (or boy).

In tracing coming-of-age narratives in the *Specials*, I am not arguing that they, or any other form of rehabilitative edutainment, illustrate a "real" psychological developmental process. Rather, I argue that they are constitutive texts in a cultural process, one that produces the figure of the teenager as a developing citizen.[4] The *Specials*' ableist approach operates by mapping "immaturity" onto disability and "maturity" onto rehabilitation, a problematic association that continues to limit the ways disability and disabled people are culturally represented. ABC's *After*

School Specials cast teenagers as proto- or "infantile" citizens, temporarily disabled by their own adolescence, sexually at risk, and in need of rehabilitation.[5] This new "rehabilitative" approach to teen citizenship and teen television programming fused the impulses of social consciousness, educational, and sexually themed programming of the era with the values of an emergent self-help culture. In so doing, it created a new, hybridized approach to television content and narrative structure that would address teenagers *proactively* rather than protectively. This mode of address found cultural and political traction because it imagined an impressionable and angst-ridden teen audience whose exposure to the "problems" of disability, disease, and death—even if only in a fictional universe—would instantiate emotional growth into a stable and responsible adulthood.

While I argue that the content and narrative structure of the *Specials* contained a rehabilitative logic with respect to teen characters and viewers, debates about the value of the programming itself also actively participated in bolstering this logic. As television increasingly became part of American lives, the *Specials* emerged amid the exponential growth of children's programming and concomitant debates about television's potential role in youth education. Amid pervasive accusations of its sexual immorality and vapidity, the television industry reformed its own reputation through this representational mode by offering socially conscious storylines and asserting that television was a valuable instructional tool for teen viewers. In contrast to a well-documented 1950s-era discourse of television as a "threat" to children, rehabilitative edutainment emerged as a new way of "domesticating" the television to make it suitable and perhaps even healthy for a young viewing audience.[6] ABC's *After School Specials* were among the earliest programming to target a predominantly teenaged audience rather than subsuming them within a family or children's audience. Rather than censuring television as damaging to young people, rehabilitative edutainment like the *Specials* participated in debates over the educational value of television by configuring commercial shows—not just public television—as having edutainment value for viewers.[7] Finally, by closely examining two episodes of ABC's *After School Specials*, "The Skating Rink" (1975) and "Heartbreak Winner" (1980), this chapter shows how these episodes link heterosexuality with able-bodiedness as the "healthy" or natural outcome of development. This narrative formula reaffirms a broader cultural process that Robert McRuer has named "compulsory able-bodiedness," or the set of diverse cultural rules that continually establish heterosexuality and able-bodiedness as pre-discursively natural in contrast to disability and queerness, which appear as mutually reinforcing and undesirable aberrations.[8] In analyzing how the *Specials* bolstered compulsory able-bodiedness in gender-specific ways, this chapter reveals the complex and surprisingly intricate ways the logics of protection and rehabilitation played out in the content of a series that was, at the same time, groundbreaking in its attention to teen sexuality.

Contestation over television's educational value affected 1970s television offerings and was formative of television's rehabilitative approach. Assailed for its violent content in the 1950s and 1960s, television had come under fire again by the 1970s for its increasing sexual explicitness. In the context of the era's new family dynamics, including increased divorces, working parents, and latchkey kids, teens were considered at risk in historically specific ways, and with parents increasingly out of the home, youth television viewing practices were less supervised. Earlier television regulations had assumed that parents would be the primary regulators of children's television intake. However, this era witnessed a new approach to teen television that presumed absent parents who would not oversee their children's relationship with television. Thus, the *Specials* assumed a role as educator that was formerly imagined to be the province of parents, and episodes reflected this shift by depicting mainly divorced, absentee, or otherwise incapacitated parental figures. Although it is tempting to read rehabilitative edutainment's cultural impulses toward sex education and sexual television programming as inherently progressive or liberalizing, I argue that these impulses, both in the classroom and on television, form a novel rehabilitative—that is to say, a productive and disciplinary—approach to teen sexuality and teen bodies that redefined teen engagement with popular culture as productive rather than damaging.

Disability Dramas and the After School Audience

In their 23-year run, ABC's *After School Specials* won numerous awards and prizes, including eighteen Emmys, three Blue Ribbons in the American Film Festival, and the prestigious Peabody Award.[9] The *Specials* debuted in 1972 amid bitter controversy over a perceived lack of quality in children's programming and a simultaneous war over the heightened visibility of sexuality on television (and in culture more generally). Viewers often remember the shows as much for their hokey didacticism as for their unique mode of address. According to National Public Radio (NPR)'s Sarah Lemanczyk, ABC's *After School Specials* addressed teenagers "not as children or adults, but as something in between" in their serious treatment of relevant teen issues.[10] NPR's retrospective piece coincided with the DVD release of select *Specials* episodes and featured man-on-the-street–style interviews with adults who had watched the series as teenagers. One man recalled that he was "forced" to watch the *Specials* in health class and remembered "Scott Baio freaking out on drugs and getting hit over the head in the water."[11] Another man laughingly reminisced about a *Special* involving an illiterate basketball player and the unlikely chain of events that constituted the story's dramatic climax: "[S]omehow I think it was his little brother burnt his eyes with some bleach and this basketball player couldn't read [*laughter*] the back of the bottle to get him some help . . . and I think Kareem Abdul-Jabbar was somehow a guest star on it."[12]

Now infamous for their unabashed preaching and often hyperbolic approach to teen problems, the shows were usually dramas but occasionally featured comedies or "dramedies." According to the *Specials'* producer, Martin Tahse, the series explicitly targeted teenagers and was pitched initially as a way "to cover the distance between the Saturday morning ghetto for kids and prime time" because "teenagers were not being addressed" in either venue.[13] The network intended the shows to be viewed when teens returned home from school, usually around 4 p.m. Although the *Specials* are now considered overly moralistic, Tahse said he and other creators never intended to "wa[g] fingers" but rather to approach "topics that normally were not being done at all." "And we were being entertaining," he added.

Drawing storylines from the era's young-adult problem novels, the *Specials* generally devoted each episode to a single dilemma facing teenagers. To stay abreast of emerging teen literature, Tahse subscribed to *Publishers Weekly*, sought advice from the American Library Association (ALA), courted new young adult authors, and negotiated with publishers to buy the rights to novels he felt would make timely *Specials*. Storylines often featured first-time young adult novelists, because for Tahse, they "present[ed] different problems with a reality to it" and used "realistic dialogue." However, Tahse also admitted that reliance on novels formed part of a strategy for managing and minimizing potential network reticence to tackle sensitive issues, because "walking in [to ABC] with a book lent credence to the story you wanted to tell." Noting the scarcity of shows addressing "serious" issues in the 1970s, Tahse argued that soap operas were one of the few venues that dealt with "drunk driving, homosexuality, [and] pregnancy" and added that they were "getting away with murder" in comparison to more staid adult-oriented prime-time shows, whose content was not nearly as racy.

When asked whether or not the *Specials* had a "formula," Tahse responded that he was "very interested in kids getting out of ghettos." This did not necessarily mean "a black ghetto," he clarified; rather, it might be "living on a farm" and imagining "how . . . you get from the farm to college and see another kind of a life than what your father has been doing."[14] Indeed, many of the *Specials*, especially those devoted to young boys, reaffirmed a "metronormative" narrative of sexual coming of age by spotlighting tensions between "conservative" provincialism, mapped onto rural spaces like farms or rough urban neighborhoods, and "liberal" cosmopolitanism, signified by boys' choices for artistic careers like figure skating or ballet (which were configured as potentially feminizing).[15] In other words, teen coming-of-age stories were at the center of the series. The *Specials* imagined coming of age as a process of developing liberal individualism by offering lessons in tolerance to citizens-in-development, often by emphasizing the tolerance of gender non-normativity or racial otherness in narratives of overcoming disability. Lessons in tolerance rehabilitated individuals—prejudiced or cruel teenagers—into liberal open-minded adult citizens, even as such lessons generally elided the large-scale social and political reality of structural inequities wrought by systemic racism, sexism, and ableism.

Dolores Morris, then ABC's East Coast director of children's programming, asserted another important guideline: "The protagonists are always young people, and in almost every instance, the problems in question are solved by the young people themselves."[16] Tahse recalled "very few rules and regulations" apart from the directive that "adult[s]

can't solve the problem" facing the teen protagonists. Problems and solutions were gender-specific, and the solutions often presented themselves through heterosexual partnering. While it is certainly true that
problems were often solved by teens themselves, it is notable that male
protagonists often actively solved problems without assistance from
female peers, whereas girls often cared for and sought assistance and
advice from their male and female peers. Thus even as they dealt with
teen sexuality in novel and frank ways, the *Specials* reinforced fairly traditional gender roles and enforced heterosexual relationships, not only
as desirable but also perhaps even necessary to facilitate coming of age.

The *Specials'* issue-driven narrative strategy circulated within and
reinforced emerging theories of psychosocial development, most notably Erik Erikson's universalizing notion of "identity crisis" as a staple of
adolescence.[17] Ideally, rehabilitative edutainment invited teen viewers
to actively participate in their own citizenship training by channeling
their emotional and behavioral responses to various crises into "healthy"
choices. Thus, an empathetic teen viewer, trained to react in appropriately liberal and cosmopolitan ways to the episode, would experience
viewership as part of his/her development into a "good citizen": a heterosexual, able-bodied, normatively gendered, and emotionally stable
adult. The *Specials* participated in configuring the resolution of teen crisis as a cultural process that was simultaneously personal, national, and
emotional.

Disability was not always considered a problem in need of rehabilitation like other social problems on the series, though characters with
disabilities were a mainstay especially of the early *Specials*. However, the
series always presumed a middle-class white (and likely suburban) audience of "normal"—able-bodied and heterosexual—youth viewers. More
often than not, the *Specials'* disabled characters were white teen boys
rather than teen girls.[18] Such emphasis on male protagonists, at least
in the earliest *Specials*, occurred partially by design, because, in Tahse's
words, "the idea was that the boys would watch a boy show but not a girl
show, whereas a girl would like a boy show too."[19] Again, assumptions
about gendered behavior and development were at work, even behind
the scenes.

Disability figured into the content of the *Specials* in a variety of ways.
It was sometimes presented as a penalty for "bad behavior." For example,

in "A Mile from Here to Glory" (1978), Early MacLaren's (Steve Shaw) all-consuming desire to break school track records rather than be a team player leads him to injury. Early sulks after failing to break the school's record, and as he returns to the bus, a car hits him and breaks both of his legs. The show depicts the accident as a penalty for Early's selfishness: had he boarded the bus with the rest of the team rather than brooding, he would have avoided the accident. While learning how to walk again, he learns the value of teamwork rather than only personal investment.

Furthermore, in a formulation typical of many teen dramas about sexually transmitted diseases (STDs), disease functioned as a penalty for "promiscuous" sex. The earliest *Specials* about STDs—the majority of which were about gonorrhea—often featured a teen cheating on their long-term significant other and then infecting their unsuspecting partner, configured as the innocent party. "A Very Delicate Matter" (1982) highlighted female sexuality as exceptionally dangerous when a female doctor argued that boys were "lucky" in manifesting physical symptoms of gonorrhea, as opposed to a girl, who could "spread gonorrhea without ever knowing that she has it."[20] The narratives construct sexually active teen girls as endangering unsuspecting boys, rather than endangered by asymptomatic diseases.

Finally, at least three episodes dealt with cognitive disability: "Sara's Summer of Swans" (1974), "Hewitt's Just Different" (1977), and the semi-biographical "Kid Who Wouldn't Quit: The Brad Silverman Story" (1987). The *New York Times* television reviewer John J. O'Connor criticized "Sara's Summer of Swans," an adaptation of a Newberry Award–winning Betsy Byars novel featuring a cognitively disabled boy, for downplaying the character's disability. He argued that the episode portrayed the boy as "little more than extremely shy," although his disability was "the real reason for the book's Newberry award."[21] In the other two episodes, Hewitt Calder and Brad Silverman appeared as teenagers with cognitive disabilities.[22] Notably, although sexuality is generally either avoided or pathologized in narratives of cognitive disability, the *Specials* emphasized Hewitt's and Brad's teenaged heterosexual desires for able-bodied women and used them to evidence their similarity to "normal" teenaged boys.[23] However, all of the episodes about cognitive disability featured white able-bodied actors playing disabled characters rather than disabled actors in the roles.

This growing televisual focus on disease and disability narratives—or what television critics named "disease-of-the-week" shows—was significant for several reasons. First, it demonstrates that disability was a predominant cultural concern and a cultural language not only for addressing and entertaining teen viewers but also as advice for channeling teens into good American adult citizenship—which is to say, traditionally gendered, heterosexual, able-bodied, and white. While many episodes used disability to teach empathy and tolerance of difference by gently castigating able-bodied youths who teased or exploited disabled protagonists, disability also entered rehabilitative edutainment as a metaphoric language for educating teens about overcoming adversity. This narrative use of disability often presumed that occupying a state of disability was both natural and pathological for developing teens until they "came of age" into able-bodied heterosexual adults. As David T. Mitchell and Sharon L. Snyder argue, physical or cognitive anomalies, used as textual signifiers for "individual or social collapse," become the "materiality of metaphor" by providing a tangible body for the "textual abstraction" of metaphor.[24] Rehabilitative edutainment corporealized the intangible psychological process of coming of age through the physically disabled body and its overcoming. In multiple cultural locations both on-screen and off, teen proto-citizens were increasingly constructed and addressed as always-already under development, as disabled subjects in need of rehabilitation. While imagining teens as constantly "in the process" of resolving their inherent disabilities, rehabilitative edutainment, infused with emergent self-help philosophies, placed the responsibility for "treatment" squarely in the hands of teenagers themselves.

Second, the series premiered in a watershed year of the disability rights movement. Through a combination of deinstitutionalization efforts, the passage of significant federal legislation (especially Section 504 of the Rehabilitation Act [1973] and the Education for All Handicapped Children Act [1975]), and highly visible political protests in San Francisco, New York, and Washington, DC, disability emerged as a politicized identity in the 1970s. Although generally not included in traditional histories of youth political activism, the disability rights movement and its campaign for autonomy and self-determination for disabled people formed within 1960s youth political activism that galvanized young citizens and fundamentally redefined the contested category of "youth." At the University of California–Berkeley, fiery critiques of the *in loco parentis* policy launched by the free speech movement cross-pollinated with the independent living movement in leveraging distinct but interrelated critiques of paternalism. Thus, the rehabilitative approach in the *Specials* was part of a wider cultural redefinition not only of disability but also of the boundaries between "child" and "adult," inflected by youth activism of the 1960s and 1970s, including the disability rights movement. Disabled people were becoming culturally visible in new ways—as political actors, as returning Vietnam veterans, as young people demanding access to education and public space—while disability narratives increasingly emerged on television in the *Specials* and elsewhere.

In the context of new conceptions and images of disability, the *Specials* operated under fundamentally ableist assumptions. Functioning pedagogically to train teen proto-citizens, the *Specials* presented overcoming disability as a metaphor for coming of age. However, this rehabilitative logic relied on the problematic infantilization of disabled people by equating adulthood with able-bodiedness and heterosexuality, even as it challenged paternalism by addressing teenagers as self-actualizing citizens. Through its overcoming narratives, the *Specials* produced a discourse of rehabilitative citizenship through the linkage of "compulsory able-bodiedness" with "compulsory heterosexuality"—as the equivalent of "growing up."

"Required TV"? The Birth of Edutainment

Parents, lawmakers, and media producers all shaped the discourse about youth, television, and sexuality in the Cold War era. Grassroots efforts through petitions to the Federal Communications Commission threatened to bring more regulation into children's broadcasting to combat sex-themed programming, entertainment without educational value, and overabundant advertising. Meanwhile, networks took evasive action with new regulations and new socially conscious programming, such as Norman Lear's adult fare, *All in the Family* (CBS, 1971–1979), *The Jeffersons* (CBS, 1975–1985), and *Sanford and Son* (NBC, 1972–1977). Alongside television producers, lawmakers also responded to concerns about youth television intake. Broadcasters and policy makers codified television's role in national educational reform efforts during the Cold

War. Specifically, Title VII of the National Defense Education Act (1958) funded the promotion of the educational use of media, which made the use of audiovisual media coterminous with educational reform.[25] William Harley, president of the National Association of Educational Broadcasters (NAEB), firmly linked educational and media reform to America's geopolitical position when he hoped that Russia would "not have to launch the equivalent of a sputnik [sic] in the use of television for educational purposes in order to bring the breakthrough which American education so desperately needs if it is again to seize a position of world leadership in education."[26] Cold War anxieties heightened television's stake in affecting the nation's youth and effecting educational reform, and in this milieu, commercial television was assailed as a "vast wasteland."[27]

As Cold War educational bills increasingly linked television to American national educational reform, journalists, educators, politicians, and concerned parents configured the embattled medium as a crisis necessitating intervention. Amid the thrust to repair its deficient educational system, the nation also began to debate the place of sex in education, both in schools and on television, as the public imagined television's potential role in providing sexual instruction for young people in the wake of sexual liberation movements of the 1960s. There were two primary targets for regulation: first, commercial programming that was either "wallowing in sex" or reveling in violence, and second, advertising during children's programming. These threats materialized as imperiling to all young viewers, although teenagers were increasingly addressed as distinct from child or family viewers in this period, both in regulatory discourses and in an economic trend toward niche-market segmentation.[28]

Positioned as an unavoidable and potentially indispensable element in a developing youth citizenry, television was implicated in national crises over citizenship and the youth in whose name regulatory efforts were undertaken. Concerns over youth passivity surfaced amid familiar debates about certain activity, namely, the dangers posed by exposure to mediated violence. While a 1972 *Science Digest* article asked, "Does Video Violence Make Johnny Hit Back?," *Time* reported the link between "TV violence" and the "national nightmare" of rising "teen-age violence."[29] This linkage sparked a national panic and a plethora of studies, including a $1.8 million, five-volume report from the surgeon general, *Television and Growing Up: The Impact of Televised Violence* (1972), that emphasized a causal relationship between increased televisual and teenaged criminal violence and voiced concerns about the sexual content of shows, commercials, and even scantily clad talk-show guests.[30]

Amid a multipronged disparagement of commercial television, edutainment became a method by which networks could market their own programming as having educational value, thus refuting the charge that they were turning young viewers into violent or sexualized beings. ABC's *After School Specials* arrived on the television scene amid a flurry of edutainment offered as a healthier alternative to Saturday morning cartoons, including the launch of shows such as *Mister Rogers' Neighborhood* (PBS, 1968), *Sesame Street* (PBS, 1969), *The Electric Company* (PBS, 1971), *Schoolhouse Rock* (ABC, 1973), *CBS Library* (CBS, 1979), *3-2-1 Contact* (PBS, 1980), *Mr. Wizard's World* (1983, Nickelodeon), and *Reading Rainbow* (PBS, 1983), as well as the rise of cable networks specifically targeting a youth audience, such as Viacom's Nickelodeon (1979) and MTV (1981). Allison Perlman argues that educational television, by coaxing the viewer to be (in Wilbur Schramm's words) "active, striving, achieving, trying to better himself, participating in social interaction and public affairs," carved out its own identity in opposition to commercial television.[31] ABC's *After School Specials*, as a new mode of rehabilitative edutainment geared nearly exclusively to teenagers, represented a complex negotiation between educational broadcasting (imagined as culturally uplifting and socially responsible) and commercial programming (imagined as vacuous and irresponsible).

While newspapers and grassroots organizations repeatedly asserted that children's television intake was problematic, a new cultural construction of television as potential "teacher" presaged the incorporation of television in school as an acceptable teaching tool. In a 1978 article entitled "Required TV for Students," which featured a cartoon of a television feeding an eager child viewer, the *Washington Post* writer Larry Cuban questioned the wholesale vilification of television. Since "the short- or long-term impact of TV" on youth was "self-evident," rather than "damning the tube or calling it a drug," Cuban asked, "why not mandate home viewing for children as a teacher second to school and make it accountable?"[32] Instead of "required reading," Cuban noted that many television shows might already fit into a "required television" curriculum for youth.

The *Specials* represented one such possibility. In contrast to what he termed the "rotten eggs" that constituted Saturday-morning children's programming, John J. O'Connor praised the *Specials*, saying that "[o]nly ABC has made a serious and impressive effort to venture a bit further than typical series for young people," and lamented that such quality programming appeared only once or twice a month.[33] O'Connor noted that the *Specials* formed with "remarkable speed" to address the many "loud" complaints leveraged by the grassroots Action for Children's Television (ACT) "about cartoon gluts and violence overdoses" in programming for young people.[34] While the resounding discourse of television reform, especially of children's programming of the late 1960s and early 1970s, took issue with televised violence and sexuality as they related to teen viewers, educational television's importance—in both devoted educational programming and commercial television that had "turned toward relevance"—was a method of disciplining the technology by making its content safe for youth consumption. Television negotiated its own disciplinary role for teen viewers through its rehabilitative approach to proto-citizens on-screen as well as in offscreen regulatory debates.

Amid these debates, the combination of educational value and sexual titillation in ABC's *After School Specials* merged two dominant impulses of 1970s TV—"relevance" and sex-themed programming—by simultaneously offering moral lessons about sexual responsibility and profiting from the incitement of teen sexual desire. The regulatory power of the era, as transmitted through the *Specials*, produced rehabilitative visions of teen sexual containment (via compulsory heterosexuality and able-bodiedness) rather than solely sexual endangerment.

Skating toward Normal

As a historically specific mode of addressing teenagers, the *After School Specials* employed a rehabilitative logic, which combined emergent "flexible" gender roles espoused by the feminist movement with frankness in sexual education in the wake of sexual liberation. Rehabilitative citizenship depended on an anxiety over a perceived "loss" and a belief that it could be masked or repaired. Commercial television, according to its harshest critics, had apparently corrupted or perhaps even "disabled" teenagers by adversely impacting their development. While this betrayed nostalgia for teens untouched by the dangers of television or of a new, sexualized culture, rehabilitative edutainment proposed rehabilitation as a middle ground, a disciplinary project that would incorporate difference while productively (re)making teens identical with the desired citizen-image of the 1970s—one characterized by flexible, heterosexual, able-bodied patriotism and tolerance. This "enforcement of normalcy," to borrow Lennard Davis's term, occurred by policing gender and sexual norms through the linkage of compulsory heterosexuality with compulsory able-bodiedness.[35]

"The Skating Rink" (1975) and "Heartbreak Winner" (1980, also known as "The Gold Test"), two critically acclaimed, award-winning stories about ice skating, illustrate the sexual and gender politics at work within disability narratives. "The Skating Rink" deals with a boy's stuttering problem, while "The Gold Test" explores a female athlete's juvenile rheumatoid arthritis (JRA). While there are obvious differences between a stutter and JRA, the episodes (and television review articles about them) collapse the distinction, describing both as "handicaps" that impede coming of age. Rehabilitative edutainment's logic of effacement collapses differences among disabilities, molding their specificities into interchangeable metaphors for developmental challenges, or "overcoming" the disabling condition of adolescence itself.

Described as "the story of a teenage boy who rises above the handicap of his stuttering," "The Skating Rink," one of ABC's earliest *Specials* and a *New York Times* "Recommended Viewing" program, meditates on issues of proper heterosexual development and disability.[36] Set in a small Midwestern farming town, this "icy tale with a happy ending" follows the teenaged Tucker "Tuck" Faraday (Stewart Peterson) in a coming-of-age story about overcoming teen awkwardness and earning paternal respect.[37] Although Tahse never noticed that many of his *Specials* focused on characters with disabilities, he said that this storyline fit into his desire to depict kids "getting out of a ghetto" or "who have a dream of wanting to do something and are held back by their parents' prejudice or lack of understanding." When asked about shows featuring disability, he immediately referred to "The Skating Rink," saying that Tuck's stutter "is not that dangerous—it's not multiple sclerosis," but argued that his focus on disability was "without question" a "teaching tool" so that "other kids watching with slight disabilities could identify with it and see that somebody could overcome it." Tahse hoped viewers would identify with Tuck even if they did not stutter: "'I don't stutter, but I have a limp' or 'I wear glasses but [Tuck] got over it and became something.'" The *After School Specials* used disability as "the materiality of metaphor" and as a "teaching tool," but scarcely imagined "severely" disabled viewers as audience members.

Tuck was described in the *Washington Post* as "a cornflake-faced country kid, tousle-headed and snubnosed, with a Colgate smile."[38] Although the show focused on Tuck's hardships with girls, the review noted his sex appeal. He may look "like the kind of golden boy for whom life is a breeze," the review states, but although "all the girls should like him," Tuck's stutter renders him "an alltime loser." Synopses of the story do not describe "The Skating Rink" as a story of overcoming a "handicap" or disability; rather, they summarize the plot with such phrases as "overcoming shyness" or "a gawky lad learns to skate."[39] Thus, the narrative presents Tuck's stutter as an explicit "handicap," and the stutter signifies adolescence itself. It is at once a "normal" indicator of teenaged awkwardness and an unnatural condition, a disability induced by the trauma of witnessing his mother's drowning in a flood when he was a child.

Tuck's disability functions narratively as an impediment to his development of heterosexuality and manhood. The narrative not only shows that his overcoming disability and achieving heterosexuality rely on one another but also indicates that his individual overcoming has broader significance to national health. In one scene, his teacher calls on him to answer a question about President Franklin Roosevelt. Apparently uniquely positioned as a stutterer to speak about the disabled president, Tuck is symbolically and visually linked with Roosevelt. The camera focuses on him while his elderly teacher, Mrs. Bayliss (Molly Dodd), recounts Roosevelt's heroic stewardship of the country through the Depression and World War II, adding that "the amazing thing about this man was that in spite of the fact that both his legs were paralyzed, he was able to rise above this affliction to become one of our greatest presidents." Focusing on Mrs. Bayliss from a low angle, the camera replicates the attentive students' perspective and aligns the viewer's gaze with those of the students. Throughout her lesson, the camera continuously crosscuts from her to Tuck, as he concentrates diligently on her words while his peers' attention wanes. When the camera cuts to a pretty blonde girl, Elva (Cindy Eilbacher), she smiles at an unnerved Tuck, who fails to return the gesture. In the shot's foreground, a book on the teacher's desk clearly reads *Voices of a Nation*, implying that the "voices" are meant to be the students'. After waxing poetic about Roosevelt's virtuous overcoming of polio to assume strong leadership over a nation in crisis, Mrs. Bayliss asks Tuck to provide more historical insight into this national hero. As Elva eyes him amorously, Tuck stands and stutters nervously that he did not complete his homework assignment, a lie meant to help him avoid talking in class more than is absolutely necessary. His voice comes out haltingly, while the students' vicious laughter drowns out the teacher's futile scolding. The scene's final image is of Elva, laughing mercilessly as a defeated Tuck takes his seat.

This episode immediately establishes its narrative preoccupation with disability, sexuality, and masculinity through Tuck's and Roosevelt's overlapping overcoming narratives. Roosevelt's story, a famous national as well as personal overcoming narrative, provides an idealized image of powerful masculinity "in spite of" the presence of disability. The scene also links Tuck's disability to heterosexual failure and emasculation, in that Elva's initial interest devolves into laugher at his stutter. Later, when he walks Elva home, he avoids talking entirely despite her teasing ("Cat got your tongue?"). While they sit together, she sidles up to him flirtatiously and threatens to leave if he does not speak. In a last-ditch effort to remain silent, Tuck tries to kiss her. Screaming, "Dummy!," Elva slaps Tuck's face, revealing that she was only flirting with him to win a bet that she could make him talk and that usually she "can make boys do anything [she] want[s]." As if her laughter and stinging rejection were not horrible enough, we also learn from Tuck's little sister that Elva is not the only one calling him names. Tuck does not ride the bus home, she says, because other kids "pick on him and call him dummy." Upon hearing this story, their unsympathetic father, Myron (Rance Howard), growls at Tuck, "Looks like you just can't stand to act like everybody else! Gotta be different, like you's tetched." These insults link Tuck's stutter to mental illness ("tetched"), inferior intellect ("dummy"), and insufficient masculinity, emblematized by his inability to stop the bullying, model bravery for his little sister, or be a viable sexual prospect for Elva.

However, Tuck's inability to conform also becomes a unique virtue, as long as it can be productively channeled within the rehabilitative norms of heteronormativity and overcoming—or in other words, into the normative expectations of healthy adulthood. Roosevelt's image links Tuck's overcoming disability to national heroism, in which a masculinist and ableist overcoming narrative leads to the development of white patriotic American citizenship. However, his sexual failure with Elva represents his disability as an obstacle to heterosexuality and adulthood. This narrative figures disability as an essential "adversity" that teen subjects must overcome to come of age as adults and citizens by equating compulsory able-bodiedness and heterosexuality with Americanness and adulthood. This narrative rendering of compulsory able-bodiedness positions Tuck within a patriotic framework of "overcoming disability," intimating that Tuck will develop his voice, while the other "voices of the nation," the student-subjects on-screen and in the audience, will learn from his struggles.

Everything begins to change for Tuck when Pete Degley (Jerry Dexter), a former professional figure skater and owner of a new ice rink, gives him private skating lessons, boosting his self-confidence and transforming him into an economically productive man. Pete's immediate interest in Tuck initially seems suspicious, as if he might take advantage of a vulnerable and isolated young teen. The two are often completely unsupervised, as Pete gives Tuck a tour of the rink. When Tuck says that he cannot skate, Pete quickly offers to give him his first skating lesson at night, if he comes back alone. Tuck, ashamed, tells him that he cannot afford to pay for lessons, but Pete insists, "Nobody said anything about paying, . . . but listen, keep it under your hat, huh? I wouldn't want anyone knowing I was giving lessons before the rink opened, especially not for free . . . right?" At nightfall, Tuck sneaks from his house to the rink. Pete skates over to him, puts his hand on the back of Tuck's neck, and guides him back to choose a pair of rental skates. Arguing that he will be cold in his light clothes, Pete offers his own sweater to keep Tuck warm.

Pete's special attention toward Tuck proves to be innocuous, but initially seems vaguely homoerotic, since his attentions are clandestine and focused so exclusively on Tuck. Although the narrative later abruptly introduces Pete's wife, initially Pete is single, new in town, and without friends his own age. The ice rink's positioning in a rural space already serves to isolate Pete, while the contrast of Tuck's hard labor on the farm codes figure skating as a frivolous and feminine luxury activity.[40] Already queered by his emasculating stutter, Tuck tells Pete that his parents would think he was "loony" if he were found to be, in his little sister's words, "skating like a girl." While a 1970s audience might have presumed Pete's heterosexuality, Tuck's and Pete's association with the feminized sport of figure skating necessitates an active narrative recoding, or "rehabilitation," of their perceived compromised (or queer) masculinity that recasts them as heterosexual, able, masculine men.

Pete divulges that he is disabled as well and offers his own overcoming as a positive example for Tuck. Discussing the knee problem that ended his professional skating career, he tells Tuck matter-of-factly, "It's a handicap—there's no doubt about that. I guess everyone has some sort of handicap to wrestle with. I'm lucky it's just my knee. Look at me. I got my own skating rink, right?" The narrative links Pete's and Tuck's figure skating explicitly to their respective disabilities, as they bond over their mutual status as "handicapped." Skating becomes a means not only to overcome disability but also to achieve normative heterosexuality and masculinity. Tuck eventually finds his true talent in figure skating after realizing he "do[es]n't have to be a good talker to skate."

The narrative rehabilitates Pete and Tuck into masculine men by spotlighting their skating not as a passion or hobby but rather as a pathway to economic productivity and romantic relationships with women. Described by one *Washington Post* reviewer as "brave-mouthed . . . handicapped fellow[s]," Pete and Tuck, coded as queer/disabled, are both rehabilitated into "better" heterosexuals than Tuck's lackadaisical brothers, Tom (Billy Bowles) and Clete (Robert Clotworthy), or his severe father, Myron.[41] Prior to the show's climax, in which Tuck performs publicly in front of the entire town, Pete's heretofore unmentioned wife, Lily (Devon Ericson), arrives and quickly explains that Pete was her former doubles partner and that she has been caring for his ailing parents in another city. Pete arranges for Lily to be Tuck's partner for the rink's opening night festivities. At the Faraday dinner table, Tom and Clete rib Tuck about looking "kinda spiffy" and ask tauntingly whether he has a date. They burst into laughter before Tuck can reply.

The rink is quickly established as a space of heterosexual courtship, as Tom and Clete playfully grope their respective girls on the ice, falling down gawkily and laughing. Their inability to function on the ice will stand in stark contrast to Tuck's nimble athletic prowess. During Tuck's and Lily's flawless performance, images of an incredulous and awestruck Myron punctuate the footage of Tuck's routine. Even Tom and Clete smile in wonderment at Tuck's hidden talent. Ecstatic over their performance, Pete says excitedly to Tuck, "I thought I was going to have to carry some of those screechin' girls out tonight! Tucker Faraday, from now on, you're going to have to beat those girls off with a club!" Introducing Pete's wife to the story resolves any vagueness about Pete's sexuality and displays Tuck's athleticism (read: able-bodiedness) and heterosexuality to the entire town. Although Tuck has been a successful singles skater throughout the narrative, he needs a female "partner" in order to demonstrate his heterosexuality, masculinity, and able-bodiedness, and in the end, viewers are signaled that he will need to beat away gaggles of determined girls rather than avoid their gazes or their ridicule.

Tuck also gains his father's respect as an economically productive and responsible family man through the narrative recoding of skating from a feminine leisure activity into a masculine "job." Pete pays Tuck one hundred dollars for his performance and offers him a teaching job at the rink. Turning most of the money over to his speechless father, Tuck tells him to buy his stepmother a coveted new stove without revealing the source of the extra cash. Just as Pete's disability is overcome by his ownership of the rink, Tuck's skating is recast as productive work rather than indulgent art. Although "prancin' around that skatin' rink with a girl" can hardly be considered "workin'," says Myron, the money is "honest" and "appreciated." Thus, Pete's and Tuck's economic productivity recodes them as masculine, while their artistic labor differentiates them from other more traditionally masculine men in the narrative.

Pete's and Tuck's masculinity is a rehabilitated version of traditional masculinity, a flexible "new masculinity" that David Savran argues became "hegemonic" in the 1970s.[42] This softer masculinity involved "a reconsolidation of the characteristics and fantasies associated with a residual, entrepreneurial masculinity combined with an avowal of certain qualities traditionally associated with femininity."[43] Rather than asserting figure skating as a masculine activity, the narrative presents rink ownership and skating lessons to legitimate skating as masculine productive work. Still, Tuck represents a healthier, more flexible masculinity than that of his father or brothers. By the end of "The Skating Rink," Tuck's difference no longer means that he is "tetched" or a "dummy." Rather, he will now have to "beat away" countless "screeching girls" while his new job will earn extra cash for the family. Together, these sexual and economic changes render permissible his participation in skating without compromising his heterosexuality or masculinity. In the end, Tuck's flexible masculinity and able-bodiedness are inextricably linked to his heterosexuality: he is construed as being at his healthiest and most mature when his solo skating becomes co-ed pairs skating. While skating *like* a girl might have feminized Tuck, skating *with* a girl masculinizes him by making him a heterosexual man and by replacing his stutter, the primary element of his characterization, with athleticism, economic productivity, and overcoming.

Five years later, the *After School Specials* broadcast "Heartbreak Winner," which follows figure skater and Olympic hopeful Maggie McDonald (Melissa Sherman) from her unbeatable performances on the ice to her diagnosis with juvenile rheumatoid arthritis. "All is not Olympic gold that glitters," stated the *Washington Post*, describing the central lesson of the "'Heartbreak' tale" as "giving is more important than victory or gold."[44] Comparison of the ice skating episodes highlights how the *Specials'* representations of coming of age were explicitly gendered. While Tuck's task in "The Skating Rink" was to become an appropriately masculine citizen by overcoming his disability and asserting his heterosexuality, Maggie's prime developmental task in "Heartbreak Winner" is to rehabilitate her femininity by disciplining her (masculine) sports ambition into normatively feminine caretaking rather than individual achievement. To do so, the narrative requires Maggie not only to secure a heterosexual pairing with a boy but also to nurture others and to "accept" rather than overcome her disability. This more passive (read: feminine) acceptance involves her focusing less on her skating career and more on her social life, specifically directing her interest toward another male figure skater, Bobby (Chris Hagan), and helping Joey Taylor (Mark James), a young African American wheelchair user with severely injured legs, to walk again. While Tuck's heteronormativity is linked to his overcoming into able-bodiedness, it is only when Maggie accepts her disability as a limitation (aided by Bobby's compassionate insight into her condition) that her heteronormative coupling can occur. In the end, the movie emphasizes Maggie's acceptance of bodily limitation and the subjugation of individual desires in favor of collective goals. Although McRuer's theory of compulsory able-bodiedness does not explicitly discuss gendered differences in its expression, juxtaposing "Heartbreak Winner" with "The Skating Rink" reveals that the gender politics of compulsory able-bodiedness work to construct normative "adult" masculinity in terms of economic productivity and individualistic pursuits while it constructs femininity in terms of caretaking and the sacrifice of individual goals in favor of nurturing others.

The episode simultaneously valorizes and labels excessive Maggie's dedication to skating, because her rigorous practice schedule inhibits her ability to partake in traditional teenaged life events—most importantly, the pursuit of boys. The narrative actively contrasts Maggie with Cindy (Tammy Taylor), a fellow figure skater who lacks Maggie's discipline and consistently chastises Maggie for being an antisocial "gold medal bore." While bad-girl Cindy skips practice, dates boys, and goes to parties, "Miss Perfect" Maggie puts in countless hours at the rink to perfect her skating routine. Cindy dons fashionable clothing and makeup and wears her hair long, while Maggie appears more masculine, with a short haircut and tomboyish dress. Maggie's mother asserts that Maggie takes after her father "with her drive and determination," while Maggie's father jokingly advises her not to "marry an attorney" like himself. Both parents implicitly reaffirm heteronormativity and traditional femininity as ideals. Moreover, though the narrative valorizes Maggie's commitment to her sport by constantly comparing it to Cindy's poor work ethic (which Maggie earnestly helps to improve), it also subtly critiques Maggie's myopic pursuit of the gold medal at the expense of a "normal" teen girl's life, even before her JRA is discovered. Indeed, this *Special*'s early establishment of some "unhealthy" masculine aspects in Maggie's personality helps to set up a somewhat surprising, if utterly characteristic, narrative operation: disability, represented as a developmental obstacle, not only incites Maggie's coming of age but also rehabilitates her, as she is forced to shift her priorities from a focus on herself (i.e., the advancement of her skating career) to a focus on caring for others as romantic partner, mother figure, and mentor.

During a skating competition, Maggie's knee buckles during a crucial jump and sends her crashing to the ice. When Bobby offers help, Maggie indignantly yanks her arm from his grasp. Courageously finishing the routine, Maggie wins the competition in spite of her fall. Standing in the middle of the ice amid resounding applause, she collapses and is rushed to the hospital. Maggie continually lies to doctors and her parents about her pain level and vehemently denies her disabled status. One evening she sneaks out to skate against the doctor's orders. Her transgression lands her back in the hospital with a flare-up, and she snarls at the nurses, "I hate hospitals! They're for people with something wrong with them. Sick people. Not me." Before and after her diagnosis, Maggie expresses contempt for other disabled patients and exhibits "bad patient" behavior, constantly undermining medical authority and resisting rehabilitation.

Her inability to "get well," the story tells viewers, stems from her selfish inability to identify as sick and submit to the care and management of her body by male doctors and her blossoming love interest, Bobby. Maggie's acceptance of JRA occurs through her relationship with two boys in the story: Bobby, who becomes a quasi-boyfriend, and Joey, an African American disabled child and fellow patient. Becoming a girlfriend to Bobby and a symbolic mother to Joey facilitates Maggie's rehabilitation, productively channeling her competitive energy into her mentoring of others rather than into more "selfish" individualistic pursuits.

At first, Joey's hopeful "can-do" attitude, emblematized by his postrecovery plans to play for the New York Knicks, positions him as the ideal patient, in contrast to the pessimistic, self-hating Maggie. When he tries to cheer her up, she dismisses him from the room and snarls that she and Joey are "losers" and "failures" who will never be able to fulfill their professional athletic dreams. However, Nurse Pearl (Lillian Lehman) argues that Joey's optimism is just "slick street talk" to "cover" his fear that an upcoming operation will not fix his legs. Pearl tells Maggie that Joey "do[es]n't need the wheelchair" and that the doctors have high hopes that he will walk again. As Pearl speaks, Maggie is visually linked to another woman, who stands in the foreground. The woman is never introduced to Maggie or the audience, but she and Maggie share the same hair color and style and wear nearly identical hospital robes. Nurse Pearl and this woman conduct a conversation in ASL, and the deaf woman not only enjoys a positive relationship with the nurse but also "cleans up" after Maggie by wheeling her empty wheelchair back into the hospital. Maggie's linkage with a deaf woman, who seems compliant and conversational with the medical staff, foreshadows Maggie's eventual acquiescence to medical authority—and her resultant happiness and maturity.

However, until the doctors' machinations succeed in allying them, Maggie and Joey's unruly resistance to rehabilitation exasperates the doctors. They are puzzled that, although they have been "medically successful" with Joey's and Maggie's bodies, the patients have not been emotionally responsive to or participatory in their rehabilitation. Joey "still won't try to walk," and even though Maggie heals from her recent flare-up of JRA, she will not "accept that she'll never compete again." Rather than a failure of medicine, their failure to rehabilitate reflects a failure of will. The doctors develop an alternative strategy—enlisting Maggie's help with Joey's rehabilitation in the hopes that it will spur both of them to rehabilitate themselves.

Before Maggie can participate in this plan, she must first accept, with Bobby's assistance, that she "ha[s] JRA" and "learn how to live with it." In other words, the narrative depicts rehabilitation as the admixture of heteronormative romance and female passivity. Armed with a bouquet of flowers and a night's reading about JRA, Bobby sneaks up flirtatiously on a sulking Maggie and pleads that JRA "doesn't mean that . . . life is over or that you can't teach somebody else to be the best skater in the world. It just means it won't be you, Maggie." She screams, "Why don't you go and kick some other cripple when they're down! . . . I hate being a failure, and I can't stand being a cripple!" to which Bobby replies, "Then stop being one!" Positioning disability as antithetical to achievement and overcoming as a mere matter of willpower, the series' rehabilitative logic shows that, just as teens can willingly inhabit rehabilitative citizenship, they can also actively "cripple" themselves.

Only after being picked up and kissed by Bobby after she crashes to the ground does she accept her diagnosis. In choosing to "stop being" a cripple, she also actively distances herself from other disabled people, who are construed as at fault for their failure to achieve rehabilitation, as she says triumphantly, "I'm not a cripple, and I'm not a failure. . . . I've got JRA, and I've gotta learn to live with it." Maggie's budding relationship with Bobby links heterosexual love with the hospital's rehabilitation efforts. Although the logic of compulsory able-bodiedness required Tuck to overcome his disability and challenge patriarchal authority by asserting his masculinity and heterosexuality, Maggie must submit to medical and patriarchal authority in order to rehabilitate herself.

While overcoming narratives like "The Skating Rink" proclaim individual triumph over disability rather than interdependence, "Heartbreak Winner" valorizes interdependence, but only through a reassertion of heteronormativity and a traditional femininity characterized by passivity and nurturance. Maggie's coming of age occurs not only through acceptance of her disability, the help of male doctors and peers, and her own physical and emotional rehabilitation, but also through her participation in the rehabilitation of others—namely, Cindy and Joey. This overcoming narrative also transforms her body and her JRA into an object of knowledge for Bobby, like the doctors, to "figure out" as her friend and potential love interest. Finally, Maggie secures lackadaisical Cindy's rehabilitation as well. Cindy commits to practicing hard with Maggie as her coach. In keeping with gendered differences in the operation of compulsory able-bodiedness, Joey is expected to overcome disability, while Maggie is encouraged to accept hers while sublimating her individual desire to assist in the rehabilitation of others.

The scene in which Joey walks for the first time evokes the visual iconography of Christian faith healers and the American telethon, as crowds of people chant encouragingly to a nervous Joey to "get up out of that chair." A scene of multicultural solidarity, Joey's struggle to walk provides a liberalizing rallying point for racial harmony and heterogeneity, as Indian, white, African American, and Asian American hospital kids become his cheering section. In spite of Nurse Pearl's coaxing that "[c]rutches are better than a wheelchair any day," Joey crashes to the ground in a heap. Everyone falls silent except Maggie, who emerges from her room to encourage Joey's persistence. Once resistant to medical authority, Joey and Maggie now not only represent the ultimate rehabilitating-citizen-subjects but also embody the triumph of liberal antiracism. They yield to the will of the doctors, partner across the color line, and provide inspiration to able-bodied people around them. Finally, in this scene, the narrative also signals the transcendence of racial difference through the materialized metaphor of disability. Here disability, as what Mitchell and Snyder call "narrative prosthesis," works to depoliticize racial and gender differences as well as differences in ability by emphasizing a shared humanity, fully realized in overcoming.[45] Thus, Maggie's mentoring relationship with Joey reconstructs her, through her own volition, as more feminine—docile, maternal, and less ambitious—while Joey and the rest of the nonwhite crowd in "Heartbreak Winner" appear as an emblem of racial harmony achieved through individual will to overcome disability.

Tolerance and Rehabilitative Citizenship

The *After School Specials'* demise is generally blamed on the rise of syndicated talk shows coupled with the proliferation of teen issue–based edutainment in movies and 1990s prime-time teen TV series, such as *Beverly Hills, 90210* (Fox, 1990–2000).[46] Although Disney discontinued the *Specials* upon its purchase of ABC, their didactic, issue-driven formula lives on in traces today, for instance, in the issue-driven "very special episode" format of contemporary teen television dramas. Comedy Central's *Strangers with Candy* (1999–2000) was a satirical take on the *Specials,* and its nostalgic humor indicates that some 1970s teen viewers likely resisted the *Specials'* earnest rehabilitative narratives. In spite of its status as a contemporary object of ridicule, the series' place in television history in addressing teens as a serious audience distinct from children, its innovative educational format, and its lasting legacy on teen programming should not be understated. As rehabilitative edutainment, "instructive" television programming traded on and reshaped cultural conceptions of television as a medium as well as ideas about audiences and the ideological work of narratives.

Intervening in our views of television's role in society, rehabilitative edutainment endeavored to train teens into proactive, responsible citizens via racy commercial fare. Although emerging contemporaneously with educational television, the *Specials* and similar shows represented unprecedented departure from educational TV and its objective to democratize access to high art by offering televised theater and opera to "uplift" adult viewers.[47] Its edutainment approach was an invention of the commercial market rather than something desired solely by industry professionals or activists proclaiming the virtue of educational television. As television continued to negotiate its place in the American family in tumultuous times, this rehabilitative logic not only expected to mold teen viewers, as subjects, through progressive edutainment but also hoped to reform commercial programming's image from damaging and frivolous to healthy and educational.

By trading on and shaping our views of teenagers, ABC's *After School Specials* were an entirely new television offering for a brand new audience segment, and it is important to analyze and historicize the specificities of teen viewership rather than consider audience solely in the binaristic terms of "child" versus "adult" or subsumed within the catchall "youth." Specifically geared toward teens, this rehabilitative model dramatized coming of age in disability narratives and positioned them in relation to national iconography, transforming coming-of-age stories into rehabilitative citizenship stories. In the television content of the 1970s and its biopolitical engagement with teen bodies both on- and offscreen, this was never a relationship of total submission. Rather, televisual rehabilitative edutainment invited and required the participation of teenagers in their own overcoming or acceptance, encouraging liberatory "exploration" rather than submission to authority figures, even while assimilation to traditional norms of gender, sexuality, and ability evidenced an adulthood achieved through struggle rather than assured in advance. With their bittersweet and incomplete endings, the *Specials* indicated that a teen's ability to solve a given problem was not a permanent cure. Rather, the series presented coming of age as a constant negotiation, a self-surveilling construction process, while teen sexual exploration was both encouraged and safely contained within romantic, heteronormative love and disciplined by the danger of imminent sexually transmitted disease. Rehabilitative logics, while ableist and oppressive, opened up possibilities for sexual openness regarding teen sexuality and constructed a new, active rather than passive, teen television viewer and proto-citizen.

Finally, by incorporating rather than stigmatizing difference, the *Specials* relied on a universal human resonance of their developmental narrative of overcoming while granting center stage to white, middle-class, able-bodied teens, who stood in as universal developmental models. In representing and redefining heteronormativity and able-bodiedness as central and related objectives for American citizens, the *Specials* spotlighted difference to use it ideologically and pedagogically. Yet the *Specials* also eschewed structural critiques of the prejudices and problems they presented by containing difference within overcoming narratives that promoted the transformative power of individual will. Furthermore, by locating extreme prejudice in rural spaces and people, like Tuck's farmer father, the series largely failed to implicate its middle-class white audience in the problems of racism, ableism, sexism, or homophobia.

The *Specials* mobilized narratives of overcoming or accepting disability as a teaching tool. This narrative strategy did important and unacknowledged historical and cultural work in conceptualizing adolescence and citizenship and in establishing a rehabilitative promise of tolerance. Wendy Brown argues that although tolerance has been constructed as a "transcendent virtue," it is instead a "historically protean . . . vehicle for producing and organizing subjects" that had become a dominant mode of governmentality in the United States by the 1980s.[48] Likewise, McRuer refers to the celebration of "flexible" able-bodied and heterosexual individuals, who "are visible and spectacularly tolerant" of disabled and queer others, as a primary effect of neoliberalism.[49] The acquisition of tolerance is used as a developmental milestone in coming-of-age narratives because tolerance is future-oriented: tolerance depoliticizes identity and effaces difference by emphasizing empathy and "betoken[ing] a vision of the good society yet to come."[50] Scholars of media and cultural history would do well to historicize tolerance's emergence as edutainment, its *a priori* good in the emotional and political realms of citizenship, and its role in normalizing visions of teen crisis and "healthy" development.

Popular culture has long been a venue to teach tolerance to children and teenagers. However, it is also important to consider how disability narratives and teen subjects have been employed in service to this emotional and political vision of good citizenship and its recuperative powers. Although Brown and others consider the important historical and cultural work of tolerance in constituting identity, we should also think about its emergence and role, historically, as a mediator of various forms of identity crisis—both generational and political. Such crises point to the centrality of adolescence and disability in rehabilitative visions of the individual and the nation. Rehabilitative edutainment, as a method of biopolitically producing and managing citizens, emphasized tolerance's rehabilitative role in emotional growth by mapping overcoming disability onto coming of age and casting coming of age as, among other things, becoming tolerant of otherness and questioning (but, crucially, without altering) existent hierarchies—or, in the tidy summation of one review of "The Skating Rink," by demonstrating that "grit and natural-born goodness win out [and] everybody is worthy, in his way."[51] In this way, tolerance and rehabilitation emerge historically and cooperatively, through figurations of adolescence and disability, as modes of governmentality within the media and cultural history of neoliberalism.

NOTES

This essay is a shortened and revised version of chapter 2 of Julie Passanante Elman, *Chronic Youth: Disability, Sexuality, and U.S. Media Cultures of Rehabilitation* (New York: New York University Press, 2014).

1 *On the Media*, "After School Specials," Sarah Lemanczyk, WNYC Studios, New York, NY, June 10, 2005.

2 The exact title of the show changed over its television run and then again in video release: *After School* or *Afterschool, ABC* or no *ABC* in the title, etc.

3 The series dealt with homosexuality implicitly, in episodes about AIDS and in one episode about ballet dancing (*ABC's After School Specials*, "A Special Gift," ABC, October 24, 1979). On racism, see "Color of Friendship," November 11, 1981; "Class Act: A Teacher's Story," March 18, 1987; "Taking a Stand," January 19, 1989; "Girlfriend," April 15, 1993; and "Shades of a Single Protein," January 28, 1993. On teen pregnancy, see "Schoolboy Father," October 15, 1980; "Jacqui's Dilemma," June 2, 1994; and "Too Soon for Jeff," September 12, 1996. On child molestation, see "Don't Touch," November 6, 1985. On child abuse, see "Please Don't Hit Me, Mom," September 19, 1983; and "Terrible Things My Mother Told Me," January 20, 1988. On physically abusive teen relationships, see "Love Hurts," September 16, 1993. On divorce, see "What Are Friends For?" March 19, 1980; and "Divorced Kids' Blues," March 4, 1987. On sexual harassment, see "Boys Will Be Boys," September 15, 1994. On rape, see "Did You Hear What Happened to Andrea?" December 27, 1983; and "Date Rape," September 15, 1988. On teen suicide, see "Amy and the Angel," September 22, 1982; and "Face at the Edge of the World" (a.k.a. "A Desperate Exit"), September 19, 1986. On illegal drugs, see "Stoned," November 12, 1980; "Tattle: When to Tell on a Friend," October 26, 1988; and "Desperate Lives," March 3, 1982. "Stoned" starred Scott Baio, while "Desperate Lives" featured a young Helen Hunt as a drug-using teen who, in a scene that has achieved cult fame, vaults from a window while high on PCP.

4 I treat psychological ideas about adolescence and their codification of universal "normal" developmental stages as one historical context for the *Specials*, but I would argue that the establishment of universal psychological norms of develop-

ment are invested in what disability studies scholar Lennard Davis has named as the historical and cultural process of "enforcing normalcy." See Davis, "Constructing Normalcy," 3–17. For a disability studies critique of theories of childhood development and their use in education, see Ferri and Bacon, "Beyond Inclusion."

5 "Infantile citizenship" is Lauren Berlant's term. See Berlant, *Queen of America*.

6 See Spigel, *Make Room for TV*.

7 The *After School Specials* had many clones, including *CBS Schoolbreak Special* (1984–1995), CBS's *Afternoon Playhouse* (1981–1983), NBC's *Special Treat* (1975–1986), and HBO's *Lifestories: Families in Crisis* (1992–1996).

8 McRuer, *Crip Theory*, 2.

9 Establishing the total number of ABC's *After School Specials* is nearly impossible, since no complete archive of the series exists. Individual episodes were produced by small production companies and then sold to ABC. The Internet Movie Database records 154 episodes. Individual episodes of the *Specials* are scattered throughout the country in different libraries and museums, and some have been released on DVD. New York's Paley Center for Media boasts the largest (unindexed) collection.

10 *On the Media*, "After School Specials."

11 Ibid.

12 Ibid.

13 Martin Tahse, telephone interview by author, February 22, 2007, Washington, DC (written notes). Unless otherwise cited, all quotes from Tahse are from this telephone interview.

14 Psychological theories of separation from the family of origin and its essential relationship to individuation, identity formation, and coming of age emerged from the late 1960s through the early 1980s, most notably by psychoanalyst Margaret Mahler. See Mahler, Pine, and Bergman, *The Psychological Birth of the Human Infant*. See also Blos, "The Second Individuation Process of Adolescence."

15 Queer scholars have used "metronormativity" to describe how sexual liberation has been linked to a compulsory migration from rural to urban spaces and critique the oversimplified association of rural spaces with backwardness and sexual repression. See Herring, *Another Country*; Gray, *Out in the Country*; Halberstam, *In a Queer Time and Place*; Tongson, *Relocations*. On metronormativity and disability, see Clare, *Exile and Pride*.

16 Leslie Garisto, "Why 'Afterschool Specials' Are Special," *New York Times*, August 5, 1985, H21.

17 Discourses of developmental psychology in the late 1960s and early 1970s were one of many cultural locations that codified and reproduced the notion of adolescence as crisis. Lawrence Kohlberg's theories of moral development and the problem-novel formula share many similarities. See Kohlberg, "Stage and Sequence." For a historical analysis of identity politics and youth in reference to Erik Erikson's work on identity crisis, see Medovoi, *Rebels*.

18 No episodes about cognitive disability feature disabled girls, and very few episodes about physical disability feature a female protagonist, except "Blind Sunday" (1976) and "Run, Don't Walk" (1981).

19 Tahse's notion of girls liking a "boy show" (but not vice versa) cohered with dominant developmental psychological ideas about adolescence, which were presented as universal but generally based on white, able-bodied, all-male subjects. Carol Gilligan's work became influential in shifting attention to the specificities of adolescent female development by the late 1980s. See Gilligan, "In a Different Voice."

20 See "A Very Delicate Matter" (1982) and "Private Affairs" (1989). I did not see any episodes dedicated to herpes, HPV, or chlamydia, although all were also prevalent at the time. The series devoted at least three episodes to HIV/AIDS: "Just a Regular Kid: An AIDS Story," September 9, 1987; "In the Shadow of Love: A Teen AIDS Story," September 18, 1991; and "Positive: A Journey into AIDS," December 7, 1995. "In the Shadow of Love" featured a disclaimer for parental discretion uncharacteristic of the *After School Specials*. "Don't Touch," an episode about child molestation, seems to be the only other *Special* that featured a parental warning about the episode's disturbing content, suggesting that narrative renderings of certain issues of sexuality, HIV/AIDS, and child molestation, were deemed more controversial than episodes that dealt with non-sexual child abuse or STDs that were not so closely associated with homosexuality.

21 John J. O'Connor, "Those Adaptations—Faithful or Fudged?" *New York Times*, February 29, 1975, D29.

22 Although Brad Silverman, an actor with Down syndrome, appeared at the end of "The Kid Who Wouldn't Quit" to address the audience, different able-bodied actors played Silverman at various stages of life. An able-bodied actor also played Hewitt in "Hewitt's Just Different."

23 In "Hewitt's Just Different," Hewitt's younger friend, Willy, finds a sexy poster of a scantily clad blonde woman and ridicules Hewitt, "Wow! Hewitt! Gonna hang it in a special place? . . . Got a crush on her?" Hewitt angrily yanks the poster away from Willy, who apologizes. Meanwhile, "The Kid Who Wouldn't Quit" establishes Brad Silverman's coming of age through his bar mitzvah and his energetic flirting with able-bodied high school girls. He flirts openly with a cheerleader without realizing that she is making fun of him to her friends. An African American basketball player rescues Brad, encouraging him to "be cool" rather than coming on so strongly to the girls.

24 Mitchell and Snyder, *Narrative Prosthesis*, 48–49. Mitchell and Snyder importantly note that disability's centrality to representation poses a problematic conundrum: the ubiquity of disability as a "symbolic figure" in representation rarely results in its depiction as "an experience of social and political dimensions."

25 Clowse, *Brainpower for the Cold War*, 162–167.

26 Hearings before the Committee on Interstate and Foreign Commerce, United States Senate, Eight-Sixth Congress, January 27–28, 1959, 67, in Allison Perlman, "Reforming the Wasteland," 25.

27 The phrase "vast wasteland" originated in FCC chairman Newton Minow's 1961 address to the National Association of Broadcasters. One report, *The Impact of Educational Television* (1960), described commercial television as "encourag[ing] chiefly passivity and minimum effort rather than activity, a minimum of social interaction, a concern with fantasy rather than real life, and living in the present rather than concerning oneself either with self-improvement or the problems of tomorrow." *The Impact of Educational Television*, ed. Wilbur Schramm (Urbana: University of Illinois Press, 1960), 26 in Perlman, "Reforming the Wasteland," 36.

28 See Perlman, "Reforming the Wasteland."

29 "Does Video Violence Make Johnny Hit Back?," *Science Digest*, January 1972, 57; "Ending Mayhem," *Time*, June 7, 1976. See also Office of the Surgeon General, *Television and Growing Up: The Impact of Televised Violence. Report to the Surgeon General, United States Public Health Service* (Washington, DC: National Institute of Mental Health, 1972); Frederic Wertham, "How Movie and TV Violence Affects Children," *Ladies' Home Journal*, February 1960, 58–59; V. B. Cline, "TV Violence: How It Damages Your Children," *Ladies' Home Journal*, February 1975, 75; and E. Kiester, "TV Violence: What Can Parents Do?," *Better Homes and Gardens*, September 1975, 4.

30 Levine, *Wallowing in Sex*, 82.

31 Schramm in Perlman, "Reforming the Wasteland," 36.

32 Larry Cuban, "Required TV for Students: A Proposal for Home Educational Programming," *Washington Post*, May 21, 1978, B8.

33 John J. O'Connor, "Saturday Is No Picnic for the Kids," *New York Times*, September 30, 1973, 137.

34 John J. O'Connor, "ABC's 'No Greater Gift' about Organ Donorship," *New York Times*, September 10, 1985, C22.

35 Davis, *Enforcing Normalcy*.

36 "TV Highlights," *Washington Post*, February 5, 1975, B11.

37 Emily Fisher, "An Icy Tale with a Happy Ending," *Washington Post*, February 5, 1975, B9.

38 Ibid.

39 IMDB describes the story as one of "overcoming shyness." See *ABC's After School Specials*, "The Skating Rink," *Internet Movie Database*, www.imdb.com. Netflix's description of this episode on the DVD sleeve features the description, "A gawky lad learns to skate."

40 My analysis of the representation of rural space is deeply informed by Victoria E. Johnson's work. See Johnson, *Heartland TV*.

41 Fisher, "Icy Tale."

42 See Savran, *Taking It Like a Man*. My use of the term "flexible" derives from Emily Martin's work. See Martin, *Flexible Bodies*.

43 Savran, *Taking It Like a Man*, 125.

44 "'Heartbreak' Tale: All is Not Olympic Gold that Glitters," *Washington Post*, February 10, 1980, TV43.

45 Mitchell and Snyder, *Narrative Prosthesis*, 48–49.

46 ABC's affiliates were actually part of the show's success and its demise. Tahse noted that "once critics started reviewing the shows, the affiliates really joined in and made it all possible," because "every city started showing them, and then the advertisers jumped in." However, the *Specials* were always economically precarious, because they were "really at the whim of affiliates" that had to voluntarily "give up" hour timeslots for the *Specials* rather than filling that time with more profitable commercial programming. From Tahse, telephone interview.

47 I thank Laura Cook Kenna for illuminating this significant distinction.

48 Brown, *Regulating Aversion*, 11.

49 McRuer, *Crip Theory*, 2.

50 Brown, *Regulating Aversion*, 5.

51 Fisher, "Icy Tale."

PART II

Disability and Race

3

Throw Yo' Voice Out

Disability as a Desirable Practice in Hip-Hop Vocal Performance

ALEX S. PORCO

Alex S. Porco argues that vocal disability is a desirable, if unacknowledged, practice in hip-hop vocal performance. His materialist approach to vocal performance resists reducing voice to a metaphor for race, oppositionality, or liberation; it reveals, instead, the physiological and social processes that render hip-hop voices unique, particular, and audible. Porco emphasizes the agency hip-hop artists possess in performing disability and assuming disabled identities for aesthetic and political ends. The chapter demonstrates how integrating disability, music, and media technologies can produce fresh and important new insights about this well-studied genre.

I want to speak about bodies changed into new forms.
—Ovid, *Metamorphoses*

but I sound better since you
cut my throat. the checkerboard is also a
chess board. it's also a cutting board and a
sound board. it's also a winding sheet and a
sound booth.
—Fred Moten, "Rock the Party, Fuck the Smackdown"[1]

In 1886, Sir Morell Mackenzie, M.D., published *The Hygiene of the Vocal Organs: A Practical Handbook for Singers and Speakers*. The study was based on the doctor's 25 years of medical and therapeutic fieldwork in London, "ministering to diseased throats, and every singer or actor of note in this country."[2] "I have thus had very unusual opportunities," explains Mackenzie, "of studying the conditions which affect the voice for good or for evil."[3] As part of the period's general obsession with hygiene (from "ladies' under-clothing" to "the problems of drainage and sewage"),[4] his Victorian-era handbook outlines "common-sense rules for the culture and management of the voice":[5] he identifies staccato and tremolo as "evils" to be avoided;[6] he advises against performing outside or, similarly, inside buildings "of bad acoustic construction";[7] and he warns "ladies of an impressionable nature" that "violent and prolonged weeping is likely *to dull the voice.*"[8] On the one hand, Mackenzie recognizes that, both in everyday life and in artistic performance, one's voice is not simply a given—it is subject to contingency. Physical and moral labor, as well as the unequal distribution of economic and cultural capital, marks each body and, therefore, each voice differently and at different times. On the other hand, he clearly treats the voice as an object to be disciplined in the face of such contingency: in a world that divides neatly into good and evil, the success or failure of the voice is ultimately based on its edification. The *right* voice is an index of good, clean, and purposive living.

Mackenzie's handbook means to erase any difference through the implementation and administration of best practices related to the well-being of the body politic and the sounding of its uniform, representative voice. A century later, and a continent over, however, in the South Bronx, hip-hop artist KRS-One proudly makes those differences of labor and capital audible.[9] In the culture of hip-hop, the wrong and bad voice may, in fact, be the right and best voice. In a revealing couplet from Boogie Down Productions' 1987 recording "Criminal Minded," KRS-One raps, "Everything that flows from out of my larynx / Takes years of experience and bottles of Beck's." Time ("years of experience") permits KRS-One to hone a vocal style characterized by steady pacing and over-enunciated strong stresses as well as the occasional slip into his mother's Jamaican *patois*. But the rigors of touring (e.g., repeat performances in venues "of bad acoustic construction")[10] and the indulgences of party and club culture—represented by Beck's beer—take a toll on his body, of which the "larynx" (voice box) is a synecdoche. That toll is constitutive of his voice's uniqueness. Touring and party culture provide experiential *gravitas*, or what Roland Barthes calls "the grain,"[11] and the grain authenticates and authorizes KRS-One's voice and position in the field of hip-hop.

KRS-One's couplet casts his response to the disabling performance context of early hip-hop in heroic terms. However, the physical demands and emotional pressures of performing are not always readily available to such self-mythologizing or, for that matter, reducible to a neatly rhymed couplet. For example, in 1997, as a result of excessive drinking and smoking while on tour, Run-DMC's Darryl McDaniels began to suffer from spasmodic dysphonia. The disorder causes involuntary movements of the larynx; as a result, the voice continually gives out, making it impossible to rap with any consistency. As Ice-T explains, in a conversation about McDaniels, "You're a rapper. Your tool is your voice. . . . If you lose your voice, it's like being a piano player and losing your fingers . . . how cruel is that? That's the worst thing that can happen to you."[12] McDaniels's vocal disability, in conjunction with his alcoholism, led to a period of suicidal depression.

That said, without romanticizing disability or minimizing its real physical and emotional effects, I would like to suggest that vocal disability is, to an unacknowledged degree, a desirable practice in hip-hop performance. Disability refers to a history of intersecting medical, legal, and cultural meanings related to health, citizenship, and stigma, respectively. Following Joseph N. Straus, I define disability broadly as any form of "culturally stigmatized bodily difference,"[13] including impairment. It is a socially determined "minority identity" as opposed to an exclusively physiological condition.[14] Disability is not a problem in need of correction but a positive resource, especially as it pertains to aesthetics.[15] By conceiving of disability as a practice, however, I mean to propose three separate yet related qualifications. First, the meaning of disability depends on the dynamic relationships, dispositions, and (unequal) power distributions within a given field of production[16]—in this case, rap music and hip-hop culture. Second, disability includes those individuals who are defined as such by external agents and legislative forces, yes, but also those individuals who actively seek out and assume disabled conditions and identities. Third, disability is temporal insofar as it involves physiological, social, and political processes. Disability as a practice, then, marks out differences of degree, agency, and time.

In "The Organ of the Soul: Voice, Damage, and Affect," Laurie Stras astutely observes, "The damaged voice continues to be accepted, even preferred, in many genres within popular music, to the point of optimum levels of damage appearing suitable for different types of singing: the gravel-voice of the rock singer is not interchangeable with the subtle hoarseness of the jazz vocalist. Many singers have learned to simulate or manipulate damage in the voice, so further revealing the affective value of the sound; and in a reversal of what might be considered normate associations, damage here seems to be linked with concepts of authority, authenticity, and integrity."[17] Hip-hop exists beyond the purview of Stras's essay, which focuses on blues, rock, and jazz vocalists from the mid-twentieth century; as my next section outlines, hip-hop's aesthetic and ethical relationship to disability is autonomous from those other musical genres. Nevertheless, Stras's essay makes the important case for an "essential" relation between disability and vocal performance in general terms: "Trauma typically forces a disjunction between body and voice . . . but the integration and healing of trauma is achieved through reestablishing narrative, through giving voice to the trauma. Nonetheless, the disrupted singing voice cannot help but tell of trauma, for the damage leaves its trace at sublinguistic levels."[18] That "trace" *affects* listeners, initiating "a process of catharsis."[19] Stras is correct in noting that disability throws into sharp relief the "sublinguistic" aspects of vocal performance, or what Steve McCaffery calls the "protosemantic" (e.g., "the full expressive range of predenotative human sonorities: grunts, howls, shrieks, and hisses").[20] However, Stras's "hermeneutic of trauma" remains too restrictive because it negatively frames disability as inevitably injurious, diminishing the importance and positivity of play, style, and pleasure (including humor) for the hip-hop artist and listener, respectively.

Disability is a desirable practice in hip-hop because it stamps the "sound iconicity" of vocal performances. "Sound iconicity" is a phrase coined by Charles Bernstein,[21] and it refers to those features of vocal performance that escape signification: pitch, register, tempo, amplification, etc. But sound iconicity doesn't just happen. Rapped vocals represent interpretive acts and aesthetic decisions materially grounded in the body and the recording studio. Put another way, I am interested in the provenance of hip-hop's vocal poetics—the "habits and practices of thinking and making"[22] mediated, in particular, by disabled bodies and disabling spaces. This means I will *not* be reading the voice as a metaphor for race, oppositionality, or liberation. Metaphor silences, mystifies, and dematerializes the vocal performance. In addition, following from Barthes once more, I will resist—as much as possible—the impressionism of the "adjective."[23]

Vocal performances are audible, incarnate, and particular. But to hear and appreciate them as such means attending to where voices actually come from. Thus, the convergence of disability studies and hip-hop prompts a timely methodological break: it turns the listening ear's attention to the otherwise hidden, inaudible, or unknown.

* * *

Hip-hop culture is a form of vernacular theory and practice.[24] The vernacular is rooted in an archive of everyday language and images shared by disenfranchised citizens. The vernacular is grounded in local communities and concerns yet, in accordance with the logic of late capitalism and globalization, transmissible and adaptable to distant locales. The vernacular is also synonymous with improvisation, which requires sensitivity to, and awareness of, changing situational exigencies. Finally, the vernacular is a renewable resource, perpetually engaged in the dialectical process "of tearing down old vocabularies and proposing new ones."[25] In hip-hop culture, the idiomatic phrase *flip the script* describes an act of tactical resistance to dominant power structures: to invert or, at least, interrupt the value system that privileges certain language rules, technological imperatives, cultural spaces and objects, and master narratives. As vernacular theory and practice, hip-hop *flips the script* on disability, transforming a physical condition and social stigma into a desirable aesthetic value.

The history of hip-hop provides numerous analogous instances of *flippin' the script*. In 1988, recording duo Eric B. and Rakim released "Follow the Leader," an Afrofuturistic riff on the Pied Piper of Hamelin legend. The song includes Rakim's oft-quoted couplet, "I can take a phrase that's rarely heard, flip it, / Now it's a daily word." Rakim's punning turn of phrase establishes the relationship between language, style, and currency. More importantly, it speaks to the influence of hip-hop slang on contemporary popular culture: it's ubiquitous—from the playground to the classroom, from the stoop to the White House. Hip-hop culture's influence on the English language is more formally recognized through governing bodies like the editorial board of the *Oxford English*

Dictionary (*OED*). In recent years, the *OED* has made headlines by including "crunk," "bling," "jiggy," "dope," "phat," and "balla." Rappers have used these words and invested them with hip-hop-specific meanings.

Hip-hop culture also adopts and transforms instruments of new media. Consider the record player. As Jonathan Sterne explains, "The turntable is a classic case of people making a 'virtue' of necessity. . . . [T]he lower-class (and mostly non-white) 'turntablists' convert a playback medium into a musical instrument in a world where musical instruments were very hard to acquire."[26] Hip-hop *flips the script* on the technological and commercial imperatives of record player manufacturers. Through trial and error, early hip-hop deejays—Kool Herc, Grandmaster Flash, and Grand Wizzard Theodore—developed a musical aesthetic with a repertoire of techniques such as the break-beat, the scratch, the crossfade, the backspin, and clock theory.[27] Since the mid-1980s, turntable manufacturers have worked with deejays to "co-create" products that meet their changing artistic interests and formal demands. The more recent relationship between rappers and Auto-Tune likewise illustrates how "[technologies] cannot come into existence to simply fill a pre-existing role"—and this has consequences, especially, for the rapping voice.[28]

Antares created Auto-Tune software to correct "pitch problems in vocals and other instruments" during studio performances, concert performances, and post-production.[29] Auto-Tune also includes a throat-modeling feature, in which any one of the throat's five constitutive features may be reshaped, changing the vocal apparatus and, by extension, the sound iconicity of the voice. Contemporary hip-hop artists (e.g., Kanye West, Lil Wayne, and T-Pain, among many others) apply Auto-Tune to the voice—but *not* for the purposes of pitch correction. Using the device's in-built phaser effect, these artists generate vocals that modulate *in* and *out* of tune, in waves, tapping into quarter- and semitones. The resultant timbral quality is typically described as robotic and synthetic, or, as Alexander Weheliye puts it, "posthuman."[30] The software is used by hip-hop artists to disable the vocal apparatus and, thus, to denaturalize the voice.

Hip-hop culture reterritorializes institutional spaces, too. Promotional flyers for early hip-hop events in the South Bronx reveal how students transformed public school gymnasiums into performance venues.[31] The symbolic disciplinary power of the school during the day is countered by personalized expression at night. Official knowledge in the form of core curriculum is countered with embodied, affective knowledge communicated through music, dance, graffiti, and fashion. Moreover, in an instance of nimble improvisation, the promotional flyers cleverly incorporate school yearbook photos to put a face to the performer's stage name. They demonstrate how early hip-hop performers infused the school with local artistic pride—independent of authorized educational forms (class timetables, lectures, tests) and authorities (teachers, principals, administrators).

Finally, hip-hop culture *flips the script* on strategies of representation, too. Rappers provide alternative or "minority" perspectives on significant political events, historical figures, and cultural objects and symbols.[32] So, for example, Public Enemy's "Fight the Power" interrogates representations of popular history that advocate exclusively for white cultural heroes:

> Elvis was a hero to most
> But he never meant shit to me you see
> Straight out racist that sucker was
> Simple and plain
> Motherfuck him and John Wayne
> Cuz I'm Black and I'm proud
> I'm ready, I'm hyped plus I'm amped
> Most of my heroes don't appear on no stamp[33]

Chuck D proposes a new black hero rescued from the sediment of popular culture. In response to (white) *visuals*, he presents (black) *audio*: "the sounds" of James Brown's "funky drummer," designed to generate racial pride and inspire social change. Thus, Chuck D situates his listener at what Jennifer Stoever-Ackerman calls "the sonic color-line . . . a socially constructed boundary where racial difference is produced, coded, and policed through the ear."[34] His witty rhyme, "amped" and "stamp," highlights the competition between audio and visual epistemologies.[35]

The foregoing genealogy of hip-hop's *flip the script* aesthetic and ethic is meant to situate hip-hop in unique relation to disability as a practice and disability studies as a field. Hip-hop artists emphasize that cultural

meanings, norms, and values—including (but not limited to) ableism—
are open to social agents and processes that stage "the intersection of
different 'accentings' in the same discursive terrain."[36] But to quote Tricia Rose, "Without historical contextualization, aesthetics are naturalized, and cultural practices are made to appear essential to a given group
of people. On the other hand, without aesthetic considerations, Black
cultural practices are reduced to extensions of sociohistorical circumstances."[37] Disability is a key "vanishing mediator" between the hip-hop
aesthetic and its social-historical context.[38] This essay aims to make
disability present and audible as a mediating practice; it proposes that
hip-hop's self-conscious acts of transvaluation challenge the discursive
dominance of ableism.[39]

* * *

Every hip-hop MC possesses a unique vocal apparatus: oral, nasal, pha-
ryngeal, and laryngeal cavities, as well as the lungs, sternum, and stomach
muscles.[40] The vocal apparatus calls and responds to the rest of the body
and its constantly changing dispositions *and* to contexts of production.
The vocal apparatus is involved in recursive involutions of physical and
existential labor: "To speak is to perform work, sometimes, as any actor,
teacher, or preacher knows, very arduous work indeed. The work has the
voice, or actions of voice, as its product and process; giving voice is the
process which simultaneously produces articulate sound, and produces
myself, as a self-producing being."[41] The MC expands or contracts the
mouth cavity to control attack. He projects from the diaphragm for more
volume. He inhales and exhales, using his breath to delimit the length of
prosodic units. He flexes the tongue to affect dialect and uses the throat
to add vibrato. Through the use of what Marcel Mauss calls "body techniques,"[42] the MC's *physis* is expended, expanded, and—sometimes—even
disabled for the purposes of art and commerce.[43]

Shouting, for instance, places "acute stress" on any voice.[44] Chuck D
developed his particularly aggressive shouting style of rapping through
his experience in the Long Island club and party circuit of the early
1980s, when he was an undergraduate student at Adelphi University: "I
had the strongest voice of anybody around me and that was key, because
most sound systems were cheap. You had to be able to cut across a cheap

system. Guys like DJ Hollywood and Melle Mel had no problems with something like that. . . . Me and Flavor was blessed with having voices on two different ends of the spectrum, and they could both cut across any live situation very easily."[45]

Acoustic design—or lack thereof—shapes Chuck D's identifiable vocal style and skill, and his ability to overcome otherwise disabling conditions situates him in a prestigious hip-hop genealogy à la KRS-One's "Criminal Minded." His insistence on the *sprezzatura* with which he is heard against all spatial and technological odds is a source of masculine pride, and it implies that less successful rappers are rendered—and gendered—silent and weak. This anecdote is useful for two reasons. First, it reveals how conceiving of disability *as a desirable practice* in hip-hop culture means accepting its simultaneously positive and negative presences. Second, it historicizes Chuck D's voice: only later in the decade, as a member of Public Enemy and in the context of that group's militant iconography, is Chuck D's shouting style transformed into a politicized instrument of anger and figured as an ideological critique of R&B singers who use their voices to sing "senseless songs to the mindless."[46]

Like Chuck D, rappers Percee P and Big Pun similarly test, exceed, and valorize the voice's limits. In 1992, Percee P released the single "Lung Collapsing Lyrics." As the title suggests, he purposely exposes the vocal apparatus to risk and, ultimately, system failure:

> I'm the capital P-E-R-C double E dash P P dash double E-C-R-E-P in
> me
> Shots in top lyrical fitness that's why you bit this
> Get this, I got a witness and I won't quit this
> And flip flop, get dropped, shit I'm in tip-top shape
> Lyrics escape, can't even catch him with tape . . .
> I cold-grip the mic, strike then rip his life
> My rap dilapidate adversaries with kryptonite
> Hit you with a verse, make you disperse but first
> Call up a hearse cuz Perc' leave you worse than this
> Brain cells shatter, MCs scatter
> I splatter them all with something that ain't even matter[47]

Percee P's high-speed delivery matters more than the lyrical content. Extended periods of uninterrupted breath units signify the dialectic between athletic exceptionalism ("tip-top shape" and "lyrical fitness") and disability ("lung[s] collapsing"). At the same time, Percee P argues for the inimitability of his vocal style. If another hip-hop MC should try to "bit[e]" his vocals (i.e., *to steal* in hip-hop parlance), that MC risks the health of his "lungs" ("My rap dilapidate adversaries with kryptonite"). While Percee P's disabling condition remains in the realm of metaphor, the late Big Pun's does not, unfortunately. Big Pun struggled with obesity throughout his life. When he died in 1999 while recording his second album, he was close to seven hundred pounds. At that weight, even everyday activities (e.g., walking and talking) are physically exhausting—to say nothing of rapping. Thus, his signature, virtuoso delivery, which relied on uninterrupted breath units extended over multiple musical bars, sounds out a Freudian death drive by purposefully placing his body under conditions of duress.

Disability is a desirable vocal practice in hip-hop, then, only to the extent that it doesn't eventually result in total vocal failure or death. Rappers Fat Joe, Raekwon, Guru, and Coolio, for example, have voices distinguished by aspirated timbre connected to chronic asthmatic conditions. Or, consider Erick Sermon of the popular late-'80s group EPMD. He began to rap in high school and developed what he calls a "slow" vocal style.[48] He performed slowly in order to better control and hide the conspicuousness of his lisp. Other rappers celebrate and accentuate the lisp: Biz Markie, Kool G Rap, The Notorious B.I.G., Cappadonna, Cormega, Mos Def, and R.A. the Rugged Man. In fact, R.A. the Rugged Man views his lisp as an inheritance from his father, creating a special bond across generations; it is the auditory trace of the Vietnam War's violence.[49] Ghostface Killah suffers from diabetes, as did the late Phife Dawg of A Tribe Called Quest: dietary restrictions imposed by the disease alter the body's processes. Grillz—designer gold teeth—change the physical make-up of the mouth cavity and its resonance, as the vocal iconicities of Ol' Dirty Bastard and Lil Wayne indicate. But perhaps the most extreme medical case is that of MF Grimm, shot multiple times in 1994 and paralyzed: "He couldn't see, hear, or talk properly . . . larynx damage affects his speech to this day."[50] More recently, Eminem revealed that he had to relearn how to rap after kicking prescription drugs: "I actually had to learn how to say my lyrics again—how to phrase them, make them flow, how to use force so they sounded like I meant them. Rapping wasn't like riding a bike. It was [as much] physical as mental. I was relearning basic motor skills."[51]

In 2000, 50 Cent was (in)famously shot nine times in front of his grandmother's house in South Jamaica, Queens. One bullet entered his left cheek, resulting in the loss of a wisdom tooth and a disfigured tongue. The event changed his mouth cavity and, by extension, his vocal style. If we compare a pre-shooting track like "The Hit" with a post-shooting track like "What Up Gangsta," we hear "a difference"—but not "a deficit," to borrow from Joseph N. Straus.[52] In the former, 50 Cent has a penchant for bursts of well-articulated speed rap. His words and phrases are clearly defined units. In the latter, 50 Cent possesses a conspicuous slur or drawl. The start and end of words and phrases are unclear. Thus, many early listeners mistakenly assumed he was a Southern rapper, a confusion of significance in hip-hop, where identity and geography are inextricable, the sources of *topophilia* and, sometimes, *topophobia*.[53] Temporally, his post-shooting elocution is slightly behind the beat, as compared to the more mechanically precise performances from earlier in his career. Despite the gravity of the event, 50 Cent manages to mine what Ralph Ellison calls the "near tragic, near comic lyricism"[54] of the blues from his experience: "I've been shot nine times . . . that's why I walk funny / Hit in the jaw once, that's why I talk funny."[55] Moreover, 50 Cent adduces a lesson of perseverance from it: "A few words for any nigga that get hit the fuck up / My advice if you get shot down, is get the fuck up."[56]

In October 2002, as Kanye West prepared his debut album, *The College Dropout*, he was involved in a serious car accident, his jaw broken in three places. Adding insult to injury, hospital staff at Cedar Sinai in Los Angeles wired his jaw incorrectly, forcing doctors "to break it again and put it in the right place":[57] "I had nasal fractures—I'd be talking to people and my nose would start bleeding. Even to this day, I could start choking because spit will go down the wrong path. That whole area is messed up. But right now I'm healing, I'm just learning how to pronounce words like, 'What's up' with the 't' and the 's' together without it being slurred, so I can rap again."[58] West decided to allow listeners access to his rehabilitation process: only two weeks after the accident, with his jaw still wired and his face significantly swollen, he composed and recorded "Through the Wire." Listening to the track, one notes a lack of expressive range in terms of pitch, articulation, accent, and speed. West even acknowledges and apologizes for the disabled performance:

> I really apologize how I sound right now man
> If it's unclear at all man
> They got my mouth wired shut . . .
> I had reconstructive surgery on my jaw
> I looked in the mirror, half of my jaw was in the back of my mouth[59]

However, like 50 Cent, Kanye manages to derive some humor from the situation: "I drink a Boost for breakfast, an Ensure for dizzert / Somebody ordered pancakes, I just sip the sizzurp." He *flips the script* on pain, even imbuing his voice with metaphysical overtones: "I turned tragedy to triumph / Make music that's fire, spit my soul through the wire." West and 50 Cent both illustrate how vocal performance helps control how the representation and meaning(s) of disability circulate.

* * *

Between the final recorded product and the listener's ear, there exists a whole world—the recording studio. Studios are technological *and* social spaces that shape the sound iconicity of the voice. In the case of the former, gewgaws and gadgets, such as Auto-Tune, fill the studio with aesthetic, expressive, and rhetorical potentiality. A high signal-to-noise ratio foregrounds a rapper's voice in the mix. Compression ensures clarity and balance from a line's start to finish. Engineers minimize or maximize the smack of lips. They can adjust speeds, too. Multi-tracking enables vocal layering. Pitch-shifting allows rappers to create multiple dramatic personae. Echo and reverb create the illusion of space. As producer for the Wu-Tang Clan's *Enter the Wu-Tang (36 Chambers)*, RZA recalls how "each Wu-Tang MC had their own compressor set to a certain setting. I had nine compressors, each on a setting. So whoever came over, they could just grab a mic and rip it. That's why on the earlier music of Wu-Tang, everybody sounds like themselves—they're more recognizable."[60] Studio technology shapes and shades vocal contours, just as camera type, lens, aperture, and shutter speed shape and shade a photograph. The concept of an unmediated or pure voice is only an illusion of ableist ideology.

The recording studio is where friendships are made (and broken) and ideas and feelings are shared (and rejected). In *The Audible Past*, Jonathan Sterne points out that recording studios have always been characterized by an "irreducible humanity."[61] They are eminently social spaces. Like a club or block party from hip-hop's early days of the 1970s, a studio has an active audience, which doubles as collaborators: childhood friends, family, lovers, crews, label mates, producers, engineers, executives, A&R reps, journalists, filmmakers, athletes, and sycophants are watching and listening. Record executive Dante Ross recalls the social atmosphere that accompanied the making of De La Soul's *3 Feet High and Rising*: "[It] was a magical time. . . . The list of people who came by the studio when they were making tracks was insane. Biz Markie, the Beatnuts, Jungle Brothers, Ultramagnetic, even Melle Mel. Hip-hop was a smaller, tighter community back then, everybody didn't know everything yet. I can't remember one iota of bad vibes."[62] The performers *and* audience acquire, share, and refine tacit knowledge about what works and what doesn't, aesthetically speaking. In addition, as with much postmodern art, the distinction between performer and audience is blurred amid the constant exchange of "vibes" between intimate bodies.

An informed studio audience disables "those habits and practices of thinking and making"[63] to which a performer is predisposed to return— his vocal *habitus*. In this sense, disability as a practice is, in part, desirable because it is connected with what the Russian Formalists called *ostranenie* [defamiliarization].[64] For example, East Los Angeles group Cypress Hill's B-Real possesses one of hip-hop's most iconic voices: it is high-pitched and nasal, complemented by excessive staccato and off-beat accentuation. B-Real's voice signifies a drug-altered state and his cultural heritage: his group's iconography draws heavily on West Coat cannabis and Latino cultures, respectively. But B-Real's rapped voice is *not* his natural voice: "The nasal style I have was just something that I developed. *My more natural style of rapping wasn't so pleasing to those guys' ears*, so they wanted me to try something different, and it just stuck."[65] Through negotiation with the tastes of Cypress Hill's other members, Sen Dog and DJ Muggs, B-Real is asked to throw his voice out and he complies, recreating his sense of self and artistic identity along the way.

The studio is also the site of what Daniel Tiffany refers to as "infidel poetics": it houses "the hermetic yet expressive communities, certain social underworlds, within the global fabric."[66] Inevitably, the indulgences of hip-hop's street, house, and club party ethos are also transposed into the studio underworld. Alcohol and narcotics circulate and, when consumed, have physiological *and* aesthetic consequences. Thus, the playful, otiose, and even wasteful voices heard on a given record are anything but sonic signs of aural or moral fidelity. What is heard are the voicings of *altered states* and of *alterity*, which "defy the seemingly inexorable logic of transparency and continuity" as well as the logic of ableism.[67]

For example, in 1985, Philadelphia-based rapper Schoolly D went into a classical music studio to record the single "P.S.K. What Does It Mean?"—one of the earliest gangsta rap recordings. Schoolly D *flipped the script* on the prestige, aura, and protocols associated with a "classical music" studio: "One other thing with the recording back in those days is that we was hiiiiiigh. It was like—puff puff—more reverb! More reverb! . . . We stayed at that studio working and smoking all night, until like six in the morning, and when I woke up at one or two the next day I played it and was like, 'What the fuck is this?' But I played it for the crew and they went ballistic. It was instant."[68] According to Fredro Starr of the group Onyx, their debut album, *Bacdafucup*, was composed and recorded with members "on LSD the whole time, straight up. We was dropping papers, taking meth tabs, during that whole album. That's just the creative side of making music."[69] Starr's comments help explain why the vocals on the album's hit single and the group's most famous song, "Slam," sound like a grab bag of guttural screams and barks. Similarly, Shock G, of Digital Underground, admits that that group's 1990 concept album, *Sex Packets*, was recorded under the influence: "There are a lot of shrooms and Ecstasy that went into some of the thinking on that album, too. I even wrote some of that stuff on these mescaline 'yellow giggle drops.'"[70] More recently, in a 2009 *New Yorker* profile of Daniel Dumile/MF Doom, journalist Ta-Nehisi Coates notes how Dumile's recording process involves "beer" and "Grey Goose vodka," the consumption of which helps Dumile assume his persona of MF Doom.[71]

The case of Digital Underground is especially interesting because the disabled voice is explicitly connected to disabled identity. *Sex Packets* yielded a smash hit called "The Humpty Dance." That single featured the group's newest, most popular, and most recognizable member: Humpty Hump. Humpty Hump was an act of "hip-hop ventriloquism."[72] Shock G generated Humpty Hump's character and voice by putting on a prosthetic Groucho Marx nose and oversized glasses. The prosthetic pinched Shock G's nose, cutting its airflow. This created his nasal-sounding voice. In addition, like Daniel Dumile/MF Doom, Shock G needed to be intoxicated in order to successfully embody the Humpty Hump character. As Digital Underground group member Money B recalls, "The demo of it was really hot, and we kept trying to recreate it but just couldn't do it. . . . Fuze and Shock were fucking around with the song, and they were like: 'What's missing?' And I figured it out. It was Hennessy! So I went to the store, got some Hennessy, got Shock drunk, and then Humpty came right out, just like magic."[73] Subsequently, Shock G tried to have people believe that he and Humpty were different people through paratextual devices. He credited Humpty Hump as a group member on the album's liner notes, for example. He developed and disseminated a back story, too: "I started the myth of Humpty during a college radio interview. I said that he was my brother from Tampa, an ex-lounge singer who got in a grease accident in the kitchen. *He stood as a hero for all handicapped people around the world, because you can overcome anything.*"[74]

The character of Humpty Hump lacks any sort of hip-hop fashion sense. He typically wears a plaid dinner jacket and a white, Daniel Boone–like hat. He's "ugly," with a disproportionately large nose. He describes himself alternately as "skinny," a "fool," a "freak," and a "drunk." Humpty's look has corollaries in his behavior and language: he revels in having sex in a Burger King bathroom or engaging in juvenile antics such as grabbing girls "in the biscuits." His language veers into nonsense: "I get stupid, I shoot an arrow like Cupid / I use a word that don't mean nothin', like looptid." Even the eponymous "Humpty Dance" is contrary to the physical dexterity and athleticism upon which much hip-hop dance typically depends:

> It's supposed to look like a fit or a convulsion
> Anyone can play this game
> This is my dance, y'all, Humpty Hump's my name
> No two people will do it the same
> Ya got it down when you appear to be in pain[75]

As a supplement to his slurred, nasal vocals, Humpty's disabled dance style ("crazy wack funky") assumes value as a symbol of democracy in action—a celebration of the relationship between the one and the many ("Anyone can play this game . . . / No two people will do it the same"). And in rendering "pain" as foundational to democracy, Humpty Hump formalizes disability as a constitutive force within the body politic—rather than external or detrimental to it.

* * *

In describing disability *as a desirable practice* within hip-hop music and culture, my intention is not to treat in a sentimental or cavalier manner what are most certainly difficult emotional, physical, and economic realities of hip-hop performers who live with disabilities; nor do I wish to downplay the racial, legal, and political contexts that certainly exacerbate said difficulties. At the same time, however, by casting disability *as a desirable practice*, I do wish to invest hip-hop performers with a sense of agency and invention when it comes to vocal styles rather than "reducing" vocal styles to a racially informed "pathology, compensatory behavior, or creative 'coping mechanisms,'" as Robin D. G. Kelley laments is too often the case in discussions of rap and hip-hop culture.[76] In *Blackness and Value*, Lindon Barrett observes that the "singing voice" is "the primary means by which African Americans may exchange an expended, valueless self in the New World for a productive, recognized self. It provides one important means of formalizing and celebrating an existence otherwise proposed as negative and negligible."[77] Disability studies provides a useful critical lens that stresses those material and political values of vocal performances suggested by Barrett. Disability studies prompts a methodological shift away from the "hermeneutic level of statement,"[78] which emphasizes hip-hop's lyrical content exclusively, thus exposing it to the discourse of moral panic and conservative attack. When voice is rendered audible and particular, and when it is treated as a process rather than an object, it is more positively recognizable as the means by which hip-hop artists imagine alternative ways of occupying and interpreting the world they live in, of sounding out and sounding off. The voice is where struggles over authenticity, originality, and realness—signs of cultural and economic capital in the field of hip-hop—play out.

On his 2006 recording "Hip Hop is Dead," rapper Nas quipped, "Most intellectuals will only half listen" and, therefore, most intellectuals only half understand. But close listening and the dream of *total* understanding means extending the critical discourse beyond formal taxonomies of pitch, register, tempo, and timbre (though such taxonomies are very useful) and attending to vocal provenance, especially the disabled body and disabling recording practices, technologies, and social relations. Otherwise, if we follow Nas's deathly conceit to its logical conclusion, we risk transforming the music and culture into a graveyard of voiceless corpses.

NOTES

This essay originally appeared in slightly different form in *Disability Studies Quarterly* 34, no. 4 (2014), http://dsq-sds.org.

1   Moten, "Rock the Party," 23.
2   Mackenzie, *The Hygiene of the Vocal Organs*, ix.
3   Ibid., x.
4   Ibid., 2.
5   Ibid., 3.
6   Ibid., xii.
7   Ibid., 102.
8   Ibid., 102; emphasis added.
9   In this essay, I use the terms *hip-hop* and *rap*. The two terms have complex histories and are not always synonymous. Lovebug Starski, for example, coined the neologism *hip-hop* in the mid-1970s while living and performing in the South Bronx. *Rap*, on the other hand, is a term with a long and rich history in the African American expressive tradition, originally referring to "romantic talk from a black man to a black woman for the purposes of winning her emotional and sexual affection" (Smitherman, *Talkin and Testifyin*, 69). Some performers and listeners use *hip-hop* and *rap* to communicate divergent values: the former embodies an original or pure spirit/aesthetic and celebrates grassroots, community-oriented political action; the latter embodies culture-industry imperatives and celebrates the logic of "C.R.E.A.M." (Cash Rules Everything Around Me). Rap is the most popular form of hip-hop performance. I will use *hip-hop* to refer, broadly, to a cultural field that involves multiple artistic practices, including—but not exclusive to—rap. I will use *rap* to refer to a genre of music (i.e., rap music, whose recorded history begins in 1979 with the release of the Sugarhill Gang's "Rapper's Delight") and a performance style (i.e. rapping) located somewhere between everyday speech and song.
10   Mackenzie, *The Hygiene of the Vocal Organs*, 102.
11   Barthes, "The Grain of the Voice," 181.

12 Nicole Villeneuve, "Darryl 'DMC' McDaniels Opens Up about Health Problems, Depression in New Doc," *AUX*, Blue Ant Media, July 12, 2011, www.aux.tv.

13 Straus, *Extraordinary Measures*, 3.

14 Siebers, *Disability Theory*, 4.

15 See Siebers, *Disability Aesthetics*, for in-depth discussion of disability's centrality to the making of modern art.

16 Bourdieu, *The Field of Cultural Production*, 30.

17 Stras, "The Organ of the Soul," 174.

18 Ibid., 176.

19 Ibid., 179.

20 McCaffery, *Prior to Meaning*, 172.

21 Bernstein, "Introduction," 17.

22 Jarvis, "For a Poetics of Verse," 932.

23 Barthes, "The Grain of the Voice," 178.

24 See Baker, *Blues, Ideology, and African-American Literature*, and Gates, *The Signifying Monkey*. Both studies consider how African American literary and cultural production depends upon the vitality of the vernacular. My thinking on the vernacular is indebted to both scholars.

25 Magee, *Emancipating Pragmatism*, 9.

26 Sterne, "Bourdieu, Technique, and Technology," 373.

27 See Chang, *Can't Stop Won't Stop*, and Brewster and Broughton, *Last Night a DJ Saved My Life,* for excellent descriptions of early DJ culture.

28 Sterne, "Bourdieu, Technique, and Technology," 373.

29 "History: A Brief History of Antares," *Antares*, 2014, www.antarestech.com.

30 Weheliye, "'Feenin,'" 22.

31 Cornell University's Hip Hop Collection is home to the largest collection of promotional flyers and posters. A significant portion of these materials are available as jpegs via the collection's website (Katherine Reagan, ed., "Hip Hop Party and Event Flyers," Cornell University Hip Hop Collection, Cornell University Library, 2013, http://rmc.library.cornell.edu/hiphop/).

32 As Tricia Rose writes, the "unofficial truths" expressed by rappers "produce communal bases of knowledge about social conditions, communal interpretations of them and quite often serve as the cultural glue that fosters communal resistance" (*Black Noise*, 100). Like Rose, Gwendolyn Pough qua Habermas imagines hip-hop as a "counter-public sphere": "[hip-hop artists] disrupt their way into and make themselves visible in the public sphere with the goal of not only speaking for disenfranchised Black people but also claiming both a voice and a living for themselves in a society bereft of opportunity for them" (*Check It While I Wreck It*, 27).

33 Public Enemy, "Fight the Power," *Fear of a Black Planet* (Def Jam, 1990). CD.

34 Stoever-Ackerman, "Research Project," par. 1.

35 Ultimately, Chuck D's lyrics proved prophetic: on January 8, 1993, three years after "Fight the Power" was released, the United States Postal Service released its com-

memorative Elvis Presley stamp. The USPS finally released a James Brown stamp in 2015.

36 Hall, "For Allon White," 298.

37 Rose, "Black Texts/Black Contexts," 223.

38 Jameson, "The Vanishing Mediator," 26.

39 As Moya Bailey notes in her essay "'The Illest': Disability as Metaphor in Hip-Hop Music," "In the liminal spaces of hip hop the reappropriation of ableist language can mark a new way of using words that departs from generally accepted disparaging connotations" (142). Though an interesting and important contribution to the larger discussion of hip-hop and disability, the purview of Bailey's essay is limited to metaphors of disability. She does not take up my specific concerns with the material relationship between disability, performance, and aesthetics.

40 MC is a term in hip-hop used to refer, specifically, to the rapping artist.

41 Connor, Dumbstruck, 3.

42 Mauss, Sociology and Psychology, 104–5.

43 Mauss defines "body techniques" like so: "The body is man's first and most natural instrument. Or more accurately, not to speak of instruments, man's first and most natural technical object, and at the same time technical means, is his body. . . . The constant adaptation to a physical, mechanical or chemical aim (e.g. when we drink) is pursued in a series of assembled actions, and assembled for the individual not by himself alone but by all his education, by the whole society to which he belongs, in the place he occupies in it" (104–5).

44 Stras, "The Organ of the Soul," 173.

45 Quoted in Coleman, Check the Technique, 349.

46 Public Enemy, "Caught, Can We Get a Witness?," It Takes a Nation of Millions to Hold Us Back (Def Jam, 1988). CD.

47 Percee P and Ekim, "Lung Collapsing Lyrics," promotional copy (Big Beat, 1992). 12" single.

48 Coleman, Check the Technique, 190.

49 Cf. R.A. the Rugged Man's verse on Jedi Mind Tricks's "Uncommon Valor."

50 Ben Westhoff, "Private Enemy," Village Voice, October 31, 2006, www.villagevoice.com.

51 Quoted in Gil Kaufman, "Eminem: 'I Had to Learn to Write and Rap Again,'" MTVnews, September 4, 2010, www.mtv.com.

52 Straus, Extraordinary Measures, 7.

53 Forman, "Represent," 78.

54 Ellison, Shadow and Act, 78.

55 50 Cent, "Fuck You," Guess Who's Back? (Full Clip, 2002). CD.

56 Ibid.

57 Shaheem Reid, "Kanye West Raps through His Broken Jaw," MTVnews, December 9, 2002, www.mtv.com.

58 Quoted in ibid.

59 Kanye West, "Through the Wire," The College Dropout (Roc-A-Fella, 2004). CD.

60 RZA, *The Wu-Tang Manual*, 208.

61 Sterne, *The Audible Past*, 236.

62 Quoted in Coleman, *Check the Technique*, 149.

63 Jarvis, "For a Poetics of Verse," 932.

64 See Shklovsky, "Art as Technique."

65 Quoted in Coleman, *Check the Technique*, 123; emphasis added.

66 Tiffany, *Infidel Poetics*, 11.

67 Ibid., 12.

68 Quoted in Coleman, *Check the Technique*, 408.

69 Quoted in ibid., 296.

70 Quoted in ibid., 181.

71 Ta-Nehisi Coates, "The Mask of Doom," *New Yorker*, September 21, 2009, www.newyorker.com.

72 Coleman, *Check the Technique*, 183.

73 Quoted in ibid., 184.

74 Quoted in ibid., 183; emphasis added.

75 Digital Underground, "The Humpty Dance," *Sex Packets* (Tommy Boy, 1990). CD.

76 Kelley, *Yo' Mama's Disfunktional!*, 17.

77 Barrett, *Blackness and Value*, 57.

78 Brennan, "Off the Gangsta Tip," 672.

4

How to Stare at Your Television

The Ethics of Consuming Race and Disability on Freakshow

LORI KIDO LOPEZ

Lori Kido Lopez considers the ethics of watching *Freakshow*, a reality television show that aired on U.S. cable channel AMC from 2013 to 2014. Taking into consideration the racial and disability politics of historical freak shows, Lopez closely analyzes three African American performers and their relationships to the white male proprietor of the Venice Beach Freakshow. This chapter moves beyond representational critiques and offers "listening" as a way to ethically engage with media that offer seemingly exploitative or depoliticized visions of intersectional marginalized identities.

The pilot episode of *Freakshow* begins with a conversation between two men—Todd Ray, the owner of the Venice Beach Freakshow, and George Bell, a very tall African American man. Ray is trying to convince Bell that his height of 7'8" makes him freak show royalty,[1] and thus he should join the performers in Venice Beach. Bell resists, claiming that he doesn't see himself as a freak and takes pride in thinking of himself as a normal man. Although Bell's protestations are clear, the show positions Ray as the winner when we later see him enthusiastically introducing Bell during a performance as "The Tallest Man in America." Moreover, it is proprietor Ray's perspective that takes center stage throughout the unscripted television series. His voice provides the central motivation for the show as he carries out his goals of developing a modern-day sideshow and working to reclaim the word "freak" as one of pride and celebration, rather than shame and fear.

In updating the classic circus sideshow from the days of P. T. Barnum, *Freakshow* presents a new opportunity to reconsider the meanings of this cultural form. Scholars have traditionally analyzed the freak show through the lens of disability studies, asking whether the display of people with disabilities offers the potential for agency or is merely exploitative.[2] While much of the important work on disability that has come out of gender and literary studies has been useful, analysis of texts such as *Freakshow* benefits from a media studies approach that asks what it means to encounter these performers via mediated representations, rather than during an in-person encounter or live performance. This is important because *Freakshow*'s visual display of unusual human bodies is not new; programs like *Ripley's Believe It or Not!* (various incarnations since 1930), *The Undateables* (Channel 4 [UK], 2012–2016), *Taboo* (National Geographic, 2002–present), *Abby & Brittany* (TLC, 2012), *Little People, Big World* (TLC, 2006–2015), and many others focus on similar subjects.[3] Yet by focusing on a single text that so closely remediates the traditional freak show, we can better understand how we should respond to such programs and their entanglement with the history of this challenging cultural institution.

Within media studies scholarship, the privilege of being represented is seen as a double-edged sword. On the one hand, social change cannot occur without some degree of recognition of a community's existence—making the fight for increased visibility a central tool for underrepresented minorities, such as people of color or queer people. Yet visibility accompanied by harmful stereotypes or other oppressive ideological constructs can contribute to political setbacks or further marginalization.[4] Within disability studies, we must also consider that, for people with disabilities, being the object of the gaze can be an uncomfortable and unwanted part of daily life. There can be no easy connection between mediated visibility and liberation for people who consistently experience the discomfort of being gawked at; as David Gerber argues in his moral critique of the freak show, "The feeling of being on display is something with which almost all disabled people have had to deal; it is, in fact, a singular form of oppression—the oppression of unwanted attention—that disabled people share with few others."[5] Moreover, when people with disabilities are deliberately put on display, particularly with the goal of financial profit for others, visibility can be evidence of exploitation. Although theorists like Rosemarie Garland-Thomson have argued that people with disabilities can gain power through "looking back" and confronting the starer,[6] this personal exchange is impossible when that stare is mediated through the television or movie screen. Mediation may not foreclose opportunities for any kind of disruption to the privileged gaze, but it does mean that we need to theorize such encounters differently than interpersonal encounters. When looking at the representations contained within *Freakshow*, then, we must consider these contradictory concerns about the ways that increased visibility can both expand and limit political potential, particularly for those who inhabit multiple underrepresented identities.

In this chapter I use insights from disability studies, critical race studies, and media studies to move beyond representational critique and develop an ethical form of viewership in which we can all participate. I first explore the way that people of color are depicted on *Freakshow*, demonstrating that its depictions of racialized bodies complicate assumptions that we may have about the show's potential to liberate or empower those who make a living off of their bodily difference. By focusing on the show's three African American performers—hostess "Amazing Ali" Chapman, "True Living Giant" George Bell, and modification artist Marcus "The Creature" Boykin—we can see how histories of exploitation and oppression cannot be divested from the contemporary freak show. I also look at how *Freakshow* ultimately disavows race as a salient marker of difference, reinforcing a rhetoric that points to physical disabilities or medical conditions as markers of being a "freak" and weakens the show's claim to politicize the term. Yet rather than simply condemning the show for its problematic representations, I use this discussion of intersectional identities to establish the grounds for an ethics of engaging with televised acts of exploitation and depoliticization. This "ethics of staring at the television" expands upon Garland-Thomson's discussion of staring at bodily difference by incorporating media studies' considerations of moral consumption and viewing practices. I challenge the notion that visibility is necessarily connected to empowerment and theorize the viewing—and listening—practices of the audience as a potential site for negotiating a more ethical relationship with raced and disabled bodies on screen.

AMC's *Freakshow*

Freakshow premiered in 2013 on AMC with eight episodes and was renewed for a second season of sixteen episodes. The unscripted show provides an intimate look at Todd Ray; his wife, Danielle; daughter, Asia; son, Phoenix; and all of the performers at the Venice Beach Freakshow. Each thirty-minute episode blends two kinds of footage—informal, "off-stage" moments such as dinners at the Rays' house, and the cast's "onstage" performances to live crowds. One of program's recurring themes is Ray's quest to procure new acts and curiosities for the show. This includes seeking additions to his Guinness-record-setting collection of two-headed animals, such as a two-headed snapping turtle or the two-headed bearded dragon that provides the impetus for a party in the pilot.

But Ray does more than build his collection of preserved and living animals; he is also constantly seeking to add to his menagerie of human performers: beyond "True Living Giant" George Bell, over the course of the show Ray also works to add "The Bearded Lady," "A Strongman," "The Serpent Lady," and "The Illustrated Man." Ray routinely conflates people with objects in troubling ways, such as the two-headed baby whom he casually refers to as a "specimen" that belongs in his collection of "two-headed animals." In exploring the way that he convinces performers to come on board, we unearth further complications, such as the misleading patter used to describe performers and the distribution of financial benefits. In interviews throughout each episode, Ray explains his fascination with the history of freak shows and his desire to live up to and eventually exceed the accomplishments of P. T. Barnum's sideshow. He proudly shares his collection of historical pitch cards advertising each performer, often using them to convince individuals to join the show:

> RAY [IN CONVERSATION WITH BELL]: I don't know if you know much about the history of giants in the sideshow. Back in the day they literally were like royalty [shows pitch cards]. . . . So to the people it was like a mysterious person from a faraway land, a giant.
> [CUT TO RAY INTERVIEW]: People like me collect these photos, museums put them up with pride. I look at them all the time.
> [RETURNS TO CONVERSATION WITH BELL] So to have our own giant, it is a dream come true. Well, George, that's where we're at.
> BELL: The one thing you're missing is a tall person.
> RAY: Yes, a giant. A true living giant. And you know that's why you're so important.[7]

This conversation begins to reveal the motivation behind Ray's business venture. In some ways he is attempting to give people with different or extraordinary bodies a platform for being celebrated and admired, rather than ridiculed or feared. Yet his desire goes far beyond the simple rewriting of how we understand bodily difference. In his descriptions of what "The Giant" meant within the lore of the sideshow, he attributes characteristics of the foreign and the mysterious—the former being a falsehood, and the latter reminding us that performances such as these are not about humanizing people like Bell. Rather, they seek to put "the freak" on a pedestal that rises above the ordinary humans—much like royalty—where they can no longer be mocked, but they also cannot be understood. Framed by deliberately misleading patter, these individuals are made to seem even more exotic and unusual than they already are.

This specific kind of talk has always been associated with freak shows; as Robert Bogdan explains, "The actual life and circumstances of those being exhibited were replaced by purposeful distortions designed to market the exhibit, to produce a more appealing freak."[8] He notes that these deceptions largely serve to make the performer more exotic, or aggrandize details to enhance the status of the freak. Although we do not see significant deception in the way that Ray presents the stories of performers at showtime, it is certainly his role to talk up each performer—and in doing so, to emphasize their difference and guide the audience into being more astounded by what they see. During their televised performances, the camera always pans to the audience to capture mouths agape, children covering their eyes, or audible gasps of shock. In witnessing such moments, the viewing audience at home is doubly reminded that what we see is intended to be shocking, astounding, or otherwise abnormal. Although Ray actively promotes his campaign to "Say No to Normal" and works to establish non-normative identities as ideal, his treatment of Bell reminds us that this rhetoric is often literally fantastical—Bell already stated that he sees himself as normal, and it is Ray in his role as owner and barker who goads the audience into looking upon his body with shock.

Ray's methods of recruiting new performers also elide the reality that he is the primary beneficiary in these acquisitions. Procuring "A True Living Giant" for his show is important to Ray but has nothing to do with how Bell views his own life or desires. This is not to say that performers do not truly benefit or are necessarily being duped, but simply that such elisions may lead viewers to believe his motives are purely altruistic or that increasing his "collection" is a benign desire. It is important to note that, as with nearly all freak show owners, Ray himself does not fall into the category of the freak—he is a heterosexual, middle-class, normate white man who does not seem to be disabled in any way. Thus, although he purports to champion the cause of rewriting the term "freak" as a badge of pride, the term could not be used to describe him or other members of his family who participate in running the show. Of course there is nothing wrong with individuals championing a cause that does not align with their own identities, and certain social changes could never occur without buy-in from the majority. Yet in the case of Ray, we cannot neglect the self-interest that motivates him—as he states, he wants to live out his own dream of collecting every specimen from his pitch cards. Moreover, Ray financially profits from the success of his show. As a Grammy-winning former music producer, it's clear that he is both an entrepreneur and a savvy businessman; with the increased value of his brand, financial benefits will accrue as well. Indeed, by the end of the series he has strengthened his business enough to expand into a second location in Las Vegas—also a move that is framed as the realization of one of Ray's childhood dreams. Thus we see the impetus behind the collapsing of important moral differences: between objects and humans, between Ray's acquisitions of a six-legged goat, a two-headed baby, or a live human "giant" all for himself.

Race and the Freak Show

Although Ray harkens back to early sideshows as an ideal that he aspires to re-create and celebrate, scholarship on the history of such shows is not always so rosy. Freak shows have long been targeted by disability rights activists who seek to shut them down in order to restore dignity to their exploited participants, many of whom could be classified as mentally or physically disabled.[9] Robert Bogdan's *Freak Show* provides an in-depth look at the rise of the phenomenon, exploring in particular its moral quandaries.[10] In telling the story of Otis, a limbless man known as "Frog Man," Bogdan argues that we cannot understand the perspective of those who participated. Nevertheless, while the social construction of the "freak" can give otherwise powerless individuals the opportunity to make a living and achieve a form of independence, it does so at the cost of affirming the inferiority of its performers. Indeed, the morality of the freak show has long been one of its central objects of inquiry, as its portrayal of human beings as objects for amusement is ripe for critique.

Although much of this conversation about freaks centers on disability and those who possess bodies that are noticeably different, race and ethnicity have also been featured and turned into spectacle within freak shows. The history of racism and the fear of racial difference can be connected to the exploration of new lands by white settlers from Western Europe. When colonists encountered native tribes and racialized bodies on their excursions, they immediately saw an opportunity for profit and exploitation. Mass enslavement and the transatlantic slave trade were some of the consequences of these encounters, but another was the use of dark-skinned people as performers for white audiences. One of the most well-known examples is Sara Baartman, who was taken from her home in South Africa and brought to Britain at the turn of the nineteenth century. The Khoekhoe woman was given the name "Hottentot Venus," and her performances consisted of walking onto a stage, singing a song, and allowing spectators to poke her with sticks. Her large buttocks were described as a marvel of nature, and she was marketed to emphasize her sexuality and racial identity as freakish and strange. Although there is much debate about whether Baartman had agency as a free woman or was coerced as a form of slavery, it is clear that this kind of performance is dehumanizing.[11] At the end of Baartman's life, scientists made plaster casts of her genitals and buttocks, further reducing her personhood to nothing more than her body parts.

This interest in non-Western peoples is deeply embedded within the culture of freak shows. Bogdan notes that displays of "primitives," "exotic people," "native villages," and "savages" were part of the earliest world's fairs.[12] Such exhibits, meant to provide an ethnological look at other cultures, "laid the groundwork for native people's becoming sideshow exhibits at later fairs and helped to legitimize the practice for showmen."[13] Although the performers were carefully framed as authentic representatives of a primitive culture or even of a pre-human species, in reality these performers were often simply locals with dark skin who had been dressed up as foreigners. When the performers were actually non-Westerners, their real lives were always embellished to seem much more foreign and exotic. Many exhibits made frightening claims about the performers participating in cannibalism, alongside dramatic tales of the extreme violence or absurd practices that their native cultures supposedly condoned. We can see through the prevalence of these kinds of exhibits that racial difference has historically been emphasized as freakish in a similar manner to visible physical disabilities. In both cases, these individuals were seen as having been born with a condition that could be marketed as a visual spectacle for audiences.

Racialized Freaks Today

There are many ways in which these discourses have changed over the years, particularly with the rise of activist interventions such as the Civil Rights Movement. In contemporary society, it has become generally unacceptable to point out racial or cultural difference as grounds for calling one a freak. With the rise of critical race studies arguing that race is a social construction rather than a biological category,[14] and the recognition of systemic racial oppression, we now understand it to be offensive to call African Americans "primitive" or "savage" simply because of their physiognomy. But more broadly, the rise of postracial discourse has contributed to a widespread sense that racial difference is no longer meaningful, as it is presumed that we have moved beyond a social system that would condone the parading of brown bodies for white viewers.[15] These assumptions are of course false, as both institutional and interpersonal forms of racism clearly persist in multiple overlapping forms. Yet if the discourse surrounding difference has indeed undergone shifts with regard to race, the existence of the Venice Beach Freakshow reveals that there still remains a desire to put other forms of bodily difference on display. Over the course of the show we still see tall people, little people, people with missing limbs, people who display non-normative gender characteristics (e.g., "The Bearded Lady"), and people with medical conditions such as ectrodactyly or hypertrichosis.

In addition to some specific forms of bodily difference, a separate category of freak that remains acceptable for display is the self-made freak: those who learn a skill or modify their bodies in ways that turn them into freaks. Among Ray's performers, there are both "born freaks" and "self-made freaks." For instance, both Morgue and Murrugun "The Mystic" are shock artists who learned various kinds of performance— including fire-breathing, pushing steel rods through their flesh, regurgitating billiard balls, and pulling hooks through multiple facial orifices. Two of Ray's female performers, daughter Asia Ray and Brianna Belladonna "The Indestructible Woman," also perform tricks like swordswallowing, eating light bulbs, using their bodies as electricity conduits, and lying on a bed of nails. These self-made freaks appear able-bodied and white but clearly decided to give themselves the label of "freak" through the skills they developed and publically perform.

These self-made freaks may escape the moralizing that we have worried about for the "born freaks" who are made into spectacles simply for existing within a society that deems them abnormal. Yet, another member of the Venice Beach Freakshow, Marcus "The Creature" Boykin, provides a slightly different take on the spectacle of the self-made freak. Boykin is a body-modification artist who is covered from head to toe in tattoos that he performed on himself. His face is barely visible behind a mask of piercings dangling from his forehead, cheeks, lips, and other bits of skin. In one conversation with Ray about his decision to become a body-modification artist, he specifically discusses his race as an African American man (figure 4.1):

> BOYKIN: In this industry of the tattooing and body modification, there's always been limits on black or minority skin and I wanted to break that boundary.
> RAY: You were the first person I saw that was covered with tattoos but was a black man. It was amazing.
> BOYKIN: But that's as an African American male. As far as the whole thing goes, it was The Great Omai. He's my main inspiration for me being Creature.
> RAY: The Great Omai is one of history's most incredible tattooed men. One of the first to fully cover his body, including his face. But the difference with Creature is that Creature tattooed himself. From his head to his toes.[16]

Boykin raises his racial identity as part of his motivation for becoming a freak—he wants to show that people of color can participate in body

Figure 4.1. Body-modification artist Marcus "The Creature" Boykin chats with Todd Ray, owner of the Venice Beach Freakshow.

modification too. It is unclear why he believes there is a shortage of African American tattoos and body modifications, given the prevalence of tattoos on the bodies of African American celebrities such as athletes and hip-hop artists, but it is significant that he mentions his racial identity here, as race is not discussed at any other point in the show. Boykin argues that his decision to become a tattooed man is political, demonstrating that African American men can participate in all forms of cultural expression.

Yet we cannot ignore the second inspiration for his decision to cover his body with tattoos—following in the footsteps of a man they call "The Great Omai." Omai was a Polynesian warrior who was brought to Britain with Captain Cook in 1774. There he was seen as a curiosity, paraded and exhibited throughout upper-class London so that wealthy members of society could marvel at his tattooed body. William Cummings argues that the exhibition of tattooed bodies exemplifies the corporeal dimensions of Orientalism, where representatives of "the East" are seen as alien and clearly inferior to the dignity of "the West." He describes the fascination with Omai's tattooed body as examples of this ideology: "Westerners read in the tattoos of Omai and Lee Boo an account of exotic primitives living on distant tropical islands that needed no independent confirmation, for the truths which they saw were evident in the 'tawny flesh' before their very eyes. . . . Clearly too, tattooing capitalized on a fascination with race and racialized bodies."[17] In these stories we can see a connection between the parading of the "tattooed man" and the display of "primitives" and "savages" discussed earlier. It is important to read the display of Boykin's racialized body and its shocking modifications within the context of this history, particularly since he explicitly names Omai as his inspiration. When he displays his body as part of the freak show, his performance invokes this history of the exploitation of people of color and reinscribes the image of African American men as inferior, threatening, and "other." His self-given name of "Creature" also seems to reflect stereotypes of African American men as animalistic or non-human, but he does not mention this naming as an agentive act of resisting this history; from the descriptions featured on the show, his performance and name are left to simply affirm these histories and characterizations.

This reading of his body affects more than the way that Boykin is understood as a performer—the show also depicts Boykin's struggles to fit into society. His story includes attempts to reach out to his five-year-old daughter, whose mother thinks that his appearance is too frightening for a child to understand. He is also shown hunting for an apartment, but three different landlords turn him away because of his looks. In response to the failed apartment search he explains, "Once they see this, they're fearful, not even trying to understand I'm a human being. That's an everyday struggle with me. To me, when I look in the mirror, I'm beautiful. I don't see the beast or the mockery or the finger-pointing. I love what I represent because it's hard work."[18] In this statement we hear him voice his frustration with the negative consequences of his decision to modify his appearance and its resultant optics. What we do not hear him reflect upon is the way that these struggles to find housing in a discriminatory market, or to avoid stereotypes based on appearance, are consistent with the way that African American men are treated within society at large. As with the explanation of The Great Omai, Boykin's story again fails to address how racial identity can overlap with other discourses of bodily difference in ways that challenge the notion that mere visibility leads to empowerment.

Performance versus Display of Difference

Beyond his racial identity, Boykin stands apart from his fellow shock artists and other self-made freaks at the Venice Beach Freakshow in his performance style. While performers like Morgue, Murrugun, Asia Ray, and Brianna Belladonna have learned skills that they perform during the live show, it is unclear how Boykin's body modifications contribute to a performance. In the biography provided on AMC's website, he states, "As far as my role in the Freakshow, I just tell people to look at my body and ask me what's new. Because every time you see me, there's something new."[19] From what we see during the show and also in this statement, we get the idea that Boykin's performance is simply to exist and be looked at—much like the Venus Hottentot and The Great Omai. There is clearly a difference in that Boykin has made his bodily adornments more noticeable than his racial identity—it is his piercings that make him a spectacle, not simply his race—yet he does claim that to do so as an African American man is part of his goal.

This distinction, between being looked at because you have a skill to demonstrate and being looked at because you are simply "different," is unfortunately reflected in the two other African American performers as well. Neither George "True Living Giant" Bell nor "Amazing Ali" demonstrate any special skills during the show; their entertainment value seems to come solely from their visual appearance. This becomes particularly evident during the camerawork leading up to a performance, where viewers are guided through the entryway and into the interior of the showroom. The camera focuses on a number of different performers who start to take action. In one episode, we see a man with no hands write a note with his feet, a man with no eye stick his finger through his mouth and wiggle it out his eye socket, and a man with no lower half of his body do a handstand. Each of these gestures marks the fact that these individuals are here to perform—to demonstrate specific skills designed to shock or delight. But then the camera pans to Bell, who simply smiles and gives a peace sign. We already know that his story involves leaving behind his day job as a police officer, so perhaps there is no reason to expect that he will behave in the same manner as those who make their entire livelihood from street performances. Yet this moment underscores the fact that there is truly nothing extraordinary about this man; he is there only because others want to look at him.

The same can be said for "Amazing Ali" Chapman, an African American little person who is introduced as the host for the Venice Beach Freakshow. Yet on the show we never see her acting as a host in any capacity; in the first season we mostly see her casually chatting with other performers. There is also an entire episode dedicated to her wedding, which brings some important issues to the fore. During this episode, we are introduced to Chapman's partner, "Wee Matt," also a little person, and learn that they recently became engaged. Ray immediately wants to showcase their wedding as part of his show and tries to convince Chapman:

> CHAPMAN: You know that sounds so great and amazing, but I had originally planned for just us and a minister, something private. I'm just not sure I really want to do this wedding here at the freak show. . . . Being a little person, there's definitely gonna be a lot of people looking, watching. It's definitely something I'm struggling with. Being with Matt, we get a lot of attention and most of it's positive but sometimes, you know, we do get negative attention.
> RAY: I think the big way's the better way. You know why? When you go grand, people will remember it forever, and you will too. [Shows pictures of the wedding of Tom Thumb and his wife] Look how elegant they looked. A whole 'nother era. They literally were like royalty.[20]

In this conversation, Chapman makes it clear that she had not intended to have her wedding become a public, and certainly not a televised, attraction. On the contrary, she fears the additional attention that she and her partner will engender and expresses discomfort with this situation. Chapman's reluctance to have a public wedding reminds us that strangers constantly mark her as different through their gaze, and that being stared at can be uncomfortable and undesirable. Moreover, there is no discussion of the additional element of participating in an interracial marriage with her white partner—a decision that, while increasingly accepted, is still considered taboo by some Americans and leads to increased surveillance and discrimination.[21] Ray manages to convince Chapman that she is playing an important role in history by getting married at her workplace, but her initial discomfort with this arrangement is evident. As we have already seen, Ray's nostalgic connection to the history of freak shows is already suspect in its potential for redemption—as with the acquisition of new performers like Bell, the potential for alienation is wiped away with the promise of uncritically "making history."

Chapman's presence also reinforces the persistent need for all bodies to become productive within the demands of the neoliberal governmentality of late capitalism. That is, capitalist modes of production and consumption driven by market priorities naturalize the conflation of one's identity with the ways that one can market and profit off of that identity—a disciplinary process that ultimately serves to contain any radical critiques of capitalism. While this kind of (potentially exploitative) work can often be some of the only profitable opportunities available to people with particular disabilities, these examples remind us that it is the normalization of our assumptions that these disciplinary regimes are normal, or totalizing, that must be highlighted.

Gazing at the Television

In considering the politics of representation within *Freakshow*, we can already see how intersectional narratives about race contribute to troubling forms of objectification. The show's three African American performers—two of whom express a reluctance to put their bodies on display, over which the desires of their white employer ultimately prevail—provide an opportunity for viewers to look at people of color who have been expressly marked as strange and unnatural through their bodily difference. Freak shows have always capitalized on the desire to look at different bodies, as audiences are given license to stare openly and unendingly. Yet this invitation to look is not necessarily positive. As Rachel Adams explains, "[F]reak shows performed important cultural work by allowing ordinary people to confront, and master, the most extreme and terrifying forms of Otherness they could imagine."[22] They put people with bodily differences and unique skills at the center, but interacting with the subjects of freak shows is often framed as pleasurable for audiences because laying eyes upon them is marked as taboo, frightening, or shocking. In contributing to the conflation of gawking at racial minorities with participating in something socially taboo, such looking becomes worrisome.

In order to consider the ethics of engaging with *Freakshow*, we must consider more fully the relationship between the viewer and the person who is being viewed. The show clearly offers an opportunity for viewers at home to stare and gawk at the performers via their television screens.

Yet there are important differences between the act of staring via mediation such as the television screen, and an interaction between two copresent human beings. In Garland-Thomson's important work on the politics of staring, she argues that people with disabilities gain power through "looking back" and confronting the starer, which puts them in a position to take control of the staring encounter. When an interaction occurs with the disabled person on television, mediation provides an unbreachable distance between the starer and the staree, as the staree cannot participate in the kind of looking that is going on. The camera captures their performance and the viewer stares at their performance on a screen, while the staree simply performs.

The distinction between live performance and mediated performance is particularly significant for the performers on *Freakshow*, who indicate that it is through live performance that they feel empowered. In a conversation between Ray's son, Phoenix, and some of the performers, these distinctions come to the fore.

PHOENIX RAY: Is all the pain [of lifting heavy objects] worth all the people clapping?

ANDREW S: I use it for therapy. If I'm not performing I go stir crazy. I think a lot of us performers are a little bit socially awkward growing up, and the only time we get to connect with people is when you're on stage.

MORGUE: I love it, I think it's all about expression. When you're on stage people really get to connect with you in a way they can't any way else.

JASON BROTT [THE "ILLUSTRATED PENGUIN"]: In a way it's kind of like getting that approval that you never got. Being on stage and people going, "Yeah, yeah!" It's like, sweet, I'm getting that approval I always wanted, but it's from someone else other than my parents.[23]

The language that these performers use does not necessarily indicate that they are subversively staring back as Garland-Thomson theorizes—and we should not demand that they articulate the political potential in staring back in order to believe that it is possible—but it is clear that the interpersonal connection and immediate approval they desire depends on a live audience's feedback. Moreover, on the show we can see that the small venue and dramatic pauses deployed during performances frequently give performers the opportunity to look directly into the eyes of audience members, which further leaves open the possibility of staring back. When audiences view these performances on television, the potential emancipation described here is revoked, as performers can neither "look back" nor gain the feedback they desire, ever remaining the object of the stare.

One way to intervene into this complicated relationship between starer and staree is to consider the different ways that mediated individuals do have some control over their own representation. It seems clear that the individuals on *Freakshow* consented to having their lives filmed and their stories edited into televisual narratives. Moreover, the performers were undoubtedly paid for their participation, meaning that they gain money as well as fame by participating. Yet financial compensation obviously does not offer any measure of control, dignity, or moral justification, as we know from those who have criticized the institution of freak shows. Just because the abjected other is receiving financial compensation for being mesmerizing to audiences does not make the power relations that perpetuate stigma and subordination acceptable, much less moral.

How to Stare at Your TV: An Ethics of Listening

This brings us back to the moral relations of the sideshow. Even if the freak show is inherently immoral, and its re-presentation within *Freakshow* is troubling, this does not tell us how we should interact with the televised version that is available in our own homes. Must the show be avoided, boycotted, or publically condemned? Must viewers avert their eyes from all representations of those who participate in the show? These solutions are not satisfactory, as we cannot expect viewers to know what is problematic without first watching it themselves, and personal boycotts of media texts contribute little to meaningful social change.

More realistically, I argue that we must work toward finding an ethical form of engaging with such texts as we view and make sense of them. Just as Susan Sontag and Rosemarie Garland-Thomson have put forward an ethics of looking, here I also dive into the ethical project of how to stare at "freaks" on television.[24] As the reality is simply that these institutions, performances, and representations already exist and are thriving—and in fact, through increased media attention seem to be growing in number and popularity—it is more important to discuss how viewers should consume and respond to representations of both racial and physical difference than how media refusal could impact the representations themselves. Garland-Thomson argues that the confrontation between able-bodied and disabled individuals provides an ethical moment, wherein "the question for starers is not whether we should stare, but rather how we should stare."[25] Similarly, for viewers of problematic media, the question is not whether or not such images should exist, but how we should understand and respond to them.

We can begin by considering how to respond to the show's images of African Americans, which are undeniably problematic. As I have argued, the stories of Bell, Chapman, and Boykin reinscribe narratives of the long history of people of color being coerced into performances that benefit white stakeholders. Their bodies are continually displayed, exoticized, objectified, and gawked at by people with mainstream identities whose white, normative bodies remain unmarked. Yet scholars of race who focus on the stereotypical images that have systemically plagued the mainstream media remind us that critique is not our only possible response to such inequalities. Rather, even the most stereotypical images can be interpreted in counterhegemonic ways. For images such as those on *Freakshow*, we can begin by seeking out moments of resistance and subversion. As evidenced within the stories above, there are many conversations about the oppression that people with extraordinary bodies face. Bell, Chapman, and Boykin openly explain the struggles that they have faced in a society that views them as the other. We see the difficulty that they face in finding housing, maintaining romantic relationships, and securing employment. Just as Celine Parreñas Shimizu reads images of hypersexualized Asian women for their moments of resistance, or images of emasculated Asian men for their progressive potential in rewriting frameworks for masculinity,[26] we must recognize that all images can be read in multiple ways and individuals can temporarily break free from their oppressive frameworks. We must be attuned to these possibilities, as these fissures in and disruptions to the dominant narrative are important even if they are ultimately overruled.

But we can take this demand for ethical viewership further than simply looking for resistance. I argue that to be an ethical viewer of television one ought to do more than look: media consumers must also listen. It is important to characterize television as a visual medium, as it is the ability to stare and gawk and look openly that makes depictions of visible difference on television so alluring. Yet television is also an aural medium that can serve to give voice to its participants. In pointing to this capability I do not mean to privilege the auditory or vocal abilities; for those who cannot speak or hear, writing or subtitling would serve this same function. I simply want to call attention to the fact that what these individuals have to say must be taken into consideration alongside how they appear. Such an act would take up Lisbeth Lipari's call for "listening otherwise," which she argues is an ethical form of bearing witness that demands opening oneself up to otherness: "It is a kind of looking and listening without objectification or appropriation, but with a kind of awareness that makes space for the unthinkable, the unimaginable, the other."[27] This practice of open-minded and compassionate listening may be difficult, but can offer ethical ways to respond to difference and alterity that can potentially alleviate suffering.

In the case of engaging ethically with *Freakshow*, we can note that the genre of reality television is ripe for this practice of listening because its format gives viewers the opportunity to peer "behind the curtain" of the performer's lives. In addition to scenes of everyday routines and domesticity, we are also given access to "confessionals"—monologues in which we are granted access to individual performers' personal take on the unfolding situation.[28] In this way, the reality show *Freakshow* is different from the moments discussed by Garland-Thomson in her exploration of one-on-one encounters, or in looking at still photographs. In both of these kinds of encounters, what is missing is voice, or the ability to be express one's internal life.

As we have already seen in the cases of these three performers, their stories are different and their opinions are sometimes contradictory. While Boykin wants to demonstrate the beauty and uniqueness of his body, Chapman wants to be able to shy away from the spotlight. Bell wants to be seen as "just like everybody else," while Boykin proudly embraces the "Say No to Normal" campaign espoused by Ray. We can also see that their opinions sometimes change over time, and that where once they might have been hesitant to perform, now they gain great joy from interacting with fans and audiences. Garland-Thomson asks those who encounter people with disabilities in real life to be open to the possibility of joining them in activist work. But what this discussion of the individuals on *Freakshow* reveals is that there is no single activist response that can encompass the needs of those who are being stared at. When we listen, we must be open to the nuances and inconsistencies encompassed by the richness of each individual's story. Sometimes that means joining them in a cause and walking beside them toward a common goal. Sometimes that means listening to their demands to look away, or accepting that they are simply normal human beings no different than anyone else. Sometimes that means empathizing and finding commonalities, becoming filled with joy and wonder—but only if asked to do so. What this television show gives us that in-person freak shows cannot is a closer look at the individuals behind the performances. It's only a glimpse, but while they don't have the power to look back, they do have the power to share their voice—and we have the power to decide how to listen.

NOTES

1 Throughout this chapter, I distinguish between *Freakshow* (the television show), the Venice Beach Freakshow (a specific business owned by Todd Ray, located in Venice, California), and freak shows (the generic name for the classic circus sideshow that features freaks).

2 Gerber, "The 'Careers' of People."

3 van Dijck, "Medical Documentary."

4 Barnhurst, "Visibility as Paradox"; Dávila, *Latinos, Inc.*; Gray, *Watching Race*; Gross, *Up from Invisibility*.

5 Gerber, "The 'Careers' of People," 44.

6 Garland-Thomson, *Staring*.

7 "Two-Headed Bearded Dragon Birthday," *Freakshow*, AMC, February 14, 2013.

8 Bogdan, *Freak Show*, 95.

9 Durbach, *Spectacle of Deformity*.

10 Bogdan, *Freak Show*.

11 Scully and Crais, "Race and Erasure."

12 Bogdan, *Freak Show*, 51.

13 Ibid., 48.

14 Omi and Winant, *Racial Formation in the United States*.

15 Bonilla-Silva, *Racism without Racists*.

16 "Human Pin Cushion," *Freakshow*, AMC, March 7, 2013.

17 Cummings, "Orientalism's Corporeal Dimension."

18 "Tattooed Vampires," *Freakshow*, AMC, May 13, 2014.

19 "Creature," *AMC (Freakshow)*, n.d., www.amc.com.

20 "The Littlest Wedding," *Freakshow*, AMC, March 14, 2013.

21 Qian, "Breaking the Last Taboo."

22 Adams, *Sideshow U.S.A.*, 2.

23 "Strongman Competition," *Freakshow*, AMC, March 21, 2013.

24 Sontag, *Regarding the Pain of Others*; Garland-Thomson, *Staring*.

25 Garland-Thomson, *Staring*, 185.

26 Shimizu, *The Hypersexuality of Race*; Shimizu, *Straitjacket Sexualities*.

27 Lipari, "Listening Otherwise," 56.

28 Aslama and Pantti, "Talking Alone."

PART III

Disability and Gender

5

Prosthetic Heroes

Curing Disabled Veterans in Iron Man 3 *and Beyond*

ELLEN SAMUELS

Ellen Samuels examines *Iron Man 3* (Shane Black, 2013), arguing that this film's representations of veterans and disability reflected the social context in which increasing numbers of disabled veterans were returning to the U.S., with their futures uncertain. Drawing on longstanding cultural roles of veterans as "heroes" or "villains," this superhero film ultimately positions cure as both violent and mandatory, suggesting little cultural tolerance for veterans' ongoing disabilities and the resources that such conditions would require. Bringing a disability studies reading to a Hollywood blockbuster, this chapter demonstrates the pervasiveness and power of disability narratives.

The 2013 release of the third film in Marvel's blockbuster *Iron Man* series, starring Robert Downey, Jr., as the titular hero, coincided with a growing public concern in the United States about the increasing numbers of disabled veterans returning from the wars in Iraq and Afghanistan. In this essay, I consider the content and reception of *Iron Man 3* to argue that the difficult reintegration of these veterans into 21st-century American society is reflected in popular media depictions as a tension between possible cultural roles of veterans as "heroes" or "villains," and that disability plays a key role in these representations.[1]

The United States and other modern nations have repeatedly reaffirmed and reinvented themselves through the figure of the disabled veteran. National identity, gender and class structures, technological advances, and social relations have all been transformed by—and mediated through—depictions of disabled vets. Furthermore, this figure often becomes the locus of social anxieties about the transition from war to peace and the challenge of rehabilitating and reintegrating non-normative bodyminds into a normalized society.[2] Of the post–World War II era, David Gerber observes, "With a sharply divided consciousness that both honored the veteran and feared his potential to disrupt society, Americans in 1945 prepared to receive and reintegrate millions of demobilized men. The return of the disabled veteran gave rise to particularly acute anxieties. . . . On the one hand, the veteran's heroism and sacrifices are celebrated and memorialized, and debts of gratitude, both symbolic and material, are paid to him. On the other hand, the veteran also inspires anxiety and fear and is seen as a threat to social order and political stability."[3] This divided consciousness lies at the heart of *Iron Man 3*, and thus this Hollywood blockbuster is a useful cultural text for thinking through the material circumstances of returning veterans in 21st-century America.

Such an analysis also illuminates the study of superhero culture, which often acknowledges but rarely theorizes the constitutive origins of superheroes within the major military conflicts of the twentieth century.[4] Ramzi Fawaz convincingly argues that "innovations in the creative uses of the superhero in the mid-1970s politicized the figure by making explicit the mutually constitutive relationship between fantasy and political life."[5] Like Fawaz, I seek to position the popular superhero film "along a continuum with the broader political categories that drive the putatively humanist values of the nation-state."[6] However, while Fawaz locates revolutionary potential in superhero comics, especially Marvel's *X-Men* books of the 1970s, I find the strand of superhero culture typified by *Iron Man 3* less liberatory and more broadly reactionary, tending toward the normalization rather than the diversification of bodily and political states of being. Here I make a supplementary and corrective gesture to the tendency within superhero cultural studies to pay little attention to Iron Man because he is viewed as a conservative figure who is less intriguing—and certainly less of a focus for progressive identification—than the X-Men, Spider-Man, the Hulk, or other superheroes characterized by outsider status and social precarity.[7] In contrast to these outsider heroes, Tony Stark/Iron Man is a multi-billionaire, aligned with the military-industrial complex, who originated in comics as a staunchly patriotic anti-Communist.[8] In this sense he more closely resembles DC Comics' Batman than the paradigmatic Marvel Comics antihero, and it is notable that the most successful solo superhero movies of the post-9/11 era have been Christopher Nolan's *Batman: The Dark Knight* trilogy (2005–2012) and the *Iron Man* films, both of which feature wealthy heroes employing military-derived technology to restore—or impose—order on an increasingly terrifying and chaotic world.

This world has also been shaped by more than a decade of near-continuous warfare, particularly in Afghanistan and Iraq, subsumed under the concept of a global and unlimited War on Terror. Higher survival rates for injured soldiers engaged in these wars have produced unprecedented numbers and visibility of disabled veterans in the United States. In 2013, when *Iron Man 3* was released, more than 2.5 million Americans had served in the Iraq and Afghanistan wars, and 1.6 million of those had transitioned to veteran status.[9] Within that group, rates of combat-related disability are higher than in any other postwar population in the United States, with over 600,000 disability claims filed and research suggesting even higher rates of actual impairment.[10] Inadequate mental health services for these veterans have been widely criticized, particularly in the context of sharply rising suicide rates among Iraq and Afghanistan veterans.[11] These conditions are a key context for understanding *Iron Man 3*'s inclusion of disabled Iraq and Afghanistan veterans among its key characters, and the central role disability plays in the film's narrative impetus and thematic conclusions.

Traumatic Stress and the Divergence of *Iron Man 3*

Iron Man 3 was the seventh installment in the series of linked superhero films comprising the Marvel Cinematic Universe (MCU), widely considered the most critically and commercially successful superhero movie franchise ever created.[12] With sixteen films to date, which have grossed more than $11 billion globally and continue to reach millions of viewers, the MCU's influence on the cultural imaginary has been powerful and wide-reaching. The MCU was launched with *Iron Man* in 2008, and Iron Man remains its most popular hero. Premiering in 2013, *Iron Man 3* was both well reviewed and extremely profitable.[13]

I will discuss various plot points of *Iron Man 3* in detail throughout this essay. In brief summary, this film continues the story of Tony Stark, a billionaire engineering genius who operates a superpowered metal suit energized by a nuclear arc reactor implanted in his chest, which also keeps him alive by drawing shrapnel away from his heart. Stark openly bears the identity of Iron Man and, in this installment, faces two foes: an Osama bin Laden–like terrorist named the Mandarin (Ben Kingsley), and the real villain behind the Mandarin, engineer Aldrich Killian (Guy Pearce). Killian has developed a powerful bio-energy called Extremis, which can cure disease and regenerate limbs. Killian has recruited injured and traumatized Iraq and Afghanistan veterans to be infused with Extremis and then serve as his villainous lackeys. Extremis also confers super-strength, near-invulnerability, and the ability to generate intense heat with a touch; it has the unfortunate side effect of causing some of its subjects to explode like bombs. With the help of two allies from the earlier films, Col. James Rhodes (Don Cheadle) and Pepper Potts (Gwyneth Paltrow), Stark ultimately defeats Killian and stabilizes Extremis for safe use.

Despite the film's success, diehard fans of the MCU quickly filled the blogosphere with discussions of the radical discontinuities between *Iron Man 3* and the previous MCU films.[14] Indeed, *Iron Man 3* changed the rules of Iron Man within the MCU in two crucial and interrelated ways. First, while previous MCU films presented the Iron Man armor as a unified whole inextricably connected to Tony Stark's body, *Iron Man 3* transforms the armor into a set of fragmented pieces that often operate independently of Stark. Second, and more disturbing to fans, is the film's conclusion, in which Stark undergoes surgery to remove the previously irremovable shrapnel from his chest, meaning that he no longer needs the embedded arc reactor that had constituted both the origin and the *raison d'être* for his identity as Iron Man. Both of these changes seem to separate Tony Stark, the man, from Iron Man, the hero, in new and unpalatable (to some) fashions.

I suggest that these changes are not merely arbitrary, nor should they be dismissed as the producers simply ensuring that different actors can play the role after Downey.[15] Instead, they must be understood as signifying in a wider cultural plane than that of MCU fandom. I contend that these radical changes to the rules of the Iron Man body and universe reflect a new interrelationship between the onscreen heroes and villains of the MCU and the hero/villain figure of the returning Iraq/Afghanistan veterans whose disabled bodies and minds were becoming increasingly present in both the streets and the imaginations of everyday Americans.[16]

The *Iron Man* movies have been concerned with the War on Terror from their inception. In the first film, Stark's origin story was displaced from its original comic book setting in Vietnam to Afghanistan, where he was taken prisoner by a quasi–Al Qaeda terrorist cell who attempted to force him to build weapons.[17] Instead, he constructed the first Iron Man suit and escaped, but seeing his own military technology in the hands of the terrorists led Stark to abandon his lucrative career as a weapons developer. In 2010's *Iron Man 2*, although Stark refused to share his Iron Man technology with the U.S. military, he was ultimately recruited by the international super-spy agency S.H.I.E.L.D., suggesting that there is no place for a post-9/11 superhero outside of the military-industrial complex. In this film, Congress's demand for Iron Man technology is expressed as a fear that enemies of the U.S. government—specifically Iran and North Korea, members of the so-called "Axis of Evil"—will develop their own Iron Man armor, producing an arms race within the War on Terror. *Iron Man 3* continues this theme, as the supposed villain, the Mandarin, employs suicide bombers against civilian targets in retaliation for acts of U.S. imperialist aggression. That the Mandarin turns out to be a fraudulent cover for Killian, an American, does not neutralize the impact of his depiction as a jihadist-style terrorist, but rather emphasizes the point that villainy in the early 21st century is increasingly legible only when framed in terms of quasi-Islamic foreign terrorism.[18]

The consistent throughline of Middle East conflict and terrorist threat in the *Iron Man* trilogy may be contrasted, however, with the radical shift in its treatment of combat-related trauma and disability. In the first film, Stark has the sort of experiences we might expect to produce classic post-traumatic stress disorder (PTSD): He is attacked, injured, tortured, and held captive for months, barely escaping with his life. Yet upon his return to the U.S., Stark shows no signs of post-traumatic stress but focuses with laser-like clarity of purpose upon his new goal of becoming a superhero. In *Iron Man 2*, Stark is dying from poisoning caused by the arc reactor in his chest and again experiences life-and-death conflicts close at hand; yet, while he acts out in various psychologically morbid ways, Stark never shows any of the classic symptoms of PTSD, such as flashbacks, nightmares, sleeplessness, panic attacks, or avoidance of past experiences. By contrast, in *Iron Man 3*, Stark shows all of these symptoms, indeed displaying such a textbook case of PTSD that, even without the diagnosis being explicitly named, reviewers frequently identified it as a key feature of the film.[19]

So why did the creators of the MCU find the notion of Stark's PTSD so compelling that they made it a hinge point of both plot and theme in the third *Iron Man* movie, after having utterly ignored it in the first two? The answer, I suggest, has a great deal to do with how the MCU, and the *Iron Man* films in particular, have reflected and shaped the American cultural imaginary in the wake of the 9/11 attacks.[20] I suggest the first phase of MCU films, beginning with *Iron Man* and culminating with *Marvel's The Avengers* (Joss Whedon, 2012), may be viewed as an imagined representation of the American psyche leading up to the 9/11 attacks, in which injury does not produce trauma and the roles of heroes and villains are clearly defined. The battle of New York at the end of *Marvel's The Avengers*, then, evokes the 9/11 attacks, as seen vividly when uniformed New York police and firefighters struggle to evacuate survivors from buildings laid waste by foreign (alien) attackers who crash large armored vehicles into skyscrapers with abandon.[21] In *Iron Man 3*, the merest mention of the words "New York" sends Stark into a full-blown panic attack, suggesting that his individual trauma mirrors that of the nation and that any recovery he may achieve will also then be applicable to the national psyche. Thus I contend that *Iron Man 3* marks the point where the MCU begins not only to reflect the post-9/11 world, but to become symptomatic of it, in the sense that Tony Stark's post-traumatic stress becomes the stress of the viewers themselves, and the movie attempts to offer solutions that will be curative not only of the character but also of the audience and the nation.[22] Yet such solutions will inevitably be both partial and unsatisfying, just like the repeated and failed efforts by the U.S. government to resolve the conflicts in Iraq and Afghanistan and exit the region.

In this era of wars that take place far from the homeland, the visible signs of the conflicts in Iraq and Afghanistan are the bodyminds of American veterans returning home. In 2008, the same year of the first *Iron Man*, the country's new first lady, Michelle Obama, and Dr. Jill Biden, wife of the vice president, founded the Joining Forces initiative, declaring that they would focus upon the welfare of returning Iraq and

Afghanistan veterans during their husbands' tenure in Washington. In the bitterly divisive 2014 elections, better care of injured vets emerged as one of the few bipartisan issues on which a majority of Americans could agree.[23] Yet since the inception of the wars in Iraq and Afghanistan, the state agencies charged with caring for disabled vets have been plagued by scandal and stories of woeful incompetence, lack of resources, and exclusionary discrimination. From the wretched conditions at Walter Reed Army Medical Center, to the discharge of thousands of vets with misapplied personality disorder diagnoses, to the backlog of hundreds of thousands of Veterans Administration disability claims, to the revelation that the V.A. concealed the actual waiting times for veterans' medical appointments, the national institutions meant to ensure the care and rehabilitation of veterans have repeatedly and profoundly failed to do so.[24] In response, a number of non-governmental organizations have arisen, including Iraq and Afghanistan Veterans of America (IAVA) and the Wounded Warrior Project, which advocate for better services for veterans and also provide direct services such as peer counseling.

Both governmental and non-governmental responses to the unprecedented numbers of disabled veterans returning from Iraq and Afghanistan are shaped, as noted above, by a fundamental tension between perceptions of disabled vets as heroic warriors or dangerous outsiders. Today, these perceptions often map onto veterans through the figure of the amputee—whose wound is visible, incontrovertible, and prosthetizeable into a semblance of normalcy—and the "mentally ill" individual—whose wounds are invisible, nebulous, and a persistent threat to normalcy and social reintegration. The visibility of the amputee as the primary representation of the injured soldier dates back at least to the American Civil War. In the twentieth century, as Gerber observes, "[W]e find amputees garnering attention vastly out of proportion to their relatively small numbers, and in effect, becoming representative of all disabled veterans. The drama of their injury crowds out everything else about them, and about others, with different, less visible injuries or illnesses."[25] Yet this visible figure has not always carried positive associations. The late-twentieth-century figure of the heroic amputee-soldier was produced in direct and reparative response to perceptions of amputees as "potentially troubled and socially maladjusted."[26] Indeed, in the 1940s, "[E]ngineers routinely gave potential prosthesis wearers a battery of psychological tests, all of which assumed that amputees suffer from war-related neuroses."[27] This neurotic and socially dangerous amputee-soldier, then, needed to be rehabilitated not only through prosthetic technology but also through a reconception of the relationship of disability to mental health and upright citizenship. Thus, observes David Serlin, "[I]n the patriotic aftermath of World War II . . . American media regularly circulated stories about amputees and their triumphant use of prostheses. The circulation of such unduly cheery narratives of tolerance in the face of adversity implied a direct relation between physical trauma—and the ability to survive such trauma—and patriotic duty."[28] By the 1950s, we find the figure of the amputee-veteran emerging as the pinnacle of socially venerated patriotic and heroic sacrifice, with its previous connotations of mental instability and social threat expunged.

Meanwhile, the devastating psychological effects of combat upon soldiers continue and have been amplified by higher rates of physical survival amid atrocity: "In the twentieth century . . . the physical has been factored out increasingly, and we are left with war's destruction of the mind."[29] This trend has only heightened in the 21st century: While "five out of every eight seriously injured soldiers in the Vietnam War survived their injuries," that number has risen "to seven out of eight in the Iraq and Afghanistan Wars."[30] Veterans returning from Iraq and Afghanistan show extremely high rates of psychological trauma due to surviving or witnessing severe injury, with estimates ranging from 20 to 60% of returning veterans being affected by PTSD and related conditions.[31] Concerns about the social threat posed by these veterans are produced and reflected by news stories that, while often sympathetic, also often present veterans with PTSD as threatening figures who may harm their families or go on shooting sprees.[32] Thus we see how the antisocial pathologies of the amputee-veteran figure in the mid-twentieth century were displaced onto the emergent figure of the traumatized veteran, who is even more dangerous because his/her body bears no sign of the threat it contains within.[33]

The tension between these two figures can be read in a public service announcement (PSA) produced by the Wounded Warrior Project in 2013, which aired on national television and was downloadable on their website.[34] In this thirty-second film, a veteran named Norberto Lara describes losing his arm in Iraq while visuals depict him donning a technologically sophisticated prosthetic arm. These images construct Lara as the heroic and normatively masculine amputee-veteran, with close-ups of his uniform and medals, as well as pre-injury wedding pictures. Only after establishing this figure does Lara's voiceover narrative shift, as he explains, "We do have a lot of guys that have post-traumatic stress disorder." This narrative thus attempts to shift the terms of discussion regarding disabled veterans by opening up public conceptions of "wounded warriors" to include those with PTSD and other stigmatized and non-visible injuries. This voiceover continues over footage of Lara's prosthesis and empty sleeve, using his visible "heroic" body to validate his claims regarding the equal heroism of other kinds of wounds, and culminating in his final statement: "Yes, I do suffer from post-traumatic stress disorder. But [pause] I'm OK." The PSA ends with a graphic from the WWP featuring the slogan, "Don't suffer in silence."

Certainly, the PSA's goal of reducing stigma regarding combat-related PTSD and encouraging veterans with PTSD to seek help is laudable. But the PSA also presents a rich ground within which to consider the complex tensions in cultural representations of disabled Iraq and Afghanistan vets, as simultaneously heroic figures to be supported and pathologized figures to be feared. Having opened up this tension, the PSA attempts to resolve it with the statement "But I'm OK," which may strike the viewer as simplified and incomplete. Thus, the PSA, released the same year as *Iron Man 3*, represents the terms within which the film will explore the same tensions and attempt the same kind of simplistic resolution.

Prosthetic Meaning in a World without Prostheses

As described above, the first radical discontinuity in *Iron Man 3* involves the relationship between Tony Stark and the Iron Man armor, the "high-tech prosthesis" (*Iron Man 2*) that functions both to sustain Stark's physical body and to transcend that body by giving it superhuman powers. Until *Iron Man 3*, the MCU presented Stark as inseparable from his armor, linked to it by the arc reactor implanted in his chest. This narrative explicitly asserted the coherence of the bond between the suit and the man, as shown in Stark's frequent declarations that "I *am* Iron Man." The films repeatedly drive this message home, as in *Iron Man*, when Stark tells his friend Col. James Rhodes (Terrence Howard) to stop the military from firing on an unidentified flying object. Stark says, "It's me!" and when Rhodes misunderstands, repeats, "It's me, it's me, the thing you see is *me*." Similarly, in *Iron Man 2*, Stark testifies before Congress that "I am Iron Man. The suit and I are one."

Yet in *Iron Man 3*, this narrative is fractured, literally, as the singular, unified Iron Man armor is replaced by a squad of apparently interchangeable armored suits. These suits are themselves fragmented into individual "body" parts such as hands and feet that Stark can control separately and that can function independently—both of the armor as a whole and of the presence of Stark's body inside them. As one fan blogger observed: "[O]f the three *Iron Man* movies, this is the only one that treats the suits as inherently disposable. In *1* and *2*, there are multiple suits, but Tony exchanges them the way that a lobster exchanges its carapaces. Each is his skin until he discards it, and there's really only one viable suit at a time. Here, though, he exchanges them pretty much the way we exchange our clothes, which are necessary for daily life, but not *part* of us. The fact that the suits can move around on their own . . . surely reinforces this point."[35] This change transforms the armor into a series of prosthetics that both extend and solidify Stark's own status as an organic, human body without special powers. The only remaining element of unfractured heroic technology is the arc reactor embedded in Stark's chest, a point to which I will return below.

Understanding the Iron Man armor as prosthesis places it within a history of prosthetic technology that historians have located squarely within the modern military-industrial complex,[36] not only because the armor functions as a "high-tech prosthesis" compensating for Stark's shrapnel injury, but more fundamentally because of Stark's (and his father's) role as a weapons designer for the U.S. government. Conceiving the Iron Man armor as prosthesis also drives home Alex Romagnoli and Gian Pagnucci's observation that "Iron Man makes the superhero a technological construct, and in the 21st-century world of technology in which we live, this brings the possibility of being a superhero almost within reach."[37]

Since the science-fiction appeal of prostheses is that they supposedly "offer the utopian prospect of infinite choices and endless replacement of damaged or aging body parts," the seemingly endless array of armored pieces available to Stark in *Iron Man 3* reinforces the sense that

Figure 5.1. Still from *Iron Man 3* illustrating Stark's powerful red-and-gold prosthetic hand, extending up his forearm.

the fracturing of his bond to the armor only increases his ability to actualize its potential.[38] Indeed, at various points in the film, Stark has only a mechanical hand or foot attached to his body, and the film delights in foregrounding the contrast between his impotent and vulnerable body and the powerful ability of his prosthetic hand equipped with repulsor beams or prosthetic feet that enable flight (figure 5.1).

This foregrounding of the pieces of armor as limb prostheses is especially notable when we consider the complete lack of prosthetic limbs available to the several amputee characters in the film, and indeed the film's plot turns upon the presentation of amputation as an intractable injury that cannot be prosthetically compensated and thus reintegrated into society. Instead, in the world of *Iron Man 3*, amputation inevitably produces antisociality and, in its most extreme forms, villainy and destruction, thus casting us back to the pre-1945 conception of amputee-soldiers as mentally unstable.[39] In this sense, the absence of prosthetics functions as what David Mitchell and Sharon Snyder call "narrative prosthesis": the introduction of disability into a plot to move the narrative forward without becoming a fully realized subject of that narrative.[40]

This narrative function is most notable in the brief glimpse of a young girl, presumably the vice president's daughter, who is shown in a wheelchair with the stump of a below-the-knee amputation visible. This "reveal" of the girl's amputee status exposes and explains the vice president's alignment with the film's villains, since he presumptively supports their pursuit of a cure for amputation through Extremis. That an otherwise able-bodied-appearing and clearly affluent child with a unilateral below-the-knee amputation is using a wheelchair rather than a functional limb prosthesis is a necessary piece of this narrative logic, but it marks a clear break between real-life disability and that of the film's world without prosthetics.

This break is even more startling when we consider the film's portrayal of amputee Iraq and Afghanistan veterans, such as Ellen Brandt (Stéphanie Szostak), shown with a visible arm stump and no sign of the prosthetic limb that would invariably have been provided by the military-medical complex in the real world. Indeed, providing prosthetic limbs is the area in which military medicine and the V.A. have most succeeded in serving disabled veterans, performing the work of not only functional but also social rehabilitation.[41] As Serlin observes, "[F]or doctors and patients, prosthetics were powerful and anthropomorphic tools that reflected contemporary fantasies about ability and employment, heterosexual masculinity, and American citizenship."[42] Thus the absence of prosthetic limbs in the film's portrayal of disabled veterans signals a lack of reintegration into legible and useful citizenship, symbolically reinscribing them as villains who threaten, rather than represent, the national body.

This portrayal of a world without prosthetics is especially striking in a 2013 film that explicitly features Iraq and Afghanistan amputee-veterans. Just a year earlier, broad national attention had turned toward one such veteran, Rep. Tammy Duckworth, as she pursued and won a seat in the U.S. Congress. Duckworth generally appears in public wearing at least one of her two prosthetic legs, and in select media appearances uses both prostheses and a cane (at other times, she uses a wheelchair or scooter). Duckworth is probably the most visible and recognizable disabled veteran of the recent wars, and she uses her prosthetic legs not only to walk, but also as text to convey national identity. One of her legs is painted with military camouflage and a "Fly Army" insignia, while

Figure 5.2. Tammy Duckworth sits, wearing a red blazer, with her red-white-and-blue and camouflage leg prosthetics visible, March 2010. Copyright: U.S. Army; used under a Creative Commons share/adapt/attribute license; uncropped original available at www.flickr.com.

the other is decorated with the stars and stripes of the American flag (figure 5.2). Her functional legs do not pretend to approximate "normal" legs, but instead foreground both the altered conditions of Duckworth's body and the national character of that alteration. Within the distinctly nationalistic context of the American flag, Duckworth presents her disabled body as sacred object, literally that which must not be desecrated. This presentation is a stark contrast to the portrayals of disabled veterans in *Iron Man 3*, discussed below, as willing to subject their bodies to Extremis in order to cure their disabilities.

Duckworth's nationalistic prostheses are also striking as they attach to the body of an Asian American woman, a figure whose membership in the national project has long been contested.[43] In *Iron Man 3*, the decision to transform the War Machine armor into the "Iron Patriot" for this film means that its occupant, Col. James Rhodes (now played by Don Cheadle), becomes a literal embodiment of Duckworth's red-white-and-blue prosthesis, his body enclosed in the armor that has now been transformed into a symbol of Americanness.[44] Rhodes's racial identity is significant here: If a flag prosthesis can interpellate an Asian American female body into national iconography, it would seem that an entire suit of flag armor is needed to resignify the Black male body toward the national purpose. And indeed, that resignification is Rhodes's downfall, as his armor is taken over by Killian and he becomes literally unable to control the national narrative within which he is trapped. The armor can then be occupied by a villain who uses it to kidnap the U.S. president. Thus the Iron Patriot armor is shown to be able to contain a range of national subjects without altering their inherent identity.

How does this portrayal mesh with the idea of that Tony Stark *is* Iron Man? Unlike Iron Patriot, Stark has forcefully rejected any form of nationalistic identity, asserting instead the primacy of capitalism and property rights. But by the end of the film, with the league of suits that appear now entirely interchangeable and fragmentable, it is clear that Stark is shifting his allegiance. Normalcy, rather than capital, becomes his guiding principle as he destroys all of his suits and undergoes curative surgery for the sake of a "normal" life.

Curative Violence in Extremis

Here we come to the second seemingly inexplicable change to the Iron Man narrative. Previously, the MCU had been clear that Stark must have the arc reactor in his chest or die from the shrapnel it kept at bay. Indeed, in *Iron Man 2*, Stark came close to dying from poisoning from the arc reactor until S.H.I.E.L.D. provided effective treatment. Yet, at the end of *Iron Man 3*, the film abruptly declares that surgical removal of the shrapnel was possible all along and implies that it was only Stark's psychological attachment to being Iron Man that had kept him dependent on the reactor.[45] In other words, the work of *Iron Man 3* is to transform

Tony Stark from an incurable to a curable (and eventually, cured) subject. After the curative surgery, Stark's voiceover tells us that he will "always be Iron Man"; however, how the armor will function without the biologically embedded arc reactor is left unresolved.[46]

In fact, everyone is cured by the end of *Iron Man 3*, yet the movie makes it clear that not all cures are equal. In the early part of the film, Killian has an unnamed neuromuscular disability—he has tremors, walks with a cane, and appears to be in pain—which he later cures with Extremis. The revelation that Killian's corps of Extremis-powered fighters are formerly disabled Iraq and Afghanistan veterans occurs when Tony Stark remotely accesses Killian's computer system and views footage of veterans Ellen Brandt and Eric Savin (James Badge Dale). In the footage of Savin, we see a clean-cut young white man shown in tight close-up. Killian, offscreen, asks, "What would you regard the defining moment of your life?" and Savin replies, "That would be the day I decided not to let my injury beat me." Having thus established Savin as a heroic disabled veteran committed to a stereotypical overcoming narrative, the footage moves to a shot of Brandt, a white woman with dark red hair, wearing a tank top that reveals the above-the-elbow amputation of her left arm. Over scenes of Savin, Brandt, and other figures assembling in a laboratory, Killian's voice proclaims: "Once misfits, cripples, *you* are the next iteration of human evolution." We then see Brandt strapped onto an upright gurney ready to receive the Extremis infusion. As Extremis enters her body, shown as waves of bright orange light erupting under her skin, her arm regenerates in a burst of fiery energy. This is meant to be the "aha" moment for the viewer, the reveal that explains why these once-heroes turned into murderous villains at Killian's behest: He offered them a cure. That this cure comes at a heavy price is immediately conveyed as the camera pans to the man on the gurney next to Brandt's, whose face and torso become suffused in the fiery Extremis energy before his entire body explodes. The risk of cure, then, is not only the transformation of hero into villain, but the possibility that cure will destroy both the cured subject and the world around him. Watching this footage, Stark solves the mystery of the bombs that have been exploding around world and killing civilians: They are actually people, disabled veterans exploding because they can't regulate the Extremis energy in their bodies.

The equation of the disabled veteran with a bomb liable to explode and destroy those closest to him resonates again with broad social fears regarding the unpredictability and potential violence of traumatized veterans, especially toward their own families.[47] Thus, the Extremis cure functions to transform the heroic amputee-veteran into the dangerous traumatized veteran. Indeed, the motivation for the vets to use Extremis is presented as somewhat more complicated than simply regrowing their missing limbs. The missing limbs also stand in for the veterans' inability to readjust to civilian life: When Stark first investigates one of the mysterious "bombs" that was supposedly set off by a suicidal veteran, he discovers that the veteran was rumored to be "crazy," a rumor apparently confirmed by his suicide, which also killed five others. He had, in fact, simply exploded. The physical and emotional injuries of war are blurred here, and it is implied that Extremis is sought to regenerate the untraumatized mind even as it regenerates arms and legs. In practice, it has the opposite effect: Once the veterans have assimilated Extremis, they are presented as mono-dimensionally evil figures devoid of morality, empathy, and even will, functioning entirely to carry out Killian's commands.

Extremis thus instantiates what Eunjung Kim calls "curative violence," a concept that encompasses both the overriding imperative for cure as the only response to disability and the physical violence and destruction often inherent to such cures.[48] In Killian's case, he was able to use Extremis to transform himself from an uncouth, unattractive, tech wannabe into an upright, handsome, and successful tech mogul: He was not only cured but also rehabilitated. But for the veterans, Extremis only offers cure, not rehabilitation, and certainly not an end to their trauma. Extremis transforms them into figures of inchoate violence, barely human— and those are the ones who survive. Yet, as we recall, the vice president was willing to betray his country for hope of just such a cure for his daughter. Cure in the film is both imperative and flexible, presented as wholly destructive and miraculously good in the same cinematic breath. The only possibility the film's narrative entirely forecloses is that of rejecting cure and embracing difference.

In this context the end of the film makes a certain sense, as Stark seeks his own surgical cure in order to have a more normal life, and specifically, a more successful heteronormative relationship with Pepper Potts. The implication that Stark's surgical cure may have been enabled by his own assimilation of Extremis further complicates the film's narrative logic, however, and makes a kind of tortured sense only through the imposition of a reactionary normativity of both gender and heterorelationality. Here, Potts takes center stage as mediator of the tension between the miraculous and destructive potentials of cure. Killian kidnaps Potts and subjects her to Extremis, but Potts survives the infusion and uses her Extremis-fueled powers to defeat Killian and save Stark's life not once but twice in the film's climactic battle. Since Potts's role in previous *Iron Man* battles mostly involved shrieking for help and being rescued, this emergence of a powerful, combat-ready Potts is a welcome change. However, the empowered Potts lasts only long enough to prevail over Killian, then immediately turns to Stark in search of a cure, asking plaintively, "Am I gonna be OK?" Thus, Stark's original impetus to stabilize Extremis is to restore the hetero- and gender-normative order in which he is the powerful male super-hero and Potts is the damsel in distress. This restoration resolves the threat throughout the film that Potts could encroach on Stark's male realm: Not only is she now CEO of Stark Enterprises, but in an early scene she dons Stark's armor to protect him. Even in her final defeat of Killian, Potts utilizes both her Extremis powers and a detached repulsor arm from an Iron Man suit, demonstrating again the prosthetic nature of the suit's technology and its disconnection from Stark's identity. It might seem logical that, once Extremis is stabilized, Potts could and would become a superhero in her own right. Instead, the film insists, all she wants is to be "normal" again, "fixed," and as Stark assures her, "That's what I do, I fix stuff."[49]

The stabilization of Extremis, the film implies but does not directly state, also enables Stark to undergo surgery to remove his shrapnel. His voiceover during the surgery scene explains: "As promised, I got Pepper sorted out. It took some tinkering. But then I thought to myself, why stop there? Of course there are people who say progress is dangerous, but I bet none of those idiots ever had to live with a chest full of shrapnel, and now, neither will I." The triumphalism of Stark's cure narrative again blurs physical and emotional states of being, as Stark, recovered from his nightmares and flashbacks, tells us that the surgical anesthesia gave him "the best sleep I'd had in years." Stark's voiceover concludes that "I'm a changed man" as he throws the arc reactor over a cliff into the Pacific Ocean, then drives away from the ruins of his former home. Stark's trauma, it appears, has been cured as well, and thus he is able to emerge from the cocoon of his armor into a newly whole, unfragmented, and normal life. Despite his closing insistence once more that "I am Iron Man," it remains unclear how, given that he destroyed all of his suits and threw out the arc reactor. If, as I have argued in this essay, *Iron Man 3* functions in the cultural imaginary as a working through of national post-9/11 trauma and the disabling effects of the War on Terror, then the answer the film ultimately offers is a quick surgical cure, a removal of the parts that make us different or remind us of vulnerability, and a return to coherent, organic, and unfractured wholeness. In the end, the film insists, the world around us may be in ruins, and actual disabled veterans may be beyond redemption, cured into oblivion, but all that really seems to matter is that Tony Stark is "OK."

As a national allegory, *Iron Man 3* forecloses the possibility that disabled Iraq and Afghanistan veterans can be successfully reintegrated into American society, and offers instead a pessimistic view of the future in which cure is at once imperative and destructive. The generally positive responses to the film, then, suggest that this view reflects perceptions broadly, if unconsciously, held among the viewing public and American culture at large. Most disturbingly, the film offers the allure of a quick fix for a problem that needs complex and open-ended responses, and thus its role in both shaping and reflecting cultural attitudes toward disabled veterans is both significant and unsettling.

NOTES

1 Film blogger Stokes observes that *Iron Man 3* "features disabled characters more prominently than any other blockbuster action movie I can think of" ("Theorizing Disability in Iron Man 3," *Overthinking It*, May 9, 2013, www.overthinkingit. com). See also blogger Gabalicious, "The Myth of the Supercrip, Disease, Ableism, and 'Iron Man 3,'" *American Dramedy*, May 10, 2013, http://americandramedy. blogspot.com. Yet the original 2005 comic book on which the movie is based did not feature disability or include Iraq/Afghanistan veterans (Warren Ellis [w] and Adi Granov [i], *Iron Man: Extremis* [New York: Marvel, 2005]). In contrast, *Iron Man 3* is suffused with plots and subplots regarding disability and cure and features disabled Iraq and Afghanistan veterans as key characters. On disability and comic book superheroes, see also Alaniz, *Death, Disability, and the Superhero* and Foss, Gray, and Whalen, eds., *Disability in Comic Books and Graphic Narratives*.

2 I follow here Margaret Price's foundational text *Mad at School*: "I use the term *bodymind* to emphasize that although 'body' and 'mind' usually occupy separate conceptual and linguistic territories, they are deeply intertwined" (240).

3 Gerber, "Heroes and Misfits," 70–71.

4 See for example: DiPaolo, *War, Politics and Superheroes*; Johnson, *Super-History*; Romagnoli and Pagnucci, *Enter the Superheroes*.

5 Fawaz, "'Where No X-Man.'"

6 Ibid., 360.

7 On Spiderman and the Hulk as outsider heroes associated with the counterculture, see Fawaz, "'Where No X-Man,'" and Wright, *Comic Book Nation*.

8 "Iron Man was perhaps the most conservative of all the Marvel superheroes. . . . Although by the mid-1960s Tony Stark began to question the American government and the Vietnam conflict, he remained committed to a traditional conservative understanding of the U.S.'s problems, both at home and abroad" (Johnson, *Super-History*, 98). Iron Man creator Stan Lee reportedly created Iron Man as a conservative hero deliberately, to see if Marvel readers would still identify with him (DiPaolo, *War, Politics, and Superheroes*, 27).

9 Chris Adams, "Millions Went to War in Iraq, Afghanistan, Leaving Many with Lifelong Scars," *McClatchyDC*, March 14, 2013, www.mcclatchydc.com.

10 Ibid.; Williamson and Mulhall, "Invisible Wounds."

11 See also Martha Franklin et al., "2014 Wounded Warrior Project Survey: Report of Findings," *Wounded Warrior Project*, July 30, 2014, www.woundedwarriorproject.org.

12 The Marvel Cinematic Universe was created in 2007 by Marvel, in cooperation with Paramount Pictures, with the innovative and influential decision to plan a franchise of interlinked superhero films shaped around the Avengers (Sharon Waxman, "Marvel Wants to Flex Its Own Heroic Muscles as a Moviemaker," *New York Times*, June 18, 2007). As of 2014, the MCU was the second-highest-grossing film franchise of all time, just behind the Harry Potter films ("Marvel Cinematic Universe," *Box Office Mojo*, www.boxofficemojo.com). On the creation of the MCU in the context of media franchises, see Johnson, *Media Franchising*, 96.

13 As of this writing, *Iron Man 3* has a 79% rating on Rotten Tomatoes (rottentomatoes.com), with 231 positive and 61 negative reviews in English-language media. This is not as high as *Iron Man* (94%), but better than *Iron Man 2* (72%). The audience rating for *Iron Man 3* on rottentomatoes.com is 78%. The film grossed over $400 million in the U.S. and $1.2 billion worldwide, as much as the first two *Iron Man* films' worldwide revenues combined (boxofficemojo.com).

14 See for example Stokes, "Theorizing Disability"; Rob Hunter, "9 Big Questions Left Unanswered by Iron Man 3," *Film School Rejects*, May 4, 2013, https://filmschoolrejects.com; Colin Liotta, "5 Burning Questions from *Iron Man 3*," *Huffington Post*, May 7, 2013, www.huffingtonpost.com.

15 Kyle Smith in the *New York Post* complained, "Tony's suit pops on and off, in pieces, for no reason except the director likes the way the special effects look"

("'Iron Man 3' Doesn't Iron Out Its Kinks," April 30, 2013). See Liotta, "5 Burning Questions," for speculation that this change sets up the possibility of a non-Downey Iron Man.

16 The ninth MCU film, *Captain America: The Winter Soldier* (Anthony and Joe Russo, 2014), features the character of Falcon (Anthony Mackie) leading a support group for traumatized Iraq and Afghanistan veterans at the V.A., while another main character is a former U.S. Army soldier who wields a metal super-prosthetic arm. Similarly, the 2013 spin-off ABC series *Marvel's Agents of S.H.I.E.L.D.* features a protagonist who not only has PTSD from being brought back from the dead, but eventually loses his hand in combat and acquires various superpowered prosthetics. In *Avengers: Age of Ultron* (Joss Whedon, 2015), Stark's PTSD, supposedly resolved in *Iron Man 3*, leads him to create a new army of robots (the "Iron Legion") to fully prosthetize his desire to protect the world.

17 See Romagnoli and Pagnucci, *Enter the Superheroes*, 197.

18 *Iron Man 3* addressed the dilemma of how to include the Mandarin—Iron Man's traditional foe, whose portrayal evoked racist stereotypes of Asians—by having Ben Kingsley play a quasi-Arab/Asian terrorist who turns out to be a drug-addled British actor covering for the real Mandarin, Aldrich Killian, a white American with Chinese dragon tattoos.

19 See for example Smith, "'Iron Man 3'"; Richard Brody, "'Iron Man 3': A Shell of Himself," *New Yorker*, May 6, 2013, www.newyorker.com; David Edelstein, "*Iron Man 3* Succeeds by Skimping on the Iron Man," *Vulture*, May 2, 2013, www.vulture.com; Rene Rodriguez, "'Iron Man 3,'" *Miami Herald*, May 2, 2013, www.miami.com. Joshua Rothkopf at *Time Out* amusingly cited "postwormhole traumatic stress," referring to the purported cause of Stark's PTSD: his flight into an inter-dimensional wormhole to save New York City in *Marvel's The Avengers* ("Iron Man 3," April 30, 2013, www.timeout.com). Like Chris Vognar of *The Dallas Morning News*, I do not find these "scarcely explained reasons" convincing within the narrative of Stark's character in the MCU, especially as he underwent so many more potentially traumatizing experiences in *Iron Man* without trauma ("'Iron Man 3' Veers Wildly between the Frivolous and the Consequential," May 2, 2013, www.dallasnews.com). See also Andrea Letamendi, "'Iron Man 3': Does Tony Stark Have PTSD?" *Hollywood Reporter*, May 10, 2013, www.hollywoodreporter.com.

20 A number of writers have considered the impact of 9/11 on superhero culture. David A. Lewis suggests that mainstream comics became increasingly militarized post-9/11, but without addressing Iraq or Afghanistan directly (Lewis, "Militarism"). Lewis, Johnson, and DiPaolo all point to Marvel's 2006–2007 Civil War storyline as a reflection of post-9/11 concerns about terrorism, security, and civil rights (DiPaolo, *War, Politics, and Superheroes*, 98–99; Johnson, *Super-History*, 181; Lewis, "Militarism," 230). Jeff Geers argues that "one of the lasting cultural effects of 9/11 was the insufficiency of the American superhero and the subsequent creation of a new post-disaster superhero mythos" that included an acknowledgement of the inadequacy of "traditional" superheroes such as Superman and Spiderman to pro-

vide security in a post-9/11 world (Geers, "'The Great Machine,'" 251). In contrast, DiPaolo claims that superhero culture "enjoyed a notable resurgence of popularity in the period following the terrorist attacks of September 11, 2001" (1). Similarly, Jon Favreau, director of the first two *Iron Man* films, when asked in 2008 why it was such a good time for superhero movies, responded that 9/11 led American audiences to crave representations of good and evil that would allow them to process their emotions in escapist ways (Scott Huver, "Jon Favreau on the Iron Man Franchise!," *SuperHeroHype*, September 12, 2008, www.superherohype.com).

21 This is the thrust of Manohla Dargis's largely negative review of *Iron Man 3*, which focuses on how the film "at once invokes Sept. 11 and dodges it" ("Bang, Boom: Terrorism as a Game," *New York Times*, May 2, 2013, www.nytimes.com).

22 See Dargis, "Bang, Boom," who cites Steven Soderbergh's claim that, post-9/11, "the country still has post-traumatic stress disorder" that American cinema has failed to seriously address, instead offering "escapist entertainment" like *Iron Man 3* that exploits the trauma of 9/11 with "a wink and a smile."

23 See http://www.whitehouse.gov/joiningforces. On the 2014 elections, see Brian Naylor, "Veterans' Care Emerges as a Key, Bipartisan Issue in Campaign Ads," *National Public Radio*, September 10, 2014. For further details on injured and disabled Iraq and Afghanistan vets, see Williamson and Mulhall, "Invisible Wounds"; Franklin et al., "Wounded Warrior Project"; and Ainspan and Penk, *Returning Wars' Wounded*.

24 On Walter Reed Medical Center, see Michael Winerip, "And This Was Called Care? The Walter Reed Story," *New York Times*, September 30, 2013. On the misapplied diagnoses of borderline personality disorder, see Joshua Kors, "How Specialist Town Lost His Benefits," *Nation*, March 29, 2007. On the backlog of V.A. disability claims, see Josh Hicks, "House Panel to Examine VA's Progress with Backlog of Disability Claims," *Washington Post*, July 14, 2014. On the 2014 scandal regarding misreported waiting times and secret waiting lists for V.A. care, see Scott Bronstein and Drew Griffin, "A Fatal Wait: Veterans Languish and Die on a VA Hospital's Secret List," *CNN*, April 23, 2014. For further details on veterans' difficulties in accessing mental health care, see Franklin et al., "Wounded Warrior Project," and Williamson and Mulhall, "Invisible Wounds."

25 Gerber, "Introduction," 2.

26 See also Panchasi, "Reconstructions," 109–140.

27 Serlin, *Replaceable You*, 46.

28 Ibid., 28.

29 Gerber, "Introduction," 3.

30 Rodney R. Baker, "Benefits for Veterans: A Historical Context and Overview of the Current Situation," in Ainspan and Penk, *Returning Wars' Wounded*, 9.

31 Ibid., 11; See also Hendricks and Amara, "Current Veteran Demographics."

32 See, for example, David J. Morris, "War Is Hell, and the Hell Rubs Off," *Slate*, April 17, 2014, www.slate.com; Soledad O'Brien, "For Veterans, the War Comes Home," *CNN*, August 8, 2011, www.cnn.com.

33 At the close of World War II, "the possibility of millions of men exhibiting lasting, unpredictable, irrational behavior that might take antisocial forms [due to mental disability] . . . inspired dread" (Gerber, "Heroes and Misfits," 73).

34 The video was originally posted at the Wounded Warrior website and is currently available as "Wounded Warrior Project Norberto Lara PSA," *YouTube*, November 17, 2010, www.youtube.com.

35 Stokes, "Theorizing Disability."

36 Serlin, *Replaceable You*, 50–51; Ott, "The Sum of Its Parts," 18.

37 Romagnoli and Pagnucci, *Enter the Superheroes*, 170.

38 Ott, "The Sum of Its Parts," 23.

39 As Mick LaSalle in the *San Francisco Chronicle* notes, the film offers "no explanation as to why someone with a brand-new arm should turn evil" ("'Iron Man 3' Review: Not a Strong Suit," May 2, 2013, www.sfgate.com). The trope of the bitter amputee whose villainy proceeds from the intolerability of his missing limb is traceable back to such characters as Captains Hook and Ahab and is prominent in science fiction and fantasy film and television of the 2010s, such as the 2012 reboot *The Amazing Spider-Man*, featuring the Lizard, the villainous alter-ego of amputee Dr. Curt Connors.

40 Mitchell and Snyder, *Narrative Prosthesis*.

41 Serlin, *Replaceable You*; Ott, Serlin, and Mihm, *Artificial Parts*.

42 Serlin, *Replaceable You*, 27. See also Panchasi, "Reconstructions."

43 On the perception of Asian Americans as "perpetual foreigners," see Lowe, *Immigrant Acts*.

44 The Iron Patriot of Marvel Comics was not James Rhodes/War Machine, but rather a character created by Norman Osborne meant to combine features of Iron Man and Captain America. Since the transformation of War Machine into the Iron Patriot for *Iron Man 3* has no roots in the comic book universe, this particular aspect of the film clearly invokes the War on Terror's symbolic language, such as the PATRIOT Act of 2001 and the Patriot missiles deployed in Iraq in 2003.

45 This turn of events provoked much discussion and some confusion in the blogosphere. In the words of blogger Rob Hunter, "Why Has Stark Waited through Four Movies to Have the Shrapnel Removed from His Chest If It Was This Damn Easy?" Similarly Colin Liotta called this the "burning question" left unanswered by the movie. In comments, however, attentive fans pointed out small clues in the film suggesting that Stark was able to stabilize Extremis and use it on himself to enable the shrapnel to be removed. This interpretation most closely fits the outcome in the Extremis comic book. Additionally, fans with access to extra scenes included in the China release of the film pointed out that one of those scenes includes a phone conversation between Stark and a Chinese surgeon, Dr. Wu, that suggests that the doctor has developed a new surgical technique that could cure Stark. However, these fans generally seem to be in the minority, as most bloggers and commentators shared a sense of surprise and confusion at the film's ending. See Hunter, "9 Big Questions," and Liotta, "5 Burning Questions."

46 This question is left unaddressed in Iron Man's next cinematic appearance, 2015's *Avengers: Age of Ultron*.

47 In another example of a person-as-bomb in the film, the U.S. president sends "the Patriot" against terrorists in the Middle East, referring to Col. Rhodes as the Iron Patriot, but also clearly evoking President George W. Bush's deployment of Patriot missiles in Iraq in 2003.

48 Kim, *Curative Violence*.

49 In the comic book, Stark permanently assimilates Extremis and uses that energy to power the suit (Ellis and Granov, *Iron Man: Extremis*). If this is indeed the case in the MCU, it certainly begs the question why Stark could not similarly stabilize Extremis for Potts so she could keep her superpowers, rather than "fixing" her by removing Extremis.

6

"It's Not Just Sexism"

Feminization and (Ab)Normalization in the Commercialization of Anxiety Disorders

D. TRAVERS SCOTT AND MEAGAN BATES

Here, Scott and Bates analyze television advertisements for anti-anxiety medications. Through close textual analysis, informed by Foucauldian theory and political economy, they demonstrate the intricate ways that femininity, disability, and normalization inflect and reinforce each other in contemporary discourses around mental health. These ads do not merely target women, they argue, but in fact construct femininity itself as inherently pathological and in need of medical intervention. At the same time, however, parodies of these ads reveal resistance to their pathologizing tropes and point the way toward greater appreciation for neurodiversity.

Today, forty million Americans are diagnosed with anxiety, with women twice as likely to be diagnosed as men.[1] Popular media often promote "female" propensities toward anxiety with headlines like "Nervous Nellies," "Why Are Anxiety Disorders among Women on the Rise?," "Anxiety Causes Women's Brains to Work Harder than Men's," and "It's Not Just Sexism, Women Do Suffer More from Mental Illness."[2]

The growth of disability studies has influenced our understanding of such headlines as symptoms of a society, rather than individuals, needing change. Mental impairments (cognitive, sensory, and/or emotional conditions) are currently debated as to their appropriateness for disability studies.[3] This chapter explores a disability studies engagement with these impairments through an examination of representations in popular media. In this chapter, we examine television advertisements for pharmaceuticals prescribed for medications used to treat anxiety, finding themes of pathologized femininity, social pollution, and gender stereotypes. We conclude by arguing that mental impairments are represented as a normal part of femininity, not an aberration.

Through this, we will argue for a mutually productive engagement with issues of mental impairments across disability studies, cultural studies, and feminist scholarship. Rather than dismiss medical categories of mental impairments—particularly emotional impairments such as depression and anxiety disorders—as conspiracy-driven social constructs, we wish to draw on the tradition in disability studies and cultural studies of "studying from below." That is, instead of positioning ourselves as detached scholars looking down to study a phenomenon or population, we acknowledge that we *are* that population: the authors, although of different ages, sexes, sexual orientations, and backgrounds, share diagnoses of anxiety-related conditions and have been prescribed pharmaceuticals as part of our treatments. Rather than starting from the premise of detached objectivity, which would hold that these diagnoses hopelessly bias our research, we operate in the more subjective paradigm of situated knowledges, arguing that our experiences offer us unique analytical insights when studying the medical discourses and institutions "above us."

Television commercials in the United States offer a unique extension of media discourses around mental impairments, as the U.S. is one of only two nations (with New Zealand) that allow direct-to-consumer (DTC) pharmaceutical advertising. In 1997, in response to the deregulatory political spirit of the times, the U.S. Food and Drug Administration released *Draft Guidance for Industry: Consumer-Directed Broadcast Advertisements*, making DTC pharmaceutical advertising significantly easier. The response was drastic: DTC television advertising rose from $310 million in 1997 to $664 million in 1998, and then to $3.2 billion by 2014.[4] Beyond DTC, other modes of marketing have begun affecting the cultural status of pharmaceuticals around the world. For example, Watters has described marketing efforts for SSRIs in Sri Lanka, and depression as a diagnosis in Japan, all as part of a larger, devastating Western imperialist exportation of mental illness diagnoses and treatments.[5]

In this chapter, we examine advertisements for the medications Cymbalta, Zoloft, and Abilify, which are used to treat a range of symptoms from depression to chronic pain. Our original intent had been to examine ads for drugs explicitly intended to treat anxiety disorders. However, unlike the use of tranquilizers or benzodiazepines for situational anxiety or panic attacks, we found that no drug exclusively targets persistent, chronic anxiety. The symptoms and causes of anxiety disorders are so inseparably related that drugs typically have multiple purposes. Even though people commonly speak of "anti-anxiety medications" and "antidepressants" as if they were distinct categories, the same medications are used to treat both conditions.

Surprisingly, no matter what extensive list of disorders these drugs can be used to treat, they were primarily marketed to the consumer for depression. Commercials that targeted anxiety above depression were rare. Several well-known anxiety medications, such as Xanax, do not seem to have any television advertisements. Furthermore, unlike Cymbalta and Zoloft, Xanax is not currently approved for treatment of anxiety. Abilify was the sixteenth most commonly prescribed drug in 2011 and had come to our attention due to heavy advertising on television. Although not yet approved for anxiety, it was being prescribed unofficially for anxiety and undergoing testing for use with treatment-resistant anxiety.[6] Social forums for anxiety sufferers indicate that Abilify was often used to combat the fatigue of other antidepressant medications.[7]

Cultural Studies of Medicine: Pathologizing and Feminizing

Medicalization is the process by which medical authority annexes bodies, actions, attitudes, and behaviors ranging from the everyday to the "deviant" as medical conditions.[8] This is typically negative, but not exclusively: cosmetic surgery, for example, represents the medicalization of beauty enhancements; "battered woman syndrome" medically justifies women who attack their attackers. We employ the term *pathologization* to specify negative medicalization, marking something as sick or sickening, simultaneously demarcating health, and often drawing on and reinforcing social stereotypes.[9] Feminist scholars have examined pathologization in conditions such as premenstrual syndrome[10] and postpartum disorders.[11] Gilman describes pathology as "a central marker for difference"—a line drawn between that which is of the Self, and that which is of the Other, and thereby threatens order and control, whether bodily or social.[12] Indeed, the individual body frequently operates as a symbol of the social body.[13] Moreover, a particular physical disease or impairment can become socially metaphoric or signify cultural anxieties,[14] as has been explored in Asiatic cholera, breast cancer, loss of limbs,[15] blood diseases,[16] hysteria,[17] accident proneness,[18] HIV/AIDS,[19] neurasthenia,[20] and, conversely, resistance to disease.[21]

Pathologization is thereby a form of subjectification. Michel Foucault's extensive investigation into the constitution of subjects and subjectivities examined several pathologized subjects, such as deviants, prisoners, the insane, and the sick, showing their cultural and historic contingencies. In *The Birth of the Clinic*, he described how, during the Enlightenment, various elements of pathology were reconceived and redefined, and the ontology of disease moved from outside agents to the diseased individuals themselves. In this "welding of the disease onto the organism,"[22] disease changed from an outside to an internal aspect, from an invasive thing to individuals' reactions to something in their environment: "the *being* of the disease disappears."[23] Here, sickening diseases become sick persons.

Once subjectified in this way, social demarcations of sick/healthy, as with disabled/abled, participate in other social hierarchies, such as gender, race, and class. As Turner describes this process, "The concepts of 'illness,' 'disease,' and 'health' inevitably involve some *judgment* which ultimately rests on a criterion of statistical frequency or an ideal state. The 'average individual' does not exist. . . . Disease is not a fact, but a *relationship* and the relationship is the product of classificatory processes."[24] For example, one author found a tabloid report of "housewife syndrome," which pathologized feminists for constructing "normal" women as sick.[25] Feminist scholars have shown how routine functions of the female body or psyche are pathologized, reinforcing male privilege, such as Maines's history of the vibrator as not an aid to female orgasmic pleasure, but a medical device for physicians to stimulate sick women into therapeutic convulsions.[26] Laqueur argues that pathological roots inform the very understanding of sex and gender, demonstrating the history and ongoing salience of a "one-sex model" in which women (and the feminine) are a lesser, abnormal version of men and masculinity, rather than an exclusive opposite.[27]

Arguably, pathology is inherently feminizing. Gilman writes, "pathology is disorder and the loss of control, the giving over of the self to the forces that lie beyond the self."[28] In sickness, a person is *de*masculinized to some degree through their loss of bodily control, physical integrity, mental acuity, and/or individual agency. Moreover, sickness is often associated with the private, indoor spaces of curtained hospital rooms, sick beds, rest cures, bedrooms, and the like; an association that maps onto the private sphere of domestic labor associated with femininity, creating a mutually reinforcing zone of private feminine pathologization, such as the long-standing trope of the lonely housewife.

Of course, there are exceptions: feminine pathologies can be idealized (Romantic-era consumptives, contemporary anorexics), and pathologies can be masculine (sports injuries, hypertension). What we are asserting is that there is a long history of associating femininity with disease, and, therefore, social processes of marking persons, attributes, or acts as sick or sickening—pathologization—also feminize them to varying degrees.

Disability Studies and Mental Impairments

The interrogation of constructions of normal and abnormal bodies lies at the heart of disability studies. In one sense, a norm implies that the majority must fit within its umbrella, a bell-curve scenario where most reside under the curve, but the extremities offer unacceptable deviations. However, this sense of "the norm"—i.e., the typical or most common—is often entangled or conflated with the "normal" in the sense of an ideal, a social construct, the discourses about normalcy that position subjects and within which subjects take up positions. Particularly relevant in terms of medical culture, this sense of the normal also carries connotations of the natural and healthy. Through these meanings, demarcations between normal and abnormal come to stigmatize the abnormal.[29] Disability becomes the embodiment and hallmark of abnormality and otherness. In this medical "deficit model," persons with disabilities are viewed as a having a problem that needs "fixing" through medicine, rehabilitation, or education. When a deficit is not fixable, the disabled individual is left permanently abnormal and stigmatized. Discrimination is justified through their deviation from other social norms; for example, the perceived inability of disabled persons to be economically productive frames their lives as without significance or contribution.[30]

McRuer conceived of a "crip" critique of such compulsory able-bodiedness as itself manufacturing disability, drawing on the queer critique of compulsory heterosexuality.[31] Today, the word *crip* "has grown to include individuals with sensory and mental impairments."[32] We see this as a particularly needed inclusion for, as Gilman argues, "of all the models of pathology, one of the most powerful is mental illness."[33] However, the relationship between disability studies and mental impairments, particularly those of mood or emotion, is currently unresolved. One concern is that including them could reinforce stereotypes that collapse mental into physical impairments as standard features of disabled bodies. A scientific research tradition looks to confirm such presumed connections, for example, in studies on physical disabilities and anxiety and depression.[34] Associating disability with mental illness risks further pathologizing people with disabilities and suggests medical "cures" for those with mental impairments.[35] However, from the perspective of the neurodiversity movement, originating with autism but expanding to other neurological conditions such as ADHD and dyslexia, what are commonly regarded as impairments can be reconceptualized as natural variations.[36] Although not yet as consolidated of a movement, there are similar perspectives on emotional impairments, such as clinical depression, that suggest they are largely social constructs that pathologize mere differences in human emotional temperaments and should be embraced as part of a continuum of "affective diversity" or "emotional diversity."[37] A disability studies perspective based on the social model of disability could strive to reconceptualize the impairment, not as deficiencies in the learning capabilities or emotional state of the depressed person, but as the obstacles a prejudiced society places in their way, challenging social processes of (ab)normalization.[38] This perspective works well for mental impairments such as Down syndrome or "high-functioning" autism, in which persons may want to be treated as "normal," with no impetus for "cure," only an acceptance of what unique challenges—and gifts—their impairment entails.

However, we argue this fits a little too neatly, such that it seems to present the model for *all* mental variances, eclipsing those that do not fit in so well, such as emotional variance. For example, the authors' complex experiences with anxiety disorders have found them to bring gifts—such as productivity, hyperfocus, avoiding procrastination, heightened energy—in addition to challenges—such as physical pain, insomnia, irritability that damages personal relationships, avoidance of social situations, and the unpleasant state of near-constant fear. Exploring treatments has involved a difficult weighing of impacts across these areas. Indeed, there is no easy "cure," and our variances draw both social stigma and rewards.

Emotional variances can be very different, and they can occur situationally or constantly. While a one-time bout of depression, for example, can be understood as akin to a physical injury from which one recovers, living in an ongoing state of continual or episodic depression is an impairment. However, it is rarely consistent, and the intensity is constantly shifting for many persons. This lack of equilibrium makes it difficult to "settle in" to one's emotional nature and accept it as a characteristic state. Inconsistency breeds uncertainty and apprehension, which are unpleasant. So are depression and anxiety. Suggestions to embrace an "affective rainbow" deny the diversity of mental impairments, privileging those whose emotional variances do not involve high degrees of pain.

The relationship between pain and disability is complex. As Patsavas relates, there is a long history of ableist use of pain as justification for oppressing disabled persons, whether through pity or forced methods of pain relief, as well as an ideology in which chronic pain "naturally" leads to a desire to die. In addition to oversimplifying the diverse experiences of persons living with pain, this also presumes to know what that experience is like. Patsavas, in developing a standpoint-based cripistemology of pain, examines cultural representations with her own experiences with chronic pain and, notably, "deliberately resist[s] drawing distinctions between psychic and/or physical pain."[39] While this work and others importantly locate discourses of pain within power hierarchies, there is a delicate flipside to the conversation. Although pain should not be an excuse to abnormalize someone or force attempts at amelioration, this does not mean that seeking pain relief is inherently co-opting to ableism.

We must be careful to avoid, explicitly or implicitly, creating a hierarchy which suggests that those persons whose mental impairments are extremely painful should, in essence, buck up and learn to love it (see also Magnet and Watson, in this volume, on the "tyranny of cheerfulness"). In cases of emotional impairment and also, for example, chronic pain, we argue that to deny the individual's desire to have their suffering alleviated creates a problematic moral hierarchy. It evokes a Protestant stoicism that suggests a moral inferiority in those who cannot duly accept and embrace their impairment.

Ultimately, the distinction between physical and mental impairments is untenable. For example, Down syndrome is clearly organic, with cognitive ramifications, but anxiety, depression, chronic pain, chronic fatigue, and the like can come from biological, psychological, and/or social causes. Moreover, their cultural meanings, particularly those dimensions that are stigmatized and or venerated, can vary wildly across cultures and social groups. Scholars can run the risk of reifying a mind/ body dualism, as well as hierarchizing impairments of bodily origin as somehow more worthwhile of reconceptualization, if careful attention is not paid to the complexity of experiences that constitute mental and emotional variance. For example, the related field of mad studies at times describes itself in part as a "movement," including "activists and psychiatric survivors," that "challenges dominant understandings of 'mental illness,'" and connects "mad activism" to other human rights and liberation struggles.[40] While not contesting this position, our aim in this chapter is to argue for the diversity and multiplicity of the experiences of those with mental and emotional impairments, such that those who find relief or benefits through psychiatry, medication, or other contested practices are not stigmatized within or alienated from the beneficial insights of fields such as disability studies or mad studies.

For example, consider a case of when the bodily origin is neurological: a person with "high-functioning" autism, in the name of neurological diversity, may reconceive their impairment as a unique combination of sensory perception and processing. That is fine, but would we ask someone in chronic pain to reconceive their suffering as nervous diversity? Furthermore, as with chronic pain, mental impairments are typically not cured; they are managed. Symptoms are alleviated in various ways to varying degrees, and this often changes over the years, but it is an ongoing state of awareness of and struggle with one's condition—an impairment.

Anxiety Disorders

Anxiety is an umbrella term for a variety of disorders involving nervousness, fear, worry, and severe apprehension. The worry is unspecific (unlike phobias), and not due to substance abuse or another medical condition. Anxious during and with daily tasks, persons experience an almost uncontrollable fear that something is going to go wrong. They struggle to relax and find it difficult to concentrate, often experiencing physical symptoms such as headaches, fatigue, lightheadedness, irritability, nausea, and twitching. Symptoms range from mild to encumbering but are severe enough to interfere with daily functioning. Sometimes medical providers do not connect symptoms to anxiety, and individuals suffer for a long time without help.

Current etiology of anxiety disorders focuses on imbalances in the neurotransmitters serotonin, norepinephrine, and gamma-aminobutyric acid. In previous decades, treatment relied on benzodiazepines (e.g., Xanax, Klonopin), which now are used mostly for situational and short-term treatment. Today, selective serotonin reuptake inhibitors (SSRIs) are more effective, less sedating, and better tolerated by patients. Meta-studies show that current medications are more effective than placebos in relieving symptoms and preventing relapses, and have become the U.S. and European "clinical standard of care for all types of anxiety disorders."[41] However, neither SSRIs nor cognitive behavioral therapy (a common non-pharmaceutical treatment for anxiety) has consistently been shown to be more effective than the other over the long term.[42]

Antidepressants are often suspect in popular culture, viewed, for example, as part of a profit-motivated conspiracy on the part of pharmaceutical companies,[43] which some see as resulting in overprescription of SSRIs, in turn linked to suicides and spree shootings.[44] Users of antidepressants have reframed their drug use to counteract the stigma, describing antidepressants "not as a failure to handle life but as a means of taking responsibility for it—and for the well being of others."[45] While acknowledging the reality of some degree of over- and misdiagnoses, overmedication, and profit seeking, we also note that, when the DSM-5 increased the duration of symptoms and number of episodes needed to qualify for a diagnosis, this ran contrary to the economic interests of pharmaceutical companies.[46]

Anxiety disorders have gendered associations. The website of the Anxiety and Depression Association of America states that, from the onset of puberty until approximately age fifty, a woman is twice as likely to contract an anxiety disorder as a man. A partial explanation is that "the brain system involved in the fight-or-flight response is activated more readily in women and stays activated longer than in men, partly as a result of the action of estrogen and progesterone."[47] At the onset of anxiety, fight-or-flight mechanisms are enacted, which give the sufferer the overwhelming sensations of fear.[48] This is the same in both men and women; however, due to higher levels of estrogen and progesterone, this reflex is more easily triggered and harder to deactivate in women. These physiological differences manifest in cultural expressions such as hormone imbalances being widely diagnosed as causes for anxiety issues for women, but not men. Progesterone is a soothing component of brain chemistry; however, when progesterone levels drop during certain normal moments in female experience (menopause, menstrual cycles, childbirth, etc.), the female body is pathologized as being incapable of calming down. The woman is "strung out" over minimally important matters without the "proper" brain chemistry to restabilize her physiology.

In many instances with women, depression co-occurs shortly after the onset of anxiety. However, despite anxiety being the earlier onset trigger or first warning, research on anxiety in women has been largely neglected in comparison to the extensive research on depression in women. Moreover, much of the understanding of women and anxiety seems to be anecdotal, with some research focusing on biological difference and socially assigned gender roles.[49] With either cause, this has implications for men as well. The association of anxiety with femininity stigmatizes male sufferers for failing to live up to ideals of masculinity, which could inhibit their seeking diagnoses and treatment.

Television Advertisements for Anxiety Medications

We began by looking broadly for antidepressant and antianxiety medication advertising, using searches on YouTube, Google, and Bing, ultimately focusing on twenty commercials for three medications: Cymbalta, Zoloft, and Abilify.[50] We also examined fan comments, parodies, and other information online that directly related to these ads. The ads examined included seven commercials for Cymbalta, in which women and men suffering from depression, anxiety, or pain find relief through the medication. Although Cymbalta is marketed to two different groups—those suffering from depression and those suffering from osteoarthritis—the commercials are part of a unified brand and campaign in their aesthetics, tone, style, and presentation. Soft-focus, slow-motion scenes of discomfort in a variety of indoor and outdoor, private and social settings, ultimately give way to tentative smiles and optimistic expressions. Five of the six Zoloft commercials have a completely different approach, using an animated little blob that mopes then bounces around to illustrate the progression of a person suffering from mental impairments receiving treatment. Three of the seven Abilify commercials were similar to the Cymbalta commercials. Four, however, featured an animated woman who "just can't shake" her depression and often "feels stuck" until freed by her doctor.

Pathologized Femininity

In various ways the commercials associated pathology with femininity and medical authority with masculinity. The commercial that introduced Zoloft, "Rain," appeared in 2004.[51] It opens with a white blob sitting in the middle of the screen under a raining cloud; it appears depressed and sad. While ostensibly not gendered, the blob could also be read as an egg, connoting femininity, and indeed it is referred to as an egg in user comments and parody videos. In "Zoloft Party"—one of the few commercials to directly describe and address an anxiety disorder rather than depression—a pink blob quivers nervously at the door to a party at which other blobs are dancing and celebrating (figure 6.1). The blob sweats, and the voiceover discusses a racing heart. The color suggests flushed Caucasian skin, and pink is widely associated with femininity. In "Spotlight," the blob, although white at first, blushes at a party. Blushing is traditionally feminine, as is shyness, the pre-medicalized version of social anxiety. Both here are symptomatic of illness. At times the Zoloft blob has vocalizations that sound male, but it is in a demasculinized state: whimpering, moaning, and sighing. To amend the old song, "big blobs don't sigh." Finally, while the Zoloft protagonist may be sexually ambiguous, the target of the ads is not, as the drug's co-marketing partners demonstrate: two Zoloft commercials direct viewers to "see our ad in *Shape* magazine"—a women's fitness and health publication—while another directs viewers to the celebrity gossip

Figure 6.1. Zoloft's blob, now pink, sweats and quivers at the entrance to a party, in the drug's only commercial directly targeting social anxiety disorder.

magazine *People*. Similarly, Cymbalta directs viewers to the women's publications *Redbook*, *Family Circle*, and *Ladies' Home Journal*. Abilify's "Blue Robe" directs to *Health*, a women's magazine that focuses on beauty, diet, and fitness.

The association of women and femininity with anxiety is consistent throughout the Cymbalta commercials. They regularly open with the image of a woman suffering from some sort of depression, anxiety, or pain (referring back to the idea that these drugs treat more than one mental illness). The women almost always appear alone, emotionally detached, and physically and/or mentally powerless to interact with others. In Cymbalta's "Simple Pleasures," a woman with disheveled hair and in what appear to be her clothes from the previous day is so depressed that she can barely manage to sit up in bed, despite the bright light streaming through her window. "Sunrise hurts," reads the title. This crosscuts with a Latino man who has managed to attend a house party, but is lingering uncomfortably on the periphery of a festive conversation group. In some ads, women are represented almost exclusively. Other ads have an apparent gender balance, but notably, these are frequently the ads targeting osteoarthritis rather than depression. However, as in "Simple Pleasures," in these commercials women are shown in group contexts less frequently than men and shown alone anywhere from exclusively to twice as often as the men. Therefore, even though men and women were both represented, women were shown as more isolated in their pain: across the commercials, solitude is sickness.

In Cymbalta's "Laptop," three college-age women are shown, variously, in a bedroom using a laptop, running at a gym, and working in a library. Two similarly aged men are shown: one walking alone and the other eating alone in a cafeteria. The commercial alternates among these five characters, with the women garnering more cumulative screen time. At the end, three of the four indoor characters, in a montage of repeated shots, each exit a door to come outside. All then converge at a new indoor location, a public event where a table of smiling peers all reach out to shake their hands. As noted earlier, solitude and privacy have long been associated with pathology, evoking the feminization of private spheres. Similarly, in Zoloft's "Cave 1" and "Cave 2," the blob, when sick, hides in its private cave like a recluse or shut-in, a longstanding trope of pathologization with often gendered components.[52] In Cymbalta's "Simple Pleasures," those suffering from anxiety and depression are alone with house pets as their only friends.

Although we did not design this project using an intersectional framework, race did seem at times to have significant inflections on gender. For example, Zoloft's blob is either white or pink, never black or brown. As research on stereotyping and representations has shown, often stereotypes operate in paradoxical and contradictory ways, and stereotypes in one social category serve to reinforce those in another.[53] For example, in Cymbalta's "No One," the one man explicitly suffering from anxiety is African American, as is the most prominently featured man in the "Closet" ad. Rather than a stereotype of black male hypermasculinity, here they seem to suggest feminized men, suffering in doorways, with smooth shaved heads and sad expressions, suggesting that healthy masculinity is racialized as white. Indeed, one of the two men in the "Laptop" commercial is Asian, and across all of the videos men tended to be distanced in some way from their power and privilege: they were typically older, youthful, and/or non-white. In contrast, the doctors were largely white men—or women of color.

In Abilify's "Umbrella" and "Chalkboard" (and its edited-down version, "Side Effects"), we see women of color as healthcare practitioners. Here, race seems mobilized to reverse effect. Although these are women in positions of power, the ads suggest that anxiety is associated with white femininity in particular. They feature a degree of racial diversity in a non-threatening way that does not risk alienating or provoking disidentification among audiences of white women. Along similar lines, Cymbalta's "Stairs" includes a middle-aged African American man and young Latina. However, they are both light-skinned and appear in only two short shots each, among a dozen characters in the minute-long spot, many of whom receive more screen time, and all of whom are shown in an upper-middle-class setting of large houses, parks, boutiques, and a flock of white doves. White women—there are eight in the commercial—need Cymbalta, but the inclusion of four men and two persons of color prevent the ad from overtly pathologizing white women as a category. Yet the soft-focus, slow-motion ad relies on an aesthetic of stereotypical white femininity like that associated with romantic comedies. The possibility of poor persons needing this medication, let along poor persons of color, is avoided in a way that homogenizes and limits difference.

Social Pollution

The separation of pure from impure, Mary Douglas argues, is one of the fundamental organizing structures of human cultures. Pollution taboos literally shun dirty things that threaten physical bodies and metaphorically shun "dirty" threats to social bodies. Societal "dirt" is any person, attribute, action, or thing that threatens social order: "Dirt offends against order."[54] Douglas sees pollution taboos mapped to gender, associating women and femininity with impurity and disorder.

In several Cymbalta commercials we see literal disorder in the pre-medicated women's disheveled hair and clothes. One, "Closet," begins with a woman staring forlornly at her disorganized clothes. Here, anxiety appears as a type of social dirt, an impure threat to cultural boundaries and order. Across all of the commercials, social disorder is the threatening pollution because social order is what is restored by the medication: we see sufferers rejoining family roles, jobs, friendship circles, and other activities. For example, in all four of the animated Abilify commercials, a previously isolated woman is reintegrated into her nuclear family after a visit with her doctor. With a soft, pastel aesthetic that suggests sensitive greeting cards, in three of these ads, a woman's depression is anthropomorphized: a blue bathrobe grabs her; a hole in the ground partially swallows her; rain falls on her from inside an umbrella, which forcibly jerks her around, and then transforms into another hole in the ground.[55] Then, medical intervention removes the pollution. In one ad, a white male doctor literally pulls the woman from her hole of depression; in another, the white male doctor removes the robe. In all, through the help of medication she returns to her normal societal duties. In the doctor's office, the previously unruly anthropomorphs sit alongside the woman, mirroring her attentive listening and note-taking. As the voiceovers suggest, "my depression" is presented not as an external affliction, but as a part of the woman herself that she has externalized. Although metaphoric, this does not negate that the externalization evokes hysterical hallucinations and schizophrenic delusions, as well as general feminine stereotypes of excessive emotion and lack of control, which are contained by the medications and restored to order.

In the Zoloft ads, social disorder is suggested when a male narrator discusses how the sufferer feels "different," "emotional," "not normal," "lonely," and "secluded," but then reassures the viewer that "you deserve better." In "Rain," the blob is initially seen alone underneath a pouring raincloud, suggesting the disorder through its exposure to the elements and not having the sense to seek shelter. In "Spotlight," "Cave 1," "Cave 2," and "Party," the blob cannot effectively participate in social functions or interact with other blobs. Once the blob receives medical treatment, it not only rejoins the social order but also reconnects with the environment, noticing that flowers are growing and birds are chirping. This suggests normalization in the sense of naturalization, being at harmony with a way of being that is perceived as pure, "natural," and by implication, of divine design. The masculine technology of medical treatment has restored balance to the gendered social order.

Gender Role Stereotyping

In the beginning of Abilify's "Terri and Team," the sufferer is sitting alone in bed, too depressed to get up and put on her morning makeup. A helpful prescription pill offers her up a tube of lipstick that she is too sad to use. Once they go to the doctor together, she is able to go to work and, afterward, stares lovingly at her husband during their son's soccer game. Her impairment keeps her from successful performance of her femininity, until she is restored by the doctor.

Social order, as suggested in these ads, relies on traditional gender roles and stereotypes. For the most part, women are the sufferers of anxiety, appear weak and frail, and need a man or masculine medical authority to be rescued. Once a woman is healed, she is able to fulfill her gender roles more effectively as a caring spouse or mother. Consistently throughout these ads, the protagonist, usually a woman or a feminized abstraction, is alone when "sick" and interacting with a relational partner of some sort when "healthy"—unsurprisingly, as predispositions toward and skills at relational maintenance are stereotypical feminine traits.

The helplessness of female patients is also stereotypical, as is the contrasting agency of masculine savior. Anxiety, as a form of "dirt," cannot be self-purified. Masculine medical authority must remove it. These advertisements often glorify the role of the physician (typically, a white male, or, less often, a woman of color) for "helping" the women through medication. This is in contrast to other forms of pharmaceutical advertising, noticeably those for male erectile dysfunction (ED) or birth control advertisements, in which doctors are rarely present.

In several Abilify ads, a woman is sitting while her male practitioner speaks to her, standing, exemplifying a power differential. A return to social functioning for women is illustrated through traditional feminine activities: nurturing her children, spending time with her spouse, or gardening. In Abilify's "Umbrella," the doctor's office morphs into an orchard, where the woman is joined by her husband and child in picking apples, suggesting a restored balance and order. In this, the white male doctor is replaced by a woman of color, suggesting the homogenization of differences described earlier. This is also the case in "Chalkboard," in which the white woman suffering from depression is shown consulting with an African American female professional. But they are shown seated, conversing face-to-face, the professional is thus on more of an equal playing field with the sick woman. Moreover, the professional appears to be a counselor or psychiatrist, lacking a lab coat or doctor's office setting, typical signifiers in other ads for more scientific, "masculine" medical doctors.

Cymbalta's "Window" opens with the image of a woman gazing through her kitchen window with her young son watching; she speaks of the guilt she suffers from not being able to properly nurture her son as a "good" mother should. At the end of the advertisement, the woman has conquered her issues though medication and is now capable of caring for her child. The scene cuts to the woman and young boy cuddling and laughing together. "Closet" features an emphasis on gendered standards of appearance. It opens with a young woman looking sadly at her messy closet and an older woman, dressed slovenly, wandering through a grocery store. Meanwhile, one man ignores his son and another watches TV; unlike the women, neither is depicted as "deficient" based on their appearance. Once the commercial has played through, and all have recovered through medication, the women have smart new haircuts and clothes, one arriving at work and the other snuggling a kitten. The men, however, appear largely the same, but the first is now working in a home workshop and the second is playing sports with his son.

Gender stereotyping is the punchline of many user-made parodies of Cymbalta ads. Cymbalta's rigid conventions make them ripe for satire, and some of the parodies reveal the gendered conventions of the originals by flipping gender roles as their source of humor. One emasculates former House speaker John Boehner by poking fun at his tendency to cry and be overcome with emotion; this is underscored by presenting him as a sufferer of depression. Two others use existing Cymbalta voiceovers and product shots with slow-motion images of a young man playing with his dog, or another drinking soda and depressed on the couch. Nothing explicitly humorous is presented except for switching the gender role of the commercial voiceovers from talking about women to talking about men. In such parodies, we can see the contestation of dominant discourses of mental illness and gender that feminize conditions such as anxiety. However, they generally did not seem to explicitly interrogate discourses of femininity as much as they criticized pharmaceutical advertising for its crude exploitation of gendered stereotypes.

Normalization

The reinforcement of gender stereotypes enhances normalization by making its pathologization familiar, and therefore legible to all women, able-bodied or otherwise. In short, anxiety and depression may be mental impairments, but they are a normal part of femininity, not an aberration. The patterns of symptoms shown have been familiar for nearly two hundred years, echoing nineteenth-century diagnoses of neurasthenia, a disease largely discredited in the West today, but which famously had highly gendered symptoms and treatments.[56] Diagnoses of neurasthenia in the U.S. slowly began declining throughout the twentieth century, often giving way to that of schizophrenia, but linger in the popular concepts of a "nervous breakdown" or having "raw nerves"—states of heightened anxiety.

Moreover, a cumulative effect of the themes described is the reinforcement of a medical-deficit model of mental impairments. Something is wrong with the individual, and medical authority offers an ongoing treatment option to "fix" the disabled person, or at least bring them closer into social functioning; the contextual discourses of medication management, assistive medications, new medications, and nonmedical treatments—not to mention celebrity reassertions and relapses of mental impairments—make clear that one can never hope to regain normalcy. Absent is any suggestion of social accommodation or reconceptualizing their impairments. Their impairments are normalized.

Commercialization is part of this process. For pharmaceutical manufacturers and advertisers, there is a financial imperative for sufferers to *stay* sick: comfortably sick, familiarly sick, normally sick. Conditions such as anxiety and depression are more profitable when conceived of not as temporary deviations from the norm to be cured, but part of the normal. Anxiety's conflation with depression in the ads also normalizes by broadening the number of people to whom such conditions—and therefore such ads—apply. Furthermore, DTC pharmaceutical advertising increases their visibility and, thereby, familiarity.

By drawing on historical patterns, commercialization, medicalization, and well-established gender stereotypes, these ads can be seen as contributing to a discourse that normalizes the seemingly abnormal. That is, mental impairments are presented as a typical part of femininity. Feminist scholars such as Angela McRobbie and Sarah Banet-Weiser have examined a similar process in the realms of body image, eating disorders, and postfeminist culture, where being ill becomes a normal part of femininity.[57] One author (Scott) has argued elsewhere that conditions such as carpal tunnel syndrome suggest a normalization of illness as part of technological usership.[58]

We feel it is productive for disability studies to engage in discussion and analyses around mental and psychological health with related fields, such as research on health and medicine in cultural studies, gender studies, and feminism. The shared theoretical perspectives and interests in discourse, constituted subjects, social categories, and (ab)normalization will only be enriched by mutual engagement. As the title of this chapter suggests, feminine pathologization in these ads is "not just sexism." They suggest much more complex processes of co-constitutive, subjectifying discourses of disease, health, gender, and ability. The advertising of the pharmaceutical industry, as we have shown, does deploy feminine stereotypes as one part of commercializing treatments for anxiety disorders. However, our position is not merely to point out another set of examples of sexist media representations, but to explore the complexity of intersecting discourses at this site. Ultimately, following this complexity leads to larger issues raised regarding mental and emotional variances, their appropriateness for disability studies, and critiques of the practices of psychiatry or commercialization of anxiety disorders.

We conclude, then, arguing for diversity—the diversity of experiences of impairment. In the cases of emotional impairments, chronic fatigue, chronic pain, and other variances, the fact that people desire and take action to mediate their pain does not deny the reality of their impairments nor render them "bad" disabled persons who refuse to embrace their impairment. Nor does it make them dupes to or capitulators with an inherently evil pharmaceutical industry. Like a prosthetic, talk therapy and medications are tools we use to function in the world with our impairments. They are not signs of our weakness or moral laxity, stereotypically "feminine" traits. Although advertising may reinforce this and other negative gender stereotypes, only by embracing the complexity and diversity of experiences and discourses can we avoid unknowingly replicating them ourselves.

NOTES

1 "Facts," *Anxiety and Depression Association of America*, n.d., www.adaa.org.
2 Taylor Clark, "Nervous Nellies," *Slate*, April 20, 2011, www.slate.com; Shaun Dreisbach, "Why Are Anxiety Disorders among Women on the Rise?," *NBC News*, October 15, 2010, www.nbcnews.com; Michelle Castillo, "Anxiety Causes Women's Brains to Work Harder than Men's," *CBS News*, June 7, 2012, www.cbsnews.com; Daniel Freeman and Jason Freeman, "It's Not Just Sexism, Women Do Suffer More from Mental Illness," *Time*, July 18, 2013, http://ideas.time.com.
3 Davis, "Depression and Disability"; Goodley, *Disability Studies*, 97; Price, *Mad at School*, 12; Thomas, *Sociologies of Disability and Illness*, 131.
4 Donohue, "A History of Drug Advertising"; Tracy Staton, "Pharma's Ad Spend Vaults to $4.5B, with Big Spender Pfizer Leading the Way," *FiercePharma*, March 25, 2015, www.fiercepharmamarketing.com; Tracy Staton, "Pharma DTC Ad Spending Sinks 11.5%, a $2B Slide from 2006 Peak," *FiercePharma*, April 2, 2013, www.fiercepharma.com; Larry Dobrow, "Pharma DTC Spending Jumps Almost 21% in 2014," March 23, 2015, www.mmm-online.com.
5 Watters, *Crazy Like Us*.
6 Katzman, "Aripiprazole."
7 "Adding Abilify 2.5mg for Depression and Anxiety," *Anxiety Space*, February 23, 2013, http://anxietyspace.com.
8 Conrad, *The Medicalization of Society*; Dubriwny, "Television News Coverage."
9 Ewen and Ewen, *Typecasting*; Gilman, *Difference and Pathology*.
10 Bell, "Premenstrual Syndrome."
11 Dubriwny, "Television News Coverage."
12 Gilman, *Difference and Pathology*, 23.
13 Douglas, *Purity and Danger*; Turner, *The Body and Society*.
14 Bartholomew and Wessely, "Protean Nature of Mass Sociogenic Illness"; Glassner, *The Culture of Fear*; Sontag, *Illness as Metaphor*.
15 O'Connor, *Raw Material*.
16 Wailoo, *Drawing Blood*.
17 Maines, *The Technology of Orgasm*; Showalter, *The Female Malady*.
18 Burnham, *Accident Prone*.
19 Treichler, "AIDS, Gender, and Biomedical Discourse."
20 Lutz, *American Nervousness, 1903*.
21 Cohen, *A Body Worth Defending*.
22 Foucault, *The Birth of the Clinic*, xix.
23 Ibid.
24 Turner, *The Body and Society*, 176, emphasis added.
25 S. Krajewski, "4 Housewives in 5 Suffer Ailment Caused by Women's Lib," *National Enquirer*, March 15, 1983: 26.
26 Maines, *The Technology of Orgasm*.
27 Laqueur, *Making Sex*.

28 Gilman, *Difference and Pathology*, 24.
29 Davis, *Enforcing Normalcy*; Foucault, *Abnormal*; Gilman, *Difference and Pathology*.
30 Mairs, "Sex and Death"; Garland-Thomson, *Extraordinary Bodies*.
31 McRuer, *Crip Theory*.
32 Sandahl, "Queering the Crip," 27.
33 Gilman, *Difference and Pathology*, 23.
34 Lenze et al., "Comorbidity of Depression and Anxiety Disorders"; Ormel et al., "Outcome of Depression and Anxiety"; Pittion-Vouyovitch et al., "Fatigue in Multiple Sclerosis."
35 McRuer, *Crip Theory*; Wendell, "Feminist Theory of Disability."
36 Armstrong, *Neurodiversity*; Jaarsma and Welin, "Autism as a Natural Human Variation."
37 Davis, "Depression and Disability"; Häyry, "Neuroethical Theories"; Lisi, "Found Voices," 206; Meynen and Widdershoven, "Emotionality and Competence"; Barsade, et al., "To Your Heart's Content."
38 Davis, "Depression and Disability."
39 Patsavas, "Recovering a Cripistemology of Pain," 207.
40 LeFrançois, Menzies, and Reaume, *Mad Matters*, jacket copy.
41 Bespalov, van Gaalen, and Gross, "Antidepressant Treatment in Anxiety Disorders," 361.
42 Bespalov, van Gaalen, and Gross, "Antidepressant Treatment in Anxiety Disorders"; Scott, Davidson, and Palmer, "Antidepressant Drugs."
43 Blaskiewicz, "The Big Pharma Conspiracy Theory."
44 Davis, "Depression and Disability."
45 Mairs, "Sex and Death," 164.
46 Jennifer Gibson, "New Diagnostic Criteria for Generalized Anxiety Disorder," *BrainBlogger*, March 25, 2011, www.brainblogger.com.
47 "Facts," *Anxiety and Depression Association of America*, n.d., www.adaa.org.
48 Ibid.; "Facts & Statistics," *Anxiety and Depression Association of America*, 2012, www.adaa.org; Marcelle Pick, "Depression, Mood and Anxiety Disorders," *Women to Women*, 2011, www.womentowomen.com.
49 Lewinsohn et al., "Gender Differences in Anxiety Disorders."
50 In most cases, no official name of the commercial is available. The user-posted titles tended to be interchangeable: "Cymbalta commercial," "Abilify," "Zoloft Commercial," etc. The authors created the titles used in this chapter to easily identify each clip. They are indicated below in quotations.
Cymbalta:
    "Simple Pleasures": http://www.youtube.com/watch?v=o5cwqkuHwr4, https://adpharm.net/displayimage.php?pid=34013
    "No One": http://www.youtube.com/watch?v=OTZvnAF7UsA
    "This Day Calls You": https://www.youtube.com/watch?v=R__QUtq1KFQ
    "Closet": http://www.youtube.com/watch?v=kX-RryzCG8E

"Window" has been removed from the web. We viewed it originally at http://
www.youtube.com/watch?v=7d6Raon2pUA. However, a description of the
video (Cymbalta #2) remains as of June 2016 at http://jezebel.com/5991534/
ladies-be-moody-the-sad-sack-women-of-anti-depressant-commercials
"Stairs": http://www.youtube.com/watch?v=5RiTpGqt8nY
"Laptop": http://www.youtube.com/watch?v=aT6Vvxh5R20
Zoloft:
"Rain": http://www.youtube.com/watch?v=twhvtzd6gXA
"Cave 1": http://www.youtube.com/watch?v=ioYovUijswU
"Cave 2": http://www.youtube.com/watch?v=pB6_6DlXFoQ
"Party": http://www.youtube.com/watch?v=bbV6URQq2e4
"Spotlight": http://adland.tv/commercials/zoloft-social-anxiety-disorder-
spotlight-2003-060-usa
"Pill": http://www.youtube.com/watch?v=51MVDaFh65I
Abilify:
"Robe": http://www.youtube.com/watch?v=oGQcibFC9qo
"Hole": http://www.youtube.com/watch?v=tGymr78FtbU
"Magic Pill": http://www.youtube.com/watch?v=pSw9yVU5dvM
"Umbrella": http://www.dailymotion.com/video/xs622l_abilify-commercial_
shortfilms
"Terri and Team": http://www.ispot.tv/ad/7fla/abilify-terri-and-team
"Party": http://www.youtube.com/watch?v=Uv2hS_NulHU
"Side Effects": http://www.youtube.com/watch?v=25fGWKZFLIY
"Chalkboard": http://www.youtube.com/watch?v=fW2H8bVXLPs
"Pier": http://www.youtube.com/watch?v=JsqJju3ePJU

51 Dates for ads are difficult to ascertain as the YouTube upload dates do not reflect
their actual broadcast dates. In this case, however, we were able to find news
coverage of the Zoloft campaign in Kate Aurthur, "Little Blob, Don't Be Sad (or
Anxious or Phobic)," New York Times, Jan. 2, 2005, www.nytimes.com.

52 See Kirkpatrick, this volume.

53 Gilman, Difference and Pathology; Ewen and Ewen, Typecasting.

54 Douglas, Purity and Danger, 3.

55 As with the Zoloft egg, the gendered connotations of "hole" are rather overt; as
Douglas argues, pollution taboos often center on vulnerable openings, places
where social and bodily boundaries can be transgressed.

56 Beard, "Neurasthenia, or Nervous Exhaustion"; Lutz, American Nervousness, 1903.

57 McRobbie, The Aftermath of Feminism; Banet-Weiser, "Branding the Post-
Feminist Self."

58 Scott, "Ergonomic Diagrams, Medical Perception."

PART IV

Disability and Celebrity Culture

7

One of Us?

Disability Drag and the Gaga Enfreakment of Fandom

KRYSTAL CLEARY

Pop musician Lady Gaga has become both symbol of and spokesperson for freaks and outcasts, championing and often embodying cultural difference along lines of sexuality, gender, and dis/ability. Yet Gaga's role as "Mother Monster" is complicated by the different histories and statuses of the marginalized groups for whom she claims to speak, as well as the class, racial, gender, and able-bodied privilege that enables her performance of outsiderness. In an analysis that brings disability and queer studies into dialog with several subdisciplines within media studies, most notably star studies and reception studies, Cleary explores the complicated nature of Gaga's freakery.

From her outrageous costuming to the titling of her second international tour, "The Monster Ball," the universe of pop-shock performance artist Lady Gaga is full of freaks and monsters. As a self-identified freak and self-appointed mentor, Lady Gaga has adopted the role of "Mother Monster" and claims to offer refuge, hope, and inspiration to her fans. Within this framework, her fans, whom Gaga affectionately calls "little monsters," are imagined as outsiders inhabiting the margins of society. Despite the fact that she has achieved worldwide success and occupies many positions of social privilege along lines of race, class, gender, and ability, the Gaga-as-outcast persona enables her to assert a (maternal) kinship with those who experience social exclusion and oppression. In this chapter I employ an interdisciplinary theoretical framework that puts pop culture studies, feminist and queer theory, and critical disability studies in conversation to analyze the circulation of freak discourses in not only Lady Gaga's multifaceted star text but also her fan community. Not all fans embrace this freakish family narrative wholesale; Gaga, many assert, is not "one of us,"[1] as she proclaims. In particular, Gaga's use of disability as a performative trope has been challenged by people with disabilities, many of whom resist this enfreakment as a reductive act of appropriation that perpetuates ableist notions. In constructing her star persona as a freak and imagining her fans as freaks as well, I argue that Lady Gaga's performances must be understood through the lens of critical disability studies as a revision of the cultural spectacle of the freak show of the late nineteenth and early twentieth centuries. I assert that the liberatory promise and political critique that Gaga's freak rhetoric draws from the margins and interjects into the mainstream problematically conflates a subject position marked by social ostracism (but that is otherwise socially privileged) with one marked by systemic oppression.

Lady Gaga has dominated the popular music scene since her freshman album *The Fame* was released in 2008. With her long blond locks and synthesized beats, Gaga struck many as a catchy but ultimately unoriginal (and perhaps slightly less talented and conventionally attractive) version of myriad other female recording artists. Thereafter, Gaga quickly rose to fame and emerged as a controversial, deliberately strange star. However, the accusations that Gaga lacks originality persist. As Rebecca M. Lush notes, Gaga's persona and performances borrow generously from a plethora of pop cultural predecessors, particularly Madonna. Lush is quick to point out that Madonna, too, "created an image based on appropriation and reinterpretation of images from the past that demonstrated a depth of cultural referents."[2] Gaga is an interesting pop cultural figure not because she is wildly original, but because her visual and musical quotation of previous cultural figures serves as a performative bricolage that creates something that feels both curiously familiar and brand new. The very notion that a performance can be "original" is a myth, and Gaga, who has "described her entire career as a sociological study of fame," cleverly highlights the fabricated, constructed nature of performance and fame itself.[3] Moreover, Gaga's various and ever-changing performative modes inspire volumes of intense and contentious cultural discourses related to sex, gender, sexuality, dis/ability, and embodiment. Lady Gaga and the discourses that surround her persona, fame, and performative moments are therefore ideal entry points into broader considerations of our contemporary cultural moment and the politics of identity.

Such an analysis requires that we understand the celebrity figure as a complicated, polyvalent text. Susan Murray asserts that we must analyze star personas as mobile, multidimensional, and intertextual commodities whose so-called real identities and performances across various media platforms are inseparable entities.[4] It is necessary, Murray insists, to "focus on the star as a text unto itself . . . a text that moves across media, acquiring deeper and often contradictory facets as it extends itself through numerous characterizations."[5] Moreover, the machinery of celebrity is designed to produce iconic figures, not provide transparent access to personhood, even when it tries to convince us otherwise. Reading the star as a multifaceted text complicates the division between a performer's "authentic" offstage and fictional selves by revealing the celebrity image as a constellation of performative roles in which the star's "real" self is but one of its many constructed and potentially contradictory facets. It is through this analytical prism that I wish to view Lady Gaga's persona, which stretches across a plethora of media platforms: Gaga is not only a recording artist, but also a frequent guest on television shows such as *American Idol* and *Saturday Night Live*; a fashion icon who graces the cover of *Cosmopolitan*, *Vogue*, *Bazaar*, and *Vanity Fair*; an entrepreneur with her own signature fragrance, called "Fame"; enough of a mainstream star to solo at halftime during the 2017 Super Bowl; and, like Michael Jackson before her, a producer of mini-movie music videos such as the nearly ten-minute-long "Telephone." Gaga is also a vlogger, with over forty episodes of her web diary "Gagavision" available on both her website and official YouTube channel, and a notoriously active social media figure who frequently updates her (as of this writing) over sixty million followers on Facebook and tweets to her over fifty million followers on Twitter. Thus, Lady Gaga's star text spans widely across our media landscape.

This chapter cannot hope to account for the full expanse of Gaga's star text; the performative moments and public discourses surrounding them that I examine here are unified by their explicit engagement with disability. Yet disability is deceptively difficult to define. It is simultaneously identity, politics, culture, embodiment, lived experience, and socio-medico-legal status. As an umbrella category, disability is perhaps best defined by its capaciousness for vast physical, mental, and psychological diversity that exists outside of arbitrary and shifting cultural notions of what constitutes a "normal" body and mind. Lady Gaga's star persona and performative aesthetics hinge upon the unusual, and thus both often evoke the slippery image of disability. A disability studies discourse analysis of Lady Gaga could therefore include the horn-like prosthetics adorning her body in the "Born This Way" music video; the recurrent themes of mental health, medicalization, and institutionalization in her performances; and her rebirth as a swan-woman in the music video for "Applause," reminiscent of Tod Browning's 1932 film *Freaks*, in which sideshow performers vengefully transform the villainous Cleo into "one of us," a bird-woman who becomes the freak show's newest star. In this chapter, however, I limit my discourse analysis to Lady Gaga's uses of mobility aids such as wheelchairs and crutches as performance props, and to responses to these uses from the disabled community online. I do so because these instances have been consumed by audiences as most legibly and explicitly pertaining to disability and have in turn sparked the most pointed and frequently articulated critique.

Gaga's performative play with disability mobility aids, and the responses to it, constitute an archive of cultural artifacts that is simultaneously shaped by and reflective of contemporary relations of power. I examine articles on news websites as well as political and cultural commentary sites (such as *Bitch* magazine), but I foreground blog posts authored by people with disabilities and focus on backlash from the disabled community. In these discourses, Gaga's performances are critiqued as reductive acts of appropriation that undercut the political project of disability rights and recognition. Sites such as *Bitch* are heavily trafficked commercial websites, while the personal blogs are generally created and authored by one individual and attract fewer readers. Such a methodology centers the voices of people with disabilities who are responding to cultural texts. As producers of knowledge who theorize from their own lived, embodied experience of disability, these bloggers provide invaluable insights about identifying and confronting ableism both in the world at large and within our media landscape. Of course, this discourse analysis cannot hope to account for the full range of viewpoints expressed by people with disabilities. The number and intensity of these posts, however, suggest that many who embrace a politicized disabled identity are attentive to pop cultural appropriations of their experiences and produce critical, nuanced interpretations of them.

Lady Gaga, Fellow Freak

From unofficial biographies to personal interviews, an enormous amount of media attention has been dedicated to uncovering the "real" woman behind the bizarre Lady Gaga persona, as if we were gaining access to Stephanie Germanotta the person rather than consuming the Gaga star text and its surrounding discourses. These various sources all recount a similar narrative: Lady Gaga, born Stephanie Joanne Angelina Germanotta in 1986, was raised by a well-off Italian family in New York City. As a young adult, Germanotta experienced herself as an eccentric social outcast who found solace in musical expression. In a 2010 interview on *20/20*, Barbara Walters asked Gaga, "What's the biggest misconception about you?" to which she responded:

> That I am artificial and attention-seeking, when the truth is, every bit of me is dedicated to love and art, and I aspire to try to be a teacher to my young fans, who felt just like I felt when I was younger. . . . I felt like a freak. I guess what I'm saying is I want to liberate them. I want to free them of their fear and make them feel that they can create their own space in the world.[6]

This claiming of an authentic self is inconsistent with numerous other assertions of hers, such as, "Every time you see me, it's performance. When I'm sleeping, it's performance."[7] Gaga appears at first to be contradictorily invested in notions of both authenticity and theatricality, yet the narrative of "realness" is itself a part of her constructed performative identity. Resisting the impulse to uncover the "truth" about Germanotta's life before and outside of her persona as Lady Gaga, the "real" Lady Gaga can instead be understood as one constructed and mediated component of her ever-changing, polymorphous persona. We simply cannot know whether Gaga did or does indeed experience a sense of outsiderness, because the machinery of celebrity makes this inaccessible to us as audience members.

What we *can* know is that Lady Gaga (and the media industries that help to construct her image) has carefully crafted the Germanotta-as-adolescent-freak origin story, which serves to substantiate her role as "Mother Monster" by establishing a shared experience of outsiderness between her and her fans. It is the crucial, legitimizing foundation from which Lady Gaga asserts herself as both a peer and advisor to fans who experience themselves as outsiders. "For many of her 'super fans,'" Ann T. Torrusio explains, "Gaga has created a perfect come-as-you-are subculture. She instills in her 'super fans' the belief that they are important, beautiful, and unique; they will find their place in the world in the cultural margins."[8] Lady Gaga's fans are therefore imagined to exist (and encouraged to imagine themselves as living) on the outskirts of normative society. The "real" Germanotta-as-adolescent-freak persona insists that she too grew up on the margins, and, despite ostracism, came to embrace her freakishness. Purportedly Gaga is not only *like* her fans, she *is* a fan—positioning herself as fan is another way in which she constructs an identity shared by her and her audience. In her song "Paparazzi," for example, she channels the voice of the stereotypical obsessed fan discussed by media scholars Henry Jenkins[9] and Joli Jenson[10] when she sings, "I'm your biggest fan/ I'll follow you until you love me/ Papa, paparazzi." Additionally, Gaga is an adoring fan of her fans; not only does she speak their praise and her thanks in most of her public appearances, but she also has "Little Monsters" tattooed on her forearm and the iconic monster paw (or "claw," fig. 7.1) on her back in homage to her loyal fan base. Additionally, in 2014 the Bio section of Gaga's Twitter profile read, "Spreading love with every intention, forever devoted to the kingdom of monsters."[11] Though the reigning queen, Gaga's use of the word "devoted" demonstrates both a sense of membership in and subservient loyalty to her little monster fan base. Fans imagine celebrities, as Richard Dyer reveals, to be simultaneously like us and not like us,[12] and the supposedly shared experience of freakishness breaks down the boundary between Gaga and her little monsters. At least narratively speaking, this disrupts the hierarchal relationship between the two: Gaga is at once articulated here as queen/ mother, peer, and deferential adorer.

As a vocal supporter of gay rights, occasional drag performer, and perhaps the first major artist to use the word "transgender" in a chart-topping song ("Born This Way"), it is not surprising that Lady Gaga resonates with queer youth in particular, a relationship reinforced by her public disclosure of having been intimate with women. Beyond her explicit allegiances to the LGBTQ community, her performances also

Figure 7.1. Lady Gaga performs at a piano, making a hand gesture that approximates the "monster claw."

tap into many of the key elements of queer culture that Richard Dyer identifies in his examination of why many urban, white gay men of the 1950s were drawn so strongly to Judy Garland: a special relationship to ordinariness, and an emotionality of suffering and strength. Dyer writes, "The ordinariness is a starting point because, like Judy Garland, gay men are brought up to be ordinary. One is not brought up gay; on the contrary, everything in the culture seems to work against it."[13] In a similar vein, he posits that Garland's performances expressed an emotionality of suffering and survival that resonated with gay men's experiences of social marginalization. Lady Gaga appears to be making similar connections to her little monsters. Though she has a special relationship to LGBTQ youth, her fandom is imagined as extending beyond the gay community and consisting of "freaks" more broadly conceived. As such, I am cautiously extending Dyer's argument to suggest that in Lady Gaga fandom, the special relationship to ordinariness and the emotionality of suffering and survival that drew gay men to Garland is meant to attract not only queer folks but also those occupying other marginalized social locations to her performances. These two interlocking features are succinctly communicated in the lyrics of the title track of her album *Born This Way*, where Gaga belts:

> Whether you're broke or evergreen
> You're black, white, beige, chola descent
> You're Lebanese, you're orient
> Whether life's disabilities
> Left you outcast, bullied, or teased
> Rejoice and love yourself today
> 'cause baby you were born this way
> No matter gay, straight, or bi,
> Lesbian, transgendered life,
> I'm on the right track baby, I was born to survive.[14]

Like her little monsters, Lady Gaga insists that she too faced social pressure to be ordinary and therefore understands what it is like to be a freak. Her persona and work speak of suffering, but more importantly, of survival, and the potential for the outcasts of the world to celebrate their differences.

Shiny Spokes or Ableist Appropriation?

Gaga's conjuring of marginalized identity is evident not only in her personal narratives and imagining of a fan community that exists on the margins of society, but also in her performative modes. For instance, Gaga debuted her gender drag as Jo Calderone, a chain-smoking, heartbroken greaser, in her music video "Yoü and I" and then again at the 2011 MTV Video Music Awards, where she kinged during her musical number and the duration of the show, including her acceptance of the Best Female Video Award. Though many American audience members looked on in bewilderment, queer communities largely embraced Gaga's gender drag as a display of her ongoing LGBTQ advocacy. Writers on prominent queer blogs, such as AfterEllen.com, glowingly praised the performance for making "the kind of positive political statement I'd been longing for."[15] For some, then, Gaga signals a new era of gender and sexual politics. Queer theorist J. Jack Halberstam, for instance, recently declared Gaga a mascot of feminist activism in *Gaga Feminism: Sex,*

Gender, and the End of Normal. Gaga feminism, Halberstam explains, "is a form of political expression that masquerades as naïve nonsense but that actually participates in big and meaningful forms of critique."[16] As a feminism "gone gaga," it is invested in revolt rather than reform and embraces the unreal, improvisational, and monstrous. Although Halberstam insists that Lady Gaga is not the first so-called gaga feminist and that the concept is not limited to her performative archive, the shine of her star text is the book's illuminating example. With Gaga's unmistakable silhouette on the cover, Halberstam's book regards Lady Gaga as both the contemporary site of promise and the signpost of a "free-falling, wild thinking, and imaginative reinvention" of gendered and sexual conventions and politics.[17]

Jo Calderone is not Gaga's only dabble in drag; her repertoire also includes the performance of disability, which has come to be known as disability drag. First in her 2009 "Paparazzi" video, then in several performances and promotional photos since, she has rolled across the stage in ornate wheelchairs, stumbled around in sleek forearm crutches, and accessorized with neck braces. In "Paparazzi," Gaga is pushed off of a balcony by her lover and later assisted back into her mansion by African American butlers. Her dancing servants lift a stiff, neck brace–wearing Gaga into a customized jewel-encrusted wheelchair, then help her remove the neck brace along with most of her clothes. Underneath, she is wearing bronze metal lingerie and a helmet, and is handed matching forearm crutches. She proceeds to stumble down the walkway, intentionally contorting her legs along the way.

Gender drag, as a self-aware and theatrically staged exaggeration of gender performativity's[18] more mundane workings, is a fixture in queer culture, whereas disability is conversely regarded in the American imagination as a self-evident and fixed corporeality that is resistant to performative play. As Petra Kuppers elucidates, actors with disabilities are often not offered jobs because their performances are interpreted as "authentic" presentations of the self that do not require performative skill, while "non-disabled people can prove the mastery of their craft by 'acting disabled.'"[19] Though these performances are lauded in the entertainment industry as a marker of high artistic achievement, Tobin Siebers is adamant that disability drag is an irrefutably ableist caricature of the disabled experience "similar to white face performers who put on black face at minstrel shows or to straight actors who play 'fag' to bad comic effect."[20] Further, disability drag "transforms disability by insinuating ability into its reality and representation," implying that disability can be overcome or cured as easily as one can disrobe from a costume.[21] Siebers calls disability drag an "an exaggerated exhibition of people with disabilities" that "acts as a lure for the fantasies and fears of able-bodied audiences and reassures them that the threat of disability is not real, that everything was only pretend."[22] Although this chapter cannot fully map out the reasons why sex/gender and disability are not regarded as equally available for performative play, the jarring difference in response to Gaga's two drags indicates a grave failure in analogy between disability and other axes of identity and power. They cannot be conflated, even as they mutually constitute each other as analytics and lived experiences.

Indeed, unlike her gender drag, Gaga's performances of disability drag have not been so warmly received by her audiences.[23] In July 2011, Gaga took the stage in Australia costumed as her character Yuyi, a wheelchair-using mermaid à la Bette Midler's Delores DeLago, and was reportedly egged by angered fans.[24] This disdain is not solely evidenced by a few splattered yolks; on the blogosphere, people with disabilities have written volumes of critique in response to Gaga's disability drag. Arguing for an intersectional analysis of Gaga's relationship to her little monsters, Renee at *Womanist Musings* asserts in a blog post titled "Hey Lady Gaga, Wheelchairs Are Not Your Fun Accessory":

> [N]o matter how many times she advocates on behalf of the GLBT community for justice and equality, she is just as prone to failure on other isms. Due to the fact that all isms are interconnected, this means that she has failed some of the very same people that she claims to advocate on behalf of, because I am quite sure that there are disabled GLBT people who saw her little wheelchair performance and were not amused. You cannot truly be a leftist because you advocate for justice for one group of marginalized people. Justice and equality means challenging your privileges not perpetuating them when it is convenient or can be seen as edgy.[25]

Renee acknowledges the special kinship Gaga asserts with queer communities, but insists that an intersectional understanding of her fan base would reveal that Gaga does not always resonate so strongly with her audiences and that her performances can be interpreted as offensive to those experiencing other "isms," such as ableism.

Indeed, Renee finds Gaga's disability drag offensive. Elsewhere in the post, she fires:

> For GaGa [sic], a wheelchair can just be some fun toy because she doesn't need it to function as her legs. When her show is over, she can put on her ridiculous hobbling heels and strut . . . to her next gig. She will not have to go two or three extra blocks because there are no curb cuts for her to cross. She will not have to wave her arms frantically to get attention because a business owner has decided that they couldn't be bothered to install an automatic door opener. And finally, she won't get glares or accusations of faking when she stands up, because as an able bodied person, she functions as a gatekeeper to those of us who are disabled and therefore understood as "other."[26]

Similarly, disability blogger Wheelchair Dancer asserts that Gaga evacuates the lived experience of ableism from the representation of disability, and in the process actually serves to reify oppressive notions about the disabled body. She blogs, "Lady Gaga rolling around in a chair or using crutches or having a non-disabled dancer use a chair does not materially change our world. It doesn't raise awareness around disability and disability issues. . . . In some ways, the lived experience of disability appears even more unsexy when contrasted with the Lady Gaga image."[27] After seeing the "Paparazzi" video, Annaham, a self-identified disabled feminist, wrote an article for *Bitch* titled "The Transcontinental Disability Choir: Disability Chic? (Temporary) Disability in Lady Gaga's 'Paparazzi,'" in which she argued the biggest problem with Gaga's performance of disability is that it is so short-lived. She writes, "The overall message: Disability can be 'cool,' but only if it is temporary, *not* shown to the public, and that [sic] your eventual recovery from it can be portrayed through the timeless medium of dance!"[28] Annaham suggests that, in ditching her wheelchair mid-act and resuming her position as an able-bodied performer, Lady Gaga perpetuates the ableist notion that the disabled body is uninhabitable and must ultimately be corrected or overcome. For Renee, Wheelchair Dancer, and Annaham, Gaga's performative tropes of disability obscure the realities of ableist oppression and can actually intensify ableist attitudes about disability.

Unlike Siebers's discussion of disability drag, the critique leveled by Annaham, Wheelchair Dancer, and other bloggers cited above is not grounded in a notion of disability authenticity. In other words, Gaga's able-body is not the sole or main reason they perceive her disability drag to be problematic. Revealing that her able-body is not the heart of the critique, the controversy over her attention-grabbing mobility devices was reignited in 2013 when Gaga became a temporary wheelchair user after hip surgery. Though necessitated by injury, her extravagant gold-plated wheelchair, nicknamed "the chariot," was interpreted by some as an offensively lavish display that revived her uses of disability as a performative prop. Aspire, a UK support organization for people with spinal cord injuries, posted a short video to their YouTube channel insisting Gaga auction off her excessively ornate chair and donate the money to grants that help people with disabilities afford mobility devices.[29] Whereas Gaga's admissions of same-sex intimacy bolstered her status in queer communities (which does not seem to be undercut by her 2015 engagement to actor Taylor Kinney), her medically required (though brief) time as a wheelchair user did not improve but rather further tarnished her credibility with disabled audiences. Even when physically impaired, Gaga was not imagined by many people with disabilities as "one of us." The bloggers do not imply that able-bodied performers can *never* accurately capture the lived, embodied experience of disability or ableist oppression. There is, after all, no *one* disabled experience and the very notion of authenticity, particular when pertaining to polyvalent star texts like Lady Gaga, is a fiction. Rather, bloggers focus on *how* Gaga employs mobility aids in ways that perpetuate ableist ideologies and thus undermine the political project of disability visibility and social justice.

Mainstream Sideshows

Through her construction of a fellow freak persona and performative tropes of disability, Lady Gaga is orchestrating a contemporary freak show that reworks the formal conventions of the nineteenth-century version. In the context of sociopolitical anxiety over shifting notions of national and individual identity at the turn of the nineteenth century, the social function of freak shows was to dramatize a normal/freak binary and stage an opportunity for normative spectators to reaffirm their status as normal, autonomous, and mobile American citizens in opposition to their freakish counterparts. For this to happen, an enfreaked figure had to be constructed. David Hevey coined the term "enfreakment" to name the process of dehumanization of people with disabilities as the "voyeuristic property of the non-disabled gaze" in photography.[30] Extending Hevey's argument beyond the disabled body and its depiction in photographs, critical disability studies scholars use the term "enfreakment" to refer to "the process by which individual difference becomes stylized as cultural otherness."[31] To compose a character of cultural otherness that both animated and contained normative audiences' fears of disability, the nineteenth-century freak show's processes of enfreakment highlighted cultural otherness through character construction, promotional narrative, costuming, and set design much akin to contemporary media industry practices of producing mediated pop cultural texts. Though by the mid-twentieth century the popularity of the freak show had waned, Rachel Adams argues that it never fully met its demise. On the contrary, Adams asserts, the cultural spectacle of the freak show has proliferated in the realms of visual and performance art, literature, and popular culture, adapting to shifting cultural ideologies and (re)taking the stage in a diversity of mediatized spaces.

In constructing her star persona as a freak and imagining her fans as freaks as well, Gaga and her performances must be understood as a contemporary revision of the cultural spectacle of the historic freak show. Gaga becomes both ringmaster of the contemporary freak show and one of its monstrous spectacles on display for her fans. This freak show is, in theory, one by and for freaks that blurs the boundary between the normative spectator and non-normative performer. The Gaga enfreakment of fandom is not intended to strip the freak of his or her humanity, nor create distance between performer and spectator; however, as their blog commentary articulates, many people with disabilities feel profoundly alienated by Gaga's performances of disability. It attempts to bring the freak in all of us to the fore and in turn highlight a common humanity, but in doing so it flattens the realities of ableism and reifies ableist notions of the disabled body. According to bloggers' critiques, Gaga's enfreakment of fandom is therefore a failed project.

The failure of Gaga's enfreakment of fandom is largely facilitated by her privilege as a (temporarily) able-bodied economically, racially, and gender-normative subject.[32] Despite Siebers's fierce critique of disability drag, Christopher R. Smit argues that Gaga's performative tropes of disability embody what Siebers refers to as a disability aesthetic, an artistic adoration rather than a rejection of the disabled body. For Smit, Gaga vandalizes and deconstructs the conventional pop female body and in turn constructs a new "style" of disability, one in which disability "gains a position it has rarely had in the past—happenstance."[33] In other words, he asserts that Gaga's vandalism of the pop female body, which includes but isn't limited to disability drag, allows disability to be consumed alongside other performative tropes rather than as the focus of the representation as is typical in much mainstream media centered on the disabled body. However, Gaga's privilege along other axes positions her as a standardized blank slate. Onto this slate, a caricatured image of freakishness can be landscaped, one that troubles the notion that disability is simultaneously a culturally powerful and coincidental facet of her consumable star text.

Gaga's position as Mother Monster, the maternal, guiding figure of marginalized people, is a puzzling one. She attended high school at Convent of the Sacred Heart, an elite private school in Manhattan. She was raised by an upper-class family, and with an estimated net worth of $150 million dollars is undoubtedly affluent. While she has drawn inspiration for her performances from her Italian heritage, Gaga does not carry significant markers of ethnicity and racially reads as white. She also does not visibly read as disabled: while she has publicly acknowledged struggling with depression and post-traumatic stress disorder, and suspicions that she has lupus have circulated unconfirmed in the tabloid rumor mill, she recovered fully from the aforementioned hip surgery and possesses the privilege of participating in non-disabled dominant culture. Though she dabbles in masculinity while performing gender drag and is remembered more for her bizarre costuming than for being one of the great beauties of our time, with her slender frame, (usually) blond locks, and revealing outfits, Gaga is gendered consistently as conventionally feminine.

This is not to make claims about Gaga's "real" physical body or identity experience per se, but rather to identify the culturally legible

characteristics by which she is marked within our contemporary sociohistorical context and that confer her privilege. As the controversy
around her "chariot" emphasized, the problem inherent in her enfreakment of fandom as well as her star persona is not so much one of embodied inauthenticity (Gaga is not a "real" freak) but one of social privilege.
Her golden wheelchair, though medically necessitated, was interpreted
by some as a gross exhibition of the affluence that insulates her from
systemic ableist oppression. Despite temporary disability, her display of
class privilege magnified her overall elite status and reaffirmed for many
audience members that her use of mobility aids across her performative
oeuvre was divested from the project of disability visibility and justice.
In short, when examined through the lens of feminist theorizations of
power, Gaga is hardly an outsider, an observation that resonates with the
critiques from bloggers with disabilities.

Indeed, it is precisely the privilege that she reaps from occupying
dominant subject positions that enables her to construct her persona
as Mother Monster. Privileged subject positions, such as whiteness, are
rendered invisible and unmarked through their dominance in our culture. They are seen as the unspecified and the default, while minority
groups are imagined as being defined by their deviation from the norm
and saturated by difference. Gaga's unmarked subjecthood allows her
to mark Otherness on her privileged body through elaborate and exaggerated costuming; she embodies the image of the freakish through
horn-like facial prosthetics; she performs alternate identities and cor-
porealities on stage through gender drag and disability drag. Indeed,
I assert her performative tropes of disability and narrative framework
of freakishness do not deconstruct or vandalize the conventional pop
female body as Smit argues. Rather, it is her possession of a pop female
body defined by its normative statuses that allow her to artistically landscape a generalizable "freak" image in a way that people whose bodies
are saturated by a cultural discourse of difference, such as people with
visible disabilities, can not. The pop female celebrity body is not de-
constructed, but rather is the enabling foundation of the Gaga-as-freak
construction.

The Gaga enfreakment of fandom therefore imagines freak identity as
the province of anyone with the proclivity to claim it, despite social location. "Freak" has always been a capacious term. The freak show's pro-

cesses of enfreakment not only highlighted corporeal difference but also conflated these differences into what Garland-Thomson calls a freakery, "a single amorphous category of corporeal otherness."[34] "Freak" was thus an umbrella category that simultaneously foregrounded and collapsed intersecting differences across race, gender, and ability. The politics over the boundaries of freak identity call to mind debates within feminist and queer theory around the term "queer." For instance, Heather Love insists we "ask ourselves whether queer actually becomes more effective as it surveys more territory," and argues that "the problem with such a broad vision of queer is not only that it loses the specific experiential and historical anchors that gave it meaning . . . but also that the intention to be answerable to many different constituencies can end up looking like a desire to have ownership over them."[35] Love cautions against a notion of queerness that strays from its grounding in sexuality and not only loses its nuance but also encroaches upon other experiences, identities, and bodies of critical thought. The same critiques can be launched at Gaga's broad notion of freak. If everyone is a freak, no one is a freak. It is an appealing concept, and one that on the surface holds liberatory promise. However, the painful history of the freak show, which Eli Clare describes as one of forced prostitution,[36] makes the resignification of the term "freak" difficult despite the political and personal possibilities it can open up. In its attempt to celebrate and embrace diversity, the enfreakment of Lady Gaga fandom effectively obscures difference, therefore evacuating it of meaning and neutralizing its political critique. Lady Gaga's contemporary freak show constructs a category of otherness that paradoxically highlights and flattens difference, an updated version of the freak show's freakery in which social ostracism and systemic oppression are conflated.

Conclusion

Though Gaga and the industry powers that back her are the powerful producers, perhaps fan resistance to Lady Gaga's enfreakment can open up a space to extend Henry Jenkins's theorization of textual poaching. In his discussion of how fan production (such as fan fiction and filk music) draws from and reworks the primary media text, Jenkins explains, "Like the poachers of old, fans operate from a position of cultural marginality and social weakness. Like other popular readers, fans lack direct access to the means of commercial cultural production and have only the most limited resources with which to influence entertainment industry's decisions."[37] Jenkins's concept of textual poaching emphasizes the power differential between fans and industry powers, and asserts that the powerless fans, despite media producers' attempts to thwart their appropriations, raid the texts they adore in order to create their own cultural productions. Despite her rhetoric of freak community, Lady Gaga is the power-holder; she not only works in tandem with industry powers that propel her fame, but also occupies myriad privileged social positions along lines of class, race, ability, and gender expression. However, in an interesting inversion of Jenkins's original theorizations, Lady Gaga, a fan of her fans, poaches from the social margins at which many of her fans are located to construct her "authentic" freak persona and performances. In this analysis, she is a privileged performer culling material from the social margins. Thus, in appropriating the aesthetics and experiences of a (supposedly) "authentic" freak identity to construct her own, not only her fans but Lady Gaga herself can be figured as a textual poacher. Lady Gaga, through her textual poaching of the margins and the media spectacle of enfreakment, attempts to bring the margins into the mainstream and makes freakishness accessible to all. While a lot of people can contort their hand into the little monster paw, some critical fans, such as many with disabilities, maintain that Lady Gaga's contemporary freak show pilfers from and distorts the representation of their lived, embodied experiences as marginalized subjects. Her generic brand of freakishness is indeed spacious, but bloggers with disabilities insist that Gaga expands the sentiment of outsiderness at the expense of people with disabilities' identities, lives, and intersectional political projects of recognition and justice.

   Lady Gaga and the discourses that surround her persona, fame, and performative moments are ideal entry points into broader considerations of our contemporary cultural climate. As media disability studies scholar Beth A. Haller argues, interpersonal contact between people with disabilities and able-bodied persons is still limited in a world in which ableist ideological, educational, and architectural systems persist. As such, "mass media images still provide many of the cultural representations of disability to American society."[38] Just as the nineteenth-century freak show instructed viewers on the arbitrary boundaries between normative and non-normative embodiment, it is important to continually interrogate the messages about disability being propagated in mass media in an ableist cultural climate in which people may have limited interaction with people with disabilities. Lady Gaga, through her textual poaching of the margins and media spectacle of enfreakment, problematically evacuates freakishness of its historical context and obscures the realities of systemic oppression.

NOTES

1 An iconic text in the history of media representations of people with disabilities, Tod Browning's 1932 film *Freaks* tells the story of a community of side-show performers' revenge on Cleo, a beautiful but deceitful able-bodied trapeze artist who marries and later poisons a little person named Hans for his fortune. Prior to their knowledge of Cleo's bad intent, the matrimony between Cleo and Hans prompts the band of freaks to chantingly claim her as "one of us." This welcoming is fully realized in the final scenes of the film when the freaks, upon learning of Cleo's scheme, enact their retribution and mutilate her into a bird-woman, the freak show's new star.

2 Lush, "The Appropriation of the Madonna Aesthetic," 175.

3 Ibid., 174.

4 Murray, "I Know What You Did Last Summer," 50.

5 Ibid.

6 "Lady Gaga 20/20 Interview (FULL)" *YouTube*, January 24, 2010, www.youtube.com.

7 Switaj, "Lady Gaga's Bodies," 35.

8 Torrusio, "The Fame Monster," 171.

9 Jenkins, *Textual Poachers*, 15.

10 Jenson, "Fandom as Pathology," 9–29.

11 Lady Gaga, "Bio," *Twitter*, accessed September 16, 2014, https://twitter.com/ladygaga.

12 Dyer, *Stars*, 43.

13 Dyer, *Heavenly Bodies*, 153.

14 Just as Gaga's performative tropes of disability have caused controversy, the racial politics of her songs and costuming have raised concerns amongst audience members. The lyrics of "Born This Way," for example, outraged some fans who have responded prolifically on blogs. Blogger Pia writes, "Well this attempt falls flat on its face. And I bet that Gaga will plead ignorance to the commonly held definitions of the word that are based on stereotypes of class, race and culture promulgated by colonization and oppression. . . . I don't know about the rest of you, but as a bi-racial Mexican American I'm not comfortable buying what she's

selling." Pia, "Lady Gaga's 'Born This Way': Racist or Revolutionary," *Adios Barbie*, February 21, 2011, www.adiosbarbie.com.

15 Drummerdeeds, "The 2011 MTV Video Music Awards: Jo Calderone Just Glitter-Bombed America," *AfterEllen*, August 29, 2013, www.afterellen.com.

16 Halberstam, *Gaga Feminism*, xxv.

17 Ibid., xv.

18 Butler, *Gender Trouble*.

19 Kuppers, *Disability and Contemporary Performance*, 54.

20 Siebers, *Disability Theory*, 116.

21 Ibid.

22 Ibid.

23 This is not to suggest, however, that people with disabilities monolithically reject Gaga's performative tropes of disabilities. In fact, some bloggers with disabilities celebrate her disability drag. After seeing footage of one of Gaga's performances in Sydney, during which Gaga sported a mermaid tail and rolled across the stage in a chair, the late Stella Young, a contributor to the disability blog *Ramp Up*, wrote, "When I saw the footage on the news the next morning, I instinctively checked out her spokes and noted they were shiny. Ooohh, shiny new mobility aids . . . WANT! Was I offended she'd chosen to use a chair? No. I was momentarily jealous that hers was shinier than mine." In addition to her wheelchair envy, Young believed, "If [Gaga's] sending the message that a wheelchair is a liberating solution to a mobility impairment, whether it's a disability or a big black vinyl mermaid tail, I reckon that serves us wheelchair users pretty well." Stella Young, "Going Gaga over Wheels," *Ramp Up*, July 15, 2011, www.abc.net.au.

24 Matthew Perpetua, "Lady Gaga Egged over Wheelchair Stunt: Singer Rolled Out on a Stage Dressed as a Mermaid in Sydney," *Rolling Stone*, July 15, 2011, www.rollingstone.com.

25 Renee, "Hey Lady Gaga, Wheelchairs Are Not Your Fun Accessory," *Womanist Musings*, July 19, 2014, www.womanistmusings.com.

26 Ibid.

27 Wheelchair Dancer, "Lady Gaga and the Wheelchair: II," *Crip Wheels*, July 16, 2011, http://cripwheels.blogspot.com (access restricted).

28 Annaham, "The Transcontinental Disability Choir: Disability Chic? (Temporary) Disability in Lady Gaga's 'Paparazzi,'" *Bitch Magazine*, November 20, 2009, https://bitchmedia.org.

29 Aspire Charity, "Aspire Asks Lady Gaga to Auction her Gold Wheelchair for Charity," *YouTube*, March 19, 2013, www.youtube.com.

30 Hevey, "The Enfreakment of Photography," 519.

31 Samuels, "Examining Millie," 56.

32 Though Gaga typically adheres to conventional standards of white, affluent femininity, her gender drag as Jo Calderon can trouble a reading of her star persona as solely gender normative. Moreover, rumors that Gaga is intersex or transgender

have circulated since the beginning of her stardom, a fact she cheekily acknowledges in the music video for "Telephone."

33 Smit, "Body Vandalism," 37.
34 Garland-Thomson, "Introduction," 10.
35 Love, "Queer _____ This," 183.
36 Clare, *Exile and Pride*, 71.
37 Jenkins, *Textual Poachers*, 26.
38 Haller, *Representing Disability*, 29.

8

Disability, Global Popular Media, and Injustice in the Trial of Oscar Pistorius

KATIE ELLIS AND GERARD GOGGIN

Drawing on disability studies, media studies, and the sociology of sport, Ellis and Goggin argue that the case of runner Oscar Pistorius's killing of Reeva Steenkamp reveals the range, depth, and complexity of the cultural meanings of disability in contemporary society. Examining press accounts, legal arguments, and popular responses to the killing, they situate discourses of disability within multiple contexts, including the global sports industry and the dynamics of race and gender in a transforming South Africa. The "Pistorius affair," they suggest, makes visible the normally submerged roles that disability plays within popular culture, with implications for the ways that bodies, identities, and indeed life itself are understood.

On September 12, 2014, in the South African high court in Pretoria, the sportsman and international celebrity Oscar Pistorius was found not guilty of the murder of his girlfriend, the actress and model Reeva Steenkamp.[1] Instead, Judge Thokozile Masipa found Pistorius guilty of culpable homicide, for which he was sentenced to the maximum of five years in prison. On separate firearm charges, Judge Masipa pronounced Pistorius guilty of one count of unlawfully discharging a Glock 27 pistol (in an unrelated previous incident at a restaurant) and gave him a suspended sentence of three years. On December 3, 2015, a panel of five judges in the Supreme Court of South Africa overturned Judge Masipa's ruling and convicted Pistorius of murder. On March 3, 2016, the Constitutional Court of South Africa dismissed Pistorius's application for leave to appeal, judging there were no prospects of success. This final judgment and subsequent sentencing brought to a close the sensational, controversial, and highly publicized trial of Pistorius, a *cause célèbre* not just in South Africa, where Pistorius was a national hero, but around the world.

Central to the legal arguments and proceedings of Pistorius's case was his disability and its implications for his innocence or guilt, as well as the circumstances, events, and significance of his life. How disability mattered, and what it meant, was neither just a matter for the South African tribunals, nor simply the pivot of its legal arguments and analysis. Disability was central to the deep cultural and social underpinnings of how the death of Steenkamp and the inextricably woven actions of Pistorius were understood by their fellow South Africans, and indeed audiences around the world.

Accordingly, in this chapter, we argue that, to understand the Pistorius affair (as it became, revolving around him rather than Steenkamp), one needs to understand the dynamics of disability—and in particular, media and disability. It is no coincidence that the Pistorius trial was a major popular media event. How media represented Pistorius, the discourses surrounding the media event, how audiences responded, and what implications this had materially are interrelated and consequential matters for inquiry and debate. In short, the Pistorius affair offers an important case study of the cultural meanings of disability and the way disability is implicated in narratives of, and the governing of, race, gender, sexuality, and normalcy.[2] As such it exemplifies how disability is deeply implicated in the popular. Shaping, engaging with, and communicating via the popular is central to how "disabled" and "non-disabled" people understand, go about, and advance their lives—and how power is exercised. As we shall discuss, there is now growing recognition, and emerging evidence, of the role that government of disability and impairment plays in contemporary power—because these notions go to the heart of how bodies, identities, resources, and indeed life itself are understood.

The perspective provided by critical disability and media studies is vital to make sense of the obvious, stark issue posed by the Pistorius affair. Via fame and infamy, Oscar Pistorius became the best-known South African with a disability. Yet there is a yawning gap between what he came to represent (and the multiple meanings that he might convey) and the universe of experiences, realities, myths, fantasies, and signs of disability in South Africa as an imagined national community.

Official statistics remind us that the majority of people with disability in South Africa are non-white, female, and poor. The most recent survey data show that in 2011, disability prevalence was 7.5%. Disability was more prevalent among females (8.3%) than males (6.5%). Black Africans had the highest proportion of disabilities (7.8%), followed by whites (6.5%), with no observable variables among the Coloured and Indian/Asian population groups (although disability types vary across populations).[3] Generally, people without disabilities earn a higher income than those with disabilities; and among people with disabilities, "males earn double what females earn, regardless of degree of difficulty" imputed to impairment type.[4]

Accounts of South Africa's recent history testify to the links between impairment and colonization, the *longue durée* of disability in this part of Africa.[5] The decolonization period, which continues, was marked by the terrible decades of apartheid, its unique oppression, and systems of violence, exclusion, and exploitation that produced new forms and social relations of disability.[6] The health crisis of HIV/AIDS and the politics of its response in South Africa are another obvious area of disability experience. The liberation struggles, the dismantling of apartheid, and the dawning and great hopes of what Bishop Desmond Tutu coined the Rainbow Nation, with Nelson Mandela as president, coincided with the rise of the global disability rights movements and the recognition of disability as an integral element of social justice and democracy in South Africa.[7] A great symbol of this achievement and aspiration comes with the landmark new South African Constitution, in which disability is explicitly recognized in the definition of equality.[8] These democratic, affirmative, even at times redemptive aspects of disability in South Africa are not so well known internationally, nor have they received the kind of attention accorded the Pistorius affair.[9]

This striking imbalance—related to what David Mitchell and Sharon Snyder famously explored as the complex, contradictory, and dynamic "discontents" of representation[10]—has everything to do with disability and justice, and the heightened role media play in these struggles. In the Pistorius affair, we also wager that the "very discontent produced by representation provides a fulcrum for identifying the culture that *should be* rather than that which is."[11] In what follows, we explore how disability is represented in the Pistorius affair via readings of three parts of what is a large, complicated corpus of media texts, events, and reception. Schematically, these three parts relate to the discourses of disability that circulated in the wake of Steenkamp's killing, Pistorius's arrest, and public responses; the use of disability as a defense in the trial; and the representation of disability in the judgment and sentencing phase.

Disabled Global Sporting Icon

Disability is increasingly recognized as an indispensable category of analysis in media and cultural studies. In the representation, reception, and circulation of Pistorius internationally, disability is key to how he functions as global signifier—indeed, as we shall shortly discuss, a global icon across various genres, formats, and platforms of news and entertainment, especially popular cultures.[12] In his rise and fall, Pistorius has attracted avid interest, especially as a celebrity with disability.[13] However, what such celebrity signifies, and what the social function of disabled celebrity in particular might be, especially for different audiences in distinct places, is not so clear.

What little research and critical discussion on media and disability, let alone celebrity, we have so far—which is now finally developing apace—is centered in societies of the global north. For a long time, it has been recognized that much of the incidence of disability and impairment is in the majority world (as the global south is often termed), yet little disability research discusses this. Now there is work emerging on disability and the global south that begins to fill this gap, and in doing so changes the fundamental terms, concepts, and theories by which we have hitherto understood disability—globally, and especially in the global north.[14] From another angle, research has emerged highlighting the challenges for disability studies from taking colonialism and postcolonialism seriously.[15] This research helps us to locate a key issue in approaching popular media and disability. We know little about how Pistorius is represented across different media and is emotionally responded to in various places, especially in the global south, and in relation to the contest over the legacies of colonialism.[16]

We can see this when it comes to the avid pursuit of sport, which also traverses many of these areas of concern to contemporary culture.[17] In sport—its participation, engagement, and representation—we find many insights into the ways different identities and master narratives are created around the person with disability. The conjunction of media and sport is massive, and media have extended sport into new areas of everyday life.[18] In recent years, media sport as a networked global phenomenon has incorporated disability sports, sportsmen and women, and disabled audiences. Yet we know little about how this has played out in the global north, let alone the majority world[19]—although, interestingly, the new powerhouses in global sport are emerging from newly prosperous countries.[20] Mindful of this, while we focus on the Pistorius case as it has been represented in international media outlets outside South Africa (based from our standpoints living and working in Australia), we will endeavor also to draw upon and draw attention to salient aspects of the various South African accounts.[21]

The areas of sociology of sport and disability, as well as critical study of sport, media, and disability, are fledgling but also provide useful conceptual resources for approaching the Pistorius case. Sport media must incorporate "additional information, aesthetic or emotional in nature, which allows a particular sport to offer its audience more than mere athletic action."[22] The use of disability for emotive appeal has long been criticized in disability media studies.[23] In her account of superheroes and other stereotypes of disability in South Africa, Kathleen McDougall observes that "[n]arratives about disability are often predictable, and disability is often portrayed in a homogenous way."[24] The image of the "supercrip" in particular has been criticized by various disability theorists for dominating representations of the disabled athlete[25] and further for offering a problematic image of disability that cannot be so readily achieved in the general population.[26] The valorized image of the disabled sporting superstar is especially apt and rich for signifying the supercrip, as ex-Paralympian and scholar Danielle Peers explains from her own experience:

> I read the newspaper articles and press releases that others have written about me. I read my own grant applications, speeches and business cards. I read myself defined, in each of these, by one word: not crip, queer, athlete, activist, student, woman or lesbian, but Paralympian. I read my entire life story transformed into that of The Paralympian.[27]

As Peers evocatively explains:

> I see my origins declared, not at the moment of my birth, but at some tragic moment of my physical disablement. I read my new coherent life

narrative: my salvation from the depths of my disability by the progressive, benevolent empowerment of sport. . . . I am the heroic Paralympian: pedestal, medal and all.[28]

Peers argues that this discourse offers inclusion at a hefty social cost: fame through anonymity, and empowerment through passivity. As Paralympians are filtered through the optic of the supercrip, culturally enforced passivity and the marginal status of people with disability are perpetuated.

An important point in the construction of Pistorius as supercrip occurred when he sought to compete against able-bodied athletes at the 2008 Olympic Games. Although he did not qualify, he became a popular inspirational Internet meme (figure 8.1). Images of him on the track were paired with his words: "Through birth or circumstance, some are given certain gifts. But it's what one does with those gifts. The hours devoted to training. The desire to be the best. That is at the true heart of a champion."

In their astute account of the "cyborg anxiety" Pistorius's technology-enablement provoked, South African scholars Leslie Swartz and Brian Watermeyer argue that the idealizing discourse of supercrip is

> about some hope of a fantasy redemption from the "horror" of occupying the bottom-most rung of a social power and desirability hierarchy; it is about a sop to those who may be less fortunate but yet are inspiring. It is definitely not part of this script for one such "inspiring" character to enter the fray on (at least legally) equal terms and prove himself to be stronger, fitter, better than his well-shaped competitors.[29]

Presaging what was to come, they conclude that "the result is a confused flurry of gatekeeping, not only in top flight athletics but in defence against the cascading implications for body culture and othering which emanate from this peculiar situation."[30] The twists and turns in the cultural script of supercrip as adapted for Pistorius are explained by the late Australian broadcaster, writer, comedian, and media commentator Stella Young, responding to his sentencing in late 2014. Young contended that, in effect, Pistorius was a "cultural production," a neat disability narrative that got messy:

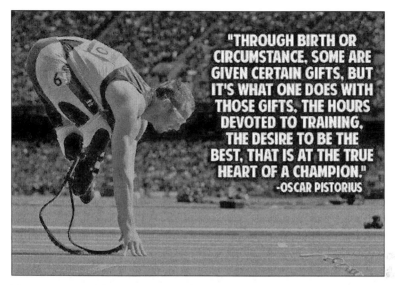

"THROUGH BIRTH OR CIRCUMSTANCE, SOME ARE GIVEN CERTAIN GIFTS, BUT IT'S WHAT ONE DOES WITH THOSE GIFTS, THE HOURS DEVOTED TO TRAINING, THE DESIRE TO BE THE BEST, THAT IS AT THE TRUE HEART OF A CHAMPION."
-OSCAR PISTORIUS

Figure 8.1. Meme featuring an image of Pistorius about to begin a sprint, with the above quotation superimposed.

This was a man who had seemingly transcended disability. He competed in both the Paralympic and Olympic games, effectively desegregating the Olympics. He sparked debate about whether the carbon fibre prosthetics he used were, in fact, better than human legs.[31]

As Young suggests:

> [Pistorius] reframed the way we thought about the disabled body. He was the ultimate supercrip. And we all love a good "overcoming" narrative, don't we? We like our disability stories nice and tidy. We're either heroes or victims, and we struggled when Pistorius suddenly proved to be neither.[32]

Young's irony plays to an international audience, indeed potentially an alternative global popular culture that embraces disability and diversity. Her supple use of "we" critiques the figure of the supercrip and intense emotional investments in Pistorius.

With the lines of this potent critique of disability, sport, and media sketched out, we now return to the consideration of how their dynamics unfold globally, as they do in the case of Pistorius. That is, what are the relationships between local or national popular cultures, in their historical and cultural specificity, and global popular cultures? What are the meanings and social functions of disability in these various dynamics of popular cultures? How much of Pistorius's anchoring in the political economy and cultural dynamics of South African society and disability has seeped into the international realm? With Pistorius, there is clearly a nice fit between the hyper-masculine, Paralympian supercrip and dominant values of sporting heroes internationally. Yet what are the emergent, subaltern discourses also circulating in global popular cultures, such as the alternative readings of Pistorius produced by disability activists and scholars, from the time of his ascension as Paralympian, or by feminists, following his killing of Steenkamp?

One handy way of condensing and illuminating these questions, which operate at the horizon of media and disability studies, is to consider Bishnupriya Ghosh's concept of the "global icon."[33] Ghosh argues that figures like Phoolan Devi (the "bandit queen" who rose from a life of crime to the Indian Parliament), Arundhati Roy (the novelist and activist), and Mother Teresa are paradigmatic examples of "contemporary global icons":

> highly visible public figures whose symbolically dense images and lives
> circulate at high speed in transnational (televisual, cinematic, print, oral,
> and digital) networks ... cultural phenomena we see every day but mostly
> dismiss as so many commodities fleetingly present in our lives. Until war
> breaks out over images.[34]

As Ghosh suggests, "As key signifiers of collective aspiration, icons that erupt into social phenomena provide further evidence of embattled responses to global modernity amid intensifying global interconnections."[35] When his star was shining brightly in the firmament, Pistorius very much operated as this kind of global icon, well suited to the age given the symbiosis of global media and sport. Yet it is unclear for many audiences the kind of social relations of disability that the iconic Pistorius served: namely, a social imaginary of disability that is "disabling" rather than "enabling"—to use the common shorthand.

The politics of disability in the case of Pistorius come to light in the inevitable phase when celebrity courts ruinous scandal. When "icon-ocrises" occur, we have an important opportunity to read such icons as "social hieroglyphics," illuminating the "social relations they constitute or destroy."[36] As we shall see, this is certainly the case with Pistorius, where idolatry is followed by iconoclasm—as his image is reviled and disavowed. Pistorius's rise and fall as covered in the mainstream media and through user-generated content provides a fascinating case study of the evolving norms of disability and media—in which journalists and the public make varying degrees of effort to recognize and deal with ste-reotypes of disability. Yet, all too powerfully, we find a fascination with disability and the still-dominant discourses in which it is either an ob-ject of fear, revulsion, and disempowerment, or something exceptional, inspirational, and heroic.

Like many stars, Oscar Pistorius's rise to fame had long been shad-owed by notoriety.[37] However, this infamy was mostly to do with the peculiar rules laid down for how athletes with disability should play fair. Such rules were tricky to apply to Pistorius, as he pioneered the use of new technology in track and field, generating controversy by his use of carbon-fiber prosthetics, which earned him the moniker "Blade Run-ner." Technology has become increasingly important to disability and is also a vexed issue in contemporary sport, where there are frequent arguments about the "unfair" advantage it is believed to give particular athletes. Pistorius had his fair share of detractors, both those who iden-tify as non-disabled as well as disabled, who criticized the extra edge his prosthetic limbs provide him.

Pistorius's bid to compete in the 2008 Beijing Olympic Games was denied because of a ruling by the world track-and-field body, the In-ternational Association of Athletics Federations, that his blades gave him an unfair advantage.[38] The ban was overturned by the Court of Arbitration for Sport,[39] but Pistorius was unable to make the quali-fying time needed—his best time of 46.25 seconds being outside the Olympic requirement of 45.55 seconds, as well as behind four other South African aspirants.[40] The crowning pinnacle of his sporting ca-reer thus far has been his pioneering dual-Olympics performance in the 2012 London games. Pistorius had been selected to compete in the

2012 London Paralympics, as a member of the South African team, and also sought to qualify for the 2012 London Olympics. Ultimately, he failed to record an adequate time for the individual 400-meter event. Despite this, because he qualified for the 4 x 400-meter relay team, the South African Sports Federation and Olympic Committee also picked him for the individual 400-meter event.[41] Perhaps not surprisingly, Pistorius's historic runs in the London Olympics and Paralympics did not exactly mark a watershed in the *cordon sanitaire* between the two events—rather they were accompanied by considerable controversy.[42] The most dramatic, controversial, and troubling events for Pistorius, however, lay off the sporting field.

Breaking the Icon

In the early hours of Valentine's Day 2013, Pistorius shot and killed Reeva Steenkamp. The 26-year-old was slain in the bathroom of Pistorius's house, located in the Silver Lakes gated community, outside of Johannesburg. Police took him into custody, and by the next day, news of Steenkamp's death and the revelation that Pistorius had been charged with murder spread around the world. In its aftermath, journalists sought to make sense of the latest development in his celebrated yet controversial life.

Early accounts typically followed the well-established pattern of Pistorius as hero, overcoming his disability. This can be seen in *Guardian* journalist Owen Gibson's article entitled "Oscar Pistorius: Athlete Who Overcame Disability to Become a Global Star":

> Not only has he transcended the world of the Paralympics, even while helping the movement grow to unprecedented heights, Pistorius is one of a rare handful of athletes to transcend the world of sport. From the moment it was confirmed that he would become the first double amputee to compete in both the Olympic and Paralympic Games, his place in history was assured.[43]

As well as his successes, crowned by his great victories in the 2012 London Paralympics and Olympics, Gibson provided a typical presentation of Pistorius as an important figure in society's embrace of disability:

In his native South Africa, he is considered one of the country's biggest sporting heroes and his ability to bridge the worlds of disabled and non-disabled sport, as well as his eloquence in fostering a shift in attitude among those confronted with his talent, have seen him twice named in *Time* magazine's list of the 100 most influential people in the world.[44]

As his fame grew, not only had Pistorius been at the heart of debates around technology in sport, but he had also been at the epicenter of deeply unsettling shifts and concerns about where disability as a category, and people with disabilities, fit into society.[45] In this light, not only did Steenkamp's death represent a "further tragic, dramatic turn"[46] in the relatively short life of Pistorius thus far; it unleashed in the media a wide range of conflicting, disturbing ideas and emotions about disability.

A relatively rare early critique was provided by South African disability leader, activist, and critical thinker Eddie Ndopu, who posed the question: "[H]ow has the construction of Oscar Pistorius as the personification of inspiration porn garnered public sympathy in reference to the first degree murder charges levelled against him?"[47] Ndopu argued that the supercrip myth ironically assisted Pistorius: "The reality that Oscar may have shot and killed his girlfriend seems almost too ludicrous of a probability for many people to fathom because for Oscar to have 'overcome' the so-called tragedy of disability means that, surely, he must be in possession of a positive disposition that (literally) enabled him to do so in the first place."[48] Ndopu contended that we can clearly see ableism at work in the reactions to Pistorius's arrest, revolving around the fact that "many people don't conceive of Oscar as an active agent in his own life"—that, in effect, "off the track, compulsory able bodiedness outperforms him."[49] For Ndopu, much of the response to the charges leveled against Pistorius was shaped by a desire to "deflect attention away from Oscar as a crip with agency and direct blame to external factors," what he saw as "psychosocial strategies" to "salvage Oscar's constructed image."[50] According to Ndopu, "what cannot be salvaged is the death of Reeva Steenkamp." As such, Ndopu understood the "real tragedy" as the "erasure of her life in the public discourse framing her murder," contending that there is "not much wiggle-room in the media to honor her memory without centralizing Oscar."[51]

Ndopu's analysis is very helpful in exploring the other dominant way that Pistorius's role was imagined—as "just another South African story." That is, the case of Pistorius shooting Steenkamp was very likely a grievous mistake that could easily occur because of the violent nature of South African society and the widespread possession of firearms and other weapons for the purpose of self-defense. This was the view taken by many South African journalists. It was also the cultural "script" widely relied upon internationally, infamously in a widely read, controversial article published in *Time*, which discussed "the killer's defense: that Steenkamp was the tragic victim of a racially splintered society in which fear and distrust are so pervasive that citizens shoot first and ask questions later."[52] *Time* journalist Alex Perry opened the article by posing the questions raised by "the murder scene itself":

> a locked bathroom within a fortified mansion in an elite enclave surrounded by barbed wire, in a country where more than half the population earns less than $65 a month and killings are now so common that they reach the highest echelons of society and celebrity. Why is gun violence so prevalent in South Africa? Why is violence against women so common?[53]

Lamenting the South African "culture of violence" borne out in so many tales of violence elicited by the Steenkamp and Pistorius episode, Perry discerned a "moral to these South African stories":

> A nation whose racial reconciliation is even today hailed as an example to the world is, in reality, ever more dangerously splintered by crime. And inside this national disintegration, however small and well-defended South Africans make their laagers, it's never enough. Father rapes daughter. Mother poisons sons. Icon shoots cover girl.[54]

That Pistorius was embroiled in these dark vicissitudes meant the extinguishment of a grand source of hope. As Perry declaimed in purple prose:

> In South Africa, Pistorius' achievements resonated deepest of all. In a nation obsessed by disadvantage, he was the ultimate meritocrat, a runner with no legs who ignored the accidents of his birth to compete against the best. Many South Africans no doubt would have seen his color be-

fore anything else. But for some, he existed, like Mandela, above and beyond South Africa's divisions. He had outraced the past and symbolized a
hoped-for future. . . . With Pistorius' arrest for Steenkamp's murder, South
Africa's dreams collided with its reality.[55]

The rub, for Perry, was that Pistorius could not escape his mooring in
South African settler culture:

> Pistorius doesn't dispute that he killed Steenkamp. Rather he contends
> his action was reasonable in the circumstances. The essence of Pistorius'
> argument is unyielding defense of his laager.[56]

Fusing race, disability, class, and violence, Perry's article drew a fu-
rious rebuke from many writers in South Africa and elsewhere. One
such critic, T. O. Molefe, argued that Perry relied upon "pre-existing,
gummed-together narratives about South Africa that, if you excise
enough contradictory information and gloss over the finer details, can
be used to explain just about any act of violence committed by rich
and middle-class South Africans."[57] In another intriguing piece, Jonny
Steinberg reflected upon "South Africa's over-involved relationship with
Oscar Pistorius":

> Something odd happened to South Africa when news of Steenkamp's
> death broke. By nightfall, the billboards of Oscar Pistorius that dotted the
> country's cities had been removed. South Africa, which had loved Oscar
> unreservedly that morning, now hated him. . . . Oscar was a symptom,
> it was said, of too many guns, of too much crime, of too much fear. . . .
> Oscar was rotten and South Africa was rotten.[58]

Steinberg suggested that to an "uncanny extent, the story the country
tells about him is precisely the story it likes to tell about itself."[59] Using
Pistorius's transcendence of disability as a metaphor for the journey of
the South African nation, he explained:

> Under apartheid, our souls were rotting. . . . Ours was a country sick with
> rancour. In 1994, as if by a miracle, we were reborn. Our capacity to make
> peace was celebrated the world over. Our president was the most-loved

human being on Earth. The sun shone on us. The world marvelled at us. Legless, we had also sprinted faster than anyone. And so, when Oscar came along, we grabbed him and owned him. Oscar was South Africa and South Africa was Oscar. Our stories were the same.[60]

Steinberg drew to our attention a story of the pain Pistorius routinely faces in slipping on his prosthetic blades to compete. Continuing with the metaphor of South Africa as disabled, Steinberg reflected:

These quiet observations are far more telling than the fast cars and the guns. Oscar is no miracle. . . . So, too, with South Africa. We are no miracle. We, too, have had to grind our stumps raw. We, too, have had to bury our shame. And so, when we heard what Oscar had done, we felt something like déjà vu. As if we always knew that his story was not quite right.[61]

Steinberg's point was that the myth-making associated with Pistorius is not helpful, either to understand Pistorius or to understand the great contradictions of South Africa, and the terrible ways in which violence is directed against women, especially. As Steinberg concluded, "It would be good if . . . South Africans could come to grasp that they are not Oscar and that Oscar isn't them."[62]

Pistorius's position in these national discourses and myths is crucial to the social function he comes to play, as a global, but also national, sporting icon. Disability also plays into these powerful social imaginaries, as does masculinity.[63] Here we have only scratched the surface of how disability plays out in these contradictory representations and debates. As the trial gathered momentum, the broad national debates—and their international reception and appropriation, represented by Perry's piece, among other commentary—took a new twist, as disability was prominently and precisely deployed.

Defenses of Disability

Amid the debate on the social meanings of Pistorius's actions and fall from grace, much international media continued to use his celebrity moniker "Blade Runner." Throughout the case, it was standard for even more considered journalism to refer to him via the icon of his prostheses.[64] What is much more interesting, however, is not the rehashing of the "Blade Runner" conceit, rather the ways in which Pistorius's prostheses figured in the juridical and media discourses of his trial.

In the initial phase, attention centered on the evidentiary potential of his prostheses. There was discussion of whether Pistorius would have found it difficult to quickly fit his prostheses in order to confront the perceived intruder. In his defense submission, he drew attention to the fact that he was without his prostheses, and that this added to his fear and belief that he had surprised an intruder, and so led him to use his gun:

> 4.5 The discharging of my firearm was precipitated by a noise in the toilet which I, in my fearful state, knowing that I was on my stumps, unable to run away or properly defend myself physically, believed to be the intruder or intruders coming out of the toilet to attack Reeva and me.[65]

Pistorius advanced his testimony concerning his lack of prostheses as evidence that, while he admitted killing Steenkamp, the deed was not premeditated. As Judge Masipa noted, this was one of the "common cause" facts (not disputed by the state), thus:

> —on 14 February 2013 shortly after 3 in the morning, screams were heard from the accused's house;
> —that the accused, while on his stumps, fired four shots at the toilet door;
> —that at the time the shots were fired the deceased was inside the toilet.[66]

After Pistorius shot at the person he believed to be the intruder, he went back to the bedroom and realized that Steenkamp was absent. He returned to the bathroom, but the door was locked. After returning to the bedroom, and screaming for help, he then "put on his prostheses, returned to the bathroom and tried to open the door by kicking it."[67] Though the use of the prostheses was not a central issue in his charges, they did figure in other aspects of the proceedings. At one point, for instance, defense advocate Barry Rioux had argued that it would be difficult for Pistorius to fly overseas: "Roux told the magistrate that Pistorius could not even pass through airport security without his prosthetic legs—and thus his identity—being detected."[68] As the proceedings gathered momentum, the prostheses receded into the background of the juridico-media terrain. Instead, Pistorius's disability figured in a different way, involving a much more explicit challenge to the charge of murder, based on a matter of enduring and cultural and philosophical debate: the relation of disability to reason.

This issue was intimated in the plea: namely, that Pistorius's impairment, especially without his prostheses, exacerbated his vulnerability due to his disability. This led to the heightened anxiety and fear that caused him to defend himself with a gun—a "fight" rather than "flight" response. Judge Masipa accepted that someone with an anxiety disorder could easily feel anxious when faced with danger; further, that it is "also understandable, that a person with a disability such as that of the accused would certainly feel vulnerable, when faced with danger."[69] However, she questioned why it would be reasonable if "without further ado, they armed themselves with a firearm when threatened with danger."[70]

Thus, in her judgment, Judge Masipa proceeded to apply the "reasonable person" test to gauge whether his conduct constituted negligence (and so supported the charge of culpable homicide). Masipa drew on case-law precedent, suggesting "a touchstone of the reasonable person of the same background and educational level, culture, sex and race of the accused."[71] She discussed the argument by the defense that the "accused's disability, among other things rendered him vulnerable hence his reaction that morning when he armed himself with a firearm and that therefore he could not be found guilty of negligence."[72]

Ultimately, Judge Masipa rejected the argument, noting that "vulnerability is not unique as millions of people in this country can easily fit into that category."[73] In her view, then, it was necessary to examine the circumstances of each case to consider its implications. In the process, she considered, and rejected, a much more common argument in South Africa (and elsewhere) that the prevalence of violence authorizes use of firearms. In Pistorius's case, his defense counsel argued that he grew up in a "crime-riddled environment and in a home where his mother was paranoid and always carried a firearm."[74] In response, Judge Masipa accepted that this was certainly an explanation, but not an excuse, pointing out that "[m]any people in this country experienced crime or the effects thereof, directly or indirectly at some time or another . . . but they have not resorted to sleeping with firearms under their pillows."[75] Similarly she was not persuaded that "a reasonable person with the accused's disabilities in the same circumstances, would have fired four shots into that small toilet cubicle."[76] Rather, she took the view that "a reasonable person with the accused's disability and in his position, would have foreseen that if he fired shots at the door, the person inside the toilet might be struck and might die as a result."[77] This was a key reason adduced by Masipa for finding Pistorius guilty of the charge of culpable homicide.[78]

The representations, uses, and reasoning of disability in Pistorius's trial have wide-ranging implications. Here we have discussed the way that the poetics of the prosthesis not only play a role in how he fashioned and established himself as a global sporting icon, but also provide meanings to prop him up, as he and his defense team crafted and revised his narratives—athlete, lover, friend, star, and accused—before the court and the tribunal of the media. Yet, as we have also elaborated, the representational work of pressing disability into the service of defense involves deep, contradictory issues at the heart of identity, action, and reason.

As well as these narratives, there is also the striking and complex affective and visceral dimension of how Pistorius behaved at a much more unconscious level throughout the trial. When he finally testified, he described his panic attacks and nightmares since Steenkamp's death as part of his apology to her family. As he did so, he cried. Elsewhere during the trial, Pistorius's reactions taken as a lack of composure were widely commented upon. On day six of the trial, for instance, forensic pathologist Geert Saayman, who conducted the autopsy on Steenkamp, testified that Pistorius had opened fire with expanding bullets "designed to cause maximum tissue damage."[79] As the pathologist spoke, "Pistorius was bent double in the dock, hands on his ears as if trying to block out the words, and violently sick."[80] Pistorius also vomited on day nine, when "gruesome images of Steenkamp shortly after her death were inadvertently shown to the packed courtroom."[81] As we shall see in the next section, these narratives, claims, signs, and affects associated with Pistorius and disability generally are not just issues for the legal profession, or established (if fraying) institutions of media. Indeed these turn out to be compelling issues for global popular culture, especially through participatory digital media.

"Playing the Crip Card"

Participatory digital media were a prominent, crucial, and fascinating element of the Pistorius affair. Initially, ordinary media users took to social media to make sense of the terrible turn of events when the news of Steenkamp's death broke. Imbued with poignancy, after the fact of her death, at 10:37 p.m. the previous night, Steenkamp had tweeted, "What do you have up your sleeve for your love tomorrow? #getexcited #ValentinesDay."[82] Steenkamp's last words were retweeted in sadness, anger, and sick humor thousands of times. Before long, a collective struggle around Pistorius as a cultural production took place on Facebook and Twitter.

As journalists and commentators dissected the image of disability previously conveyed by the figure of Pistorius and how it was being rewritten as a defense, a number of Pistorius-related trending topics dominated Twitter, initiating important conversations around disability in sport, media, popular culture, and society in general. A popular article on these issues was published in the *Washington Post* and drew a strong response from disabled Twitter users as well as many retweets. The author, Fred Barbash, argued that despite claiming he was not disabled for years, Pistorius used disability as a defense throughout his trial, describing the strategy as "audacious."[83] Barbash argued that everyone, including the trial judge, was asking "why didn't he just seek help?" when he thought there was an intruder in his home. In order to answer this question, according to Bardash, the defense team rewrote the narrative of Oscar Pistorius:

> The answers to that question were critical to the outcome of the trial. And the ones provided by Pistorius and his lawyers came more clearly into focus as the judge recounted them—and they all were excuses, all tied to disabilities of one form or the other, or disadvantage. The most obvious was Pistorius's lack of legs, which made him feel helpless that night without his prosthetics. But others were his family circumstances—their anxiety, and his, about crime in South Africa. His lawyers even argued that anxiety stemming from his disability was responsible for his erratic testimony in the trial.[84]

The story of Pistorius as the supercrip was being recast as a sham:

Far from mastering his disability, a defense psychiatrist suggested, the disability came to master him. The initial surgery to remove his legs when he was 11 months old was a "traumatic assault" that left him with an "anxiety disorder." Pressure growing up to pretend the disability was not crippling further scarred young Oscar.[85]

The notion was embraced on Twitter, with users describing the defense strategy as "playing the crip card," Pistorius himself as a "hypocrite," and the whole event as a "sad story of how Pistorius went from denying he was disabled to using it as a key part of his defense."[86]

The idea that Pistorius was picking and choosing when to emphasize his disability and that the whole defense was an offensive sham against the able-bodied, who had been duped into believing him (and by extension all people with disability), appeared in other op-eds and responses in user comments online. Take, for example, the moment when probation officer Annette Vergeer argued that prison would "break" Pistorius and he should instead be given a suspended sentence, community work, therapy, and correctional supervision.[87] Vergeer argued that his disability could not be accommodated in prison, while prosecution lawyers argued for prison time as an appropriate punishment for his crime. In response, a comment (from the poster Fred again) suggested the possibility that Pistorius was "playing the disability card":

> To point out in this way that there is no facility to cater for the accused's disability is to argue either that disabled people need special treatment (and this may not be true, such as in Pistorius' case); or to argue that certain categories of disability should excuse from prison (i.e. that disabled people should be treated "differently"). It is hard to see how these arguments square with the empowerment and normality messages of the [International Paralympic Committee], nor with Pistorius' own insistence that he is as powerful and capable a human being as Olympic sprinters. Guilty as he is of homicide, if he doesn't go to prison, what will that say about the apologetics of disability?[88]

Fred's comment raises several contradictions that surround the Paralympian as supercrip as discussed earlier in this chapter.

There is much more to be explored concerning how participatory media became entwined with, and indeed constitutive of, the discourses, tropes, and frames of disability as the Pistorius case unfolded.[89] Social media, in particular, were prominent at all key points of the affair. So, in October 2014, when news of Pistorius's five-year sentence—and its potential translation to just ten months behind bars—was handed down, the Paralympian again became a quickly trending topic on Twitter with a particularly voracious #nojustice response. In December 2015, there was the opposite reaction to the news that the South African appeals court had overturned the earlier verdict of manslaughter and found Pistorius guilty of murder.[90] What we wish to emphasize in our brief discussion here is the way that social media provided a platform for a range of interested people across the world—though clearly concentrated in particular regions, such as the U.S.—to engage with and debate the events and meanings of the Pistorius affair. This disability aspect of media and popular culture has been recognized in various studies,[91] but its precise nature and dynamics require further investigation. What we can suggest is that the Pistorius affair shows how such "hashtag" publics and politics[92] form, and re-form, around events that are the focus of intense media attention. Their bearing is global, but the obvious analysis of them can be misleading. Without further investigation, for instance, we know little about how different sections of South African publics— Twitter-invested, and otherwise—interact and participate in the conversation[93] and, especially, how they fit into the global publics, and global popular, that emerge around Pistorius's fatal and fateful actions.

Conclusion

If nothing else, the Oscar Pistorius affair shows that disability matters, in all sorts of ways. In particular, as we have sought to show in this chapter, disability is a key to unlocking the meanings, practices, structures, and power relations of society. To understand contemporary life, its struggles, pleasures, controversies, crime, justice, and death, we need to critically acknowledge and explore disability. To do this, in turn, we need tools, concepts, and research that tackle the cultural dimensions of disability, such as those we find featuring prominently in popular global media.

There are many different interpretations of the Pistorius affair, most evidently those varied and contestatory stances and interventions offered by South Africans. We have acknowledged and engaged with only a small number of these here. Similarly, we have come to grips with only a tiny part of the social relations of disability in South Africa. We have made some effort to do so, however, because we feel that the emerging, global work on disability and media—long overdue as it is—needs to constitute itself in such international contexts. This is especially important given the geopolitical coordinates of the academic disciplines and institutions that support and shape such work. The Pistorius affair is notable for the way it was received in global media, especially as it was circulated, shared, and commented upon via online and social media platforms, and in the participatory cultures associated with these, that, in relation to some countries and cultures, have been well studied. The relative visibility of these, for us, living in Australia, and experiencing the influence of Anglo-American disability and media studies, should not narrow our focus, or that of others, obscuring the complicated and rich dynamics that shape social life, normalcy, and culture all around the world.

ACKNOWLEDGMENTS

In memoriam: Stella Young (1982–2014), a great Australian media analyst, broadcaster, comedian, and activist. Katie acknowledges the support of the Australian Research Council for her Discovery Early Career Researcher award (DE130101712), and Gerard gratefully acknowledges the support of the Australian Research Council for his Future Fellowship project on Disability and Digital Technology (FT130100097), for their research and writing of this paper.

NOTES

1 *S v. Pistorius* (CC113/2013) ZAGPPHC 793 (12 September 2014), South African Legal Information Institute, www.saflii.org.

2 Barnartt and Altman, *Disability and Intersecting Statuses*; Garland-Thomson, *Extraordinary Bodies*; McRuer, *Crip Theory*; Rodan, Ellis, and Lebeck, *Disability, Obesity and Ageing*.

3 We here note the problematic nature of such racial population group categories, but these remain the official statistical concepts; in addition, there are numerous issues to be raised concerning the conceptualization of disability in the South African statistics. Statistics South Africa, *Census 2011: Profile of Persons with Disabilities in South Africa* (Pretoria: Statistics South Africa, 2014), http://beta2.statssa.gov.za.

4 Statistics South Africa, *Census 2011*, xiii.

5 See, for instance, Jones, *Psychiatry, Mental Institutions.*

6 Seedat et al., "Violence and Injuries in South Africa."

7 Watermeyer et al., *Disability and Social Change.*

8 Republic of South Africa (RSA), *Constitution of the Republic of South Africa.* No. 108 of 1996, *Statutes of the Republic of South Africa*, 1996, www.gov.za.

9 Carolyn Raphaely, "Disabled Inmates in Oscar Pistorius Prison Speak Out against Poor Treatment," *Guardian*, October 22, 2014; Carolyn Raphaely, "The Parallel Universe in Kgosi Mampuru: Inmates with Disabilities Speak," *Daily Maverick*, October 22, 2014.

10 Mitchell and Snyder, "Representation and Its Discontents."

11 Ibid., 215.

12 Miller, *Global Popular Culture.*

13 In this paper, we especially draw on Graeme Turner's account in his *Understanding Celebrity*, 2nd ed. (Los Angeles: Sage, 2014). We also draw on the wide range of work on celebrity and disability, including: Garland-Thomson, *Extraordinary Bodies*; Gerard Goggin and Christopher Newell, "Fame and Disability: Christopher Reeve, Super Crips, and Infamous Celebrity," *M/C Journal* 7, no. 5 (2004), http://journal.media-culture.org.au; P. David Howe and Andrew Parker, "Celebrating Imperfection: Sport, Disability, and Celebrity Culture," *Celebrity Studies* 3, no. 3 (2012): 270–282; Liz Giuffre, "#IsItOk to Be a Celebrity (Disabled) Comedian?: Approaching Disability with Adam Hills' Television Programme, *The Last Leg*," in Daniel Jackson, Caroline E. M. Hodges, Mike Molesworth, and Richard Scullion (eds.), *Reframing Disability?: Media, (Dis) Empowerment, and Voice in the 2012 Paralympics* (New York and London: Routledge, 2014), 66–78.

14 Connell, *Southern Theory*; Grech and Soldatic, *Disability in the Global South*; Soldatic and Grech, "Transnationalising Disability Studies"; Soldatic and Meekosha, *The Global Politics of Impairment.*

15 Barker and Murray, "Disabling Postcolonialism"; Campbell, *Contours of Ableism*; Chapman, "Colonialism, Disability, and Possible Lives"; Sherry, "(Post)colonizing Disability."

16 Wheeler, "Legacies of Colonialism."

17 Brabazon, *Playing on the Periphery.*

18 Hutchins and Rowe, *Sport beyond Television*; Hutchins and Rowe, *Digital Media Sport.*

19 Abbas and Erni, *Internationalizing Cultural Studies*; Goggin and McLelland, *Internationalizing Internet Studies*; Shome, "Post-colonial Reflections."

20 Nordenstreng and Thussu, *Mapping BRICS Media.*

21 E.g., Stadler, "Media and Disability."

22 Bertling and Schierl, "Disabled Sport," 41.

23 Barnes, "Disabling Imagery"; Haller, *Representing Disability*; Riley, *Disability and the Media.*

24 McDougall, "'Ag Shame' and Superheroes," 398.

25 Peers, "(Dis)empowering Paralympic Histories"; Silva and Howe, "The (In)validity of Supercrip Representation."

26 Ellis, "The Voice Australia (2012)"; Haller and Ralph, "Disability Images in Advertising"; Quinlan and Bates, "Dances and Discourses of (Dis)Ability."

27 Peers, "(Dis)empowering Paralympic Histories," 654.

28 Ibid.

29 Swartz and Watermeyer, "Cyborg Anxiety," 190.

30 Ibid.

31 Stella Young, "Disability and the Pistorius Sentencing Farce," *ABC News*, October 23, 2014, www.abc.net.au.

32 Ibid.

33 Ghosh, *Global Icons*.

34 Ibid.

35 Ibid., 5–6.

36 Ibid., 12. See also 104ff.

37 Pistorius, *Blade Runner*.

38 Raf Casert, "IAAF Rules Amputee Oscar Pistorius Ineligible for Olympics," *New York Times*, January 14, 2008, www.nytimes.com.

39 Joshua Robinson and Alan Schwarz, "Olympic Dream Stays Alive, on Synthetic Legs," *New York Times*, May 17, 2008, www.nytimes.com.

40 Paolo Bandini, "Olympics: Oscar Pistorius Fails to Make South Africa's Team for Beijing," *Guardian*, July 18, 2008, www.theguardian.com.

41 BBC Sport, "Pistorius to Run at London 2012," *BBC Sport*, July 4, 2012, www.bbc.co.uk.

42 Burkett, McNamee, and Potthast, "Shifting Boundaries in Sports Technology"; Smith, "The Blade Runner."

43 Owen Gibson, "Oscar Pistorius: Athlete Who Overcame Disability to Become a Global Star," *Guardian*, February 14, 2013, www.theguardian.com.

44 Ibid.

45 Cole, "Oscar Pistorius's Aftermath"; Edwards, "Should Oscar Pistorius Be Excluded"; Jespersen and McNamee, *Ethics, Dis/ability and Sports*; Norman and Moola, "'Bladerunner or Boundary Runner'?"

46 Gibson, "Oscar Pistorius."

47 Eddie Ndopu, "Oscar Pistorius: Salvaging the Super Crip Narrative," *Feminist Wire*, February 19, 2013, thefeministwire.com.

48 Ibid., 80.

49 Ibid.

50 Ibid.

51 Ibid.

52 Alex Perry, "Pistorius and South Africa's Culture of Violence," *Time*, March 11, 2013, http://content.time.com.

53 Ibid.

54 Ibid. "Laager" is a South African term for an encampment, especially formed or protected by a circle of wagons.

55 Ibid.

56 Ibid.

57 T. O. Molefe, "Myth of the Black Bogeyman," *Cape Times*, March 7, 2013, 13.

58 Jonny Steinberg, "Oscar Pistorius: The End of the Rainbow," *Guardian*, May 24, 2013, www.theguardian.com.

59 Ibid.

60 Ibid.

61 Ibid.

62 Ibid.

63 Anna Hickey-Moody makes the very suggestive argument that the "case of Oscar Pistorius is exemplary of the masculinization of carbon fibre, and the associated binding of a psychic attitude of misogyny and power to a form of violent and competitive masculine subjectivity." Anna Hickey-Moody, "Carbon Fibre Masculinity: Disability and Surfaces of Homosociality," *Angelaki* 20, no. 1 (March 2015): 139–153.

64 For example: David Smith, "Oscar Pistorius Magistrate Warns against 'Trial by Media,'" *Guardian*, June 4, 2013, www.theguardian.com.

65 *S v. Pistorius* (12 September 2014), 3285.

66 Ibid., 3288.

67 Ibid., 3307.

68 Phillip De Wet, "Oscar Pistorius Gets to Travel, and Have a Drink," *Mail & Guardian*, March 28, 2013, http://mg.co.za .

69 *S v. Pistorius* (12 September 2014), 3317.

70 Ibid.

71 *S v. Ngema*, 1992 (2) SACR 651 (D), quoted in *S v. Pistorius* (12 September 2014) 3331.

72 *S v. Pistorius* (12 September 2014), 3331.

73 Ibid.

74 Ibid., 3332.

75 Ibid., 3332–33.

76 Ibid., 3333.

77 Ibid.

78 See her restatement in ibid., 3349.

79 Claire Phipps, "Oscar Pistorius Trial: The Full Story, Day by Day," *Guardian*, October 21, 2014, www.theguardian.com.

80 Ibid.

81 Ibid.

82 Reeva Steenkamp, "What Do You Have Up Your Sleeve for Your Love Tomorrow???," *Twitter*, February 13, 2013, https://twitter.com/reevasteenkamp.

83 Fred Barbash, "The Audacity of Oscar Pistorius: The Athlete Who Said 'I'm Not Disabled' Used Disability as a Defense," *Washington Post*, September 12, 2014, www.washingtonpost.com.

84 Ibid.

85 Ibid.

86 Fiona Jarvis, "The Sad Story of How Pistorius Went from Denying He Was Disabled to Using It as a Key Part of His Defense," *Twitter*, September 18, 2014, https://twitter.com/bluebadgestyle.

87 Zjan Shirinian, "Jail Would 'Break' Pistorius, Court Told," *Inside the Games*, October 14, 2014, www.insidethegames.biz.

88 Ibid., comment from "Fred."

89 See, for instance, Scheper-Hughes, "The House Gun"; Swartz, "Oscar Pistorius"; Watson, Hillsburg, and Chambers, "Identity Politics and Global Citizenship."

90 BBC News, "Oscar Pistorius Guilty of Murdering Reeva Steenkamp," *BBC News*, December 3, 2015, www.bbc.com.

91 Ellis, "The Voice Australia (2012)"; Haller, *Representing Disability*.

92 Jeffares, *Interpreting Hashtag Politics*.

93 Cf. Hyde-Clarke, *The Citizen in Communication*; Mavhungu and Mabweazara, "The South African Mainstream Press in the Online Environment: Successes, Opportunities, and Challenges"; Wasserman, *Popular Media*.

9

Autism in Translation

Temple Grandin as the Autistic Subject

TASHA OREN

Tasha Oren conducts close readings of the television documentaries *Stairway to Heaven* (Errol Morris, Bravo, 2000) and *The Woman Who Thinks Like a Cow* (Emma Sutten, BBC, 2006) and the fictionalized biopic *Temple Grandin* (Mick Jackson, HBO, 2010). These representations of Temple Grandin—prolific author, professor of animal science at Colorado State University, and famous Autist—are used to explain shifts in popular understandings of autism in the 21st century. This chapter illustrates how close attention to film style and cultural representations can be used to understand larger social shifts in the meanings of disability.

No neurological category has captured public fascination in recent years quite like autism. The classification has spawned a rich subculture of self-identified communities ("Auties" and "Aspies"), saw the emergence of the term as a shorthand for nerd culture and personality type, and proved to be a fount of memorable literary and media depictions of lovable eccentrics, oddball geniuses, and uncommunicative savants. Along with its appearance in popular texts, autism has gained currency through the emerging political and socio-cultural notion of neurodiversity and its call to expand our understanding of cognitive difference beyond and outside the framework of disability.

When considering the emergence of Autism Spectrum Disorder (ASD) as a constellation of popular discourses, Temple Grandin's gravitational pull is irresistible. Grandin, a prolific author and professor of animal science at Colorado State University, is quite simply the most famous Autist alive. Her celebrity stems not only from her remarkable career but also from her unusual ability to communicate and explain the autistic experience to the general public. First known as an animal welfare advocate and designer of livestock enclosures and slaughter plants, Grandin emphasized what she defined as her autistic affinity with animals: a capacity to perceive the environment from a cow's point of view and be alerted to anxiety-producing elements in man-made surroundings. This unique ability propelled Grandin to professional and then public attention as a human translator of the animal mind. Yet, through her autobiographical writing, media appearances, and public advocacy, she has also become a translator of the autism experience. Grandin's comparison of her everyday experience to that of an "anthropologist on Mars" (a phrase borrowed by Oliver Sacks for a book that included a profile of her) not only expresses the fundamental sense of "otherness" that so thoroughly structures the spectrum experience for many people, but also frames its communication and study as an act of cross-cultural explanation.

As I'll explore below, Grandin's function as cross-cultural translator instructively parallels popular media's engagement with autism in the last three decades. Much of Grandin's participation in discourses about the spectrum has been on her own authorial terms—and much of the scholarly work about her has rightly focused on her own work.[1] Indeed, Ralph James Savarese suggests that Grandin's presence has been so central as to overshadow nearly all other Autists' experiences.[2] Yet I take up Grandin here as herself the subject of representation during a period when popular understandings and the cultural visibility of autism was shifting radically. The essay highlights three distinct stages of popular understanding of ASD and argues for media's role in what I call the instrumental approach to neurodiversity.

Before returning to "autism's cultural ambassador," however, let's briefly consider the startling change in Autism Spectrum Disorder's media presence and cultural currency in recent decades. Autism was virtually unknown outside a subset of the medical community when the seminal film *Rain Man* (Barry Levinson, 1988) named the condition for bewildered viewers; in the following years, autism (real and imagined) became a commonplace legibility-handle for a wide range of literary and media characters. Contemporary television teems with Autists, including Sheldon Cooper (*The Big Bang Theory*, CBS, 2007–present), detective Sonya Cross (*The Bridge*, FX, 2013–2014), forensic anthropologist Dr. Temperance Brennan (*Bones*, Fox 2005–present), amateur filmmaker Abed Nadir (*Community*, NBC, 2009–2014; Yahoo! Screen, 2015), FBI field agent Astrid Farnsworth[3] (*Fringe*, Fox, 2008–2013), and gifted child Max Braverman (*Parenthood*, NBC 2010–2015) among many—less differentiated—others.

The cultural vernacular of autism as stock character trait further infused contemporary iterations of familiar characters with retrospective legibility. Sherlock Holmes (*Sherlock*, BBC1, 2011–present) and Spock (*Star Trek: Into Darkness*, J. J. Abrams, 2013), for example, were recently textually recalibrated as characters whose abilities are entwined with their spectrum residency, and whose "quirky" difficulties with human behavioral norms are a reliable source of both conflict and humor.

Importantly, just as film and television texts increasingly represent people on the spectrum to so-called "neurotypical"[4] audiences, film, television, and web content have also been extremely important as tools of communication and cultural translation for viewers who are on the spectrum. Such viewers regularly turn to media texts not only for pleasure and leisure but also for guidance: on the largest autism discussion board, *Wrong Planet*, for example, participants discuss social behavior and interaction as depicted in television shows and films. On one such recent thread, "TV Shows to Learn Social Skills," various posters suggested programs from *Lie to Me* (Fox, 2009–2011) and *The Good Wife* (CBS 2009–2016)—"A good show to learn how to be assertive," declared poster Arrow—to *Seinfeld* (NBC, 1989–1998)—for its low-level depictions of chitchat and social interaction—as good texts for social modeling. Poster Stevenjacksonftw7 suggested *My Little Pony: Friendship Is Magic* (Discovery Family, 2010–present) or, as he suggested, "any kids show since they are specifically designed to teach social skills." Other discussants singled out programs that included spectrum characters as particularly helpful; as Armstrongclan described, "*Parenthood* has made a HUGE impact in my life. . . . It has taught me a lot about many life situations. Maybe not how to act during them, but more so just a deeper insight so I can understand and therefore sympathize more so." And for some, *Big Bang Theory*'s Sheldon Cooper was a useful model for "how not to treat people."[5] In this capacity, popular media function as travel companions and universal translators of often opaque neurotypical norms.[6]

As popular media emerge as crucial sites of two-way mediation across and among neurotypicals and people on the spectrum, they increasingly serve as an important locale for explanation, cross-cultural communication, translation, and mythmaking. How we got from *Rain Man* to Sheldon Cooper is a complex cultural narrative that involves both "real world" developments and their various uptakes within popular culture. Below, I consider some aspects and important turning points in this process through the mediated persona of Temple Grandin. From 2000 to 2010, Grandin was the subject of two TV documentary portraits and one fictionalized television biopic: *Stairway to Heaven, The Woman Who Thinks Like a Cow,* and *Temple Grandin.* This period, not coincidentally, also saw significant shifts in the cultural meaning of autism, as it transformed from minor curiosity to a central fascination. It was marked by highlights like the publication of Mark Haddon's remarkably popular novel *The Curious Incident of the Dog in the Nighttime* (2003), featuring an autistic narrator/protagonist; the founding of Autism Speaks (2005); the publication of Grandin's own *Animals in Translation* (2005); the release of *Mozart and the Whale* (Petter Næss, 2005), a romantic comedy whose protagonist-couple are both on the spectrum; the television debut of the aforementioned *The Big Bang Theory* (2007); the appointment of Ari Ne'eman as the first autistic member of the National Council on Disability (2009); and the debut of *Parenthood* (2010), with its explicit address of Asperger syndrome; and culminated in the controversial proposal to revise the *DSM-5*.[7]

Considering the three Grandin-centered films, as I do, in the context of autism's popular history highlights their widely disparate representational strategies, positioning, and narrative foci. This approach offers important insights not only into Grandin's role as a figure of cultural mediation but also into how the texts' approaches to rendering subjectivity and evoking audience engagement echo shifting understandings of autism as a cognitive difference. As I'll argue in what follows, the three films take on Grandin to, in turn, invoke wonder through the limits of representation, construct autism as a social (and gendered) problem, and advocate for social integration through representational politics. In these approaches, the films' changing regard of, and approach to, Grandin parallel the decade's evolving cultural approach to autism itself: from unknowable wonder, to social problem, and finally a bridgeable difference. As chronological touchstones, spanning the decade in which autism emerged as a major object of popular interest, these three films also offer a rough map of an evolving discourse. In this sense, this essay itself is a work of second-order mediation, focusing not on the autistic subject herself, but her *use* as a figure within this dynamic cultural process.

Temple Grandin as a subject of media representation is especially intriguing since much of her work is focused on communicating her own experience of the world to neurotypicals, and often her description of that experience relies on film and media as metaphors and material stand-ins for her perception. In the first chapter of *Thinking in Pictures*, for instance, she begins by declaring that images are her natural cognitive mode, "full-color movies, complete with sound, which run like a VCR tape in my head." A self-professed film fan, Grandin's description of her cognitive process also recalls cinema's claims to indexicality as she insists that she thinks only through specific, singular images—each with a particular "real world" materially unique correspondent.

Errol Morris's 2000 TV documentary *Stairway to Heaven* (produced as part of his *First Person* interview series for Bravo) approaches this aspect of Grandin's cognitive style head-on. The episode's introductory sequence opens with slow-moving and enigmatic winter scenes: an abandoned commercial trailer, a canted slow-motion shot of a train passing an industrial structure (a Colorado slaughter plant, as we later learn). Smoke bellows to the open top of the frame as Aphex Twin's telestic soundscape invites us to meditate on the desolate images' suggestive possibilities. Tilting from the shimmering sky downward, the frame settles on a holding pen; a cow's head emerges into focus, looking up and into the frame just as Temple Grandin's voice pierces through the hypnotic soundtrack: "I think in pictures." The sentence hangs momentarily as the screen goes black and the audio abruptly cuts off. The destabilizing equivalency between the cow's look into the camera and Grandin's "I" is startlingly resolved in the next shot, an extreme close-up of her face, as she continues, "Pictures is my first language and English, you know, is my second language." A close-up of a cow's head follows as Grandin intones, "When I read a book I translate it into a movie in my head, complete with pictures and sound." She goes on to elaborate on her cognitive process: she not only makes sense of the world in pictures, she can "replay" those images, repeatedly and from every angle in her mind's eye—"it's as if you took a video camera and plugged it in right here [she gestures to her forehead] and play the whole thing, real." This multidimensional recording/archiving capacity—already explicitly "translated" by Grandin for us as media—is linked immediately to a perceptual empathy that at once assembles the fragmented opening sequence and presents Grandin's cinematic seeing as a power to inhabit not only different coordinates in space, but different bodies and subjectivities. As a slow-motion and erratic point-of-view shot loops through a path in a narrow cow chute, she says, "I can be a cow going through that system, I can be a person walking up and down the catwalk . . . it's just that simple." The next, closing sequence returns us, in a black-and-white canted shot, to the holding pen outside the processing plant. "Nature is harsh," Grandin says; "a modern slaughterhouse is much more gentle than nature is. . . . When I get old and die, I'd much rather go to one of my meat-packing plants than have a lion eat my guts out."

In these first two minutes, Morris sets the terms by which he will employ Grandin's story through its sympathetic equivalence with his own long-term preoccupations: rendering meaning visually through continuous, repetitive oscillation between abstraction and specificity, and contemplation of death and mortality.[8] In this sense, Morris announces Grandin's role here not only as subject and "translator" of autistic experience but also a human cinematic system herself, and a figure through which cinema's own tendency toward the specific, the literal, and the indexical can be investigated and pushed.

The opening sequence also offers a condensed outline of the rest of the piece—roughly structured in three thematic parts marked by the simple title cards "Diagnosed Autistic," "The Squeeze Machine," and "Vatican City"—which moves both chronologically, through Grandin's life, and progressively outward from her specific experience to a meditation on death and meaning. Morris's familiar style of film footage insertion and penchant for slow-motion, contemplative shots of his subjects further invite viewers to ponder the parallels of approximation between Grandin's own process of concept-to-image reworking, and cinematic renderings of another's subjectivity—yet it also troubles this link and signals its limits. Of particular importance to this process is Morris's use of his own fabricated mediation device, the Interrotron. To encourage interview subjects to look directly at the camera lens—thus simulating a first–person address between interviewee and audience—Morris constructed a teleprompter-like device that projects his live video image directly in front of the camera trained on his subject. The interview is thus conducted while the subject maintains direct eye contact with the camera—through the image of Morris himself, projected directly in front of it. Eye contact, for Morris, "is a moment of drama. . . . We know when people make eye contact with us, look away and then make eye contact again. It's an essential part of communication."[9] However, one issue that unites most people on the autism spectrum is an intense discomfort with, even aversion to, direct eye contact. In close-ups, Grandin does not maintain eye contact with the camera/Morris/us, resting her gaze just to the side or above it instead—she is, in the language of the Interrotron, unknowable. This early slippage from Morris's reciprocal economy of the camera signals the tension that will undergird the piece as a whole, between subjectivity and representation, wonder and explanation.

In "Diagnosed Autistic," the film's first section, the initial sensory chaos, lack of control, and perception-overwhelm that characterized Grandin's early life are punctuated by a series of escalating jump cuts that explode—as she compares her cognitive field to "being in a pinball machine"—into an extended, dizzying black-and-white sequence inside a pinball machine, an extreme close-up shot, fast on the heels of a giant steel ball barreling through the machine's dinging and snapping innards. The ball is flung about as bells clang, flags pop up, and levers detonate in an oppressive cacophony. The section concludes with a black-and-white shot of Grandin, standing still but propelled forward on an airport moving sidewalk, completing the pinball analogy as the voiceover describes her younger self, being in a constant state of anxiety.

Yet the easy visual simile of experience-translation is challenged in the following section, "The Squeeze Machine," just as Grandin's own narrative employs it all the more explicitly. The section opens on a shot of a calf in a bright-red squeeze chute (a rudimentary steel enclosure that holds a cow immobile during an inoculation) as Grandin describes how she first observed cattle relax when they were placed in the squeeze chute device and convinced her aunt to place her in the same chute.[10] The next series of shots are of Grandin's bedroom, yet Morris rebuffs an easy entrance into the space; placing his camera outside the room, he cants the frame, slowly pulling forward. The effect distends the doorframe and the walls around it, reducing our open sightline into the room

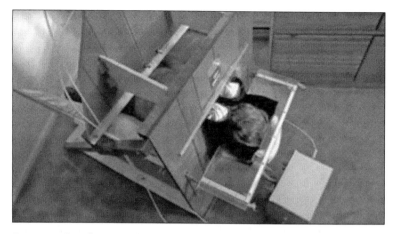

Figure 9.1. Grandin using the squeeze machine, as seen in *Stairway to Heaven*.

and positioning the viewer as a tacit observer, as if illicitly catching the goings-on. A slow-motion shot documents Grandin walking over to her squeeze machine as her voiceover continues: "And since then, working on development of more humane restraint devices, I find that if you put just the right amount of pressure on the cattle [she drops to her knees and gets inside the device] . . . and it's, like, all over their body, and it's not too tight and it's not too loose, the animal will just kind of relax." A cut now places the camera in the room and above Grandin's body, clad in a bright-red shirt, as she positions her head in the device's external rest (figure 9.1). "If you make it too tight it hurts, if you don't make it tight enough then he doesn't feel held and then he fights it." We cut to a shot below Grandin's face; it is cradled in a red headrest, and her hand extends outward, just in reach of the red control knob, as she closes her eyes. "Give in to it," Grandin tells us as she tells herself. "You gotta just give in to it." She exhales and we find ourselves no longer in her bedroom but in a dream-like, slow-moving fantasy space where Grandin, in a glowing white lab coat, moves among the cows. The image is ethereal, vintage-Morris trippy, the sky and background plains behind the pen's fence a deep void; Grandin and the cows glide and hum in warm, glowing browns and oversaturated, luminous whites. It is a vision of mysterious contentment and reverence. A close up of her fingers on the red knob follows; she holds it lightly, fingers pulsing.

Here, the effect of the visual echo of the previous shot (the calf in the bright-red chute, similarly positioned in the frame), the audio that parallels Grandin's physical experience with the cow she is describing, the off-kilter and furtive entrance of the camera into the scene, and the rhythmic pulsing of the control knob all work to destabilize, rather than clarify, our perception: do the image, sound, and movement neatly coalesce into a cross-species equivalence or mecha-sexuality? Are they riveting precisely because they don't? Are we to think of this as a moment of blissful posthuman co-being of human/animal/machine, a literal, mechanical translation, an erotic fetish? "They wanted me to give it up," Grandin's voice recalls, as an extreme close-up of her hand fills the frame, her palm lightly contracting as she adjusts the pressure on the knob, partially seen at the left side of the frame's edge. "They just made up all kinds of Freudian nonsense"—her voice rises in derision here, and Morris cuts, precisely as she disdainfully intones "Freudian," to a reframing of the previous shot. Now, the gleaming red knob fills the frame's center, with Grandin's practiced fingers nimbly pumping its side. "And I wouldn't give it up, and I'm glad I didn't."

This all-encompassing hug—that must enclose just so, too tight and it hurts, too loose and we fight it—may well remind us of cinema itself, and the work of making meaning. Morris's initial staging of the scene in the register of autoerotic practice, just as Grandin derisively dismisses this reading, further suggests the "standard" psychoanalytic approaches as insolvent in the face of such rich relational capability.

Morris's style here is further probing the question of fit as it highlights the oscillation between merging and tension in his visual conveyance of Grandin's narrated experience. As his images both bolster and undermine her account, we are caught in circles of slipping approximations and adjustments: Morris's representational strategy offers both the machine and Grandin's experience in it as simultaneously collapsible into familiar framework and beyond simile. Here the suggestive autoerotic register is both a "fix" (an explanation) and a mere counterfeit of intimacy and meaning—the fullness of which we have little access to.

In the sequence that follows, *Stairway to Heaven* draws together Grandin's retelling of her fascination with the Ames distorted room[11] and related optical illusions with an explanation of her logical thinking and need to convert words and concepts into pictures in order to "think" them. As she describes seizing on the image of a door to think through the notion of moving on and life stages, Morris pairs her narration with footage of doors opening from Alfred Hitchcock's 1945 *Spellbound*, the tale of the relationship between a psychoanalyst (Ingrid Bergman) and her repressed amnesiac patient (Gregory Peck) as she works to, as the film's opening caption proclaims, "open the locked doors of the mind" and resolve a possible murder. The sequence, ironically, is itself a fantasy and a visual translation illustrating the psychoanalytic method. Famously, the film features a Salvador Dalí–designed dream sequence and centers on the psychoanalyst's work of "translating" this dream imagery. The dizzying manifolding of multileveled translations underscores the scene's ironic recalling of Grandin's battle, recounted only minutes earlier, to keep her squeeze machine in defiance of school psychiatrists and their "Freudian nonsense."

"I wanted to find out what happens when you die. Regular religion was way too abstract . . . but the slaughterhouse was real," Grandin tells us in the opening of "Vatican City," the last, longest, and most openly contemplative section in the film. Here, the elements Morris introduced us to earlier come together: Grandin explains her slaughter plant design—using her insight into cows' perception—to minimize anxiety and create a smooth flow of movement and a painless, instant death for the cows. She argues that thinking solely in language is a key obstacle in people's ability to recognize and imagine animal subjectivity and cognition, and reiterates her belief that using animals for food is ethical as long as we "give those animals a decent life and . . . a painless death. We owe the animal respect." This section parallels Grandin's self-presentation most closely, and follows the narrative logic she presents in her own biography, which tightly links her cognitive processes, her work, and her ethics. Both the languid score and images that accompany this section's conclusion—stills of Grandin smiling, surrounded by cows; footage of her striding, content and purposeful, toward us in slow motion—enforce a sense of agreement, correspondence, and conclusive wholeness. As the section cuts to black, and the film seems to be over, Morris's own voice is suddenly heard, asking Grandin to explain naming her first ramp system design the Stairway to Heaven. The name, it turns out, was the title of a prayer penned by her blind college roommate; Grandin adjusts her face in close-up—guided by Morris's offscreen help—and reads the prayer, her face illuminated by a bright light from above, affecting celestial radiance. Here again, Morris is constructing the scene with evocative contrariness as he foregrounds his own agency and production artifice within this culminating moment of would-be transcendence. "Are you afraid of death?" Morris asks Grandin as molasses-slow-motion images of cows dreamily crossing a river appear on the screen.[12] As we return, for the last time, to an image of Grandin, facing Morris's Interrotron, his voice is heard again, off screen, asking her if she ever imagined going through the Stairway to Heaven. "Oh yeah," she replies, smiling, "many, many, many times . . . if everything's just going right . . . go through the cattle and feel a conveyer pull me in and then it'd be over with . . . if everything's working right, I wouldn't feel a thing." As promised in the film's first two minutes, we end with death, as Morris answers his own apprehension of mortality with Grandin's certitude.

While *Stairway to Heaven* frames autism in terms of wonder and difference, its interest in Grandin—even within this thematic association—remains decisively individual. In this sense, Morris's film is not about autism but about Grandin's untypical cognition and its resonant links (for Morris) with cinematic representation and sympathetic approaches to questions of translation, mortality, and faith. As an early entrant into the formation of popular understandings about autism, Morris's portrait defines Grandin as a singular persona, whose autism may frame her subjectivity, but neither explains nor determines her.

Six years later, Emma Sutton's television documentary *The Woman Who Thinks Like a Cow* would frame and interrogate Grandin's experience in a radically different way, echoing the growing cultural preoccupation with the nature of autism. Airing in 2006 as part of the BBC's *Horizon* series, the film begins and ends with Grandin among the cows. In the opening shot, she climbs over a fence into a holding pen. She walks a few steps through the muddy earth, by a group of gathering cows, and abruptly lies down as the cows move back in agitation. In a voiceover, she is heard explaining, "See, there's like two main drives, you've got fear, and you've got curiosity, they're kind of curiously afraid . . . as long as [you] don't move, they'll come up to you." And the cows do; cautiously at first, they sniff, nudge, and lumber forward, slowly encircling her. This opening sequence is notable not only in its tonal difference from the rest of the film but also because much of the film is similarly driven by two conflicting impulses as it negotiates its relationship to its subject.

The sequence that follows introduces Grandin by stressing her status as specialist and icon: "a legend in the kingdom of animal behavior . . . her followers believe Temple has a magical connection with animals," a narrator claims in voiceover, before introducing Grandin's own view that there are "similarities between my autistic mind and animal thinking." Rapidly shifting from an animal environment, the film moves to footage of Grandin signing books, giving talks, and interacting with an admiring public. Her success and celebrity is also the subject of the film's latter half, which documents her adult biography, her developing interest in cow behavior, her discovery of the benefits of the squeeze machine, and the links between her autistic cognition, her professional innovations, and her public life.

Yet the first half of the film performs a nearly opposite function, positioning Grandin not as a unique persona (as Morris's earlier profile did) but a figure on which to construct an overview of autism. Using Grandin's biography, the film's first half endeavors to provide a concise history of autism in the twentieth century, from Leo Kanner and Hans Asperger's defining observations about the children in their care, to Bruno Bettelheim's "refrigerator mothers" and Bernard Rimland's intervention toward a biogenetic understanding of autism, to contemporary approaches that focus on neurological difference and brain structure. The film's narrative strategy is to intercut Grandin's early biography with this medical history to suggest their parallel improvement and mutual emergence. Here Grandin herself, through her biography, personifies the evolution of medical understandings of autism as a narrative of progress from the early (mis)diagnostic era of child schizophrenia and retardation, to the shift from a psychoanalytical to a medicalized model, and finally to the focus on neuroscience and brain-based functions. The film's attempt to construct Grandin as both its subject and an illustration, however, forces a discordant approach that first frames Grandin's success as her "struggle" and "triumph over" autism, while her own narrative, and the film's second half, elaborate on autism as a precondition of her professional skill and identity. Moreover, its use of Grandin as a "case study" binds it to an odd representational logic that invites viewers to read incidental images of her in public (posing awkwardly for a photo or walking across a busy street) as symptomatically antisocial and isolated; as the film's narration tells us, "her struggle with autism . . . makes other people, and the realm of human relationships, a mysterious and sometimes frightening place."

Sutton's initial authoritative casting of autism as primarily about social relations, interaction, and other people—its focus on the performative and the relational—reflects autism's cultural reframing and rapidly expanding visibility in the first decade of the 21st century. As noted above, this period saw a remarkable upsurge in popular texts (memoirs, novels, and articles) about autism, and an adjustment of cultural perception, expanding from a focus on the "low functioning" child to an arching understanding of a spectrum. As popular reverberations of clinical theory about behavior, mind-blindness, and systemization shaped an emergent notion of an "autistic" skill set and interests, it also produced *social deficit* as a "core" difference and a rendition of the spectrum organized along a hierarchy of social performance.

Thus, the film's structural strategy to combine incidental footage of its subject with expert commentary about current understandings of autism produces the odd demand that Grandin "enact" and illustrate the observations made about autism—yet these moments of illustration repeatedly slip into gendered categories of difference. Her professed disinterest in "relationship-type movies," for example, is offered as one such moment of proof. Another illustration of her cultural tastes is examined to an even odder result: as an expert describes the social difficulties associated with autism—invoking a lack of "theory of mind" and the inability to read facial expressions—we watch Grandin traverse an airport. She proceeds to the ticket counter as the expert's voiceover explains that such lack of access to others' thoughts and feelings can make people "very puzzling" and sometimes "very scary." On screen, Grandin enters the airport's magazine shop and stops to regard the wall of publications. "What kind of magazines do you like reading?" the interviewer prods. "Business magazines, science magazines," Grandin replies as she peruses shelves. "How about *Discover* magazine . . . that's sorta my taste in magazines." "How about all these women's magazines?" the interviewer asks suggestively, as the camera gestures to a shelf where nearly identical bikini-clad young women smile from various covers. "I never read those," replies Grandin, "they're a bore." "What's boring about women's magazines?" asks the interviewer. Grandin pauses. "Well, I'm not typically interested in cooking and reading about [inaudible] whose marriage failed; I just find it boring." We cut to Grandin standing alone, as maudlin music cues some inherent pathos in the scene. This sequence is significant in its dubious suggestion that Grandin's disinterest in fashion or gossip—her failed femininity or gendered deficit—are symptomatic. It recalls, of course, Simon Baron-Cohen's definition of autism, which mapped it onto an "extreme male brain," as the sequence sets up the failure of gender performance as a major consequence of autism for Grandin.[13]

The film's early fixation on sociability as the "core" problem of autism, paired with its narrative framing of Grandin as a success story, also produces a synecdochic misreading of her squeeze machine. Maneuvering in the cramped quarters of Grandin's bedroom—the same bedroom where Morris staged his own scene of representational slippage six years earlier—the camera scrutinizes the contraption from all sides as Grandin demonstrates the machine's use, and then enters it:

INTERVIEWER: How often do you use this machine?
GRANDIN (SPEAKING THROUGH THE MACHINE'S HEADREST):
    About once a week.
INTERVIEWER: When you're particularly stressed?
GRANDIN: Well, usually, I'm away an awful lot, so not been using it as
    much as I'd like to.
INTERVIEWER: How long do you stay in it for?
GRANDIN: Hmm, twenty minutes [the machine sighs loudly] . . .
    it's kind of a relaxing feeling of being held, helps you to have nicer
    thoughts.
INTERVIEWER: Did you mean it helps you to feel more affection
    towards . . .
GRANDIN (INTERRUPTING THE INTERVIEWER ABRUPTLY): Yeah,
    that's right, that's right. When I was a little kid, I wanted to feel the
    nice feeling of being held, but it was just too much overwhelming
    stimulation.
INTERVIEWER: So this was a . . .
GRANDIN (INTERRUPTS): I can control it . . .

Grandin's offering of "nicer thoughts" as one helpful effect of the squeeze machine is readily assumed by the interviewer to be externally directed:

nicer thoughts and affection toward other people. Yet Grandin's reply is not primarily concerned with other people. The squeeze machine helps *Grandin* feel the physical benefits of being held—a sensation she explains as the physical approximation of affection-behavior, the hug. The sensation of firm, controlled pressure calms her mind, relaxes her body, and reduces her anxiety—a self-soothing technology that counters input-overwhelm. Grandin's assertion about her physical and mental states (and the machine's ultimate purpose) do not quite align with the interviewer's grafting of these onto the realm of the social—as a benefit to other people in Grandin's environment (and, for that instant, to the interviewer and her crew).

The Woman Who Thinks Like a Cow is especially instructive as a contemporary snapshot of autism discourse early after the turn of the century, a discourse that increasingly fixated on a lack of conventional sociability as autism's core difference and character "explainer." The film's moments of incoherence thus occur precisely when it attempts to simply yoke Grandin to this explanatory narrative—she is, after all, a public figure who is seen not only engaging audiences and individuals but also excitedly welcoming children into her home for Halloween, or maneuvering successfully in public space—while explaining her subjectivity as not sourced in a social disinterest but rather extreme sensitivity, perceptual difference, and anxiety. While in its mode of conventional documentary style, Sutton's film is radically different from Morris's exploratory portrait and meditation on the failures of representation, a comparison of the two films still yields a striking difference in conceptions of autism, from interior difference to social conventions and behavioral consequences.

Further, as a historical milestone in evolving popular understandings about autism through media portraits, *The Woman Who Thinks Like a Cow*'s initial positioning of Grandin's condition as a deficit of sociability is particularly notable when read in the context of fictional media up to that point. As Stuart Murray observed, typical media depictions of autistic characters reflected back on the "normal" world by posing the character of the autistic person in relation to/against/in comparison with a typical and non-impaired character.[14] These depictions of the Autist are thus pitched toward a "normal" audience and reflected back upon a "normal" and non-autistic world.[15]

In a 2007 *New York Times* article, "Hollywood Finds Its Disorder Du Jour," film critic Caryn James observed a marked spike in media attention to autism, which, she wrote, "has become to disorders what Africa is to social issues, the celebrity cause du jour." Speculating on the cause of autism's sudden visibility, James echoed Murray's critique, observing that it is due in part to "the nature of the disorder itself. A condition that thwarts the ability to communicate and express emotions, autism seems ready-made for symbolic use."[16] As my final example—and the third film based on Temple Grandin's biography—suggests, the project of portraying Grandin's subjectivity as a mainstream narrative outside the logic of its symbolic value for a majority culture required its own delicate process of translation.

For most of its history, narrative cinema has been hailed as an empathy machine, with its apparatus, language, narrative construction, and formal conventions all trained on conveying its audiences through the protagonist's interiority, and delivering co-feeling as a story (and, indeed, pleasure) condition. While cinema's power is in its flexible subjectivity, its adaptability to various orders and kinds of sensory mingling, and its knack for inching us toward another's experience, that power is also in its ability to stop short, fruitfully fail, and invitingly refuse, helping us recalibrate our notions of subjectivity and interrogate our own process of empathic viewership. In this sense, *Temple Grandin* offers a particularly instructive popular site for how subjectivity-difference is represented. Especially noteworthy is how the film constructs its point thematically, not through its protagonist's emotional response but through mise-en-scène and the active invitation to mediate our difference through productive construction.

Temple Grandin, which premiered in 2010 on HBO, tracks a remarkably similar path to *The Woman Who Thinks Like a Cow*; like the documentary, it divides Grandin's life into discrete stages, opening at the turning point of her arrival on her aunt's farm in Arizona, the place of discovery of her own affinity with cows and the beneficial and calming effects of the squeeze chute. From this temporal locale, the film unfolds in two distinct parts as it marks young Temple's education—flashing back to her childhood—and her postgraduate move from the Eastern, sweater-set realm of college to the mud-washed Western terrain of cows and men, including her rise to prominence as a cow-enclosure and slaughterhouse designer. The film ends with a single scene that encapsulates Grandin's role as a public advocate and "inside explainer" of autism, picturing her as she takes the mic at an autism convention and begins to relate her story to an eager audience.

As in *Stairway to Heaven*, Grandin's self-described visual cognition is the aesthetic and thematic foundation of *Temple Grandin*. The film's complex rendering of its subject as the narrative's center and sympathetic anchor sets up its investment in fabrication, mediation, and translation as it endeavors to both place Grandin in the center of its plot and express her cognitive style. As a conventionally structured narrative film, *Temple Grandin* mediates its protagonist's perceptual and affective difference, providing a kind a layered legibility for audience engagement.

Claire Danes's performance is striking for its physical and vocal approximation of Grandin herself—her rigid and angular gait, the forward flexion of her neck, the piercing vocal inflection, its flat emphatic intonation—yet Danes's performance is itself, importantly, a mediation. Her rubbery-featured expressive conveyance of fear, anger, indignation, or confusion ceaselessly communicate, mapping narratively corresponding and legible responses onto autistic sensibility—a sensibility notorious for its disconnection from conventional performance of expressive affect. Grandin's perceptual subjectivity is similarly rendered in a style that both represents her sensory input and "explains" it: remembered images and film clips flash rapidly; sounds roar into earshot or pulse menacingly; new objects are captured with an audible flash-like "click" as they are stilled to single black-and-white images in order to directly invoke the photographic process; figures of speech flash as literal images for comic effect; Grandin "morphs" into a young calf as she drops to her knees to examine a holding chute; and her ability to assess, measure, and perceive three-dimensional objects is marked by a graphic overlay of a designer's blueprint, reminiscent of the credit sequence, which marks this "builder vision" and construction aesthetic as a character motif and theme. In this sense, the film manages what Anthony D. Baker has termed the "spectacularization of autism"[17] by tilting toward the illustrative. And while this plot-driven representational strategy of perception and response is conventional, the film's management of its emotional cues and spatial staging is not.

In particular, the film's narrative relies on supporting characters' (Grandin's mother, aunt, admiring teacher, etc.) points of view and emotive responses to mark the film's emotional high and low notes. Thus, repeatedly, the "scene of empathy" as Carl Plantinga terms it, where a close-up on a character's response is emphasized not mainly to communicate emotion but to invite audience empathy, is enacted by a character in Grandin's orbit who reacts, observes, or remembers it.[18]

Most notably, the film's two distinct halves (adolescence and adulthood) both conclude with a public speech by Temple (first to her graduating class and family, and, at the film's end, to a rapt audience at an autism convention) in which she affirms her own perseverance and the supportive role of friends and family. In both, her mother's teary-eyed response marks these as the film's two climatic moments, readymade staging grounds for the audience's own outpouring of emotion.[19] This strategic setting for the story pays off as public triumphs and formal appeals to interpersonal support and collaboration also affirm the film's more interesting move toward a neurodiverse ethic. Both public culminations echo the narrative's framing of Grandin's struggle as one not with autism but human ignorance, resistance, and self-centered conformity. While her perceptual subjectivity and narrative centrality throughout the film invite its audience to engage with Grandin and take up her perspective, these two climactic moments of public address firmly relocate the viewer to the (literal) bleacher seats of an audience's perspective—we are not "with" Temple; we are her audience and part of the self-same public. Importantly, this position is also employed in the film's pre-credit opening sequence, in which Grandin steps through an Ames room and addresses the audience directly with a formal introduction: "My name is Temple Grandin and I'm not like other people." Thus, at the film's beginning, middle, and end we are brought back from any artifice of unselfing or co-feeling—addressed as other people, we are put in our place.

With this positioning of its audience and elusion of easy cues of identification, the film offers a productive move toward what rhetorician Dennis Lynch has called "the rhetoric of disappointment." As Lynch reads Grandin's book *Thinking in Pictures*, assumptions about reader empathy are instructively shown their limit, where the space of co-experience is no longer possible:

> She shows us times when she has reached her limit with others; and in the course of her story, we have many occasions to sense when we have reached our limits with her. . . . She wants instead to change the spaces within which we engage in such exchanges, to make them more flexible, more giving. She wants us to become more familiar with obstinate bodies, with irreducible complexity, and with the simple act of refusal, with a "no" that does not have to end interaction forever but that admits that no one understands exactly what is happening in every situation and that no one needs to assert authority in every situation.[20]

Similarly, the film places the bulk of its thematic weight not in the empathic meeting place of emotional sharing, but in the physical space of constructed environments. It is here that the full meaning of mediation and instrumentality as agency takes shape. The film largely avoids the familiar trope that Grandin's full emotional life is merely buried or trapped "under" her autism—and can be "rescued" through emotional connection.[21] Instead, Temple Grandin's visual style and narrative emphasis suggest the limits of empathic co-feeling as the source location of change, pointing instead to structuring actions and acceptance of difference.

Inasmuch as its storytelling traces Grandin's life as a series of overcome obstacles, the first half of the narrative is focused on the squeeze machine: its discovery, its construction, Temple's battle to keep it in defiance of various institutional alarms and "expert" opposition. As her mother reiterates the college's position, speaking to Temple's aunt, "They were very clear, no devices in her room. Is there a better way to mark her as a weirdo or an oddball?" Grandin repeatedly proclaims the squeeze machine's importance and benefit to her in the face of an institution that regards the contraption as an expression of deviance and sexually focused perversion—but her assertions have no effect. Temple triumphs with her first act of neurotypical translation: she turns to the tools of psychological framework and scientific methodology (she makes the project her class term paper) that establish the machine's utility for "everyone."

The squeeze machine is not only Grandin's own therapeutic device (so important, in fact, that she credits it publicly for her success in a graduation speech) but also a powerful conveyer for the film's central

Figure 9.2. Danes, as Grandin, constructs the squeeze machine in *Temple Grandin*.

strategy of highlighting construction, modification, mediation, and perspective shifts as working models for rethinking cognitive difference.[22]

As Morris's portrait also references, an opening door was the concrete image Grandin had used to think through notions of progression and life changes. Its usefulness as a metaphor is suggested by a beloved science teacher who first grasps her pictorially based cognition, recognizes her promise, and encourages her to pursue a career in science. Since the young Temple is confused by the abstract notion of future changes, the teacher offers her, "Think of it as a door, a door that's going to open up to a whole new world for you. All you need to do is decide to go through it." Indeed, doors and constructed openings structure the film in virtually every sequence, as well as transition us from the pre-credit sequence into the film's narrative. In the film's opening, pre-diegetic sequence Grandin first appears in a close-up, addressing the viewer directly with a self-introduction as an Ames room draws itself around her and materializes. She then walks through it, and opens a door to leave the frame—as a match cut delivers us into the diegesis with a plane door yawning open, revealing a teenage Temple, just arrived in Arizona. Notably, this motif continues to mark nearly every new scene in the film. In addition to the narrative centrality of the squeeze machine, which literally references fabrication, agency, and mediation, scenes of construction and self-made objects dominate, not only ones Temple builds herself (her aunt's gate, a rudimentary transpiration cart she constructs in high school, an Ames room model, a toy airplane) but through her placement in various sites of construction: from the chaotic schoolyard scenes where fellow students race makeshift cars, to her science teacher's workshop, to the construction site at the edge of the campus, where she climbs to mark her graduation, to the sites of half-finished feed lots, plank-laid processing plants floors, scaffold walkways, and rudimentary bridges, catwalks, and passageways that crisscross the mise-en-scène. Ad hoc refittings and adjustments thematically undergird the diegetic universe, reinforcing the film's investment in modification and co-mediation of variance.

As the film suggests, taking neurodiversity seriously, like taking its media representation seriously, must mean a critical stance that interrogates neurotypical assumptions about cultural co-habitation: first, through a perspective shift from the centrality of co-feeling to the possibilities of co-being, and second, in accepting difference as the place from which we start, where we begin to construct not only bridges and passageways but also media texts as instruments.

As I noted at the outset, Grandin's media journey from representational slippage and sensorial wonder (in *Stairway to Heaven*), to a fix of social correction and performance (in *The Woman Who Thinks Like a Cow*), and finally to agency and translation (in *Temple Grandin*), mirrors autism's changing position in our cultural imagination. As cultural ambassadors and multidirectional translators themselves, media texts are crucial to a cognitively diverse community of producers and viewers; they are our own story-instruments of mediation and connection. Moreover, in our current moment, when discourses about cognitive disorders fold smoothly into a popular culture enthralled by neuroscience as root narrative, our storytelling about interior landscapes and difference is instructive and increasingly relevant to our understanding of subjectivity and the diversity of ways we see, experience, and understand our shared culture.

NOTES

1 For an analysis of Grandin's authorial construction of autism and its relationship to political claims, see Murray, *Representing Autism*.

2 Savarese, *Reasonable People*.

3 In this science fiction show, Astrid is a doubled character who is neuronormative in one universe and autistic in another.

4 The term "neurotypical" ("NT," for short) emerged within the autistic community as the preferred term for people not on the spectrum as a replacement for "normal." Its usage thus rejects the notion that a person on the spectrum is necessarily disabled, ill, or otherwise abnormal.

5 *Wrong Planet Autism Forum*, www.wrongplanet.net (thread under "social skills and making friends"), 2013.

6 In parallel with mainstream popular media texts that depict Autists, artists/activists like Axel Brauns, Alex Plank, and Amelia (Amanda) Baggs, among many others, have used visual media to represent their own fundamental estrangement from neurotypical subjectivity, offer an alternative experience of being-in-the-world, and form social and political networks through the media they produce.

7 The *DSM-5* (the *Diagnostic and Statistical Manual of Mental Disorders*) is the official publication of the American Psychiatric Association. After a much-publicized debate, the association eliminated the stand-alone classification of Asperger's syndrome in 2013, folding it into an expanded definition of "autism spectrum disorder."

8 Like much of Morris's work, *First Person* is preoccupied with death and killing. Other episodes include ones on Sondra London ("The Killer inside Me"), about her relationship with two convicted serial killers; Saul Kent, a cryogenics promoter who stole and froze his dead mother's head; Joan Dougherty, a crime scene "cleaner"; and Gary Greenberg, on his friendship with the Unabomber; as well as several other mediations on murder victims, stalkers, criminals, and forensic experts.

9 Errol Morris, "The Fog of War: 13 Questions and Answers on the Filmmaking of Errol Morris by Errol Morris," *FLM Magazine* (Winter 2004).

10 Grandin's design consists of two large padded plywood panels, connected to a simple lever mechanism, that sweep in, wing-like, to engulf the user and produce firm pressure across her body. The amount of pressure is controlled by a red knob on the lower front of the machine.

11 The Ames room (named after its inventor, Adelbert Ames) is a built optical illusion in which a room appears to have a standard square shape but is actually constructed so that the four walls form a trapezoid (where ceiling and floor walls are not parallel but angled to almost meet at one corner). Because its actual shape is hidden, a person walking across the room appears to be drastically growing or diminishing in size with each step.

12 The scene is from the Western *Red River* (Howard Hawks, 1948).

13 Baron-Cohen, *The Essential Difference*. In this work, Baron-Cohen does make a point of distinguishing between what he terms "male brain tendencies" and male and female brains, allowing that both men and women can share such tendencies.

14 *Rain Man* is a classic example of this narrative formulation.

15 Murray, *Representing Autism*.

16 Caryn James, "Hollywood Finds Its Disorder Du Jour," *New York Times*, April 29, 2007, www.nytimes.com.

17 Baker, "Recognizing Jake."

18 Plantinga, "The Scene of Empathy."

19 Other such moments (like the funeral of Grandin's teacher) are similarly public. In a scene where Grandin is tormented by a group of sexist cowhands, who cover her truck with bloody bull testicles, her reaction is pictured in a long shot, her face obscured by the soiled and bloody windshield.

20 Lynch, "Rhetorics of Proximity."

21 This logic, as Murray and others suggested, often pervades narratives about autistic people.

22 The film offers a similar, more playful use of the Ames room. Throughout the film, Temple is misunderstood and misunderstands others, but her first academic success involves the construction and explication of the Ames room to her classmates—a literal repositioning of perspective that both resolves the problem and shifts her classmates' perspective on Temple herself.

PART V

Disability and Temporality

10

How to Get through the Day with Pain and Sadness

Temporality and Disability in Graphic Novels

SHOSHANA MAGNET AND AMANDA WATSON

Shoshana Magnet and Amanda Watson focus on two graphic memoirs, *Hyperbole and a Half*, by Allie Brosh, and *Cancer Made Me a Shallower Person*, by the late Miriam Engelberg. These comics, using text, images, and the specific affordances of the genre, allow for representations of the "temporalities of disability," which are at odds with normative expectations concerning time and productivity. Such alternate temporalities, when made evident, can become the basis for broader understanding of and greater empathy toward disability experiences.

In her groundbreaking book *Ghostly Matters*, sociologist Avery Gordon argues that the truism that life is complicated is a "fact of great analytic importance."[1] In particular, she demonstrates that lives are complicated by phenomena that are visible as well as by those that go unseen or are no longer seen. Gordon uses the term "haunting" to describe how our lives remain shaped by those aspects that may not be easily detected. For example, she shows how everything from intergenerational trauma to what feminist theorist Sharon O'Brien would call the "emotional inheritances" of our families of origin haunt our present in ways that are not immediately detectible using conventional empirical methods. In this way, Gordon argues for studying those phenomena that run beneath the surface, rendering us troubled "by things [we] sometimes have names for and sometimes do not."[2] In this chapter, we argue that narratives about disability are haunted by time and temporalities. Examining two graphic[3] narratives, *Hyperbole and a Half* (2011–2013) and *Cancer Made Me a Shallower Person* (2006), we argue that an undertheorized piece of the structure of ableism is the way that people with disabilities are both shamed and haunted by time and its passing under late-capitalist narratives obsessed with normative forms of productivity and efficiency. That is, we argue that people with disabilities are made to suffer under modern temporalities, both from a too-muchness of time and from an inability to fill time in ways that are construed as normatively productive.

In this chapter, we aim to contribute to the interdisciplinary dialogue between disability studies and media studies by examining the ways that comics move us beyond the textual and provide us with a set of images for what we call the "temporalities of disability." Of course, different understandings of disabilities produce different temporalities. For example, people living with cancer are imagined to occupy a different set of temporalities from people living with depression. In fact, capitalist temporalities can produce new categories of disability altogether, as in the case of chronic fatigue syndrome, in which one becomes disabled if one cannot work a full-time work week. In our chapter, we remain interested in the ways that picturing time and disability through text and image in comics makes visible the varied temporalities that haunt disability. That is, we investigate the ways that comics showcase how people with disabilities are asked to inhabit an impossible set of temporalities, how disabled bodies fail to meet temporal requirements, as well as how people with disabilities resist meeting these demands. If, as Engelberg notes, "so much of life is really about filling up time,"[4] how might these comics showcase a crip theory that reveals strategies for filling time in ways that resist able-bodied temporalities oriented around productivity? That is, how do the graphic novels we analyze here imagine ways to spend time outside efficiency that might produce more liberating temporalities for both people with disabilities and able-bodied folks?

This chapter begins with a review of the literature on critical approaches to time and temporality, followed by a review of contemporary understandings of the possibilities of comics. Thinking about scholarly interest in comics as a pedagogical tool, we ask questions as to the productive possibilities presented by picturing disability in comics. We next detail two separate graphic accounts: the sections on depression in Allie Brosh's autobiographic comic book and blog *Hyperbole and a Half*, and Miriam Engelberg's *Cancer Made Me a Shallower Person*, a memoir about breast cancer.

Temporality and Identity

We use the term "temporality" to refer to complex cultural constructions and lived realities of time, including ones that are differentially
produced and experienced in ways connected to identity categories
such as race, gender, and sexuality.[5] In other words, we do not all experience or relate to time in the same way, and that unevenness in our
different relationships to time is often connected to social power. In
this way, temporality denotes an awareness of "power relations as they
play out in time."[6] In a related vein, Sarah Sharma's book *In the Meantime* investigates the relationships among racialization, social class, and
time. Sharma problematizes the truism that life under late capitalism
is defined by "speed up." She argues that statements such as "the speed
of life has increased" have a flattening effect, seemingly suggesting that
everyone experiences speed up as equally stressful without referencing the ways that people experience different "temporal orders" that
remain connected to their class and race positionalities. For example,
in contrasting what Sharma describes as the "temporal architecture"[7]
provided for business travelers with that lived by taxi drivers, Sharma
shows how, from sleep pods that allow business travelers to catch up on
naps to cell phones that make waiting profitable, elites live in privileged
temporalities, even if their sped-up pace of life remains stressful and
demanding. Yet these privileged temporalities remain "entangled" with
those of a temporal underclass.[8] That is, taxi drivers speed up and slow
down depending on the whims of these same business travelers, and the
drivers are regularly asked to take on both the emotional and temporal
labor associated with racing the temporal elite to their destinations. In
this way, a whole temporal architecture of laborers is there to serve the
highly paid temporally privileged, a category that, in the case of the
business traveler, Sharma shows is too often a privileged classed and
raced category, while taxi drivers remain the racialized underclass of
the current temporal moment.[9]

Thinking more specifically about sexuality and temporality in his
book *In a Queer Time and Place*, Jack Halberstam argues that queer
temporalities often usefully resist normative futurities as they have developed at least partially through a resistance to normative cycles of heterosexual marriage and reproduction.[10] As Halberstam explains, those

who refuse to look forward to the future are deemed threatening to healthy social reproduction:

> We create adolescence as something we want to mature from, and longevity as the most desirable future, applaud the pursuit of long life (under any circumstances) and pathologize modes of living that show little or no concern for longevity. Within the life cycle of the western human subject, long periods of stability are considered to be desirable, and people who live in rapid bursts (drug addicts) are characterized as immature and even dangerous.[11]

Halberstam argues that queer time can usefully disrupt the emphasis on normative future-oriented temporalities centered, in the case of his work, on marriage, children, and property ownership. We extend this argument below to think about how the temporalities inhabited by people with disabilities may also usefully resist and disrupt normative temporalities centered around futurity. Referencing communities that refuse to embrace longevity, as well as the ways that the AIDS epidemic shaped the impossibility of queer futures for some queer bodies,[12] Halberstam argues that "the constantly diminishing future creates a new emphasis on the here, the present, the now, and while the threat of no future hovers overhead like a storm cloud, the urgency of being also expands the potential of the moment."[13] Robert McRuer, in *Crip Theory*, extends this argument to disability in his analysis of queer crip artist Bob Flanagan, whose enjoyment in the relationship between S/M and the treatments that he requires for his cystic fibrosis showcases a certain reveling in the pleasures of the present despite the shadowy cloud of an uncertain future.[14]

And yet, what does this urgency in the here and now mean? Certainly, these temporalities yield new possibilities for pleasures in the present, but we must ask whether these possibilities are realized and by whom, as well as what kinds of burdens these intensified forms of living in the moment present. What are the implications of chronic pain, chronic melancholia, and the threat of no future for disabled temporalities? We turn now to explore the possibilities of comics for rethinking temporality and disability, extending existing ruminations on the ways that time is constituted in relation to racialization and sexuality in order to think about the relationship between disability and temporality, and how comics can reveal how disabilities are both challenged by and pose a challenge to normative temporalities that (re)consider productivity and efficiency as defining successful citizen-subjects.

Literature on Comics

From the histories of freak shows to objectifying representations of people with disabilities in contemporary medical texts, there are significant risks to representing disability.[15] And yet, the possibility of interrupting contemporary ableist depictions of disability through comics—especially in the genre of visual autobiography in which people with disabilities write about themselves and their lives in pictorial form—remains a helpful corrective to mainstream and commercial representations. Feminist theorists Sarah Brophy and Janice Hladki argue that "visual autobiography's critical contributions to the cultural politics of embodiment, health, disability, and agency . . . [offer] a politically hopeful account of the surge in autobiographically oriented visual cultural production."[16] As disability theorist Susan Squier writes: "In their attention to human embodiment, and their combination of both words and gestures, comics can reveal unvoiced relationships, unarticulated emotions, unspoken possibilities, and even unacknowledged alternative perspectives."[17] Brophy and Hladki follow other theorists of the form in arguing that "the medium combines gestural forms, represented pictorially, with written narrative. Since they juxtapose gestural images and text, graphic narratives are generically equipped to depict embodied conditions of illness and disability, including neurological impairment and chronic pain."[18] We argue that the graphic autobiographies we examine here serve as a form of knowledge production that showcase the ways that people with disabilities continue to both wrestle with and construct alternative temporalities.

Multimodal and manipulable renderings of time and temporality are central to comics as a genre, as explicated by theorists Hillary Chute and Marianne DeKoven:

> In comics, the images are not illustrative of the text, but comprise a separate narrative thread that moves forward in time in a different way than

the prose text, which also moves the reader forward in time. The medium of comics is cross-discursive because it is composed of verbal and visual narratives that do not simply blend together, creating a unified whole, but rather remain distinct. The diegetical horizon of each page, made up of what are essentially boxes of time, offers comics a representational mode capable of addressing complex political and historical issues with an explicit, formal degree of self-awareness.[19]

As representations of the complexities of time are central to graphic narratives, comics provide a useful medium to think about the temporalities of disability. Part of what comics allow for is a complicating of time as a linear progression. For example, a narrator may appear in the same box as her younger self or may otherwise interrupt the chronological progression of time, possibilities that are facilitated by the imaged nature of the graphic narrative.

Some of the possibilities for thinking about alternative and agentic representations of people with disabilities in the graphic autobiographies we review here can be attributed to the possibilities of memoir as a genre. In writing about the role that memoir plays in thinking about affect, Ann Cvetcovich notes that this type of writing can, for example, capture "how depression feels—the everyday sensations of depression embedded in ordinary circumstances."[20] With respect to representations of disability in comics, comics can provide different (and new) insights to textual memoirs through their picturing of the everyday lived experience of chronic pain, chronic sadness, and other forms of embodied suffering.

Memoir and autobiography have long been a staple of feminist writing. There has also been an explosion of memoirs on disability in recent years.[21] As Cvetcovich describes in *Depression: A Public Feeling*, feminist public cultures privilege confessional modes of discourse that are themselves oriented around the "expression of emotion" with the belief that this "can have a collective, often cathartic impact."[22] Graphic novels present unique possibilities for catharsis through the number of different visual methods they provide for picturing the dailiness of the lives of people with disabilities. In keeping with feminist theoretical insights that everyday experiences of oppression (such as the microaggressions of racism, sexism, homophobia, and ableism) are themselves a form of insidious trauma,[23] these graphic memoirs usefully picture the experience of being on the receiving end of ableist comments (ones that, as we will see, are often connected to misunderstandings of the temporalities associated with disability). And yet, in refusing to reify experience or to present only a coherent subject, graphic memoirs investigating ableism as form of trauma usefully "constitute forms of visual/performance culture that testify about, but do not reproduce trauma."[24] In this way, these comics provide possibilities for the development of a community of connection through the emotional recognition of the traumatic impact of experiences of everyday ableism.

The popularity of Brosh's *Hyperbole and a Half* signals a digital community of connection in the form of an enthusiastic fan base made up of many people who also struggle with depression. Here, we would briefly like to draw on reception studies in order to think about the possibility of Brosh's text for drawing together a community centered around disability. Reception studies examines audience negotiations of particular texts, including the ways that readers/viewers may consume texts (from complete embracing of the text's message to an oppositional gaze), as well as analysis of how reception may itself be a communicative act.[25] Reception studies has also theorized how differences across race, class, and gender (as well as sexuality and ability) are negotiated in the audience reception of a text.[26] Communication theorist Jack Bratich argues that audience responses to particular texts need to be conceptualized not as uniform or singular but as containing a set of ontological truths that result in these responses having "constitutive power."[27] That is, audiences can help to reshape the meaning of a particular text. With respect to *Hyperbole and a Half*, although a detailed study of audience reception of Brosh's text is beyond the scope of this article, it is clear that it helped to produce a community of readers who discursively expressed a set of beliefs about the importance of recognizing depression as a disability.

As Hillary Chute argues, quoting Cathy Caruth, one useful definition of trauma is that to "be traumatized is to be possessed by an image or event."[28] The narratives we analyze below, like all comics, appear in fragments "just as they do in actual recollection."[29] Of course, as Chute asserts, this fragmentation "is a particularly prominent feature of traumatic memory."[30] As a result, comics allow for the picturing of traumatic recollections in ways that uniquely parallel the formation of these types of memories. Part of the reason that graphic narratives so eloquently capture traumatic memory is that the visual format of these narratives provides possibilities for destabilizing the temporal coherence of the subject, a coherence that has been interrupted by trauma. For example, as noted above, comics can present the adult narrator at the same time as a younger narrator, an intervention into picturing disability and temporality that is made possible by the unique interface of the graphic novel. That is, comics allow the authors to present "temporal layers of experience while refusing to reify experience as the foundational precept of feminist critique."[31]

Comics provide other possibilities for disability studies in addition to their capacity for visually picturing ableism as a form of trauma. As Susan Squier argues in her discussion of the possibilities of comics for disability studies, "[G]raphic fictions rely on, and challenge, longstanding notions of normalcy, disability, and the comic book genre in order to articulate the embodied, ethical and sociopolitical experiences of impairment and disability."[32] Brophy and Hladki build on Squier in arguing that

> image-texts mobilize ethical spectatorship—the possibilities for learning, and learning's fraught qualities—in relation to multiple embodiments. But our interest attaches to what is unsaid in these texts as much as to what they "articulate" or bring into meaning and understanding. We are particularly interested in how graphic memoirs, through their unfixing of the meanings of illness, disability, and witnessing, wrest intersubjectivity away from a kind of mirroring that confirms what we already knew, instead testing perception and identification in relation to what is unknown and/or unspeakable.[33]

In the comics we examine, we explore how Brosh and Engelberg picture ethical responses to the challenging questions of how people with disabilities live in time. We argue that both authors write narratives that help their readers to reflect upon the possibilities for reconfiguring alternative responses to disability and temporality.

The Temporality of Mania and Depression: Allie Brosh's "Adventures in Depression" and "Depression Part Two"

Allie Brosh's *Hyperbole and a Half*[34] deals with what we might term the "trauma of everyday life," or what the book's subtitle describes as "unfortunate situations, flawed coping mechanisms, mayhem, and other things that happened." Based on her hugely popular illustrated blog of the same name, Brosh's book chronicles her everyday experiences, ranging from embarrassing childhood memories and adventures with her dog to reflections on depression and contemplations of suicide.[35] In October 2011, Brosh posted a comic titled "Adventures in Depression," after which she did not post any new updates to her blog for over a year, for reasons that she later explained had to do with the persistence of the depression described in this chapter. Approximately a year later, she posted a brief update on Reddit[36] and a few months after that posted a new comic on her blog titled "Depression Part Two." Her second blog post about living with depression as a disability garnered over 1.5 million hits in a single day.[37] The popularity of this second post, and the range of comments that expressed amazement that Brosh had gotten "inside my head," or that "I could have sworn that [she was] writing about me," or that "This has been me in the past, and I'm so glad I'm not alone,"[38] remind us how a particular text can foster a community of connection around the common experience of disability. This is also seen in the praise Brosh's work has received from health professionals, such as psychologists who expressed how much her description of her depression resonates with their patients' experiences.[39]

In her description of the possibilities of artistic production,[40] Janice Hladki notes that many feminist artists use what she terms "poetic time," rather than chronological time, to tell life stories.[41] Poetic time does "not map out a linear passage or temporality. . . . [T]he narrative components come together and disengage, connect and cut adrift, in an unraveling composed of specific details rather than a general mapping of the life story."[42] Brosh also relies on poetic time to both describe and illustrate the everyday details of living with depression. Rather than a chronology, her narrative illustrates that part of what remains so challenging about depression as a disability is the way that it makes a mockery of time as a natural and teleological progression of events.[43] In the many everyday

Figure 10.1. A three-frame sequence in which Brosh, lying on a couch, muses, "Maybe I'll go outside today," stays where she is, and concludes, "Nope. I hate myself too much." Source: Brosh, *Hyperbole and a Half*, 104–105.

Figure 10.2. Brosh, in six largely identical panels, demonstrates a flat emotional affect. Source: Brosh, *Hyperbole and a Half*, 125.

scenes of what it is like to live with depression, her life often appears to exist in a form of temporal stasis. For example, one set of images features Brosh lying stagnant on the couch in mute misery (figure 10.1). After some time has passed, her inability to move prompts her inner critic to berate her for her lack of productivity and general lack of worthiness. Referencing both the endless time that those at home suffering from depression must fill and the ways that even a moment of catastrophic sadness may feel endless, Brosh's depression mutes her world until all experiences—whether good, ordinary, or actively negative—have a similar emotional resonance.

In a second vignette (figure 10.2), Brosh draws the ways that the sun, her birthday, and even spiders, of which she remains terribly afraid, all produce the same emotionless impact for her while she is depressed. Rather than the usual ways that comics convey the progression of time, which is by showing a narrative develop from left to right as one's eyes move across the page, the images below might all occupy the same temporal period, one of stagnation in which, no matter the experience, the temporal moment of feeling numb and sad remains. This lack of differentiation between varied life events highlights the ways that depression interrupts the chronological progression of time. As even the most minute tasks become impossible, Brosh visually captures the experience of time standing still in her description of how she continues to sit on the couch, surfing the internet "on top of a pile of my own dirty laundry which I set on the couch for 'just a second' because I experienced a sudden moment of apathy on my way to the washer and couldn't continue."[44] As Brosh states, this state of depression (and we would add temporal stagnation) means that everything "leads to horrible, soul-decaying boredom,"[45] where, as she notes, the only sure thing is that nothing is again going to happen today.

As mentioned above, Chute argues that to be traumatized is to be "possessed by an image or an event."[46] In *Hyperbole and a Half*, Brosh presents the traumatic nature of her disability in ways that not only unsettle the temporal coherence of the subject but also destabilize the assertion that it is possible to have a temporally coherent experience of life. Instead, her graphic narrative illustrates that part of the trauma of depression as a disability is its interruption of the sequential progression of time. Brosh specifically excavates those traumatic images that possess her, often images in which she dramatizes the depth of her self-loathing and self-doubt. Of course, as O'Brien notes in her memoir *The Family Silver*, depression is a condition haunted by time.[47] In part, depression forces the question: how does one fill one's time when one is truly too depressed to move? In a genre of writing (depression memoir) that remains too often marked by the progression of depression until its eventual cure,[48] Brosh's comic instead pictures what the dailiness of living with depression looks like and that time may not necessarily progress linearly to recovery.

Brosh's memoir also usefully pictures how ableist reactions to her situation are an everyday form of trauma to which people with disabilities are subjected.[49] Disability theorist Brian Watermeyer argues that the field of disability studies has "avoided researching the emotional experience of disability" in part because of a fear that this would intensify existing oppressive stereotypes that people with disabilities are "helpless" and/or "damaged."[50] Brosh's memoir helps to fill this void by exploring the everyday microaggressions of ableism and their connection to the creation of psychic wounds for people with disabilities. Part of what makes her memoir helpful is that she pictures the emotional consequences of invasive ableist questions.[51] In a sequence in which she depicts what it is like to have one's disability continually called into question or made the subject of "helpful" suggestions (a frequent ableist reaction to people with disabilities, who are expected to take every suggestion seriously and leave no stone unturned in trying to "overcome" their disability), Brosh notes that a fundamental misunderstanding of depression informs so many of the responses to her situation.

As she says, "It would be like having a bunch of dead fish, but no one around you will acknowledge that the fish are dead. Instead, they offer to help you look for the fish or try to help you figure out why they disappeared."[52] Brosh draws herself holding two dead fish and, when people ask her what's wrong, repeatedly stating that her fish are dead. Various friends and family members continually ignore her assertion of the facts of her situation. One friend responds, "Don't worry! I'll help you find them! Are there any clues where they went?" When Brosh again replies, "I know where they are . . . the problem is they aren't alive anymore," her friend again suggests that they "keep looking! I'm sure they'll turn up somewhere." Other friends suggest a variety of useless and undermining solutions, including "Have you tried feeding them?"; "Fish are always the deadest before dawn"; and "Why not just make them be alive again?" As she notes, these solutions are "for a different problem than the one I have" and as such are worse than useless. Rather than recognize her pain, Brosh's friends' and family's responses to her depression only make her sink deeper into sadness as she frantically tries to get them to see "just how dead her fish are." This fundamental misrecognition of her emotional state and her friends' well-intentioned—but, we would note, ableist—attempts to get Brosh to just feel better, contribute to her feelings of isolation and loneliness and in fact only intensify the challenges of her disability as the pain of their misrecognition results in her "spending more time alone."[53]

Although Brosh's narrative does much to theorize the implications of ableism for people with disabilities, an intersectional feminist analysis means that we must simultaneously consider the ways that this memoir elides analysis of racialization. In one vignette, Brosh notes that she feels stared at because of how sad she looks: "I noticed a woman looking at me weirdly from a couple rows over. She was probably looking at me that way because I looked really, really depressed and I was dressed like an eskimo vagrant."[54] This text is accompanied by an illustration of Brosh wearing a gray hooded sweatshirt, boots, and carrying a knapsack. Her use of a racial slur to connote abjectness illustrates how a cis-woman who is racialized as white can neglect to consider how abject bodies are constantly subjected to unwanted stares. In a way, the fact that Brosh is feeling this gaze, presumably for the first time as she presents sadness, reflects her privileged position. O'Brien's memoir *The Family Silver* explores the "emotional inheritance" of depression, which she argues is marked by gendered norms of the necessary performance of niceness as well as by an inheritance of thwarted desires for a middle-class mobility. However, in her analysis of O'Brien's work, Cvetcovich argues that "it is important to note that the norm that dictates silence for women is also marked by class and race, and a fuller account of how O'Brien's narrative concerns a specifically white and middle-class femininity would be telling."[55] We would like to similarly note the possibilities for a "fuller telling" of an experience of depression that also notes how it remains classed and raced and, furthermore, that does not depend on the othering of racialized bodies as a visual technique to communicate ableism.

Cvetcovich further notes that depression is frequently cast as a form of stasis and asks how we instead might come to understand disability as a form of resistance to the increasingly impossible demands placed on us in this moment of late capitalism. As Brosh's disability renders her unable to meet normative temporal requirements oriented around work, her narrative captures that depression is a disability that takes places in time in which one remains mired in immobility and in which the achievement of everyday life-maintenance, let alone deeds that reinforce capitalist inequity, is impossible. For Brosh, it is the "the ongoingness of daily life" that she loses to her depression, as her disability becomes the source of what O'Brien terms "the blank patches" in her life.[56] In the commitment of this volume to acknowledging the power and urgency of a turn toward dis/ability in media studies, the editors struggle with the ways that new media texts produce new possibilities of thinking about disability and representation. With *Hyperbole and a Half*, Brosh innovates a way of picturing sadness—or imaging disability—when there are no words. The text plus images of the comic serve to fill this lacuna in language in ways that provide for new possibilities of representing the lived realities of chronic melancholia.

Temporalities of the Emergency: Miriam Engelberg's *Cancer Made Me a Shallower Person*

A staple of women's writing more broadly, and as we have seen, increasingly central to representations of disability, memoirs are vital in chronicling the impact of breast cancer. These include memoirs written

from a feminist perspective that investigate the intersecting consequences of racism, lesbophobia, and classism on the experience of breast
cancer,[57] many of which are graphic memoirs.[58] The genre of graphic
fiction that examines life with cancer (both breast cancer and cancer
more broadly) has been dubbed graphic pathography by disability theorist Laura McGavin.[59] These works include *Stitches*, a narrative about
breast cancer that forms a central part of the plotline of the comic strip
Dykes to Watch Out For, *Mom's Cancer*, and *Our Cancer Year*.[60] Disability theorists note the ways that comics call into question the boundaries
of ill bodies and additionally interrupt seemingly straightforward narratives around the possibilities of medical imaging to visualize cancer.[61]
We would like to extend the burgeoning literature exploring health and
illness in graphic narratives by adding in questions of temporality.

In a courageous article, "Breast Cancer Narratives as Public Rhetoric," Judy Segal argues that an overabundance of memoirs, especially in
relationship to cancer, have made memoir into a "pink genre," one that
is "so welcome in part because it is unthreatening—unlike, for example,
the genre of the protest rally or the diatribe."[62] Segal includes *Cancer
Made Me a Shallower Person* in her critique of the limited possibilities
presented by many memoirs.[63] We would like to note the importance
of her argument for thinking about this genre, and we agree that it is
crucial that the expression of one's feelings not be understood by itself
to be a radical act. And yet, we argue that, much like Brosh's resistance
to her friends who demand that she just get better and put her disability
behind her in time, *Cancer Made Me a Shallower Person* also usefully
pictures a resistance to normative demands as to how people should
live their lives following a catastrophic diagnosis through its critical response to time and temporality. Like *Hyperbole and a Half*, Engelberg's
memoir showcases how a structure of ableism partly consists of forms
of bullying about how one's time should best be spent once one has received a life-threatening diagnosis.

Cancer Made Me a Shallower Person documents different aspects of
the author's life with terminal breast cancer, ranging from her initial
diagnosis to deeper, existential questions about how to live one's life
while chronically ill.[64] Engelberg showcases many moments of the despair and isolation that accompany illness, focusing, for instance, on
how long-term sick leave often results in a lot of hours in the day to

fill. Navigating uncomfortable topics such as self-blame and a culture of responsibilization around cancer diagnoses, the graphic novel works against the suggestion found in many memoirs[65] that disability can be overcome or that it involves a pleasurably slowed-down pace of life. As she notes in the introduction, "I hadn't counted on the degree of interruption provided by cancer. What is the point of life when illness takes over and becomes the main event? When someone goes through a hard time, friends will say, 'You can get through this.' This implies a temporary state, like a Lifetime made-for-TV movie scenario, where the heroine comes out stronger in the end."[66] And yet, as this memoir demonstrates, chronic pain and nausea become the main event in an endless day in which it becomes challenging to know how to spend one's time. In *Pink Ribbons, Inc.*, Samantha King describes how women living with breast cancer are constantly exhorted to be upbeat, positive, and cheerful by media campaigns that hold that an individualized positive attitude is essential to beating cancer.[67] This "tyranny of cheerfulness," as King terms it, becomes a replacement for models of collective action, such as a more sustained look at the rise in the production of cancer-causing molecules caused by an increase in industrial production. Following King, we would like to argue that there is a specific set of temporalities that accompany the "tyranny of cheerfulness," including temporalities in which one is exhorted to live with immediacy and to cease delaying any pleasurable activities. This is a narrative that should be complicated by the intersections of gender, race, class, and sexuality, as it remains out of the reach of those who have neither the time off nor the funds to make the most of life.

And yet, as Engelberg shows, people with cancer are constantly bullied by expressions that tell them they should be making the "most of every moment" or that they should be focused only on living in the now (figure 10.3). In fact, the urgings of people around her, both cancer survivors who have internalized the "tyranny of cheerfulness" and those without cancer exhorting her to enjoy every minute of life post-cancer (with such time-focused interventions as "now I enjoy each precious minute of life—it's been a gift!" and "despite intense pain, I'm determined more than ever to continue activist work"), only serve to intensify Engelberg's feelings of worthlessness as well as to confirm her sense of the meaninglessness of her own life. As she notes that her job working

Figure 10.3. Six frames in which Engelberg reflects on the "tyranny of cheerfulness" and stages of grief. Source: Engelberg, *Cancer Made Me a Shallower Person*.

on computer databases for non-profits is not likely to change the world and that it was impossible for her to "enjoy the moment" pre-cancer, let alone with cancer, Engelberg sinks into a depression that is partially induced by her inability to figure out how to productively fill the time she has left.

Cancer Made Me a Shallower Person is also a narrative about the intersections of systems of privilege with systems of inequality. For example, that Engelberg has time that she has to figure out how to fill is also a classed and sexualized phenomenon. It is significant that she has a partner to support her and a job that seems to have some sick-leave benefits. Those with neither the support of a life partner nor those types of benefits would live out this time very differently, including in ways that might not involve any treatment at all under a system of for-profit medicine. As temporality itself denotes an awareness of "power relations as they play out in time,"[68] part of Engelberg's struggle around how to fill her time when she is at home with breast cancer in chronic pain is also a privilege of a classed form of leisure. We are not arguing that Engelberg should highlight her privilege in her graphic memoir, but rather that it remains the role of the theorist to think about the ways that this narrative also is one that is shaped by forms of privilege.

Cvetcovich argues that we need to think about the ways that both depression and apathy can work as forms of resistance to capitalist narratives encouraging us to commodify our lives into discrete chunks of time aimed at productivity and efficiency. Engelberg's memoir serves to image Cvetcovich's call to resist these normative temporalities. That is, *Cancer Made Me a Shallower Person* pictures ways of resisting capitalist temporalities that hold that a successful life consists only of the timely and productive achievement of meaningful goals. Rather than using her time to accomplish what she has "always wanted to do," Engelberg makes clear that this is a task that was impossible before the level of chronic pain that accompanies her diagnosis and certainly is not possible after.

Instead, for Engelberg, temporalities of futurity were and remain a constant source of anxiety: "If the biopsy is benign, I'm sure I'll be able to enjoy life again, just like I used to . . . I hope terrorists don't attack! Maybe we should move to a smaller city. Is that mole on my arm a melanoma? Killer bees are scary. Is my job safe?"[69] As shame and empathy researcher Brené Brown argues, time and how to deal with it are

Figure 10.4. Six frames in which Engelberg illustrates common breast cancer awareness efforts and the imperative to do what she's always wanted to, concluding with a giant question mark. Source: Engelberg, *Cancer Made Me a Shallower Person*.

a constant preoccupation for most of us during the course of our lives. Moreover, from 9/11 to the global financial crisis, the anxiety-provoking events of the past decade yielded new cultural narratives as well as new forms of collective trauma in which we are constantly being exhorted to micro-control our futures in order to stay safe.[70] That is, for all of us, anxieties about the future and how best to spend one's time are emotions with which many of must contend on a daily basis. In picturing the struggle to get through the day and visualizing a range of strategies that are not about controlling the future, Engelberg makes visible a new set of temporalities of disability. Finding that intellectual pursuits are increasingly beyond her following her diagnosis and its accompanying devastating anxiety, as well as the symptoms associated with chemotherapy and other forms of treatment that make it impossible for her to concentrate for any length of time, she draws the range of strategies that she uses to contend with the quotidian. Almost unable to read or even watch an entire movie, instead she decides to focus on puzzles and television shows such as celebrity poker, pursuits she finds to be among the very few activities that engage her, upon which she can focus, and that allow her to numb the crushing weight of her life with breast cancer. Here, her images of days filled with low-culture pursuits showcase temporalities structured by the daily rituals in which one continues to engage, rituals that represent what Cvetcovich would call some "of the many ways in which the desire to live manifests."[71] In picturing a life that is focused on getting through the day rather than the accomplishment of great deeds—the type of life that most of us lead—Engelberg pictures a way of inhabiting time that might liberate both people with disabilities and able-bodied folks from trying to lead impossibly busy lives driven only by the anxiety-provoking question of how to use one's time best.

One of the strengths of Engelberg's memoir is that she provides images that allow readers to explore the feelings associated with the crushing wait of trying to fill an entire day when one is suffering from pain and nausea. She visualizes what it looks like to live with nausea while trying to find ways to make the hours of the day pass more quickly. A particularly vivid scene shows Miriam lying in the front room where a lava lamp that her son loves is also set up. Although Engelberg does not want to diminish her son's pleasure in the lamp, its slowly moving balls of mineral oil serve only to intensify the extremity of her nausea. Capturing both the slow rolling sensation of nausea as well as the sluggish nature of a day defined solely by waiting for the release of sleep, the lava lamp comes to symbolize that painful "watching the clock" that makes Engelberg both physically and psychically ill. As we reviewed above, Sarah Sharma argues that maxims that hold that life is defined by "speed up" under this moment of late capitalism have a flattening effect. In particular, for people with disabilities, life may not be defined by speed up, but by a terrible combination of speeding up and slowing down. That is, one is both left with less time (hurtling toward a shortened lifespan) while being exhorted to make the most of every moment at precisely the time when everyday routines (such as work and family life) are disrupted. Although Engelberg notes that many of us think about what we would do if we didn't have to work every day, in fact, this question often provides us with worrying temporalities with which to contend: "If only I didn't have to work every day! I could . . . I could . . ." The next panel shows Miriam thinking with a worried expression about the various things that present themselves when she is not keeping herself busy, including her "fear of death, the void, state of the world, embarrassing memories." As Engelberg notes, life with a disability is partially structured by a frightening temporal order of a "too-muchness of time" that offers up too many opportunities to think about those possibilities that frighten us most.

Conclusion

In *Depression: A Public Feeling*, Cvetcovich observes that terms that invite further elaboration are useful to theorizing oppression; for example, she likes the term "feeling bad" as it invites further elaboration, possibly in the form of an anecdote.[72] It is precisely the gaps left in a phrase like "feeling bad" that the memoirs we analyzed above attempt to depict. Using images to flesh out what "feeling bad" might mean in relation to disability, these memoirs help to illuminate how temporalities are part of the structures of "feeling bad" produced by ableism. Heeding Cvetcovich's call for work in memoir that contains the "rough edges" that capture the messiness of lived reality,[73] both Brosh's *Hyperbole and a Half* and Engelberg's *Cancer Made Me a Shallower Person* image the untidiness of lives marked by the temporalities of disability.

As "invisible things are not necessarily not-there,"[74] disability, we have argued in this chapter, is an identity category "haunted" by time. That is, disability is accompanied by its own unique set of temporalities structured by chronic pain, chronic melancholia, and the threat of no future. In particular, we examined the possibilities that graphic fiction holds for thinking about how normative temporalities aimed at productivity and efficiency are traumatic and how people with disabilities are often compelled to resist them. In doing so, we asked how, in challenging capitalist temporalities aimed at productivity and efficiency, these narratives might produce more liberating temporalities for both people with disabilities and able-bodied folks.

Of course, part of the work of the narratives above is also about providing suggestions for how we might refuse ableist responses to disability. Rather than urging people with disabilities to live in the now or to just "get better faster," both Engelberg and Brosh call for empathetic responses to disability. These types of responses might best be encapsulated by open-ended responses that refuse easy solutions, such as that proposed by Brené Brown in response to difficult disclosures. As Brown argues, easy solutions or calls to action are rarely relevant, and instead challenging life moments would be much better encapsulated by responses along the lines of "I'm not even sure what to say but I'm just so glad you told me."[75] In our analyses of these graphic narratives, we hoped to show how these are a form of media that engage with disability studies by picturing some of the harms of systemic forms of ableism and leaving the possibility for us to think about how to image alternative responses to chronic pain, depression, and life-altering diagnoses. In doing so, we aim to contribute to the interdisciplinary dialogue between disability studies and media studies and examine the ways that graphic novels move us beyond the textual by providing us with a set of images for what we call the "temporalities of disability."

NOTES

1   Gordon, *Ghostly Matters*.
2   Ibid., 4.
3   Following Chute, we use the terms "graphic novel," "graphic fiction," "graphic memoir," "graphic autobiography," and "comics" interchangeably. See Chute, *Graphic Women*.
4   Engelberg, *Cancer Made Me a Shallower Person*, n.p.

5 Cvetkovich, *Depression*; Halberstam, *In a Queer Time and Place*; Puar, *Terrorist Assemblages*; Sharma, *In the Meantime*.

6 Sharma, *In the Meantime*, 17.

7 Ibid., 8.

8 Ibid., 21.

9 Ibid.

10 Halberstam, *In a Queer Time and Place*, 1.

11 Ibid., 4.

12 Halberstam cites poet Mark Doty, who says, "All my life I've lived with a future which constantly diminishes but never vanishes." Halberstam, *In a Queer Time and Place*, 2.

13 Halberstam, *In a Queer Time and Place*, 2.

14 McRuer, *Crip Theory*, 182.

15 Couser and Davis, "Disability, Life Narrative, and Representation"; Brophy and Hladki, "Visual Autobiography in the Frame."

16 Brophy and Hladki, "Visual Autobiography in the Frame," 5.

17 Squier, "So Long as They Grow Out of It," 23.

18 Brophy and Hladki, "Visual Autobiography in the Frame," 1.

19 Chute and DeKoven, "Graphic Narrative," 9.

20 Cvetkovich, *Depression*, 79.

21 Callahan, *Don't Worry*; Kuppers, Marcus, and Steichmann, *Cripple Poetics*; Patinkin, *Up and Running*; Sanford, *Waking*; Rushton, *It's Good to Be Alive*.

22 Cvetkovich, *Depression*, 76.

23 Rajiva, *Trauma and the Girl*.

24 Mark Reinhardt, quoted in Brophy and Hladki, "Connective Tissue," 249.

25 Philip Goldstein and James L. Machor, eds., *New Directions in American Reception Study* (Oxford: Oxford University Press, 2008); Janet Staiger, *Media Reception Studies* (New York: New York University Press, 2005); for the oppositional gaze, see bell hooks, *Black Looks: Race and Representation* (Boston: South End Press, 1992).

26 Staiger, *Media Reception Studies*; hooks, *Black Looks*.

27 Jack Bratich, "Activating the Multitude: Audience Powers and Cultural Studies," in *New Directions in American Reception Study*, edited by Philip Goldstein and James L. Machor (Oxford: Oxford University Press, 2008).

28 Cathy Caruth, *Trauma: Exploration in Memory* (Baltimore: Johns Hopkins University, 1995). Cited in Chute, *Graphic Women*, 3.

29 Chute, *Graphic Women*, 4.

30 Ibid.

31 Ibid., 6.

32 Squier, "So Long as They Grow Out of It," 72.

33 Brophy and Hladki, "Connective Tissue," 249.

34 This blog spawned a book of the same name in 2013. The book contains a significant number of the comics featured on Allie Brosh's blog, including the "Adven-

tures in Depression" narratives parts one and two. Our chapter cites Brosh's book for ease of page reference.

35 Thanks so much to our brilliant research assistant Brittany Neron for the research behind this paragraph.

36 Brosh, *Hyperbole and a Half*, 65.

37 Zaineb Mohammed, "Meet Allie Brosh, Reclusive Genius behind the Blog (and New Book) 'Hyperbole and a Half,'" *Mother Jones*, November/December 2013.

38 Brosh, *Hyperbole and a Half*, 108.

39 Jonathan Rottenberg, "What Is It Like to Be Severely Depressed?" *Psychology Today*, May 9, 2013.

40 Here, Hladki is specifically describing feminist artist Allyson Mitchell's short autobiographic video *My Life in Five Minutes*, in which Mitchell sings a short song about the everyday traumatic events that shaped her life (from getting her period while wearing white pants to struggling with bulimia). The video does not present these events in any temporally ordered way, hence Hladki's neologism "poetic time" (Hladki, "Nothing Big. Nothing Small," 18).

41 Hladki, "Nothing Big. Nothing Small," 171.

42 Ibid.

43 Time under late capitalism is held up as ideally structured by progress, success, and accumulation; see Sharma, *In the Meantime*.

44 Brosh, *Hyperbole and a Half*, 111.

45 Ibid., 125.

46 Chute, *Graphic Women*, 3.

47 O'Brien, *The Family Silver*.

48 Here we are suggesting that the most widely read memoirs on depression too often are narratives that contain a happy ending—usually brought on by drugs. Ann Cvetcovich includes as representative of this genre the popular books *Prozac Nation* and *Prozac Diary*—which, like so many others, too often present the introduction of drugs as the successful end of depression as a disability (Cvetcovich, *Depression*, 93). See Elizabeth Wurtzel, *Prozac Nation: A Memoir* (New York: Riverhead, 1994); Lauren Slater, *Prozac Diary* (New York: Routledge, 1998).

49 The term "microagressions" is used by Yosso, Smith, Ceja, and Solorzáno to describe the everyday, insidious, and damaging acts that constitute the daily fabric of life for people of color under the system of white supremacy; see Yosso et al., "Critical Race Theory." This term has been extended to facilitate thinking about the ways that everyday instances of ableism are a form of trauma for people with disabilities. See Disability Access Services Blog, *Ableism and Language* January 31, 2012, http://blogs.oregonstate.edu.

50 Watermeyer, "Is It Possible to Create," 162.

51 In her groundbreaking book *Daring Greatly*, Brené Brown argues that questions that lack empathy can themselves be traumatic. We would like to expand Brown's work to think about the impact of ableist questions that lack empathy for people with disabilities more specifically.

52 Brosh, *Hyperbole and a Half*, 134.
53 Ibid., 136.
54 Ibid., 115.
55 Cvetkovich, *Depression*, 144.
56 Cited in ibid.
57 Butler and Rosenblum, *Cancer in Two Voices*; Lorde, *The Cancer Journals*; Sontag, *Illness as Metaphor*.
58 Bechdel, *The Essential Dykes to Watch Out For*; Marchetto, *Cancer Vixen*.
59 McGavin ("Why Should Our Bodies End at the Skin?") uses the term "graphic pathography" to refer to the combination of "pathology" and "autobiography" that looms large in autobiographical comics.
60 Small, *Stitches*; Bechdel, *The Essential Dykes to Watch Out For*; Fies, *Mom's Cancer*; Pekar and Brabner, *Our Cancer Year*.
61 McGavin, "Why Should Our Bodies End at the Skin?"
62 Segal, "Breast Cancer Narratives," 17.
63 Among these narratives that don't challenge larger structural reasons for the rise in cancer, Segal includes graphic narratives such as Marchetto, *Cancer Vixen*, in which the heroine too often contends with her fear of cancer by dieting and shopping without a critique of the limited efficacy of these practices. Unlike these other narratives, a substantive critique of breast cancer as opportunity for individual consumption is contained in Bechdel's *The Essential Dykes to Watch Out For*.
64 Thanks so much again to our brilliant research assistant Brittany Neron for her assistance here.
65 Marchetto, *Cancer Vixen*.
66 Engelberg, *Cancer Made Me a Shallower Person*, n.p.
67 King, *Pink Ribbons, Inc.*
68 Sharma, *In the Meantime*, 17.
69 Engelberg, *Cancer Made Me a Shallower Person*, n.p.
70 Brené Brown and Katy Davis (Gobblynne), *RSA Shorts: The Power of Empathy*, Royal Society for the Encouragement of Arts, Manufactures, and Commerce, December 10, 2013.
71 Cvetkovich, *Depression*, 211.
72 Ibid., 158.
73 Ibid., 94.
74 Toni Morrison, "Unspeakable Things Unspoken: The Afro-American Presence in American Literature," *Michigan Quarterly Review* 28, no. 1 (1998): 1–34. Cited in Gordon, *Ghostly Matters*, 17.
75 Brown and Davis, *The Power of Empathy*.

11

Any Day Now

Queerness, Disability, and the Trouble with Homonormativity

ROBERT MCRUER

Robert McRuer considers how the film *Any Day Now* (Travis Fine, 2012) may serve as a model for bringing concerns about disability and immigration into conversations about contemporary homonormativity. Queer scholars' and activists' critiques of homonormativity, often characterized by the fight for gay marriage and adoption rights, rest on its mainstreaming goals and its erasure of alternative forms of kinship and community. McRuer reads *Any Day Now* as resisting homonormativity through its presentation of crip modes of desiring, desiring togetherness in and through embodied differences.

Let me tell you. It was quite hard to be gay and get married in 2013.

As I hope will be clearer over the course of this chapter, I mean my opening statement rather ironically, in an era when it's quite hard to be ironic about gay marriage. The statement potentially has more meanings than are immediately legible, and I'll ultimately turn to disability and/in popular media, specifically Travis Fine's 2012 film *Any Day Now*, to excavate those meanings.[1] An earnest liberal understanding of statements such as "It was quite hard to be gay and get married in 2013" is arguably well-nigh compulsory at the moment; from an activist position on the queer Left, or among queer theorists, things are potentially more complicated. To well-meaning liberals, non-gay and gay, the "fact" that it was hard to be gay and get married in 2013 focuses on certain circumstances and makes several assumptions that are unquestioned, that essentially go without saying. The circumstances are extremely straightforward: at the beginning of 2013, only eight U.S. states and the District of Columbia permitted same-sex marriage. The Supreme Court, in *United States v. Windsor*, struck down the Defense of Marriage Act (DOMA), which defined marriage as the union of one man and one woman for the purposes of federal law, on June 26, 2013. By the end of 2013, the number of states permitting same-sex marriage had doubled to sixteen, meaning that it was still officially banned in 34 states. It was not until the Supreme Court's ruling in 2015 in *Obergefell v. Hodges*, declaring state-wide bans on same-sex marriage unconstitutional under the equal-protection clause of the Fourteenth Amendment, that a right to marry was guaranteed in all fifty states and the District of Columbia. Thus, on a literal, logistical, level for most of the year, it was in fact still quite hard to be gay and get married in 2013.

If one purports to be in favor of LGBT rights, there are many things that cannot really be questioned about this history. Put differently, the liberal assumptions that indeed "go without saying" in relation to these circumstances are multiple. First, the LGBT movement is and should be moving to what is now called "marriage equality" (a nomenclature that is itself virtually compulsory in many or most LGBT or LGBT-friendly conversations about the topic). Second, before June 26, 2013, we lacked a clear "freedom" that we (those of us on, as a popular catch-phrase would have it, "the right side of history") agreed and agree that we should have. Third, in most states at the time, even as we believed wholeheartedly that eventually love would win (another catchphrase frequently used by the marriage-equality movement), we interpreted *not* having that "freedom" to marry as fairly straightforward and state-endorsed discrimination and homophobia. Even if it's not for everyone, so the argument went, lesbians and gays should have the "choice" to marry and (in yet another oft-repeated phrase) all the "rights and responsibilities" that come with that choice. In the majority of states in 2013, however, it was not only hard to be gay and get married; it was literally impossible, and we (if "we" cared about LGBT rights) were obliged to feel that impossibility deeply.

There is actually a vibrant queer history critiquing this often single-minded focus on marriage. The critique of marriage draws on feminist thought that has long questioned the ways in which marriage curtails women's freedom, particularly securing property relations that severely disadvantage women. Some have termed the LGBT movement that sustains a disproportionate focus on marriage rights (both nationally and—

now that "love has won" in the U.S.—internationally) the "corporate gay movement." In such critiques, the corporate gay movement is usually represented by the politically centrist Human Rights Campaign (HRC), the country's largest and wealthiest LGBT rights organization. I myself have participated in that important critique of the marriage rights movement, and that collective critique should be seen as the condition of possibility for this chapter.[2] A queer critique of "marriage equality," however, is still not regularly articulated in and by the mainstream media (to say the least); many liberals would in fact undoubtedly be surprised to hear that the critique is as pronounced as it is. What often goes without saying is that the gay marriage question is "a simple matter of justice"; barriers to marriage equality should (obviously) be removed.

But the phrase "it was hard to be gay and get married in 2013" has another meaning as well, perhaps unexpected and certainly buried beneath this mainstream liberal consensus. I'll introduce this alternative meaning via an anecdote. In November 2013, I sat across a dinner table from a friend and listened patiently as he provided a list of mutual acquaintances who had recently married, noting in the process the supposed irony of "all these gay guys, against marriage, getting married." I smiled and nodded, inescapably—at the time and still—caught up in this ironic category. Although I'm in print in more than one location critiquing the mainstream LGBT movement's focus on marriage, I had, a few months earlier, married my non-U.S. partner, in a double civil ceremony at the Washington, D.C., District Court House. In that double wedding, my non-U.S. ex-partner also married his (U.S.) partner. It was, in fact, the District of Columbia's first double gay wedding, and—since I regularly teach a transnational queer film class—I joked to my students at the time that it was little more than a big transnational gay date movie. Both couples had been together for more than three years and were (and are) best friends as a foursome. Within six months of the wedding, by April 2014, both couples had gone through the immigration process, and the temporary green cards recognizing both non-U.S. members of each couple as permanent residents had been approved. For one member of the foursome, it was the first time in a decade that documented status was (again) vouchsafed.

For someone who understands himself as part of the queer Left, this whole process was, to say the least, hard. In some ways (in terms of finding the language to talk about it that wouldn't generate knowing pronouncements like my friend's observation over dinner), it was sort of impossible. I anticipated that this would be the case from the day in August when we signed the initial application. For better or worse, going through the process meant navigating or enduring the implicit or explicit charge of what has come to be called homonormativity. And in fact the layers of irony were not lost on me, as I recognized that we were participating in a moment of incorporation into the state at the *precise moment* that other queers were being detained, surveilled, and incarcerated by the state. In that very week in August when we signed the application, most notably, Chelsea Manning was sentenced to 35 years in prison for revealing information about the Afghanistan and Iraq wars to WikiLeaks. Over the course of her incarceration and trial, she had been subjected to an intense campaign of discrediting that often directly invoked her trans identity. Additionally (that week), David Miranda, a Brazilian man partnered with a U.S. journalist working in the U.K., was detained and interrogated for nine hours under "anti-terrorism" laws in London's Heathrow Airport. Miranda's partner, Glenn Greenwald, had published information in the *Guardian* about the U.S. government's monitoring of citizens—information that he had obtained from Edward Snowden, a former employee in the National Security Agency. It was easy to imagine that the state, to personalize Jasbir Puar's formulation, was essentially embracing or "targeting" my partner and me, and even the queer foursome of which we were part, "for life" as other queers were simultaneously targeted for interrogation and incarceration.[3]

It was a complicated year. Given such complications, it's not surprising that by 2013, on the queer Left, "homonormativity" circulated freely in our collective vocabulary to describe various complicities with state power and conservative institutions (most prominently, of course, marriage). Anything that was an unequivocal "victory" on the liberal side (the side of the mainstream LGBT movement), was (and perhaps is) at the same time a moment for the Left to nod knowingly, certain that (yet again) we were witnessing the consolidation of that homonormativity.

One contention of this chapter is that homonormativity—even as it has been discussed in innumerable locations since (and even before) the 2001 publication of Lisa Duggan's "The New Homonormativity: The Sexual Politics of Neoliberalism"—has often not been discussed in a particularly nuanced way outside of scholarly publications, especially in the past few years.[4] We are in need of cultural texts that allow for more nuanced conversations, texts that allow us to re-member the wide range of ways that we have shaped kinship networks, disidentified with state institutions and state power, engaged in intersectional political movements that work to decenter the respectable white gay male couple as the representative face of the movement, and committed to solidarity with a wide range of other struggles not always, on the surface, directly focused on sexuality (for example, struggles for racial and economic justice, for universal health care, or against environmental degradation or war). A central premise of this chapter is that disability should be at the very center of such conversations about what homonormativity in our moment might mean.

A lack of nuance was certainly not evident in Duggan's original 2001 argument, which contained pointed and very contextualized critiques. She was specifically discussing the Independent Gay Forum (IGF), an officially non-partisan but actually center-right organization that was putting forward a supposedly alternative political vision between what they described as a "conservative" position that "gays pose [a] threat to social morality or the political order" and a "progressive" position that "gays should support radical social change or restructuring of society."[5] Duggan carefully traced the ways in which the rhetoric of the IGF, offering what they packaged, essentially, as an ostensibly rational "third way," was implicated in the cultural logic of neoliberalism, the system of capitalism that has been dominant for four decades. Neoliberalism relies on a state that protects the sacrosanct free flow of capital while dismantling public, social protections and the more collectivist mind-set that had, in previous moments, partially secured such protections. It constructs "a narrowly constrained public life cordoned off from the 'private' control and vast inequalities of economic life";[6] for Duggan, the IGF's implicit endorsement of a "third way" was akin to the explicit "third way" proffered by neoliberal politicians such as Tony Blair and Bill Clinton. The privatizing logic of neoliberalism infused the arguments of writers associated with the IGF as they sought in their rhetoric to distance themselves from a more broadly politicized and progressive LGBT movement. Their distancing, Duggan argued, constructed "a dramatically shrunken public sphere and a narrow zone of 'responsible' domestic privacy, in terms arguably more broadly antidemocratic and antiegalitarian than the [1950s] homophile movement at its most cautious and assimilationist."[7] Put differently, a respectability politics averse to radical and systemic analyses of oppression had certainly characterized earlier moments in LGBT history, but the homonormativity of the IGF marked an unprecedented complicity with the dominant economic and political ideology of the moment.

Duggan thus put forward "homonormativity" as a term useful for comprehending both the dramatically shrunken public sphere envisioned by the IGF and the ways in which that vision was anchored in neoliberalism more broadly: "The new neoliberal sexual politics of the IGF might be termed the *new homonormativity*—it is a politics that does not contest dominant heteronormative assumptions and institutions but upholds and sustains them while promising the possibility of a demobilized gay constituency and a privatized, depoliticized gay culture anchored in domesticity and consumption."[8] Duggan clearly argues that the focus that the IGF (and by extension, other conservative or center-right groups, including the HRC) placed on both marriage and integration into the military as the main (really, the only) rights for gay people to pursue is an example of homonormativity. The IGF explicitly articulated these "rights" as private rights and critiqued a more expansive and public gay or queer movement that desired and worked toward a more radical restructuring of society (that would, particularly, focus on and redress economic inequality).

The IGF, in other words, was not simply "depoliticizing" the LGBT movement as a *consequence* of their positions; forwarding a moment of advanced neoliberalism, they were *actively* calling for its depoliticization, for its transformation into a movement more focused on privacy, domesticity, and consumption. This understanding of homonormativity emergent from and germinating in specific contexts was borne out in the special issue of *Radical History Review* on homonormativity.[9] But what Duggan is not *necessarily* suggesting in her original argument is what I am arguing was the case on the queer Left by 2013, when "homonormativity" had entered common parlance: "We know what that means" *any* and every time that what looks like "gay marriage" is the topic at hand. Well-meaning students in LGBT studies classrooms (who have worked to verse themselves in the language and politics of queer theory now) at times provide evidence of how thoroughly "homonormativity" has become an easy answer that can shut down reflection about the complexities of a text or topic; when a film gets called out as homonormative in my Transnational Queer Film Studies course, for example, it often means that the students dutifully think that's all we need to say. Duggan's consideration of the term was intended to generate historicized questions: how might we account for shifts in contemporary gay politics? How might we trace those shifts in the rhetoric generated by particular groups? How and why does an economic and political system work according to a cultural logic whereby seemingly (or formerly) "marginalized" groups are put to work as primary spokespersons for that system? How might the solidarity and coalition that have characterized queer history at its best be reinvented in this historical moment? In contrast to such textured questions, "that's so homonormative" at times now functions as the seemingly obvious answer to the question of what is going on in a particular popular text. *Any Day Now*, I will argue, might be one contemporary text that challenges that easy dismissal and allows for the careful and contextualized reading that characterized Duggan's initial reflections on the concept of homonormativity.

In Homonormativity but Not of Homonormativity

The remainder of this chapter, then, examines what would, in a filmic representation of the 21st century, *usually* be considered (or called out as) homonormative: a white, same-sex couple in a committed relationship seeks recognition from state institutions (specifically the courts), and hopes to adopt a disabled child and to care for that child using private resources. The Swedish gay date film *Patrik 1,5* (2008) would be, arguably, a comparable example of such a homonormative filmic representation.[10] Made in an era of homonormativity, however, but not (my contention will be) necessarily made of the era of homonormativity, *Any Day Now* should not be so easily dismissed or contained.

Following its 2012 premier, *Any Day Now* was screened at numerous queer film festivals around the world; I myself saw it for the first time at the Mezipatra Queer Film Festival in Prague in November 2013. The film tells the story of Rudy Donatello (Alan Cumming) and Paul Fligers's (Garret Dillahunt) ultimately unsuccessful efforts to secure cus-

Figure 11.1. Marco (Leyva) sitting at a table and laughing.

tody of Marco DeLeon (Isaac Leyva), a child with Down syndrome, in 1978 Los Angeles. Marco's name arguably also lightly codes him as Latino, although the script never provides any direct commentary on that coding, and his mother, Marianna (the two "n"s already representing an Anglicized spelling), is played by the relatively well known Anglo-American actor Jamie Anne Allman. The film was inspired by one true story from the 1970s and its production and release were influenced by another when the screenplay was adapted more than thirty years later (and I will also have more to say about that in my conclusion). The melodramatic film, I argue, complicates both what we think we know as homonormativity now and what we might understand as what David Mitchell and Sharon Snyder term "narrative prosthesis": the use of a disabled figure to tell a story that is not necessarily "about" disability at all but rather something else—in this case, the contemporary formation of a privatized and state-sanctioned gay family unit.[11] That larger story of (gay) family formation was a dominant narrative (really, *the* dominant gay mythology, in Roland Barthes's sense)[12] in the U.S. when *Any Day Now* was released. Given what Mitchell and Snyder argue about the ubiquity of narrative prostheses, it would thus be unsurprising to encounter variations on such a dominant gay narrative making use of narrative prostheses (put differently, if that dominant narrative is virtually compulsory, its repetition would at times rely, invariably, on one of the most basic tools for constructing narrative that the culture has). And yet, both homonormativity and narrative prosthesis are inadequate for comprehending the cultural work of the film.

The film looks backward (to 1978) in order to look forward and, in doing so, can be read as interrupting compulsory, now-domesticated queer progress narratives. The common expression "any day now" conveys futurity, gesturing toward something that will take place at some unspecified point in the future. I ultimately argue, however, that the film cruises utopia by specifically turning to a past that has been dematerialized in the homonormative present but that nonetheless haunts that present and thus still exists as a resource for imagining alternative futures. When I say that the film "cruises utopia," I am specifically deploying José Esteban Muñoz's now well-known formulation for challenging both contemporary assimilationist and nihilist LGBT politics.[13] For Muñoz, cruising utopia means yearning for a queerness that we have not yet accessed but that is discernible if we look carefully at and for the desires we felt in the past. In other words, my argument about the film is that, in 2012, it stages characters from 1978 yearning for *what will have taken place* in the future—a future that we as viewers now inhabit but that has short-circuited, via homonormativity, many of the promises contained in the "any day now" of the past.

The queer/crip past of *Any Day Now*/1978 allows for, and indeed requires, an embrace of perversion and misfit status, of gender nonnormativity, and—most importantly—of an alliance or coalition between queer and disabled (and otherwise marginalized) subjects. It "requires" such an embrace in the sense that the central characters lose their battle in court and, hence, are literally judged perverse by a state institution. Such a judgment, however, ultimately only fuels even more a desire for the misfit alliances the film imagines. The concept of homonormativity is extremely useful for reading a range of institutions—the IGF, the HRC, and other facets of the corporate gay movement that focused, when the film was released in 2012, on an essentially privatized, neoliberal future. The compulsion to look toward that homonormative future, however, can and should be interrupted by recalling the nonnormative, freaky, and public ways of being-in-common that were born in a more radical moment for both gay and disability politics. The seductive backward glance toward public ways of being-in-common that the film generates troubles any easy reading of *Any Day Now* as itself homonormative.

Perverse Solidarity

The film opens with a shot of Marco, holding a thin doll with long, blond hair, walking down a solitary, dark street and onto a bridge (we later learn that he has named this doll "Ashley"). It is a scene that will be called back near the end of *Any Day Now*. Even without a context at the beginning of the film, the scene is legible as a representation of what Rosemarie Garland-Thomson calls the visual rhetoric of the "sentimental" for depicting disability, evoking through that rhetoric pity for the lonely child (and *Any Day Now* evokes pity unabashedly, I would say). Spatially, Garland-Thomson argues, "the sentimental places the disabled figure below the viewer, in the posture of the sympathetic victim or helpless sufferer needing protection or succor."[14] Melodrama often largely depends upon pity and, and arguably, upon the visual rhetoric of the sentimental for representing disability. Given how overdetermined the generic conventions are for this film, pity and sentiment are thus never fully counteracted in it, even if—as I will explain—they are nonetheless complicated a great deal (not least by Leyva's strong performance). The sentimental can also be supplemented by other rhetorics and affects, and—I would add, following the poststructuralist logic of the supplement—*always will be*, any day now. In *Any Day Now*, the sentimental is particularly supplemented by what we might position as (extending Garland-Thomson) the perverse visual rhetoric of solidarity. If the sentimental mode places the disabled figure below the viewer, in need of protection or succor, the mode of solidarity places the disabled figure *alongside* the (non-disabled or disabled) viewer, in need of justice.

I call the visual rhetoric of solidarity perverse with the full, strict definition of the term in mind:

> 1. (Of a person or their actions) showing a deliberate and obstinate desire to behave in a way that is unreasonable or unacceptable, often in spite of the consequences. . . . 1.1 Contrary to the accepted or expected standard or practice. . . . 1.2 *Law* (Of a verdict) against the weight of evidence or the direction of the judge on a point of law. . . . 1.3 Sexually perverted.[15]

All these elements of the perverse are ("in actual fact," to ironically invoke Michel Foucault on the *perverse*)[16] central to *Any Day Now*, from beginning to end. In our (neoliberal) moment, solidarity—borne out of coalition—is undoubtedly "contrary to the accepted or expected standard or practice"; those who engage in it, shaping alliances across difference, can indeed come across as obstinate and unreasonable, and face unwanted consequences. As I have already explained, moreover, Paul and Rudy's insistence on their desire to be with Marco is directly rebuked by judicial authority, and specifically because they are (as the state attorney argues, and as common sense would have it) sexually perverted.

The soundtrack for this perverse solidarity is openly invitational, for the characters and for viewers. With France Joli's disco hit "Come to Me" playing faintly in the background, the film cuts from the opening lonely scene with Marco to a lonely scene with Paul, outside a local gay bar where Rudy performs. Disability in film has been criticized by Martin F. Norden for presenting, across the twentieth century, a "cinema of isolation,"[17] but I would say that the loneliness of differently marginalized subjects in this film is actually central to, or foundational for, the queer/crip "any day now" they ultimately cruise. Inside the bar, with the music no longer faint, Paul is next seen drinking a beer and sitting in the shadows as Rudy and two other drag queens lip-sync to Joli's music. Eventually, it is clear that Rudy is directing the lyrics—which specifically invite a "lonely man living in a world of dreams" to "come to me"— towards Paul.

Paul, who is a successful public attorney, is closeted about his homosexuality while at work. The film, however, represents him in this opening sequence of scenes apart from work. The two men hook up immediately after Rudy's performance, with Paul receiving a blow job from Rudy in his car. As the car scene opens, both men are still breathing heavily, as Rudy sits back up in the passenger seat. The post-ejaculation conversation is founded on a particular kind of queer immediacy and intimacy. Rudy asks if it is Paul's first time (he answers yes) and whether he is married ("divorced," Paul responds). Paul then asks Rudy when he knew he was gay, and Rudy responds with a story of a gender non-normative adolescence lived out through the mandates of gender normativity (indeed, a story about mandates coming directly from his father). "My first year of high school," Rudy begins, "my father made me play football. The coach told me to line up center, bend over, and grab the ball. Donny Walsh was the quarterback. He walked up behind me, put his hand on my ass for the snap, whew, I was in heaven." He shakes his head and concludes face-tiously, "It's honestly . . . all been downhill from there."

The sex scene is significant on several levels, not least because it leads to an ironic confrontation with state power, and state power represented in a way that is atypical for many white gay men in an era of homonor-mativity: as non-benign and in fact openly hostile to queerness. A police officer walks up to the car with a flashlight. "Don't worry! Roll down the window! Let me do the talking!" Rudy insists. His interaction with the officer is full of double entendres. Rudy explains that nothing was going on and that, in fact, the two men had "actually" just been talking about playing high school football. "No, really!" he says to the officer, "And you look like you've played with a few balls in *your* time." The officer immediately becomes angry and pulls his gun, but Rudy continues to taunt him (and in fact escalates his confrontation): "Why you so angry? You want to talk about it? Big man with your big gun!" Paul's reaction, however, is the reverse, as he raises his hands and nervously tells Rudy to do whatever the officer says (Rudy does not put his hands up). As the officer becomes more enraged, Paul yells at him to wait, informing him that he's a district attorney and that if he pulls the trigger he'll be guilty of murder one: "A jury will convict you in five seconds and you'll spend the next fifty years in a jail cell with some guy who wants to play cops and robbers with you every night." The officer pulls back and tells them to move along, but not before making a snide aside that the dis-trict attorney's office would be very interested to know "about one of its own getting sucked off in a parking lot." The scene ends, notably and refreshingly, with laughter, as Rudy brushes back his long hair and asks Paul, "Oh my God, what's your name?" The connection between the two men is thus visually established from the start as one of easy intimacy, perverse sexuality (a blow job in a car when the two men didn't even know each other's names), endangerment from or harassment by state power, and (in the face of all of that) laughter. As Paul drops off Rudy at his apartment ("I'm just staying here until they finish up my place in Malibu," Rudy says), he gives Rudy a card with his office number and tells him to give him a call.

The central crisis of the film is established over the course of the next 24 hours. In the hallway to his apartment, Rudy passes his neighbor's door, from behind which loud rock music is blaring. Rudy picks up the doll Ashley, which is lying on the floor in the hallway. As he returns the doll, his neighbor Marianna angrily tells him not to give her parenting tips and calls him a cocksucking motherfucker. Through the peephole in the door of his own apartment, Rudy then observes her leaving with a man and sees Marco wander alone back into their apartment.

The next day, angry at the ongoing pounding rock music from Marianna's, Rudy (in his underwear) barges through the slightly ajar door to turn the music off himself. It is then that he realizes that Marco has been left alone and it is from that moment, to return to the *Oxford English Dictionary* definition of perversion, that his "deliberate and obstinate desire" for justice for Marco is firmly established. Rudy calls Paul's office from a pay phone, but cannot get patched through to Paul by his secretary. Undeterred, he takes Marco directly to the office, expecting that Paul as an attorney can devise a plan that would somehow protect the child. The scene in the office is chaotic, with Paul attempting to maintain appearances in front of his co-workers and Rudy insistent that something be done. The differing stances the two men take toward authority and institutions in the confrontation mirrors their initial reaction to the police officer the previous night: the one thing Rudy *can* do, Paul insists, is "*call Family Services.*" Rudy refuses: "What, so they can toss him in a foster home? Do you have any idea what they do to kids in those places?" Paul asks if Rudy needs money, but Rudy does not take it, interpreting it as a sign that Paul just wants the whole situation (and Rudy himself) to go away.

Back at Rudy's apartment building, Family Services has indeed arrived, and a social worker named Miss Martinez (Kamala Lopez) tells Marco to pack up his clothes. Miss Martinez brusquely informs Rudy that Marianna is not coming back, since she was picked up by the vice squad for drug activity the night before. As the scene closes, Rudy says, "Hey Marco wait up!" He picks up Ashley from the table and hands the doll to the boy. It is a key bonding moment as Marco and Rudy gaze at each other, and Marco takes the doll, cradling her in his arms as he exits with Family Services.

The next scene represents Marco as lonely and unhappy in a temporary foster situation, and as night falls, he climbs out of bed, and—still carrying Ashley—wanders out into the empty streets. Meanwhile, back at the bar, Rudy is again performing, lip-synching this time to Honey Cone's "One Monkey Don't Stop No Show." When Rudy realizes Paul is again watching the performance, he once more directs the lyrics in Paul's direction: "If you don't want my love, you're free to go. . . . There's lots of other guys who'd love to play your role." Paul apologizes after the performance for his behavior earlier in the day, and in a tender bar scene, the two men share a drink together and talk about their lives: "I moved here to study law and change the world," Paul explains. "How's that world-changing going?" Rudy responds, implying playfully that he believes the system is not set up to work in favor of outcasts like them. He serenades Paul with a live piano number with lyrics he composes on the spot, concluding with "we could go to your car for round two."

In the car on the way back to Rudy's apartment, however, they pass Marco wandering down the street. When Rudy asks Marco where he is going, the boy responds, "Home." "Home, to your mommy's place? You're going in the wrong way," Rudy explains. He takes the child into the car. At the apartment, the men hold each other gently on the bed and drink wine directly from the bottle as Marco sleeps on the couch. "Nothing scares you," Paul says to Rudy.

Paul rushes out late to work in the morning, leaving Marco and Rudy behind for their first extended conversation, a conversation that has perverse affinities with Rudy and Paul's first conversation in the car, since this conversation too ends in laughter. "Excuse me. I'm hungry," Marco begins. There is not much in the refrigerator, and Marco quickly makes clear that he doesn't like peanut butter, or carrots. What he really wants, he says, are "donuts." Rudy lectures him about how bad donuts are for him and makes a plate of crackers and cheese. To entice Marco to eat the food, Rudy jokes that it is what they eat in France. He points to the crackers and cheese and begins to use an exaggerated French accent. It is at that point that Marco finally smiles and breaks into laughter. The laughter again marks an easy, queer (and now crip) intimacy between the two.

The perverse solidarity between the three characters is at this point firmly established. The film contains many more scenes of laughter and play as the relationship develops. The trajectory of the remainder of the film, however, is toward defeat (and, indeed, in true melodramatic fashion, death). The two men visit Marianna in prison and convince her to sign papers granting custody to Rudy while she is incarcerated. They decide to fight for permanent custody, and to strengthen their case, Paul invites Rudy to move out of the run-down apartment and in with him. They send Rudy to school and take him for regular medical checkups.

Paul and Rudy's relationship as lovers, however, is exposed by Paul's employer (he in fact loses his job), and Marco is taken from their care. The rest of the film is largely a series of court battles, with virtually all witnesses (the teacher at Marco's school, a social worker who is sent to interview them) agreeing, sometimes reluctantly, that Rudy and Paul have been good parents. Because of their "lifestyle," however, and especially because of evidence of non-normative gender behavior that appears in court (the prosecution makes much of the fact that Marco saw Rudy in a dress and that Marco's favorite toy is a girl doll), Paul and Rudy are not allowed to keep the child. Marco is returned to foster care and, once again, with the flash-forward scene that opened the film now returning, wanders out into the dark lonely streets in search of "home."

As the film concludes, the scene with Marco on the street now emerges as part of a montage of scenes, which also includes Rudy singing an anthem (Bob Dylan's "I Shall Be Released") in a new club where he has secured a position; Paul writing a letter to the various authorities in the case, including with his letter a very brief newspaper report about Marco's death; and the various authorities (the prosecuting attorney, and the judges who ruled against Paul, Rudy, and Marco) reading Paul's letter. A voiceover of Paul reading the letter, and then Rudy singing the anthem, moves the montage forward. "Enclosed please find a newspaper article," Paul's letter begins:

> You might have seen it when it was published, although I doubt it; it was buried deep in the middle of the paper. . . . Just a few brief lines about a mentally handicapped kid named Marco, who died, all alone, under a bridge, after trying to find his way home for almost three days. Since you never got to meet him in person, and since this article is short on details, I wanted you to know who Marco really was. He was a sweet kid, and smart, and funny. He had a smile that could light up a room. He loved junk food. Chocolate donuts were his drug of choice. He was the world's

greatest disco dancer. And he liked to have a story told to him every night, as long as that story had a happy ending. Marco loved a happy ending.

As Paul's voiceover concludes, Rudy's singing comes to the foreground, with Dylan's lyrics clearly articulated. As Rudy sings, the scene moves back and forth between Marco on the bridge and Rudy onstage in the club. Echoing the opening of the film, Paul watches the performance from the audience, and at one key moment, as their eyes connect (before a final cut back to Marco), it is again clear that Rudy is directing the lyrics toward his lover.

Rudy's cover of Dylan's song (performed, without lip-synching, by Cumming himself) slightly revises the lyrics. As the piano pounds, Rudy's scene opens with him belting out the lyrics as written: "They say every man needs protection,/They say every man must fall./Yet I swear I see my reflection/Some place so high above this wall." "Any day now, any day now, any day now," Rudy sings at the top of his voice. As he comes down from the dramatic crescendo, however, with softer and slower piano accompaniment, he looks directly at Paul and slightly revises (collectivizes) Dylan's lyrics: "Yes, I see my light come shining/From the west down to the east/And I swear, I swear, I swear, my love/We shall be released." Although Paul and Rudy are clearly, at this point, a committed couple, the "we" of Rudy's performance necessarily includes Marco and, arguably, multiple others. The "we" cannot be reduced to gay people, and certainly not gay couples; across the repetition of "any day now, any day now, any day now," it identifies the unacceptability of the present for multiple misfits and calls out not for pity but for solidarity across difference and for a future marked by justice for queers, for crips, or for anyone made perverse or pathological by state power and systems that would regulate or straighten embodiment, comportment, desire, and forms of relationality.

Crip Modes of Desiring

I use the term "committed couple" pointedly, as the phrase is, in our own moment, now saturated with homonormativity. It was not saturated with homonormativity in 1978, when it did not necessarily circulate so freely as a phrase. "Committed couple" is now generally used to mark a difference between respectable, upstanding gay figures seeking acceptance and recognition and undisciplined queers having sex in public and shaping complex and unexpected kinship networks with other outcasts who are (or were, only yesterday) virtual strangers. Paul and Rudy (and Marco) "commit" to each other in and through their public struggle to sustain an intimacy that was not and could not be recognized. The film represents that commitment and public struggle and gestures in the process toward what Kateřina Kolářová terms, adapting Muñoz, "crip horizons."[18] For Kolářová, crip horizons are visible from "untidy, crooked, queer, twisted, bent, crip versions of pasts"[19]—pasts that did not resolve into the present we now occupy but that can nonetheless still be called back. My argument is that the film's crip horizon of 1978 clearly did not resolve into our present, the 2012 in which it was released, yet the film represents that lost horizon as necessarily still desirable and discernable.

Kolářová's term "untidy" is worth taking seriously when thinking about representations of the past; *Any Day Now* is indeed untidy in multiple ways. My bracketing of a homonormative reading and gesturing toward a crip horizon should not discount that untidiness. If Marco is lightly coded as Latino, that coding from one perspective adds one more layer of solidarity across difference, a layer that is played out melodramatically, moreover, in the solidarity Paul and Rudy develop with their African American attorney, Lonnie Washington (Don Franklin). Washington explicitly reads the systems through which all these characters are moving with the assessment "there is no justice," and his words resonate beyond the three main characters. It is important to note that the state institutions making Paul and Rudy perverse do the same with Marianna, and a strong reading of the film would need to insist that its imagination of an elsewhere and elsewhen does not, within the terms of the narrative we have, explicitly encompass her, even if such a reading could also insist at the very least that Marco's own initial yearning for something else is implicitly predicated on a desire for her, too, to be released. Again, Rudy's first question to Marco in the street, as he tries to make sense of what Marco is seeking and where Marco is going, is "Home, to your mommy's place?" Marco nods, but the film does not, and perhaps cannot, do more to gesture toward a desired release for Marianna.

Muñoz describes the present as a "quagmire . . . that lets us feel that this world is not enough, that indeed something is missing."[20] Queerness, for Muñoz, is "a structured and educated mode of desiring" that indicates other possibilities.[21] The mode of desiring in *Any Day Now* is both queer and crip, with "crip modes of desiring" signifying, perhaps, across the film's melodramatic story, modes of desiring to be together in and through embodied (disabled) difference. Crip modes of desiring are always proximate to queer modes of desiring in that they both always thwart expectations of proper development, gendered comportment, and appropriate alliances.

In an extended consideration of the imaginative limits of "access" in our moment, Tanya Titchkosky argues that a "politics of wonder" pauses "in the face of what already *is*" and transforms "the assumed clarity of what is already said and done into a place of questions where doubt can open on to new horizons of possibility."[22] While recognizing that *Any Day Now* is in many ways a readily recognizable maudlin disability film that includes some problematic narrative hooks and that ends with (surprise, surprise) the death of its main disabled character, I *wonder* whether it nonetheless blurs the assumed clarity of narrative prosthesis (as that which simply fixes, controls, or eliminates disability from the narrative in order to tell a larger and different story). The "heartwarming" scenes often associated with representations of Down syndrome are not absent from *Any Day Now*—most notably, the disco dancing scene where Marco loses himself in enjoyment of music and motion. Yet in the film as a whole, Marco's enjoyment of music and motion is placed alongside Rudy's enjoyment of music and motion and his "heartwarming" scenes are arguably matched by heartwarming scenes of Paul and Rudy's easy and tender bodily intimacy. Most importantly, disabled actor Leyva portrays Marco reaching for, desiring, not pity but dignity, and Marco in fact receives not pity but dignity from Rudy and Paul. The film, moreover, as I suggested earlier, establishes a parallel pattern of desire and recognition by rhyming scenes of Paul and Rudy watching each other with scenes of Marco and Rudy watching each other, or Paul watching Marco and Rudy, and so forth, with each member of the group receiving a reciprocal dignity from each other in that exchange of gazes.

As I indicated in my introduction, *Any Day Now* is inspired by a true story. Screenwriter George Arthur Bloom initially conceived the story, and drafted it in 1980, after watching the developing friendship between a disabled boy and a gay man named Rudy, both living in Brooklyn before it was gentrified in subsequent decades. Rudy "practically raised him," Bloom explains, and he began to wonder what would happen if Rudy had tried to adopt the boy.[23] At the same time, the case "mirrors" another, more contemporary story—the case of Wayne LaRue Smith and Dan Skahen, who in 2008 became the first gay men in the state of Florida permitted to adopt (and one of their two sons is disabled).[24] Fine met with Smith and Skahen as he adapted Bloom's script. It is perhaps poetic that varied queer/crip kinship networks, from two different historical moments, are in circulation around the story of the film's production. In suggesting, however, that the film is in homonormativity but not of homonormativity, I mean to caution against a reading that would imagine that the film is inspired by the supposedly "true" story of the LGBT movement's grand progress narrative, about "us" as we march toward marriage equality and adoption rights. Frankly, the popular reception of the film regularly gestures toward precisely such a reading; *ScreenDaily* is not isolated in positioning the film as "a prequel to battles over gay marriage and gay adoption."[25] My argument, however, is that the film crips the compulsory modes of desire that characterize the time of its release (modes that straighten and privatize us) and conjures up perverse solidarity—who we hoped to become, any day now, in the past. Who we hoped to become (those of "us" in a wide range of world-transformative movements for social justice) was expansive, public, and explicitly non-normative.

The trouble with homonormativity now is that its necessary (and, at times, perhaps even dutiful) identification can itself be somewhat normative if the identification does not allow us to wonder whether what appears to be "gay marriage" and homonormativity might simultaneously be haunted by a queer/crip something else, formed in and of the past (formed of that which is not "us" as we are today), that we still might access in the future. *Any Day Now*, the film, both represents something that could be called, from a certain perspective, homonormativity *and* cruises around for a utopic elsewhere. "Marriage" and "marriage equality" can't kill that cruising, although they will sometimes (perhaps quite often) make it difficult to detect. "Indeed to access queer visuality," Muñoz writes, describing (or cripping) ways of seeing or visualizing that

I am linking in this conclusion to crip modes of desiring, "we may need to squint, to strain our vision and force it to see otherwise, beyond the limited vista of the here and now."[26] Any day now, we will desire (again) disability in the ways Muñoz does here (squinting, straining vision), materializing a public and perverse solidarity beyond the constraining boundaries and relations of the here and now.

NOTES

1 *Any Day Now*, directed by Travis Fine (2012; Chicago: Music Box Films).
2 Cf. McRuer, *Crip Theory*, 77–102.
3 Puar, *Terrorist Assemblages*, 3.
4 For an important discussion of the history of the term "homonormativity" in transgender studies, see Stryker, "Transgender History."
5 Duggan, "The New Homonormativity," 176.
6 Ibid., 177.
7 Ibid., 182.
8 Ibid., 179.
9 Murphy, Ruiz, and Serlin, "Editors' Introduction."
10 *Patrik 1,5*, directed by Ella Lemhagen (2008; Stockholm: Sonet Film).
11 Mitchell and Snyder, *Narrative Prosthesis*.
12 Barthes, *Mythologies*.
13 Muñoz, *Cruising Utopia*.
14 Garland-Thomson, "Seeing the Disabled," 341.
15 Definition from the *Oxford English Dictionary*.
16 Foucault, *The History of Sexuality, Volume 1*.
17 Norden, *The Cinema of Isolation*.
18 Kolářová, "The Inarticulate Post-Socialist Crip," 264.
19 Ibid., 279.
20 Muñoz, *Cruising Utopia*, 11.
21 Ibid., 1.
22 Titchkosky, *The Question of Access*, x.
23 Kendra, "Any Day Now Tackles Gay Adoption in the 70's," *It's Conceivable*, February 10, 2013, http://itsconceivablenow.com.
24 Steve Rothaus, "Gay Adoption Film 'Any Day Now' Mirrors Case of Key West Foster Fathers," *Miami Herald*, January 21, 2013, http://miamiherald.typepad.com.
25 David D'Arcy, "Any Day Now," *ScreenDaily*, April 25, 2012, www.screendaily.com.
26 Muñoz, *Cruising Utopia*, 22.

PART VI

Disability and Technology

12

The Price of the Popular Media Is Paid by the Effluent Citizen

TOBY MILLER

An important shared interest of disability studies and media studies is the materiality of media and its consequences for differently situated subjects. Toby Miller examines both ends of the production cycle of media technologies—manufacture and disposal—to demonstrate the interconnected ways that they are physically, economically, environmentally, and politically disabling. He reveals how these modes of disablement collectively produce the liminal status of "effluent citizenship" for poor and despised laborers on the fringes of the global economy upon whom the popular media depend.

Who pays the price of the popular media, and how does it relate to disability? And what is an effluent citizen?

I shall put some of these terms under erasure as contingent and debatable, then argue that we need to turn away—for a moment, not forever—from such important issues as the production, representation, and reception of screen texts and their implications for disabled people, and toward the production of disability in the very manufacture and recycling of media technologies themselves. My case study will be Mexico's formal and informal labor force.

Disability and Price

The United Nations Convention on the Rights of Persons with Disabilities defines "persons with disabilities" as people with "long-term physical, mental, intellectual or sensory impairments which in interaction with various barriers may hinder their full and effective participation in society on an equal basis with others."[1] The Convention provides a useful starting point because it allows for disability's shifts and shocks as a social construction. We should add the constitutive role of corporate, governmental, cultural, and interpersonal ignorance and prejudice in creating and negating "disability" as part of biopower's hyper-investment in conventionally productive and reproductive bodies.

The relevant categories are of course historically, geographically, politically, theoretically, and empirically contingent, as is being able-bodied.[2] And activism has been central to altering the relevant definitions, debates, and policies. For example, anti-eugenics disability civil rights movements have challenged conventional discourses.[3] And while medical researchers engage supposed links between, for example, autism and the media in the language of illness, activists and progressive scholars argue that it should instead be regarded as a disability, or embrace "neurodiversity" as a means of understanding differences without denigrating them.[4]

So how does this connect to pricing?

In his problematization of supply and demand as the principal determinations of the price and value of goods and services, Amartya Sen says that a disabled person may have "the same demand function over commodity bundles" as an able-bodied one without deriving the same utility from them, because they have particular needs. As a consequence, setting prices through these mechanisms and ignoring different subjectivities means we all pay the same amount but get different qualities of experience in return. The capacity to increase income or transform it into social power through consumption, for example investment in human capital, may be similarly unequal.[5]

This argument lies at the heart of Sen's support for focusing social policy not just on inequalities derived from wealth and income, but capability as well.[6] Such a focus is sometimes taken to imply that the disabled cannot lead pleasurable, autotelic lives—but that is not Sen's view. Rather, he is saying that the resources required for self-actualization may be greater and more diverse for the disabled than others.[7] And it is clear that social policy enabling access to those resources does not happen in the media sphere.

Disability and the Media

"Medium," the singular form of the word "media," has been in English usage since the seventeenth century. It refers to something that lies between two objects and links them. With that in mind, I use the term "media" to cover a multitude of cultural and communicative machines and processes that connect people, processes, institutions, meanings, and power in the material world, but with a particular emphasis on film and television drama.

Like disability, media definitions are very contingent—for instance, why are the BBC and Russia Today/RT *not* "social media," when their news reports are discussed by millions of people; but a solitary web page attacking feminism and read by no one *is* "social media"? We supposedly occupy an epoch that sees *La fin de la télévision* (*The End of Television*)[8] and we are routinely told that *La televisión ha muerto* (*Television Is Dead*).[9] But such claims are empirically empty. Worldwide, the number of subscribers to television via satellite and cable increased 8% to eight hundred million in 2012.[10] In 2013, the average Briton watched about four hours of linear television a day on a TV set, and just three and a half minutes on tablets, smartphones, and laptops.[11] Indian residents are likelier to own television sets than have access to indoor plumbing, and politicians devote their advertising money to television ahead of all other options. The number of Indian TV households grew by eleven million in 2012.[12] In Mexico, as digital media proliferate, so does TV. It is the dominant medium, and if anything increasingly so.[13] In Australia, "all age groups continue to spend the majority of their screen time with the in-home TV set."[14] And the first five months of the 2016 U.S. presidential campaign saw almost three million commercials on cable TV alone, an increase of a million from four years earlier.[15]

From a textual perspective, specifically a metaphorical one, disabled people pay a heavy symbolic price in the media for their social status. The history of cinema discloses that from the earliest moving pictures, disabled bodies were objects of stigmatization and even derisive laughter.[16] These bodies remain subject to the scopophilic gaze, a psychoanalytic term used in film theory to explain the pleasure spectators may feel at watching people on screen who cannot see them—in pornography, for example.[17] But one could also think of pornography as a valued aid to sexual self-expression for the paying disabled, who meet a price in search of pleasure.[18]

On television, it is a quarter-century since the British Council of Organisations of Disabled People issued guidelines for producers on representing disabled people. They were based on intense dissatisfaction, wide consultation, and a review of relevant literature.[19] But recent studies of disability and TV, focused with equal vigor on production, text, and reception, clarify that little has changed.[20] In 2015–16, U.S. primetime TV drama's percentage of regular characters living with disabilities dropped from 1.4% the previous year to 0.9%, even though 12% of the U.S. population is disabled.[21]

Occasionally, a television series emerges that is hailed for focusing on disability as simultaneously normal, manageable, shocking, and traumatic, such as *Push Girls* (Sundance, 2012–present); but this is uncommon. Eugenic views continue to haunt Hollywood, as seen in protests regarding the film *Me before You* (Thea Sharrock, 2016),[22] and the few dramatic roles that involve disability are frequently cast with able-bodied actors.[23] The desire for more integration into storylines of both factual and fictional media texts remains strong among the disabled.[24]

This is very much in keeping with the discourse of misrepresentation and exclusion that runs through civil-rights arguments about media texts. It is a powerful position that can attain commercial, state, and media responses due to its basis in popular democracy and understanding of how to lobby and embarrass. This narrative of inclusiveness has circulated in debates about the media and disability in the United States since at least the early days of radio.

But it can also be articulated to the governmentalization of the everyday and the radical as a counter to disabled activists' fundamental critiques of the bourgeois media through their incorporation in a Faustian bargain that ensures interpellation but leaves prevailing power relations intact.[25] Talent agencies may now have diversity departments that specialize in casting disabled people[26] and Hollywood unions offer some research and services;[27] but it is an unequal exchange when disabled people pay for the media as consumers just like everyone else, yet are either ignored or exploited by them as social subjects.

Adopting a more medical model of disability, some scholars look at the price of the interaction between the media and disabled people in a different way, contending that popular culture has deleterious effects on mental functioning and bodily fitness.[28] There is a lengthy history of parents, doctors, psy-function[29] experts, officials, politicians, and community groups expressing concern about the impact of the media on developmental problems, behavioral conditions, and so on, and linking these to disability—as far back as the nineteenth century, neurological experts attributed their increased business to telegraphy, alongside the expansion of steam, periodical literature, science, and education for women.[30] Despite several decades of scholarship and activism, such positions remain prevalent in contemporary discourse about people with disabilities.

What of the newer media, as opposed to these venerable and middle-aged forms? Aren't they supposed to demolish barriers and end the confinement of social groups? Perhaps, but at a price. At a policy level, in the U.S. for example, services such as closed captioning and deafness are frequently associated with private endeavor and hence understood to articulate to consumption and telecoms policy, diminishing their standing under civil-rights legislation.[31] And the supposed capacity of the internet to break through cultural gatekeepers and permit unfiltered expression can easily lead to the attempted humiliation and commodification of disabled people via extraordinarily abusive rants.[32]

Of course, in their replication of letters to the editor, the newer media can provide a means of talking back to the bourgeois media and potentially forming a variety of counter-public spheres where disabled people and other excluded or stereotyped groups can speak, unite, disunite, exchange, disengage, and so on, instead of being fixed in place as isolated and disgruntled spectators.[33] But disabled people are among the many disadvantaged groups with less access to the internet than is the norm.[34] This dilemma inevitably directs us to questions of citizenship rights.

Effluent Citizenship

The last two hundred years of modernity have produced three zones of citizenship, with partially overlapping but also distinct historicities. These zones are the political (conferring the right to reside and vote); the economic (the right to work and prosper); and the cultural (the right to know and speak). They correspond to the French Revolutionary cry "*liberté, égalité, fraternité*" (liberty, equality, solidarity) and the Argentine left's contemporary version "*ser ciudadano, tener trabajo, y ser alfabetizado*" (citizenship, employment, and literacy). The first category concerns political rights; the second, material interests; and the third, cultural representation. Running across these are calls for ecological or environmental citizenship.[35]

I suggest we use "*effluent citizenship*" as a further category—an unfortunate one on the surface, unlike those above, as "effluent" means waste or sewage. I stumbled across it as what I assume is a typographical error made by Taylor and Francis, the publisher of an article I consulted for this chapter.[36] It got me thinking about the specific rights of those working with and as the *detritus* of society. It articulates to my earlier remark about the role of corporate, governmental, cultural, and interpersonal ignorance and prejudice in creating and negating "disability" as part of biopower's hyper-investment in conventionally productive and reproductive bodies. This effluent citizenship specifically applies to the search for rights by those who dispose of media trash, but I suggest we can also apply it to those working under abject but factory conditions in the more formal economy of media manufacturing.

In pre-industrial European towns, the anxious rich condemned the "odor of crowded bodies" and a "rising tide of excrement and rubbish." Ragpickers typified urban untouchables: "sewermen, gut dressers, knackers, drain cleaners, workers in refuse dumps, and dredging gangs."[37] Removal meant the *displacement* of waste, but not its *elimination*. As a living, malodorous reminder of urban filth, the lowly ragpicker foiled bourgeois fantasies of cleanliness that depended on "escape from and rejection of a primitive agricultural system now in a state of crisis."[38]

In the electronic waste (e-waste) era, ragpickers are statistical and managerial problems in terms of public health, income, self-sufficiency, and so on. They are effluent citizens. Indian ragpickers, who number in the hundreds of thousands, suffer a historically unprecedented prevalence of low hemoglobin, high monocyte and eosinophil counts, gum disease, diarrhea, and dermatitis.[39] In Brazil, where it is estimated that there are half a million ragpickers, extraordinary levels of physiological disorders and psychological distress are reported. Epidemiological studies frequently find ragpickers at fault for polluting their environments, and seek to outlaw them.[40]

I am concerned here, then, with how the media cause disability—not through consciousness/media effects, but as part of their real, material practice, linked to the creation of electronic technologies and their post-consumer lives. My site is Mexican workers in both the formal sector (who manufacture media gadgetry) and the informal sector (who re-cycle it). The vast majority of the world's six hundred million disabled people live in the Global South and are also among the likeliest to de-velop disabilities due to injuries at work.[41]

I focus below not on the monetary, metaphorical, or medical cost paid by consumers of media technologies and texts, but the price in terms of physi-cal health paid by the workers who manufacture and recycle the devices that consumers are forever upgrading in order to augment their pleasure and performance. Many people laboring in the *maquiladoras* of northwest-ern Mexico, whether in the formal or informal sectors, suffer remarkable physical harm that materially affects their capabilities as per Sen's account.

Mexico

When a *bracero* (guest-worker) program with the U.S. ended in the mid-1960s, the Mexican state introduced import-tax exemptions to attract external manufacturing, and Washington permitted duty-free return of components that had originated north of the border and were assembled south of it. Mexican *maquiladoras*—factories owned by foreign (especially U.S.) companies producing goods for reimportation into those countries—opened their doors. What began as a temporary initiative became of massive economic significance during the 1980s and 1990s. In 1993, *maqui-ladora* exports amounted to U.S. $21.9 billion; in 2000, the figure was U.S. $79.5 billion. The *maquiladoras'* proportion of Mexico's overall exports grew from 37.8% in 1995 to 47.1% in 2006, when they employed upwards of 1.2 million people, a labor force generated through the migration of poor rural people to the north. There was no equivalent growth in social ser-vices, education, public health, housing, or water supplies.[42]

The North American Free Trade Agreement/*Tratado de Libre Comer-cio* (NAFTA/TLC) became a key instrument of this exploitation. Since the treaty's adoption, trade between the U.S. and Mexico has grown without a comparable redistribution of wealth or economic develop-ment. Mexico boasts over eight hundred electronics manufacturers, em-ploying over six hundred thousand people. They are paid lower wages than their counterparts in Nepal and China.[43] The U.S.-Mexico frontier is characterized by "greater income disparity . . . than at any other major commercial border in the world."[44]

Women have long been at the forefront of the *maquiladoras'* electronic-labor process and its impact on health and disability. For instance, when RCA moved its radio and TV plants from Bloomington to Ciudad Juárez in search of cheaper costs, company elders sought a workforce of young, unmarried women.[45] The gendered nature of this employment has been accompanied by violence. Human Rights Watch disclosed the numerous misogynistic assaults and discrimination in *maquiladoras* in 1996. Matters have hardly improved. The Centre for Reflection and Action on Labour Issues (CEREAL) interviewed thousands of workers in 2008 and 2009 across the Mexican electronics sector, disclosing systematic sexual harassment and fundamental exploitation; one reads telling stories of each female employee preparing over a hundred central-processing units an hour in factories. They are classified as "temporary" so that employers can elude regulations and deals that govern full-time labor. Their occupational health and safety are jeopardized, just as their labor is discounted.[46]

Maquiladora warehouses, managers, and researchers are generally based in San Diego. Components are imported to Mexico from there, Germany, Korea, Japan, Taiwan, Malaysia, and Thailand. Put another way, the dangerous, dull, and poorly remunerated work is done across the border. In response, vigorous civil-society groups remind authorities of their responsibilities and encourage direct citizen activism, notably Las Voces de la Maquila,[47] the Colectivo Chilpancingo Pro Justicia Ambiental,[48] the Environmental Health Coalition,[49] and Greenpeace.[50]

Mainstream economic analyses of these industries focus on foreign direct investment, local employment, and technology transfer, largely ignoring pollution, exploitation, and gender relations.[51] An example is the *New York Times* headlining TV-set manufacture as "A Boom across the Border."[52] For such approaches, "*maquiladora* diseases . . . that bloom in wombs and spinal columns"[53] are no doubt negative externalities, to be considered—if at all—in a calculus of Paretian optimality and the most "efficient" allocation of resources.

Of course, manufacturing television sets is only one part of Mexico's electronics production. Hewlett Packard, Hitachi, IBM, Nokia, Siemens, Philips, and Motorola all have businesses there, not to mention such subcontractors as Foxconn, Solectron, Flextronics, and Jabil Circuits.[54] This abject situation has not been simply accepted by workers:

As workers and communities outside of Silicon Valley began to discover this "dark side of the chip," they also began to come together to confront its "clean" image. Community and worker based movements began to emerge in other countries—PHASE II in Scotland, Asia Monitor Resource Centre in Hong Kong, TAVOI in Taiwan, CEREAL in Mexico, etc. as the grassroots efforts began to grow into a global movement. Many of these groups are now working together internationally through various networks to develop worker training on occupational health and safety, to clean up and prevent air and water pollution, to press the electronics industry to phase out use of the most toxic chemicals.[55]

The National Coalition of Electronic Industry Workers, declares that five years after the publication of the Electronic Industry Code of Conduct: the same companies that signed the Code are the ones violating the human labor rights. The Code states (part A-7) that the signing companies should respect the workers' freedom of association. This right, in our Federal Labor Law, is constantly violated. We recall two recent cases. The first one: the dismissal of more than 10 workers of Flextronics, only because they demanded transparency on the issue of profit shares. The second case was the dismissal of Aureliano Rosas Suárez, Omar Manuel Montes Estrada [and] Vicente de Jesús Rodríguez Roa, sacked because they demanded their right to have their wages leveled. They also worked for the company Flextronics. We inform the International Electronic Industry that the members of the National Coalition of Electronic Industry Workers will continue to use this mask as a symbol of our repression. But the coalition will continue demanding and defending our human labor rights.[56]

The second quotation above comes from a group of masked activists who protest against these labor conditions. Their identities are kept secret in order to protect their employment, their friends, and their relatives. The anonymous protestors have made periodic media appearances since 2007. They offer a civil-society voice that is organic to current and former workers on the line (unions exist, but are basically inactive or corporate). They represent effluent citizenship.

And the environment? The 1984 La Paz Agreement on Cooperation for the Protection and Improvement of the Environment in the Border Area/*Convenio entre los Estados Unidos Mexicanos y los Estados Uni-*

dos de América sobre Cooperación para la Protección y Mejoramiento del Medio Ambiente between Mexico and the U.S. mandates that *maquiladora* waste return to where the relevant multinational corporation is domiciled.[57] Despite that accord, and NAFTA/TLC's environmental and labor protections, the *maquilas* have ushered in and maintained low wages, labor-law violations, and exposure to unhealthy chemicals and gases—a toxic life in every sense. Enforcement has been lax, and statistics about the environmental side effects of production and the flow of contaminated goods are spotty (the anecdotal evidence is appalling). Domestic manufacturing is similarly scandalous in the pollution of air, water, and soil, which leads to disability across industrialized population centers. The constitutive racialization of Republican Party electoral tactics routinely dogs the prospects for effective bilateral governance in the collective interests of public health.[58]

The 1992 Basel Convention on the Control of Transboundary Movements of Hazardous Wastes and their Disposal prohibits international transportation of hazardous material, even between non-signatories of the accord (the U.S.) and signatories (Mexico).[59] But powerful polluters like Japan, Canada, and the U.S. engage in "venue shopping," seeking out dumping grounds wherever feasible. They justify such actions on a neoliberal basis, invoking the doctrines of comparative advantage and the notion that every nation has a certain amount of e-waste it can bear. California alone shipped about twenty million pounds of e-waste in 2006 to various nations, including Mexico.[60] The U.S. is notorious for dispatching old batteries across the border, where clinical reports of the impact on children's development are chilling.[61]

Such waste is one of the biggest sources of heavy metals and toxic pollutants. It causes grave environmental and health concerns, stemming from the potential seepage of noxious chemicals, gases, and metals into landfills, water sources, and salvage yards. Mexico has some of the most advanced technology in the world for recycling computer monitors and television sets,[62] but profit margins are greater when unsafe methods are used in the informal sector.

Before the Spanish invasion, Mexico had many *pepenadores*—people who managed waste. Their policies and practices were disrupted by the conquest, which saw more and more urban dross accumulate over three centuries as commodification took hold and put an end to rural recycling norms.[63] Today, much e-waste recycling is done by pre-teen girls, ragpickers who work without protection to pull apart outmoded First World televisions and computers. The remains are dumped in landfills.

So a vicious cycle ensues, whereby workers in the conventional economy in a place like Mexico make the devices, fall ill, and become disabled; then after the media are deemed surplus to requirements in the U.S. and elsewhere, they are exported back to Mexico, where workers in the informal economy recycle them, fall ill, and become disabled.[64] The disposal of solid waste such as electronic equipment is responsible for over 8% of the country's greenhouse-gas emissions.[65]

The effluent citizens who deal with this waste are as liminal as the border itself. Like other global fringe-dwellers who have circled both modernity and postmodernity, they are crucial yet often invisible contributors to material and mythological life. Ironically, itinerant ragpickers are hardy perennials, supplying raw materials to cultural industries from Gutenberg to the internet. Perhaps 1% of people in the Global South live this way—approximately fifteen million worldwide.[66]

Mexican e-waste ragpickers are frequently former employees or family members of *maquiladora* workers. They operate beyond taxation, labor laws, and police, collecting, separating, cataloguing, and selling materials from spurned consumer and business products that have made their way to rubbish dumps and low-income areas. Most ragpickers do not earn wages from employers, nor are they in registered co-operatives or small businesses. As we have seen, this lack of workers' rights also characterizes the *maquiladoras*, which use temporary-employment agencies to hire people who are never deemed full-time.[67]

Like others laboring in the informal sector, they suffer three kinds of occupational harm: primary emissions expose them to dangerous substances in the objects they are recycling, such as mercury, arsenic, and lead; secondary emissions see dioxins forming during incinerations; and tertiary ones emerge when the precious metals that ragpickers seek are extracted through poisonous reagents, such as cyanide, which are left exposed in the open air. The results change the bodies and life chances of very poor, very young people forever, altering their very DNA, hormones, fertility, breathing, and other functions.[68] Ragpickers have the lowest life expectancy in Mexico[69] and labor for little—an average of

U.S. $2,500 a year.[70] And the young ragpickers exposed to e-waste frequently lack information about the dangers confronting them.[71]

In 2012, the Mexican state introduced reforms to transfer people from the informal to the formal sectors of the economy.[72] There are classically three reasons for doing this. From the government's point of view, it increases tax revenue and spreads the tax base. In terms of social services, it permits a better accounting for the who, what, when, where, and how of the nation. For workers, it can mean both greater regulation and greater protection—less freedom and flexibility, but more rights and entitlements. It is putatively designed to boost government revenues and regularize salaries and conditions. Perversely, such "reform" is really designed to disempower trade unions and make the employees they cover into flexible workers as per those in the informal sector.[73]

In addition, local public policy frequently exacerbates ragpickers' lives by mandating that they forge perverse alliances with exploitative middle-"man" brokers, even as they remain outside the law: the Mexican case saw quasi-formalization of the informal sector under the *clientelismo* of the Partido Revolucionario Institucional, which ran national and rural politics for decades through a mixture of electoral popularity, corruption, and international networks.[74]

The wider background to this story is structural adjustment as peddled by the World Bank, the International Monetary Fund, the World Trade Organization, and the sovereign states that dominate them. That neoliberal clerisy encourages the Global South to turn away from subsistence agriculture and toward tradable goods. This tendency has urged, and capitalism has driven, chaotic urban growth. The result is an informal working class that is generally disarticulated from political activity and non-government organizations, because it lacks monetary and cultural capital and organizational heft. Not surprisingly, the World Bank and its kind show no interest in actually engaging ragpickers: they want to transform them from a distance. The same applies to orthodox waste-management systems.[75]

Conclusion

Several options for regulating multinational corporations and the challenges they pose trans-territorially for citizen action present themselves as responses to the situation I have described: "soft law [protocols of international organizations], hard law [nationally based legislation], codes of conduct [transnational norms], and voluntary self-regulation" (ho ho ho).[76] But critical research argues that these strategies have so far failed to secure a nexus between "the transfer of technology" and the transfer of "practices for using it safely."[77] That outcome would necessitate universal standards of health and safety across sites, from the post-industrial core to the manufacturing periphery, in addition to contractual deals between multinationals and their hosts.[78] Guidance must come from a blend of political, economic, and cultural citizenship into effluent citizenship, recognizing those who are left out of even progressive narratives. We need to respond to this situation by connecting the materiality of media technologies to the production of disability. Our research should be as nimble as capital itself, so that we can juggle political economy, ethnography, and textual analysis and work with the relevant parties in order to set an agenda and fulfill it.

NOTES

1 United Nations, Convention on the Rights of Persons with Disabilities.

2 Asch and Fine, *Women with Disabilities*; Davis, *Enforcing Normalcy*; Linton, *Claiming Disability*.

3 Rose and Rose, "The Changing Face of Human Nature."

4 Hacking, "Kinds of People." On "neurodiversity," see Oren, this volume.

5 Sen, *Development as Freedom*, 69, 88, 119.

6 Sen, *The Idea of Justice*, 253.

7 Eagleton, *The Meaning of Life*, 84–85; Angeloni, "Integrated Disability Management."

8 Missika, *La fin de la télévision*.

9 De Silva, *La televisión ha muerto*.

10 Wayne Friedman, "Worldwide Pay TV on the Rise, Big Growth in Asia," *Media-Post*, May 23, 2013, www.mediapost.com.

11 Rory Cellan-Jones, "TV's Changing? Not So Fast . . . ," *BBC News*, February 17, 2014, www.bbc.com.

12 FICCI/KPMG, "The Power of a Billion: Realizing the Indian Dream," Indian Media and Entertainment Industry Report, 2013, www.ficci.com.

13 Rodrigo Gomez, Gabriel Sosa-Plata, Primavera Téllez Girón, and Jorge Bravo, "Mapping Digital Media: Mexico," *Open Society Foundations*, 2011, www.opensocietyfoundations.org.

14 Nielsen Australia, "Australian Multi-Screen Report: Quarter 1 2013," *Australian Policy Online*, June 27, 2013, http://apo.org.au.

15 Kate Kaye, "Cable TV Sees 2.8M Political Spots since January," *AdAge*, June 18, 2016, http://adage.com.

16 Williams, *Hard Core*, 47.

17 Aguilera, *Disability and Delight*; Elman, "Mainstreaming Immobility"; Galbraith, *Career of Evil*.

18 Shakespeare, Gillespie-Sells, and Davies, *The Sexual Politics of Disability*.

19 Barnes, "Disabling Imagery."

20 Barton, "Disability and Television."

21 GLAAD, "Where We Are on TV" (2015): 25, www.glaad.org.

22 Rebecca Sun, "'Me before You' Storyline Sparks Criticism from Hollywood's Disabled Community," *Hollywood Reporter*, June 6, 2016, www.hollywoodreporter.com.

23 Greg Gilman, "Hollywood's Disabled Actors Protest NBC's 'Ironside' Casting—When Is It Their Turn?" *The Wrap*, May 20, 2013, www.thewrap.com.

24 Hardeep Aiden and Andrea McCarthy, "Current Attitudes towards Disabled People," *Scope*, 2014, www.scope.org.uk.

25 Kirkpatrick, "'A Blessed Boon.'" See version in this volume.

26 "Diversity Department," *Kazarian/Measures/Ruskin and Associates*, 2016, http://kmrtalent.com.

27 Olivia Raynor and Katharine Hayward, "The Employment of Performers with Disabilities in the Entertainment Industry," *Screen Actors Guild*, 2005, www.sagaftra.org.

28 Lillard and Peterson, "The Immediate Impact of Different Types of Television"; Robertson, McAnally, and Hancox, "Childhood and Adolescent Television Viewing."

29 The psy-function is a shifting field of knowledge and power over the body that is comprised of psychoanalysis, psychology, psychotherapy, psychiatry, social psychology, criminology, and psycho-pharmacology, and their success in various disciplinary sites—educational, military, industrial, and carceral. See Foucault, *Psychiatric Power*, 85–86, 189–90.

30 Miller, *Technologies of Truth* and "Media Effects and Cultural Studies."

31 Ellcessor, "Captions On, Off."

32 Liddiard, "Liking for Like's Sake"; Ellis and Goggin, *Disability and the Media*, 12–14; Tom Shakespeare, "Not Just a Pretty Facebook," *Ouch!*, July 28, 2009, www.bbc.co.uk.

33 Rodan, Ellis, and Lebeck, *Disability, Obesity, and Ageing*; Ihlebæk and Krumsvik, "Editorial Power and Public Participation"; Quinn and Powers, "Revisiting the Concept of 'Sharing'"; Cavanagh, "Ladies of the *Times*"; Pedersen, "What's in a Name?"; Ellis and Goggin, *Disability and the Media*.

34 Elizabeth Rust, "How the Internet Still Fails Disabled People," *Guardian*, June 29, 2015, www.theguardian.com.

35 Miller, *Cultural Citizenship*.

36 Premalatha, Abbasi, and Abbasi, "Management of E-Waste": 1585.

37 Corbin, *The Foul and the Fragrant*, 53, 114, 115, 145–46.

38 Calvino, *The Road to San Giovanni*, 113.

39 Monocytes and eosinophil are white blood cells.

40 Silva, Fassa, and Kriebel, "Minor Psychiatric Disorders"; Ray et al., "Respiratory and General Health Impairments"; Mukherjee, *Child Ragpickers in Nepal*.

41 Sen, *The Idea of Justice*, 258–59.

42 Carrillo and Zárate, "The Evolution of Maquiladora Best Practices"; Mendoza, "The Effect of the Chinese Economy"; Reygadas, *Ensamblando culturas*; Baram, "Globalization and Workplace Hazards."

43 Centro de Reflexión y Acción Laboral, *El precio de la flexibilidad*, 8–9. Not all these firms are based near the nation's northern border and not all are *maquiladoras*.

44 Jacott, Reed, and Winfield, *The Generation and Management of Hazardous Wastes*.

45 Cowie, *Capital Moves*, 17–18; Kalm, "Emancipation or Exploitation?"

46 Centre for Reflection and Action on Labor Issues, *Labor Rights in a Time of Crisis*; Kent Paterson, "Temping Down Labor Rights: The Manpowerization of Mexico," *Corpwatch*, January 6, 2010, www.corpwatch.org; Centro de Reflexión y Acción Laboral, *El precio de la flexibilidad*.

47 "Lexmark, Voces de la Maquila | Hablan trabajadores de Ciudad Juárez," *YouTube*, February 10, 2016, www.youtube.com.

48 "Invitacion Salvemos la Playa XXI por Jovenes Pro Justicia Ambiental," *YouTube*, March 13, 2011, www.youtube.com.

49 Environmental Health Coalition, n.d., www.environmentalhealth.org.

50 García and Simpson, "Community-Based Organizing for Labor Rights"; Simpson, "Warren County's Legacy."

51 Cf. Mendoza, "The Effect of the Chinese Economy."

52 Elisabeth Malkin, "A Boom across the Border," *New York Times*, August 26, 2004, www.nytimes.com.

53 Urrea, *By the Lake of Sleeping Children*, 12.

54 Angélica Enciso, "México genera cada año hasta 180 mil toneladas de basura electrónica," *Jornada*, December 24, 2007, www.jornada.unam.mx; Greenpeace, "Tóxicos en la Producción y Basura Electrónica (e-waste)," n.d.; Rafael H. Guadarrama, "'Reciclatrón,' este fin de semana en el Valle de México," *Once TVMexico Noticias*, January 28, 2010; Guillermo J. Román Moguel, "Diagnóstico sobre la generación de basura electrónica en México," Mexico City: Instituto Nacional de Ecología, 2007.

55 Smith, "Why We Are 'Challenging the Chip.'"

56 Centre for Reflection and Action on Labor Issues, *Labor Rights in a Time of Crisis*, 28.

57 Available at http://biblioteca.semarnat.gob.mx.

58 Simpson, "Warren County's Legacy": 166–67; Perez-Maldonado et al., "Assessment of the Polychlorinated Biphenyls (PCBs) Levels"; Collins-Dogrul, "Governing Transnational Social Problems"; Pezzoli et al., "One Bioregion/One Health"; for a more sanguine view, see Mumme and Collins, "The La Paz Agreement."

59 Available at www.basel.int.

60 Mike Lee, "Our Electronic Waste Is Piling Up Overseas," *San Diego Union-Tribune*, June 19, 2007: A1.

61 Elizabeth Rosenthal, "Lead from Old U.S. Batteries Sent to Mexico Raises Risks," *New York Times*, December 8, 2011, www.nytimes.com. Of course, middle-class Mexicans also contribute to the problem—the government estimates that country generates 411 tons of e-waste a day, with an annual increase of 6%. Also see Semarnat, *Programa nacional para la prevención y gestión integral de los residuos 2009–2012*, Estados Unidos Mexicanos, 2008, 10, www.sustenta.org.mx; Marino and Rosas, *ICTs and Environmental Sustainability*.

62 Duan et al., *Quantitative Characterization*, 45.

63 Marello and Helwege, *Solid Waste Management and Social Inclusion of Waste Pickers*, 130.

64 Premalatha, Abbasi, and Abbasi, "Management of E-Waste."

65 Hoornweg and Bhada-Tata, *What a Waste*.

66 Medina, *The World's Scavengers*; Silva et al., "World at Work."

67 Medina, *The World's Scavengers*, vii, 1, 128.

68 Premalatha, Abbasi, and Abbasi, "Management of E-Waste"; Estrada-Ayub and Kahhat, "Decision Factors for E-Waste."

69 Wilson, Velis, and Cheeseman, "Role of Informal Sector Recycling."

70 Marello and Helwege, *Solid Waste Management*, 3.

71 Marino and Rosas, *ICTs and Environmental Sustainability*.

72 Centro de Reflexión y Acción Laboral, *El precio de la flexibilidad*.

73 Centro de Reflexión y Acción Laboral, *El precio de la flexibilidad*; Marello and Helwege, *Solid Waste Management*, 18.

74 Medina, *The World's Scavengers*, 133; Alma Guillermoprieto, "Letter from Mexico City," *New Yorker*, September 17, 1990: 93; Marello and Helwege, *Solid Waste Management*, 18.

75 Medina, *The World's Scavengers*, ix; Centro Interdiciplinario para Prevención de la Contaminación, *Programa de difusión y capacitación*.

76 Maxwell and Miller, *Greening the Media*, 146.

77 Baram, "Globalization and Workplace Hazards."

78 Ferus-Comelo, "Mission Impossible?"; Schatan and Castilleja, "The Maquiladora Electronics Industry."

13

Disability and Biomediation

Tinnitus as Phantom Disability

MACK HAGOOD

The medical mediation of bodily differences can be fraught, and many scholars have shown how the combination of media and medicine can produce disablement according to biopolitical norms. Mack Hagood proposes a framework for the study of biomediation that disentangles medical uses of media technologies from the medical model of disability. Using tinnitus as his case study, he demonstrates the value of this framework for understanding the complex role of media in both biological and political struggles over disability and disabled identities.

An audiologist sits behind a diagnostic audiometer. Beyond this device, which resembles an audio engineer's digital mixing board, stands a double-paned window. Beyond the window, her client sits in the sound booth, wearing headphones. The audiologist presses a button and speaks into a microphone: "If I get to a pitch that's fairly close to the sound you usually hear, press the button." The client hears the audiologist's words through the headphones, looks down at the subject-response switch in her hand, and nods. The audiologist then uses the audiometer to generate the first of many tones.

A man sits at his desk, trying to concentrate. He fears his boss is losing patience. When he told him about the terrible roaring in his ears weeks ago, the boss shrugged it off: "I have that too. Doesn't bother me a bit." The man turns up the thunderstorm from rainymood.com on his computer speakers and does yet another Google search for "tinnitus cure."

The leader of a local support group is writing a second email to the American Tinnitus Association: "The Jerry Lewis Labor Day MDA telethon started on a TV station in New York City. Need I tell you how far it's come and how much money has been raised? More people suffer from tinnitus than muscular dystrophy, but no telethon. The noise is unbearable. I see distressed and desperate people at every meeting I host. Isn't it time we took a chance?"

Disability and Media beyond Representation

The scenes above are compiled from three years' ethnographic fieldwork among Americans with tinnitus (buzzing, ringing, or other "phantom sounds" in the head or ears) and the professionals who treat them. Involving a wide array of technologies (audiometer, headphones, speakers, internet, email, television), they speak to a complex relationship between disability, healthcare, and technology, in which mediation is central to the diagnosis, treatment, representation, and social relations around a problem of the body.

That complex relationship and the sorts of experiences of disability evoked in the scenes above—moments in which individuals use media to diagnose, treat, and advocate for human bodies—have not been adequately addressed by either disability or media studies. These practices involve—yet also extend beyond—what David Serlin calls the visual culture of public health, which "arguably represents the confluence of two mutually dependent innovations: the emergence of modern medicine's reliance on sophisticated media to represent diagnosis and treatment, and the emergence of modern communication's reliance on sophisticated media to fulfill particular institutional or ideological goals."[1] In fact, the confluence of media and medicine Serlin describes goes beyond the visual and involves more than representation. When an audiologist uses an audiometer to match the pitch and volume of a person's tinnitus, this is not the representation *of* diagnosis, but the use of audio media *in* diagnosis. Similarly, when audiologists prescribe the use of rainfall and ocean sound machines to ameliorate tinnital suffering, the utility of these digital artifacts shifts from representation to treatment. When scholars study moments such as these, in which bodies and technologies interact, they shift the analytical frame from one of representation to one of *biomediation*.

This chapter advocates the study of media technology as it pertains to disability, exploring ways that biomediation can play a more central role in the critical analysis of disability and media. In 2003, Gerard Goggin and Christopher Newell proposed to "cast a critical gaze upon the very technologies that are supposed to provide the solution to disability—and show how new media technologies actually build in disability."[2] Goggin and Newell's work challenged the hype that surrounded new media at the time—even in the work of many media scholars—while also taking seriously media's potential for new kinds of agency and community when utilized by disabled people. By 2005, Goggin was calling specifically for more work to be done "at the intersection of the literatures of social study of science and technology, those of cultural and media studies, and those of critical media studies"—an intersection we might call "media technology studies."[3] In the intervening years, some important work in this vein has been done in areas such as new media accessibility and community, as well as deafness and media technologies. Nevertheless, there is work to be done in bringing together technology, disability, and media studies, as explored in the introduction to this volume.

Biomediation is one way to integrate these perspectives and promote interdisciplinary work on disability and media technologies. After discussing the recent interdisciplinary trend of closely examining media technologies as both culture and artifact, I will suggest the types of questions media technology studies can address. Next, I will propose a loose framework for the study of biomediation as it regards disability, discussing the many ways that disability, medicine, and media are being—and might be further—explored. Throughout this chapter, I will draw on examples from my own research on tinnitus to make the case for the robust study of biomediation for disability media studies.

Recent years have seen dynamic growth in media technology studies, as scholars with training in diverse fields such as sociology, anthropology, informatics, cultural studies, and media studies have increasingly investigated the material practices and technologies involved in media. Influenced by both empirically based social science and hermeneutic approaches from the humanities, media technology scholars believe that, as Sarah Kember and Joanna Zylinska put it, "questions of language and materiality, of culture and politics, have always needed to be studied together." They often draw influences from science and technology studies (STS), which "has contributed towards blurring the distinctions between the two frameworks, or 'camps'" of social science empiricists and interpretive humanists.[4] Until recently, however, science and technology studies itself tended to shy away from popular media, saving its sociocultural analysis and critique for more "serious" practices and technologies; conversely, media studies often focused on texts, audiences, and industries without giving technology its due.[5]

Over the past decade or so, the new wave of media technology scholars has integrated these approaches by "understanding communication as meaning, process, and artifact," combining "textual approaches to understanding . . . with historical, political, behavioral and social ones."[6] To cite but a smattering of examples, this sort of work includes analyses of media's roles in the assemblage of various publics and communities, the cultural nature and influence of formats and algorithms, and the ways that cultural differences and ideals get built into media technologies.[7] Media technology studies takes seriously the materiality of media but avoids deterministic interpretations in which technology "does things to us"; instead, it looks to the processes through which subjects, culture, and artifacts shape one another.

Exploring disability through a media technology studies methodology involves interrogating the epistemological, ontological, and social technologies and practices that produce lived experiences of disability. It often requires studying the institutions where disability is defined, contested, and designed for—and while one must assiduously avoid reinscribing the medical model in disability research, it is also important to critically examine medical industries, as disabled people are said to "comprise the largest and most important health care consumer group in the United States."[8] In other words, if the medical model is the dominant cultural discourse around disability, media technology scholars must visit the spaces in which the medical model is *enacted*, investigating the roles of media and mediation in biometric and obstetric screening rooms, for example.

Legibility, Visibility, and Audibility

In my fieldwork on tinnitus, I met people whose experiences seemed to complicate the question of disability and its representation. Rather than being misrepresented, my interlocutors complained of their disability being medically *illegible* and socially *invisible*, while feeling that both their tinnitus and their voices were largely *inaudible*.[9] As suggested by Colin Barnes's term "disabling imagery," disability scholars often engage media texts by assuming a certain kind of visibility in disability, in which an already-recognizable (or *legible*) impairment is shaped into a disability through cultural discourse. For example, one of Barnes's targets is "the alarming growth of TV charity shows such as 'Children in Need' and 'Telethon'—programmes which encourage pity so that the non-disabled public can feel bountiful."[10] No matter the producers' intentions, in Barnes's critique, such shows turn a legible impairment (say, muscular dystrophy or blindness) into a disability through problematic representations of it. As Paul Longmore has shown most definitively, telethons portray life with such conditions as a living hell in order to inspire charity in the public, simultaneously denigrating the value of such lives, putting disabled youth on display as "poster children," and creating a lucrative industry of televised fundraising.[11]

What are we to make, then, of the email at the beginning of this chapter in which a tinnitus support group leader—himself a tinnitus sufferer—pleads with the American Tinnitus Association to create a new telethon? He describes tinnitus as an "unbearable" torment, making the very sort of argument and seeking the very sort of telethon that Barnes describes as disabling. In effect, the group leader is *pleading to be disabled*. How might we understand this desire for disabling imagery, which would seem to affirm a medical model of disability, without condemning this man, or accusing him of a false consciousness?

This example highlights the tensions between the social and political costs and benefits afforded by the visibility of disability, and the struggles of invisibility/illegibility. As Longmore points out, "There is no single disability experience or identity; there are multiple experiences and more than one identity."[12] Many people experience isolation and despair not because their impairment is represented offensively, but because it is barely represented at all. Like its phantom sound, tinnitus's phantom social status vis-à-vis disability can be maddening to its sufferers, who often experience what Ellen Samuels calls "the uneasy, often self-destroying tension between appearance and identity [and] the social scrutiny that refuses to accept statements of identity without 'proof.'"[13] Thus, despite well-founded criticisms of the telethon and similar discourses as a disabling force inflicted upon the impaired, the tinnitus group leader and others like him are engaging in media campaigns designed not just to legitimize social claims for recognition and political claims on resources for research and treatment, but also to construct an identity of disability around tinnitus and forge networked communities around these identities.

One option for thinking through these tensions is what Tobin Siebers calls "complex embodiment," in which there is a reciprocal and interactive relationship between human bodies on the one hand and representations and environments on the other.[14] Tinnitus is a good example: otology and audiology have historically focused on the ear and auditory system as a medium for *communication*, thus framing tinnitus as a possible *symptom* of hearing problems, but not as a disability in itself. Indeed, the majority of people who experience tinnitus are unbothered by it, but this is little comfort to those who are. People who suffer from tinnitus frequently report that doctors tell them to go home and "learn to live with it," while providing no advice on how to do so. In such moments, people suffer from the *illegibility of impairment*—the fact that the bodily phenomena they contend with have not been mediated into a clearly recognizable "object" of understanding and treatment. Embodied experience must be mediated—both epistemologically and technologically—for a disability to become legible within the medical model. Through a focus on technological practices, we can gain insights into how people negotiate the complex relationships between bodies and representation: when and how are media used to make impairments legible? Which impairments are left out and why? What beliefs about and agendas for the body motivate these practices?

One might wonder whether the illegibility of disability is simply a curious and marginal phenomenon limited to tinnitus, a quirky disorder that slightly troubles the rules of disability and media theory. In fact, illegibility is a problem faced by many others with non-apparent and contested impairments, from lupus to poorly understood mental disorders.[15] Elaine Scarry observes that to be in pain is to be certain, while to hear about another's pain is to be in doubt; we might add that hearing about pain without a legible name can inspire even greater doubt.[16] Individuals impaired by unnamed clusters of symptoms often meet with impatience, indifference, and disbelief from friends, family, bosses, lawyers, and government agencies that write disability checks.

Bringing legibility to disability, therefore, can bring certain personal, social, and political gains. Internalized as a form of self-knowledge, the legible representation of disability can offer comfort to subjects—even when diagnosis does not lead to remedy. Having a name for one's physical experience helps demystify and validate it. Successful diagnostic mediation also opens the door to a new identity within an imagined community of similar others. *Legibility* through diagnosis, in other words, can lead to the *visibility* of a disabled identity and a visible community who share that identity. Like a legible disability, a visible disabled identity is something that must be constructed through acts of mediation, whether online or in books such as this one. Such acts of mediation also create spaces of *audibility*—the inclusion of disabled perspectives in social discourses. Audibility means being able to include one's physical experience in an interior monologue that makes sense within public discourse. It also means being able to express one's experience in terms that will be sensible to others, whether through dialogue or activist invective. Without audibility, there is no creation of disabled publics and thus less agency for disabled people (see also, in this volume, Lori Kido Lopez's discussion of listening).

How and why do some aspects of bodies and experiences of disability become legible, visible, and audible through media? How and why do other experiences remain illegible, invisible, and inaudible? Why have media become prostheses or salves for some kinds of impaired bodies and what are the surrounding ethics and economics? To help answer questions such as these, I propose a framework for the study of biomediation.

A Framework for the Study of Biomediation

The term "biomedia" is associated with the work of Eugene Thacker, who uses it to reference the convergence of the life and information sciences in media discourses (which rethink biological life in terms of its genetic coding) and media practices (such as genetic engineering, which turns biological life into a medium for the production and storage of biomedical products). Thacker is interested in the scientific, political, economic, and cultural dimensions of biomedia, which undermine commonsense distinctions between nature and technology: "Because biomedia are predicated on the concept of a genetic code, a concept that stitches together bios and technê, there is no primordial, biological life that is subsequently technologized and rendered into genetic code."[17] Patricia Clough expands upon Thacker's conception of biomediation to include the ways that digital media expand the affordances of the biological senses, involving humans in new ways of knowing, affecting, and laboring. For both scholars, *information*—as a paradigm that orders concepts and practices of bodies—is the center of gravity. But while genetics and new media are extremely important factors in the contemporary experience of embodiment and disability, defining biomedia digitally excludes pre–"information age" practices involving artifacts such as stethoscopes, X-ray machines, and medicinal tuning forks used to test bone-conduction hearing. Such practices persist to this day, indicating the influence of a longer and broader history of biomediation.

The following framework for studying the history and present of biomediation consists of three main aspects. First, it requires broad-spectrum definitions of media and mediation that involve a wide array of technologies and practices, understanding them "as complex, sociomaterial phenomena."[18] Second, it suggests a biopolitical research agenda that examines the roles of mediation in the production of bodily experiences, norms, practices, identities, and publics. Finally, it outlines types of biomediating practices that produce bodies of knowledge and known bodies, locating the latter in matrices of ability and responsibility. These practices include: (1) setting scientific and social norms for the conditions and abilities of human bodies generally; (2) compiling and disseminating medical knowledge; (3) sounding and screening individual bodies for compliance with the aforementioned norms and knowledge; (4) cataloging and regulating individual bodies and their access to care; (5) mediating individual bodies for corrective or therapeutic purposes; (6) advocating for group disability recognition, identities, rights, and funding; (7) shaping "accessibility" in everyday media technologies (usually according to dictates of the medical model, which often result in new forms of exclusion); and finally, (8) representing bodies and medicine in popular media.

The list is not meant to be exhaustive but rather to open up the possibility of thinking about media, medicine, and disability more systematically. Involving technologies as diverse in type and scale as MRI, feature films, quantified-self applications, databases, and algorithms, this framework affords the opportunity for scholars across disciplines to situate their research in relation to one another's work. On the one hand, it encourages more disability scholars to expand beyond textual representation and engage with scholars examining media technologies. On the other hand, current scholarship on such technologies stands to benefit from greater interaction with the unique critical perspective offered by disability theory and identity, which "stands in uneasy relationship to the ideology of ability" that these technologies so often embody—a perspective "that disturbs and critiques it."[19]

A Broad-Spectrum Approach to Media and Mediation

A first tenet of the study of biomediation and medical media would be that "media" should be defined broadly, with close attention paid to broadly defined material practices of mediation. Despite the animated scholarly and industrial conversations and prognostications around media convergence, conceptions of media technologies often remain siloed. The many screens that populate medical offices, labs, and waiting rooms, for example, are scarcely encountered in media studies. As Lisa Cartwright writes, there has often been "disregard for the cultural implications of the technological interdependency of science and forms of popular culture."[20] Cartwright examines the visual culture and practices shared by these ostensibly separate realms, showing how film technology has served in the physiological surveillance and management of the body. Similarly, Mara Mills has recounted the shared history of the telephone and the audiometer, in which the instrumental measurement of "normal" human hearing was developed to allow for the more efficient transmission of speech over telephone lines—a development that had profound impacts on definitions of deafness and hearing impairment.[21] Cartwright and Mills show us that the medical modeling of the body and everyday media technologies shape one another in largely unrecognized ways.

Charting such histories and examining their present manifestations requires interdisciplinary research that does not take popular and industry definitions of media as givens. To provide a different sort of example, ocean- and rain-simulating sound machines used by tinnitus sufferers are marketed to retailers at the International Home and Housewares Show as "health and wellness" devices, rather than at the International Consumer Electronics Show, despite the fact that they are digital audio playback machines. For media scholars to overlook such devices simply because they do not fit within popular and industry conceptions of media is to choose objects of study that, in Lawrence Grossberg's words, "remain analytically and conceptually ungrounded" and to simplify "enormous complexities, articulations, and convergences."[22] The analysis of biomediation requires and inspires the transcendence of received knowledge about what constitutes "media."

One useful strategy for breaking with preconceived definitions of media is to begin by looking for patterns in practices of mediation rather than by constructing a study around a particular medium or media—this is the rationale for the list of sociomaterial medical media practices that I will elaborate below. The shift of emphasis from media to mediation has also been recently advocated by Kember and Zylinska in their characterization of mediation as "a vital process." The authors draw on Gary Gumpert and Robert Cathcart's "biotechnological explanation of media," which conceives of media technology as an outgrowth of human biological development that evolves along the lines of biology. While Kember and Zylinska are agnostic as to the literal truth of the biotechnological explanation, they utilize this paradigm to focus on media's organic "complexity, adaptability, and specialization . . . [and] to shift the perspective of what counts as media."[23]

In hearing, for example, environmental sound is mediated by pressure waves of air molecules, cilia and fluid in the ear, and neurochemical transmitters, as "sound" is transduced from one materiality to another. In other words, there is no unmediated sound—electronic audio media simply add additional material conversions to the signal chain involved in hearing as subjectivity emerges in the interaction between biology, technology, and environment.[24] The crucial question is always this: toward what ends, according to what cultural logics, and with what results are structures of biomediation being developed?

Media and Biopolitics

The second element of the framework is therefore the organization of research around the critical examination of media technologies as they surveil, sound, normalize, classify, and regulate human bodies in accordance with prevailing forms of knowledge and power. This biopolitical research agenda is, of course, deeply indebted to the theoretical and methodological innovations of Michel Foucault. Foucault claims that modern scientific discourse and liberal governance combine to create a new form of power, one wielded not through physical coercion, but through technologies that standardize bodies and conduct. When individuals come to identify with the bodily norms established, deviations from those norms usually emerge as a disability—a hindrance to the individual freedom of choice and action we are all expected to exercise in a liberal society. Physical or mental differences that diminish this required freedom can come to be seen as dehumanizing defects— indeed, as Shelly Tremain argues, "the category of impairment [as found in the social model of disability] emerged and, in many respects, persists in order to legitimize the governmental practices that generated it in the first place."[25]

The governmental requirement of freedom has two implications for the study of biomediation. First, there is the issue addressed earlier— that those with illegible impairments or invisible disabilities are often perceived as moral failures rather than disabled people. In such cases, clinicians and sufferers alike use media to *externalize* poorly understood impairments as manageable and circulatable objects, amenable to research, treatment, prevention, empathy, and activism. In the case of tinnitus, this is evident in the audiologist's use of digital tones to match the frequency and volume of the client's tinnitus, which allows her to objectify subjective sound. Once she has isolated the tinnitus in this way, she can make its frequency and volume visible on a printout to be shared with the client and the people in her life. Mediation provides a form of validation and, perhaps, some reprieve from the full responsibilities of freedom.

Media also become a form of tinnital treatment, as in the use of the wave-producing sound machines mentioned earlier, as well as a host of other technologies such as tone-generating hearing aids and iPod-like "sound therapy" devices. These "orphic media," as I call them, are examples of a second way biomedia are used under regimes of responsibilization: as *technologies of the self*.[26] In his later years, Foucault became interested "in the technologies of individual domination, the history of how an individual acts upon himself, in the technology of self" through which individuals operate "on their own bodies and souls, thoughts, conduct, and way of being, so as to transform themselves in order to attain a certain state of happiness, purity, wisdom, perfection, or immortality."[27] Media are used as technologies of the self when they help individuals overcome perceived impairments that emerge in the context of societal, economic, and interpersonal pressures—allowing them to function as "healthy" biological, social, and economic agents. Other examples of this variety of medical media might include cochlear implants, hearing aids, relaxation tapes, fitness videos, exercise games, and numerous other ways that people try to comply with what Deborah Lupton calls "the imperative of health."[28] Through these technologies, individuals attempt to become subjects capable of bearing the responsibility of freedom, thus subjecting themselves to "a power [that] has to qualify, measure, appraise, and hierarchize, rather than display itself in murderous splendor."[29]

Practices of Biomediation

The final element of the framework is a list of modes of biomediation that have been—or might be—examined by scholars of media technologies. Drawing on the Foucauldian analysis of norms in disability, we begin with media's role in *(1) setting scientific and social norms for the conditions and abilities of human bodies generally*. Work of this kind has been discussed above: Cartwright has traced the role of film in the development of norms in physiology and Mills has recounted the history of audiometry in establishing norms for human hearing, providing examples of biomediation at work in the standardization of human bodies. An important dynamic in this form of mediation is the interplay between media and understandings of the body. As Mills shows, the development of audiometry was greatly advanced by AT&T, which wanted to set standards of human hearing for the development of more efficient telephone technology. Thus, the needs of telephony encouraged a communicative model of hearing subjects, which was then built into the testing technology of the audiometer. The audiometer brought impairments such as noise-induced hearing loss into legibility but left the problem of tinnitus illegible for decades, until neurophysiology and its scanning media began to render tinnitus as a legible impairment.[30]

Of course, norms do not work if they are not shared, so media are also deployed in *(2) compiling and disseminating medical knowledge* for use in *(3) sounding and screening individual bodies for compliance with medical norms and knowledge.* Subjects and medical personnel use media—we might call them *diagnostic media*—to help flesh out impairments, rendering them recognizable and possibly treatable. They type symptoms into search engines, consult dog-eared copies of the *Diagnostic and Statistical Manual of Mental Disorders (DSM-5)*, put bodies into computerized tomography (CT) scanners to view cross-sectional images of bones and soft tissues, or use online hearing tests. As seen in these examples, some media are used to compile and disseminate abstract medical knowledge—these diagnostic media are *epistemological* in nature and function in general accordance with the social model, representing "normal" bodies and abilities as well as deviance, damage, and disability. One advantage, I believe, of the broad-spectrum approach to media that I propose is that it allows us to view professional disciplinary practices of diagnostic mediation (consulting the *DSM-5*, DynaMed, or PubMed) as being of a piece with lay practices (consulting Google, WebMD, or watching *The Dr. Oz Show* (2009–present)). Indeed, the epistemic battles now occurring over medical practices such as vaccination may stem in large part from the proliferation of epistemological diagnostic media for laypeople.

Other diagnostic media, meanwhile, are used to bring forth aspects and defects of *specific* bodies in accordance with the scientific and lay knowledges circulated in epistemological media—this is the *ontological* aspect of diagnostic mediation. Electron microscopes, ultrasound imaging, CT scanning, PET scanning, online hearing and psychological testing, and genetic screening all mediate human bodies and minds, rendering aspects of them as legibly impaired in accordance with medical knowledge. It is important to emphasize how the analysis of this sort of mediation is different from perspectivalism (in which there is a plurality of differing perspectives on a singular, actual body) and social constructivism (in which a plurality of past possibilities gives way to a singular socially constructed body in the present). Instead, drawing on actor-network theory (ANT), we look to the way media are used to *perform the reality of disease and disability*. As Annemarie Mol emphasizes, "Rather than being seen by a diversity of watching eyes while itself remaining untouched in the centre, reality is manipulated by means of various tools in the course of a diversity of practices." Therefore, medical politics extends "not only [to] the representations of reality in information circulating as words and images . . . but also [to] the very material shaping of reality in diagnosis, interventions, and research practices."[31] In the case of tinnitus, "fleshing out" phantom sound as a matter of neurophysiology has led to new forms of legitimacy and treatment. Intriguing STS- and ANT-influenced work has been done on the biopolitics of MRI, fetal photography, mammography, and brain scanning, suggesting promising directions for disability scholarship.[32]

Another form of medical mediation with significant political relevance is *(4) the cataloging and regulating of individual bodies and their access to care*, as seen in the networked infrastructures of government and private health agencies and insurers. The convergence between new forms of medical knowledge and new media have led to concerns around medical records privacy and the potential for individuals to be genetically pigeonholed, as seen in debates around the Icelandic genome project, in which a private company has attempted to data mine the genetic history of an entire nation.[33] These are debates to which disabled people—who have long experienced subjectification through the implementation of the medical model—have much to contribute. Gaby Admon-Rick, for example, has examined "the technoscientific disability classification system" through which "impairments are classified, bodies numbered, and eligibilities determined."[34] Classificatory decisions and their implementation across information networks have serious implications for disability. For instance, because the Veterans Administration classifies tinnitus as a disability, it has become a costly source of disability payments to combat troops returning from Afghanistan and Iraq, motivating a recent wave of government-funded research into potential tinnitus cures.

The next biotechnological practice, *(5) mediating individual bodies for corrective or therapeutic purposes*, has already been discussed in some detail above. In fields such as musicology, anthropology, and media studies, there has been some research framing media as technologies of the self, but my sense is that we have only scratched the surface.[35] I believe that this is another space where media and disability scholarship have much to share with one another, in an effort to understand specifically how impairment and cure emerge within the same biotechnological power dynamics. An exciting start is Laura Mauldin's illuminating study of how cochlear implantation practices recast deafness as a neurological problem, imposing onto subjects a new responsibility to "train the brain."[36]

In the case of tinnitus, I have found that tinnitus sufferers tend to be more attracted to technological solutions on sale in the marketplace than to approaches designed to lessen suffering through acceptance of tinnitus as a part of one's embodied experience. These individuals believe they are *supposed to be free of the defect of tinnitus* and search for a technology that will take it away, despite the fact that emotional acceptance of tinnitus is the actual differentiator between suffering and not suffering from its sound. As seen in the case of the office worker who experiences tinnitus as disabling to his efficacy as a cognitive laborer, tinnitus in the United States emerges within a regime of required freedom—a regime that also offers numerous "cures" in the form of pills, sound-generating apps, websites, sound therapy devices, and hearing aids.

The last three types of biomediation in the framework have received more recognition and study from disability scholars than the preceding five. First, media provide means of *(6) associating and advocating for group disability recognition, identities, rights, and funding.* In the case of tinnitus there have been televised public service announcements, YouTube videos in which sufferers share their experiences, websites for local support groups, and message boards where people with tinnitus share stories, resources, and advice. Questions of (self-)representation and community in online spaces have been addressed by a number of disability scholars in recent years.[37] Similarly, the question of *(7) shaping "accessibility" in everyday media technologies* has continued to receive much-needed study, especially where the internet is concerned.[38] These studies sometimes demonstrate how, in the words of Ingunn Moser, "technologies working within an order of the normal are implicated in the (re)production of the asymmetries that they . . . seek to undo."[39] However, as seen in the work of Elizabeth Ellcessor, this scholarship can also point the way to new models of accessibility that accommodate a wide range of bodies without reproducing dis/abled divides (see her chapter in this volume).[40] Finally, there is the dimension of mediation most amenable to sociotextual analysis, *(8) the representation of medicalized bodies and medicine in popular media.* These representations in books, television, film, and other popular media profoundly impact public understandings of disability; however, as I hope to have demonstrated, while these latter practices of community, access, and representation in media are of great importance, they are far from the whole picture when it comes to disability and media.

Conclusion

This chapter opened with descriptions of people using media technologies to contend with the phantom sound of tinnitus. An audiologist and her client used an audiometer and headphones to turn its subjective sound into an objective impairment that others could see and hear. An office worker used his computer as a medical reference and even as a sonic salve for the roaring in his head. A support group leader advocated for a telethon to foster a disabled identity for people with tinnitus. While these moments may have seemed unusual at first, we have seen that they are, in fact, exemplary of the everyday interplay between the experience of disability and media technologies.

The framework of biomediation suggests a way to sort through and understand such moments. It presents a diverse set of media practices that articulate with one another—practices through which disability emerges and potentially becomes legible, visible, and audible. These practices of biomediation are performed with a wide array of media tools, often forged on the anvil of biopower for purposes of normalization and responsibilization. This framework is meant to encourage cross-disciplinary work that engages media both technologically and textually, furthering our understanding of the dynamics at work. With these categories of mediation in mind, we can explore how they articulate with one another: how does the categorization and regulation of bodies influence regulation and "innovation" in digital accessibility, for example? How do online disability advocacy groups attempt to influence popular representations of disability on television and in other media?

Perhaps most importantly, if we think of mediation as "a vital process" in which bodies and technologies are always engaged in a process of mutual recreation, we might begin to imagine less disabling, more liberating forms of biomediation. Certainly, this would involve moving away from the simple paradigm of technological "fixes" for disabled bodies, which both the medical model and capitalism encourage us to embrace. In the case of tinnitus, for example, the most effective treatments use audio media not to completely drown out the sound in people's heads but as part of a program to help them relax and stop perceiving their tinnitus as a threat.[41] In this case, media technology liberates insofar as it helps a disabled person accept her body just as it is.

NOTES

1 Serlin, "Introduction," xxii.

2 Goggin and Newell, *Digital Disability*, xv.

3 Goggin, *Cell Phone Culture*, 90. "Media technology studies" is the term suggested by media scholar Mary Gray for this field.

4 Kember and Zylinska, *Life after New Media*, xv.

5 Gillespie, Boczkowski, and Foot, *Media Technologies*. Even in a case such as "apparatus theory," media technologies are dismissed as inherently ideological rather than being explored in their full material and practical specificity.

6 Gina Neff, "On the 30th Anniversary of the UCSD Communication Department," *Culture Digitally*, June 17, 2013, http://culturedigitally.org.

7 Baym, *Personal Connections in the Digital Age*; boyd, *It's Complicated*; Dunbar-Hester, *Low Power to the People*; Fouché, "Say It Loud"; Gillespie, "The Relevance of Algorithms"; Gray, *Out in the Country*; Lisa Nakamura, *Digitizing Race: Visual Cultures of the Internet*, Minneapolis: University of Minnesota Press, 2007; Sterne, *MP3*; Striphas, *The Late Age of Print*.

8 National Council on Disability, "The Current State of Health Care for People with Disabilities," September 30, 2009, www.ncd.gov.

9 Although legibility, visibility, and audibility are often literal in the media practices I describe, the terms are used metaphorically here. So, for example, Deaf voices are "audible" in online message boards for Deaf communities.

10 Barnes, "Disabling Imagery," 7.

11 Elliott, "Disability and the Media," 75–76; Longmore, *Telethons*.

12 Longmore, *Telethons*, xviii.

13 Samuels, "My Body, My Closet," 233.

14 Siebers, *Disability Theory*, 25.

15 See also Samuels, this volume, and Scott and Bates, this volume.

16 Scarry, *The Body in Pain*, 4.
17 Thacker, "Biomedia," 123.
18 Gillespie, Boczkowski, and Foot, *Media Technologies*, 1.
19 Siebers, *Disability Theory*, 9.
20 Cartwright, *Screening the Body*, 2.
21 Mills, "Deafening."
22 Grossberg, *Cultural Studies*, 207.
23 Kember and Zylinska, *Life after New Media*, 24; Gumpert and Cathcart, "A Theory of Mediation."
24 For a fascinating discussion, see Moser and Law, "'Making Voices.'"
25 Tremain, "Foucault, Governmentality," 11.
26 Orpheus played his lyre to counteract the dangerous song of the Sirens and thus preserve the safety and freedom of himself and his fellow Argonauts. Much of my research concerns the ways people use sound media to combat other sounds, sonically fabricating a safe space for the self.
27 Foucault, *Technologies of the Self*, 18–19.
28 Lupton, *The Imperative of Health*.
29 Foucault, *The History of Sexuality, Volume 1*, 144.
30 For a lucid explanation of the neurophysiological model of tinnitus, see Jastreboff and Hazell, *Tinnitus Retraining Therapy*.
31 Annemarie Mol, "Ontological Politics," 77, 86. In Mol's *The Body Multiple: Ontology in Medical Practice* (Durham, NC: Duke University Press, 2002), she conceives of the disease atherosclerosis as a multiple object, with one reality that is enacted in the clinic via doctor-patient interview and another enacted through a microscope at the Department of Pathology. Though practitioners work to make their objects compatible, at times the different atheroscleroses conflict.
32 Joseph Dumit, *Picturing Personhood: Brain Scans and Biomedical Identity* (Princeton, NJ: Princeton University Press, 2004); Kelly Ann Joyce, *Magnetic Appeal: MRI and the Myth of Transparency* (Ithaca, NY: Cornell University Press, 2008); Paula A Treichler, Lisa Cartwright, and Constance Penley, *The Visible Woman: Imaging Technologies, Gender, and Science* (New York: New York University Press, 1998).
33 Pálsson and Rabinow, "The Icelandic Genome Debate."
34 Admon-Rick, "Impaired Encoding," 106.
35 Tia DeNora, "Music as a Technology of the Self," *Poetics* 27, no. 1 (October 1999): 31–56; Rosalind Gill, "'Life Is a Pitch': Managing the Self in New Media Work," in *Managing Media Work*, ed. Mark Deuze (London: Sage, 2010), 249–62; Mack Hagood, "Quiet Comfort: Noise, Otherness, and the Mobile Production of Personal Space," *American Quarterly* 63, no. 3 (2011): 573–89; Tomas Matza, "Moscow's Echo: Technologies of the Self, Publics, and Politics on the Russian Talk Show," *Cultural Anthropology* 24, no. 3 (August 1, 2009): 489–522; Pam Royse et al., "Women and Games: Technologies of the Gendered Self," *New Media & Society* 9, no. 4 (2007): 555–76.

36 Mauldin, "Precarious Plasticity."

37 Peter Anderberg, "Peer Assistance for Personal Assistance: Analysis of Online Discussions about Personal Assistance from a Swedish Web Forum for Disabled People," *Disability & Society* 22, no. 3 (2007): 251–65; Kristin Björnsdóttir and Hanna B. Sigurjónsdóttir, "The Internet's Empowering and Disempowering Qualities: Online (Re)Presentation of Disabled Parents," *Disability Studies Quarterly* 33, no. 3 (2013): http://dsq-sds.org; Ellen Liberti Blasiotti, John D. Westbrook, and Iwao Kobayashi, "Disability Studies and Electronic Networking," in *Handbook of Disability Studies*, ed. Gary L. Albrecht, Katherine D. Seelman, and Michael Bury (Thousand Oaks: Sage, 2001), 327–47; Katie Ellis, "A Purposeful Rebuilding: YouTube, Representation, Accessibility and the Socio-Political Space of Disability," *Telecommunications Journal of Australia* 60, no. 2 (2010): 21.1–12; Jin Huang and Baorong Guo, "Building Social Capital: A Study of the Online Disability Community," *Disability Studies Quarterly* 25, no. 2 (2005): http://dsq-sds.org; Estelle Thoreau, "*Ouch!*: An Examination of the Self-Representation of Disabled People on the Internet," *Journal of Computer-Mediated Communication* 11, no. 2 (2006): 442–68.

38 For example, Goggin and Newell, *Digital Disability*; Ellis and Kent, *Disability and New Media*; Jaeger, *Disability and the Internet*; and Ellis and Kent's "Disability and the Internet," special issue, *First Monday* 20, no. 9 (September 7, 2015).

39 Moser, "Disability and the Promises of Technology," 375.

40 Ellcessor, *Restricted Access*. Other works on digital accessibility include: Gary Annable, Gerard Goggin, and Deborah Stienstra, "Accessibility, Disability, and Inclusion in Information Technologies: Introduction," *Information Society* 23, no. 3 (April 26, 2007): 145–47; Kerry Dobransky and Eszter Hargittai, "The Disability Divide in Internet Access and Use," *Information, Communication & Society* 9, no. 3 (June 2006): 313–34; Ellis, "A Purposeful Rebuilding"; Goggin and Newell, *Digital Disability*; Gerard Goggin and Christopher Newell, "The Business of Digital Disability," in *Foucault and the Government of Disability*, ed. Shelley Tremain (Ann Arbor: University of Michigan Press, 2005), 261–77; Paul T. Jaeger, *Disability and the Internet*; Paul T. Jaeger and Cynthia Ann Bowman, *Understanding Disability: Inclusion, Access, Diversity, and Civil Rights* (Westport, CT: Praeger, 2008); María Rosalía Vicente and Ana Jesús López, "A Multidimensional Analysis of the Disability Digital Divide: Some Evidence for Internet Use," *Information Society* 26, no. 1 (2010): 48–64.

41 E.g., Jastreboff and Hazell, *Tinnitus Retraining Therapy*.

14

"A Blessed Boon"

Radio, Disability, Governmentality, and the Discourse of the
"Shut-In," 1920–1930

BILL KIRKPATRICK

Disability and media shape each other in often surprising ways. Through
his analysis of the discourse of the disabled "shut-in" in the first decade of
broadcasting, Kirkpatrick reveals how, in the realm of media and social policy, ideas about disability helped shape the U.S. radio system while, simultaneously, ideas about radio influenced the social meanings of disability.
Drawing on Foucauldian notions of governmentality and cultural policy,
Kirkpatrick argues that disability and media have been co-constitutive
since the birth of broadcasting, each helping to produce and regulate the
other, with subtle but significant political and cultural consequences.

In 1929, the *Chicago Tribune* published a feature on the Nighthawks, a
Kansas City jazz band that played on the radio late at night. The feature
included this anecdote about one of the band's biggest fans, a "crippled
woman" who lived somewhere in the "far north": "Being a shut-in in a
frozen wilderness, for twenty-six years, she had heard no other voice
save that of her husband, a trapper. On one of his excursions to civilization, he purchased a new fangled radio set, and one of the boys'
rollicking parties on the air was the first thing she tuned." The woman
sent fan mail to the musicians, making the coda to the story a poignant
contrast of old and new media: "Some months later, by many stages of
dog team, came her exultant letter, and thereafter she was their heroine,
serenaded and greeted every night over the thousands of frozen miles."[1]
    This tale is one of thousands of invocations of disability during the
first two decades of radio broadcasting, and it follows a typical narrative
pattern: an isolated and miserable "shut-in," bereft of all joy and of most

human contact, one day receives a radio set and—presto—instantly re-discovers the forgotten pleasures of life through the magic of broadcasting. In newspapers, in magazines, in policy documents, and on the radio itself, this discourse of the shut-in was one of the most significant—and heretofore one of the most overlooked—tropes through which Americans came to understand radio in the 1920s and 1930s.

In this chapter, I take a closer look at the discourse of the "shut-in" and its cultural and political work. Although there are many first-person accounts of people with disabilities benefiting from radio, I am primarily interested in the "cripple" or "shut-in" as a rhetorical figure: why were invocations of disability so important to early constructions of this new medium? And what were the consequences of these constructions for both the media system and persons with disabilities themselves? My study focuses on policy, i.e., how cultural and political systems generate and enforce rules, procedures, laws, and structures that govern various spheres of society. There are two areas of policy at play here: (a) media policy, or how we design and regulate the media system (including broadcasting), and (b) disability or health policy, or how we define and regulate individuals and populations as healthy, sick, able-bodied, or disabled. By looking at media policy through a disability lens, and at disability policy through a media lens, we can gain new insights into the interplay of media and disability at a critical moment for both.

I use this case study to argue four specific points. First, disability policy and the cultural production of disability/able-bodiedness influenced the shape and workings of the media system in the 1920s; as such, media policy studies are enriched when disability becomes a category of analysis (analogous to race, gender, and sexuality) through which we examine the differential exercise of social power.[2] Second, media policy in the 1920s contributed to the production of disability and able-bodiedness not only through the technologies and economies that resulted from those policies, but in and through the processes of policy formation themselves: who speaks, who is spoken for, and how that speech is managed and regulated. As such, media policy deserves a greater place in the field of disability studies. Third, the integration of disability studies and media studies has catalytic effects for our understanding of "policy" more broadly; that is, by reading media policy through the lens of disability policy and vice versa, we can better define "policy" and understand its workings. Finally, the co-construction of media policy and disability suggests new ways to think about how communication technologies are adapted to the project of social regulation and governmentality.

Governmentality is a concept introduced by Michel Foucault to describe "the conduct of conduct": the ways that our behaviors are shaped, limited, incentivized, or punished through networks of power from the state down to individuals. Foucault argues that our conduct is regulated not just by the state, but also through formal and informal systems of punishment and reward, surveillance and confession, the affordances and constraints of the physical environment, procedures of truth-making, and the enforcement of norms and processes of normalization that include our own self-discipline. These regulatory networks include prominent institutions (schools, prisons, media outlets, the medical establishment, and so forth) as well as the family and individuals: we participate by surveilling and policing our own conduct and the conduct of others. The significance of governmentality for this study is that, from a Foucauldian perspective, policy is not solely about issue-oriented politics, capitalist maneuvering, or technical specifications. It is also an effect of culture: the ways that we come to know—and regulate—ourselves and our society.

Foucault is also central to my approach to disability in this chapter, especially his concepts of biopolitics and biopower. These terms refer to the practices through which modern states manage and regulate human populations as bodies, i.e., as organisms that eat, reproduce, get sick, and die. Biopower includes the state's exclusive claim to the right to kill (including deciding who should be deemed killable and under what circumstances), as well as how the state bases its legitimacy on the health and welfare of the populace. The related concept of biopolitics refers to the extension of state surveillance and control into the lives of citizens, for example by measuring their health, monitoring and regulating their sexuality, encouraging them to eat healthily, establishing norms of physical fitness, and so on. Regarding disability and able-bodiedness, biopolitics includes the discourses, technologies, and structures through which certain individuals are identified and classified as physically "abnormal" and thus of special concern to the state: how some individuals are set apart (physically, culturally, economically, politically) as "disabled," how other individuals are encouraged through processes of normalization to disidentify with disability and strive toward bodily "normalcy," and with what effects on those individuals and society as a whole.[3]

The shut-in is interesting as a trope through which the processes and procedures of governmentality and biopower become visible, and through which broadcasting was refashioned and deployed for biopolitics. It helps us see how the structure and policies of the media—not just media content—came to help regulate conduct and establish the parameters of modern citizenship, with positive and negative implications for people understood as disabled. The historiography presented below thus transcends the specific context of 1920s broadcasting to inform more generally our study of media, disability, policymaking, and social power.

The Discourse of the Shut-In at the Birth of Broadcasting

Invoked routinely throughout the 1920s by journalists, broadcasters, and audiences (including persons with disabilities themselves), the shut-in was second only to another oft-discussed outsider, the noble farmer, as the rhetorical figure of choice in debates over the social meanings of broadcasting and the future of U.S. media. It was such a common trope that *Radio Broadcast* wrote in 1925, "It is dangerously near a bromide to say that radio has taken an almost irreplaceable part in the lives of those who are shut in."[4]

A catch-all term, "shut-ins" most frequently referred to those who by illness or injury were consigned to long periods of hospitalization or homebound isolation, prominently including tens of thousands of World War I veterans in addition to those impaired by industrial accidents or diseases such as polio. Importantly, it usually connoted people who were *physically* sick or disabled; although the shut-in's disability might have emotional consequences, the term was rarely used to describe people whose impairment was primarily emotional, mental, or cognitive. Instead, it performed something of a rhetorical sleight of hand, referencing persons with "abnormal" bodies, but simultaneously erasing those bodies in favor of the socio-spatial consequences of their difference: being a shut-in meant, above all, being cut off from the outside world. Thus the trope of the shut-in turned physical disability into a metaphor for social isolation, a quasi-disembodiment that made shut-ins especially useful in discussions of radio, which was understood as the disembodied medium *par excellence.*

Constructed as external to mainstream society, the shut-in was imagined as a silent recipient of culture rather than an active producer of it, the passive beneficiary of radio created by others. In this way, too, the shut-in resembled the farmer, though in the case of the shut-in this passivity was literally embodied through the supposed degradation of disablement, whereas the farmer was ennobled by the physicality of his toil.[5] Furthermore, while the farmer may have wanted for "human contact, human sympathy, and culture,"[6] this was due to his geographic remoteness. In contrast, shut-ins—at least in popular imagination—could not enter the social world even if they wanted to: their broken bodies made them *too* socially remote. In both cases, however, radio was constructed as a symbol of civilization, bringing culture to the literal or figurative wilderness. We see this in my opening example of the Nighthawks serenading a shut-in: only radio could cure the "crippled woman's" isolation and presumed loneliness; only radio would return to her the joys of socialization of which disability had deprived her.

While invocations of the farmer highlighted radio's ability to transcend distance and incorporate the pre-modern local-agricultural community into visions of a modern-industrial nation, the great rhetorical usefulness of the shut-in was to assert technology's ability to complete us as human beings, spiritually and physically, making disability an especially profound site for the healing power of technology. The broken or diseased body of the shut-in became the perfect demonstration of the modern technocratic repair of body and soul, helping to claim broadcasting for biopolitics: radio technology, properly deployed, could assist the modern liberal state in its duty of maintaining the overall health of the population. Both the popular press and the specialty radio press regularly touted the healing power of radio, including the therapeutic use of radio in ambulances and hospitals, entertainment and education for the blind, access to the public sphere for the physically impaired, and even hearing for the deaf, as illustrated by headlines like "Deaf Ears Hear Again through the Magic of Radio" and "Radio for the Deaf."[7] No less a personage than Helen Keller wrote of spending "a glorious hour last night listening over the radio to Beethoven's 'Ninth Symphony.'"[8] Keller was referring to her ability to enjoy the vibrations produced by the radio;

her elation seemed no less genuine—and radio no less miraculous—because of it. "Let me thank you warmly for all the delight which your beautiful music has brought to my household and to me," Keller wrote. "I want also to thank Station WEAF for the joy they are broadcasting in the world."[9] (For reasons that will become clear below, it is worth noting here that WEAF was owned by AT&T, a key player in the commercialization of radio and a pioneer of national network broadcasting.)

If radio could heal, or at least help move persons with disabilities back toward a physical norm of able-bodiedness, it could also provide spiritual uplift and repair the soul, functioning as a treatment for the side effects of loneliness, depression, and, in the case of veterans, what we would now call post-traumatic stress disorder.[10] The press eagerly shared testimonials to the therapeutic properties of radio. For example, in 1922 *Radio Broadcast* published a letter from A. J. DeLong of Lafayette, Indiana, headlined "What Radio Is Doing for Me": "Having listened to daily entertainments, I declare myself less susceptible to fatigue, more alive to everything, and a more contented person. Radio has done for me what medical science failed to do."[11] That same year, a Brooklyn medical superintendent insisted, "Think what it will mean for some poor devil, friendless, homeless, laid up with a broken back, never receiving any visitors, with nothing to do from one day to another but look at the wall and think."[12] In his account, the shut-ins in his care seem barely human prior to radio but undergo a kind of rebirth through the act of listening: "I have put headsets over the ears of many such men, and have seen them transformed in a few minutes from creatures that were just dully existing to the intelligent, interested men they once were and now soon will be again, permanently, and much quicker because of the interest, the life, the health that radiates from radio."[13]

The importance of these discourses for media and disability is profound. They help us perceive how, at a time when Americans were becoming more aware of and interested in radio, biopower came to be exerted in and through the technology. One way this happened was by using the shut-in to construct broadcasting as a new means of managing previously unmanageable bodies—recuperating persons with disabilities by "remote control" as it were. Where the modern state had previously failed to adequately provide for the inclusion of its disabled citizens—a failure made newly visible (and politically salient) by so many disenfranchised war wounded during precisely this era—broadcasting was fitted to a narrative of more effective inclusion and care. By connecting the ethereal technology of radio to the physical plight of the shut-in, the invisible airwaves could be reembodied, transforming an intangible phenomenon into one that had real, even miraculous physical consequences for the health of the populace. In that sense, the shut-in functioned as an "ideal abnormal": a paradigmatic outsider by which the state, in the form of proper media policy, could demonstrate its ability to care for all the citizenry. Viewed from the other direction, the ideal abnormal of the shut-in served to underwrite state media policy, proving the rightness and benevolence of regulation that brought "the life, the health that radiates from radio" to people with disabilities. The result was a two-way biopolitical street: abnormal bodies legitimized official radio policy; radio legitimized state responsibility for (and therefore authority over) abnormal bodies.

In the next two sections, I examine these processes more closely, looking first at how the shut-in was enlisted to support specific media policies, then at how radio was enlisted to justify specific policies pertaining to disability.

The Shut-In in Media Policy

Given all those column inches devoted to what radio could do for the shut-in, it pays to ask: what was the shut-in doing for radio? Put another way, how does a disability studies lens reveal ways that the technology was imagined at the time, conceptions that would become official policy by the end of the decade?

Three ways of "knowing" and thus regulating radio emerged through the trope of the shut-in. First, the shut-in was the perfect passive listener justifying one-to-many broadcasting. Until the 1920s, radio was largely a two-way medium—a "wireless telegraph" allowing operators to communicate around the globe. Although amateur wireless operators were the site of some social anxiety and modest regulatory work, they largely fell outside the concerns of the state as a small, relatively harmless cohort of hobbyists playing with a "toy." With the advent of broadcasting, however, the social and commercial potential of radio as a mass medium became apparent, dramatically increasing the interest of the state in its operations. If, as had been the norm for fifteen years, anyone could speak to anyone over the ether, what would prevent radio from becoming a chaotic free-for-all beyond governmental control? A full exploration of this issue is beyond the scope of this chapter, but the problems boiled down to the danger of unregulated speech and the commercial and military significance of radio to the state. The primary solution that evolved was, in essence, to separate speaking bodies from listening bodies: limit the microphone to a few hundred delegates ("licensees") approved by the state, and turn the rest of the population into audiences. This meant eliminating rights of access to the airwaves, licensing transmitters, denying legal standing to the public in disputes over content, and a host of other policy decisions from 1920 to 1934 that effectively removed the public from radio broadcasting and policy.[14] A small but undeniable feature of these discursive struggles was the elevation of passive, socially isolated listeners like the shut-in and the farmer, turning them into privileged stakeholders whose need for broadcasting superseded free speech and other rights. Tapping into commonplace notions of speech as active and listening as passive, the bedridden shut-in became the paradigmatic passive "listening body" and thus a metonym for the radio audience, helping to legitimize an understanding of radio that worked against a public right to the airwaves.

Second, the purported importance of radio to the shut-in helped allay concerns about emerging mass-consumer culture by assuring observers and policymakers that even the often "frivolous" content of radio could have a noble social purpose. As broadcasting gained popularity in the 1920s, and ever more middle-class families acquired radios, the cultural perception of the radio set shifted from a hobbyist's "toy" to a bourgeois "luxury." In this process, anxieties about mass culture and the materialism of emerging consumer culture were displaced, in part, onto the shut-in. In that sense, persons with disabilities often served as structuring others who, unlike people for whom wireless was possibly a mere fad, really *needed* radios: "Radio may prove merely a craze now," wrote one paper in 1922, but when people are "shut in and denied other entertainment . . . radio can not be said to be merely a craze."[15] Similarly, a 1922 syndicated column claimed that radio was not "a fad, a new toy or plaything," but rather "for invalids—those confined to their homes, it will come as a blessed boon . . . to pass the weary hours."[16]

The dangers of mass culture that attended to radio became more acute as the trends toward entertainment programming and commercialism intensified, as evidenced by the raft of apologists insisting on radio's social value to shut-ins in the face of "decadent" jazz music and stultifying advertising. For example, when the "Keep-the-Air-Clean-on-Sunday Society" protested WMCA's airing of jazz on Sunday evenings, WMCA fought back by claiming that "400 disabled soldiers enjoyed [this] radio hour every Sunday and would miss it greatly if it were discontinued."[17] In such ways, the shut-in's enjoyment of entertainment provided, in Paul K. Longmore's words, "the means by which nondisabled people can prove to themselves that they have not been corrupted by an egocentric and materialistic capitalist order."[18] This discourse, in turn, helped justify governmental interest in radio, something clearly so important that it required state management for the benefit of life and the well-ordered society.

The third way of knowing radio pertained to a more specific policy question: the structure of the radio system as a whole. Invocations of the shut-in were most often connected to support for a particular form of radio, namely high-powered, national, commercial broadcasting. This was a system in which a few corporate interests would dominate the airwaves, beaming a narrow range of advertising-supported content to the public, and most of the country would partake in that content. In the 1920s, this was far from a universal vision of what American radio should become.

To understand this, it helps to remember the ways that new media technologies frequently become part of nationalist projects, and that most countries created a state-sanctioned radio monopoly whose content reinforced national identity and ideology. The U.S. instead adopted a system that was dominated by private commercial concerns, funded primarily by advertising, and regulated with great deference to corporate interests. Even without an official state broadcaster, however, U.S. radio was not free from nationalist associations. Indeed, the peculiar structure of American radio quickly became known as the "American system" and was widely articulated to freedom, individualism, entrepreneurialism, and other facets of American ideology.

Importantly, the use of media to construct and defend national identity often depends on marginalization and exclusion of women, racial/

ethnic others, queer people, and others from full cultural citizenship;[19] Gerard Goggin and Christopher Newell added disability to this list, demonstrating that, in the case of mobile telephony, "people with disabilities were systematically excluded from this nation-building project."[20] By silencing or marginalizing such others, media systems could reflect and maintain hegemonic power relations within the imagined national community. However, here I want to highlight a slightly different process: while the recognition of exclusion and marginalization is critical to any understanding of media history, a disability studies perspective can also alert us to the *inclusive* discursive construction of disability at critical times in the development of national media structures. The importance of the shut-in derived from rhetorics of incorporation and privileged status: although persons with disabilities did not enjoy full cultural or political citizenship in the early twentieth century (a condition, one must perhaps redundantly point out, that continues to this day), disability was nonetheless instrumental in helping imagine and promote an inclusive vision of national radio.

How did this intersection of nation-building and disability result in specific media policies? In the early 1920s, the U.S. was enmeshed in debates over the shape of the emerging broadcasting system, including whether radio would be subject to monopoly control (like AT&T's telephone monopoly), whether it would become corporate run and advertising supported, what role state experts would play in its management, and whether it would become primarily a national or local system. Central to this question was whether there would be more local, low-powered community and nonprofit stations serving their city and region, or fewer high-powered stations, owned by national corporations with the resources to broadcast artists and events of national interest to millions of people. Closely tied to these issues was the question of transmitter power, especially as the Commerce Department moved to increase wattages for some stations (thereby increasing the geographical reach for those few broadcasters) at the expense of others. In these debates, the value of serving sparsely populated and rural areas became one way to legitimize high-powered broadcasting: the most efficient way to reach these isolated communities, which were considered way too small and remote to support local stations, was through big national stations beaming in "civilization" from the urban centers. As *Radio Digest* argued, "Northerners are beginning to consider a radio set not only a wonderful luxury but also a necessity. Being able to receive the broadcast, the voice of civilization, is insurance against stagnation of mind and depression of spirit; it dispels the loneliness even from the farthest frontier."[21] One imagines desperate, godforsaken homesteaders in a miserable shack on the barren tundra, and the only thing making life bearable is reliable reception of the Metropolitan Opera.

Similar to such tropes of geographical remoteness, the shut-in's *social* remoteness allowed advocates of high-powered broadcasting to justify special privileges.[22] A good example came in 1925, a critical time in the development of radio policy, when the Commerce Department approved "super-power" for RCA's station WJZ in Bound Brook, New Jersey. Listeners up and down the East Coast wrote to Commerce Secretary Herbert Hoover about the decision—fans of WJZ were thrilled, but because RCA was the dominant corporate force in radio, the move also fueled fears of an RCA broadcast monopoly and the disappearance of low-powered, locally oriented stations. In this dispute, defenders of high-powered radio frequently invoked persons with disabilities to argue their case: the social and physical isolation of the shut-in became evidence of the need for super-power stations and corporate mass entertainment. Ada Harrison of Newark, for example, claimed that WJZ's offerings were one of the few joys available to her blind and shut-in mother, and thus the station should be allowed to transmit at greater wattages. Contrasting her mother's legitimate needs with the selfishness of the urban dweller for whom radio was a mere luxury, Harrison pleaded, "For the sake of the older people—the *shut-ins*, the isolated ones—whose pleasures are few, and whose troubles are many, is there not *some way* by which WJZ can broadcast on super-power (reaching and bringing light and joy to these people) without unduly annoying the selfish and pleasure-loving people around New York and New Jersey?"[23]

The major broadcasters themselves routinely used shut-ins to justify greater policy privileges and make the case for bringing big-budget commercial entertainment to all parts of the country. In 1927, for example, shortly before the newly formed Federal Radio Commission reorganized the airwaves in favor of large corporate broadcasters, NBC's house conductor, Walter Damrosch, used a profile in the *New York Times* to highlight the importance of high-powered, interference-free transmissions to, of course, shut-ins: "A glance through the letters received by the conductor reveals this scattered, broken world of music lovers brought together by the notes radiating from the central broadcasting station in New York. One letter . . . came from an invalid, shut in for life on an Iowa farm. She lies in her lonely world and listens to Beethoven as played by the orchestra New Yorkers pay and ride through snow in their taxicabs to hear. And she is only one. The bedridden all over the world listen in and write Mr. Damrosch of what it means to them."[24] In case anyone missed the point—that great New York musicians can entertain the sad shut-ins of Iowa only if we eliminate low-powered local stations and clear the airwaves for NBC's super-transmitters—it was hammered home again a paragraph later: "Mr. Damrosch is naturally interested in all radio improvements. He expects governmental control to result in cleaning the air for better broadcasting."[25]

As is by now well known, governmental control did soon result in "cleaning" the air for "better" broadcasting: the Commission eliminated dozens of smaller stations, usually local and often nonprofit, and organized the airwaves to favor large corporate stations broadcasting on high-powered "national" frequencies. Of course this outcome resulted from multiple and complicated political, economic, technological, and cultural factors. Nonetheless, a disability studies lens on media policy illuminates the importance of the discourse of the shut-in to this complex process, especially by defining broadcasting in moral terms, as well as by constructing key audiences as passive and in need of "quality" national culture provided by trusted stewards of the airwaves—a vision that, not coincidentally, benefited RCA, AT&T, and other large commercial broadcasters. The modern corporate-liberal state, charged with caring for the well-being of the populace, found in the shut-in strong biopolitical justification for what became the "American system" of radio.

The Deployment of Able-Bodiedness: Radio in Disability Policy

Clearly radio was indeed a "blessed boon" for countless disabled individuals; their letters fill the archives and the newspaper columns of the day. "I cannot refrain from expressing to you how much pleasure I receive from your programs," read one typical letter by a listener who had been bedridden for 38 years. "I never dreamed, I should have such wonderful music and splendid offerings as I have—it has made me so happy! . . . May God bless you in this wonderful work, and I shall be right here to listen whenever you are on the air."[26] It is impossible to read such testimonials and not be moved by the real joy they express at the advent of broadcasting, and there is no question that untold millions of people, including many identifying as disabled, cherished their radio sets as positive additions to their lives.

At the same time, it is important to consider not just individual experiences with radio but also the social and political consequences of broadcasting's emergence and of the discourses that gave it meaning. If disability, through the trope of the shut-in, played an important role in media policymaking, how did media, through this same trope, function in disability policy? The elevation of persons with disabilities in radio's development led to an outpouring of efforts to help more people benefit from the new technology, but in ways that tended to reaffirm the ableist middle-class politics at the heart of Victorian sentimentality: the impulse for interventionist uplift and moral charity, and the impulse to use modern technology and the expertise of elites to solve social problems.

The charitable work of middle-class reformers has a long history in the U.S.; following World War I, efforts to help veterans and other disabled citizens intensified.[27] This was the era during which the "poster child" came to prominence, with professional charities using the image of the "cripple" to raise funds for the medical rehabilitation of persons with disabilities.[28] Given the purported healing power of radio, some of these charitable efforts unsurprisingly included providing radio sets to shut-ins. The New York City Visiting Committee, for example, solicited funds to outfit hospitals with radio sets through which "[e]ndless vistas are opened for the bed-ridden and shut-ins generally."[29] Ordinary citizens often donated their used sets to shut-ins; for example, the *Chicago Tribune's* "Friend in Need" columns featured letters like Harold L.'s offer of "a crystal radio receiving set (except the ear phones) I made myself and which I shall be glad to give to some poor crippled child or shut-in."[30] The column also featured requests such as: "I hope you can help me to secure a radio with a loud speaker. I am on a lonely farm in Michigan and have an infection in head and hip, which keeps me an invalid. I see only the four walls of my room, day after day, and feel a radio would mean a world of happiness to me." Added the column's editor, Sally Joy

Brown, "What an outlet into the world a radio would mean for our shut-in friend! Please let us know if you have a radio to give."[31] The double-edged nature of charity emerges clearly in these discourses. Generosity and compassion spurred the giving of radios that gave countless individuals an "outlet into the world," but those acts are inseparable from attitudes about persons with disabilities as friendless, culturally limited, socially isolated, and deprived of all pleasure.

Furthermore, the technology that brought the world to the shut-in could be used to justify the "containment" of disability in troubling ways. A brief review of the historical context will help make this clearer. As Susan Schweik demonstrates, the early twentieth century witnessed intense struggle over the meanings of disability and its relationship to "normalcy."[32] Longmore and Goldberger argue that the dominant paradigm for physical disabilities in this era was "the crippled," which joined a wider generic category of "the disabled" that included the blind, deaf, "feebleminded," and others marked as abnormal.[33] Public policy often explicitly marginalized and devalued persons with disabilities, preferring the path of segregation over integration. Such persons were routinely isolated in hospitals and other institutions, or sequestered in private homes where friends and relatives were expected to muster the resources to care for them. Courts repeatedly upheld the right of businesses, including railroads and buses, to refuse service to people with disabilities, reflecting attitudes of non-accommodation that resisted the imputation of any societal responsibility to enable access. So-called "ugly laws"—anti-panhandling ordinances that particularly targeted people with disabilities[34]—were of a piece with ableist policies of exclusion in public schools and elsewhere; in an infamous 1919 case, the Wisconsin State Supreme Court ruled that an educable student could be excluded from regular schools because his drooling and facial expressions had "a depressing and nauseating effect on the teachers and school children."[35]

The early twentieth century was also the heyday of immigration laws banning disabled aliens from entering the country, marking them as an undifferentiated class of unproductive persons representing a drain on society.[36] As Longmore and Goldberger emphasize, such persons were not just physical invalids but were socially *in*valid—not quite full citizens, and certainly not full cultural citizens: "they were represented as incapacitated for real participation in the community and the economy, incapable of usefully directing their lives, disruptive and disorderly, antithetical to those defined as *healthy* and *normal* . . . the inversion of socially legitimate persons."[37] At the extreme end of this policy spectrum was eugenics, which enjoyed a highpoint of mainstream support during this period. Courts, medical professionals, and many others used disability as a criterion for establishing not merely an individual's non-citizenship, but his or her non-personhood, leading to marriage restrictions, forced sterilization, and more.[38] The question of the nature of disability and able-bodiedness—and how society should police those boundaries—was thus an urgent issue involving high stakes for anyone identified as possessing a "disabled" mind or body.

Against this life-and-death political backdrop, the positive and negative dimensions of radio in disability policy emerge more clearly. By presenting radio as an enabler of integration into the national community as well as a technology of physical and emotional healing, the trope of the shut-in functioned as a discourse of both inclusion and exclusion. As discussed above, radio promised to give shut-ins greater access to the public sphere. By conferring partial cultural citizenship on persons with disabilities and conceptualizing broadcasting as a tool of social integration—albeit one-way and often self-serving—the voices championing radio for shut-ins were moving American society toward slightly greater inclusion for bodily non-normativity within the social fabric at a critical historical moment. While it would be a mistake to overstate this point, I argue that it was also no minor matter: at a time when eugenics was enjoying its political zenith, radio *did* play a role in more fully incorporating persons with disabilities—slightly but surely—into a vision of the modern American nation, both in political rhetoric and in fact. Through its articulation to disability, broadcasting helped advance the idea that even the severely disabled could enjoy increased cultural citizenship through effective media policy, that the social isolation understood to inhere in disability could be reduced, and that the supposedly pitiable or even valueless lives of people with disabilities could be improved and made worth living.

It may help to put this point in more Foucauldian terms. As mentioned above, disability in the 1920s revealed a politically salient gap in the modern liberal state, representing a point of failure in the biopolitical management of the health of the population. One response to this gap was eugenics, a form of disavowal and exclusion: condemn the disabled themselves as inherently unfit to live and work in modern society, and contain or eradicate them accordingly. In contrast, the trope of the shut-in helped invigorate an alternative response to this failure: through radio, pursue the "virtual" integration of persons with disabilities into society (in both senses of virtual—technologized/simulated and effective/almost). One wishes this counter-narrative could have done more; it would be many more decades, many political and cultural developments (including Nazism and the disability rights movement), and many tens of thousands of impacted lives before even the "strong" form of eugenics was widely discredited in the United States. Nonetheless, it is clear that dominant discourses about radio's potential social value participated, narrowly but significantly, in the long, slow work of resisting eugenicist policies and reimagining, in the realm of physical impairment, the relationship between the health of the individual body and the health of the social body.

Even on its own terms, of course, this virtual integration through radio remained far from a 21st-century vision of access, inclusion, and social justice. Indeed, the discourse of the shut-in simultaneously functioned as a rhetoric of ongoing exclusion, in part by allowing radio's potential for social inclusion to substitute for greater physical, economic, political, and cultural inclusion and participation. As Goggin and Newell point out, "That the social and discursive shaping of technologies proceeds via a promissory note that they will confer unalloyed benefits upon people with disabilities reveals a fundamentally flawed approach to disability."[39] For example, if allowing disabled children into school had a "nauseating effect" on their able-bodied classmates, perhaps radio could solve the problem by bringing education to the disabled. As one teacher wrote, following a series of educational broadcasts in 1930, "Most gratifying of all were the letters from the mothers of shut-in children who could have through the radio a little of school work and school life brought to their homes."[40] The prospect of education by radio, perhaps in conjunction with traditional correspondence courses, promised a technological fix to the problem of accommodating disabled students, one that asked little of mainstream society. Similarly, in all spheres of society, the discourse of the shut-in offered radio in lieu of reforms such as accessible spaces, non-discriminatory policies, or shifts in cultural attitudes. Radio thus became a way to *partially* integrate shut-ins into American life while resisting more ambitious attempts at integration that would have required adjustments within the broader society. Furthermore, by constructing the disabled as inherently passive—the "ideal abnormal" broadcast listener—there was no need to consider allowing shut-ins to produce and criticize cultural life, that is, to allow them agency or a voice on the airwaves themselves. Keeping shut-ins shut in also meant keeping them shut out.

A final way that radio and disability worked together in the early days of broadcasting was through normalization and the production of compulsory able-bodiedness. As Robert McRuer has theorized, "compulsory able-bodiedness" is the expectation that one will both agree that norms of able-bodiedness are preferable and that the good citizen strives to attain them. Enforced through "control of consciousness" (a term borrowed from Adrienne Rich) and, if necessary, through violence (sometimes lethal), compulsory able-bodiedness requires the devaluation of disability as a condition of full citizenship.[41] The role of people with disabilities in this system, McRuer argues, is to embody the abnormal condition against which the able-bodied can be measured. Adds Alison Kafer, compulsory able-bodiedness renders problematic any desire to identify oneself as disabled, "suggesting that a disability identity is to be avoided at all cost."[42] Here, too, the shut-in functioned as an "ideal abnormal," this time in a sense akin to the "model minority" trope of racial difference, since this rhetoric consistently presumed that the shut-in wanted nothing more than to be an able-bodied participant in modern consumer culture and the capitalist order.[43]

Discourses of disability harnessed radio to the production of compulsory able-bodiedness by creating and enforcing norms about usage: who could listen to what kinds of radio, when, and where. For example, it is striking how frequently the shut-in was named as the ideal target of religious broadcasting, with the corollary condemnation of the able-bodied who listened to religious programs instead of coming to church. "Radio religion is not a substitute for public worship," chided Rev. Dr. E. J. Van Etten, a popular Episcopalian pastor who broadcast services for shut-ins from his Pittsburgh church. "[Church] must become active and not passive."[44] Rev. S. Parkes Cadman of New York had a weekly program on NBC but nonetheless feared losing the able-bodied to radio:

"Many people throughout the country are only too willing to seize upon an excuse for staying away from church, and I did not care to offer them such an opportunity."[45] Similarly, Rev. J. L. Davis of Manhattan complained that radio was a "cheap substitute," making religion "too easy" by extracting it from the sociability of church.[46] Through such rhetoric, radio was constituted as a kind of spiritual prosthesis that most "normal" citizens should not need; indeed, if they leaned too heavily or often on the "crutch" of radio, they were likely to become (spiritually) impaired themselves.

The same pressures toward able-bodiedness also applied to education, as illustrated in figure 14.1's depiction of a boy feigning illness instead of going to school; he'll make up his lessons by listening to school broadcasts for shut-in children. The cartoon suggests that educational programming is fine for cripples, but children who are able-bodied had better come to class. By representing shut-ins as "allowed" to use radio this way because—and only because—their disabilities prevent them from accessing social spaces, these discourses naturalized continued non-accommodation in the physical world and enforced norms of able-bodiedness on the rest of the population. To this day, the close association of children's sick days from school with watching TV reveals the anxieties about the loss of social control introduced by the disembodied medium of broadcasting, anxieties that the shut-in helped negotiate at a critical moment in the technology's development.

As a final point in this section, it is worth noting that all this talk about shut-ins and broadcasting in the 1920s is even more striking when we consider what else was effectively absent: real technological accommodation in radio sets. I was unable to find any discussion of the practicalities of radio listenership for persons with disabilities, nor policy proposals intended to make radio itself more accessible. A radio receiver in the 1920s could be a seriously erratic device often requiring near-constant attention, including tweaking small, sensitive knobs and difficult-to-read dials. Broadcasts often veered off their intended frequency, and weather and electrical interference could make maintaining consistent reception a maddening task. On one level, the job of keeping the radio properly tuned was closely articulated to masculinity; as noted above, shut-ins occupied a feminized social space of passivity, meaning that they were already in some ways culturally "disqualified"

Figure 14.1. Compulsory able-bodiedness at work: fears that
broadcasting makes things "too easy" for the able-bodied.
Source: *Milwaukee Journal*, March 10, 1929, 6.

from mastering the technology. But many shut-ins were physically disqualified as well: the ability to access the set implies a degree of mobility that many persons with disabilities did not have; the ability to tune
implies fine motor coordination; etc. It is thus significant that, parallel
to the absence of concern with social accommodation to benefit persons
with disabilities entering the public sphere, there was almost no concern
with technological accommodation to benefit persons with disabilities
remaining within the private sphere. Radio set design and operation

remained of and for the able-bodied, requiring many persons with disabilities to enter into relationships of dependency to take advantage of the blessed boon of broadcasting.

Conclusions: Governmentality, Policy, and Biopower

Interestingly, by the mid-1930s, the discourse of the shut-in had all but died out. While people with disabilities continued to figure in discussions of media technologies,[47] it was primarily in the first fifteen years of broadcasting that shut-ins were invoked with striking frequency. Clearly the shut-in was helping Americans think about radio at a brief, crucial moment when the purposes and structures of the medium were still up for grabs. A disability lens on radio thus reveals that the shut-in, as an "ideal abnormal" body, helped legitimize the extension of state power into new realms, justify the "American system" of national commercial radio, and resolve tensions around modernity and mass culture. Similarly, radio was helping Americans think about disability at a brief, crucial moment when U.S. society was coming to terms with an influx of war wounded, the ongoing reform impulses of the Progressive movement, and the implications of eugenicist policies. A media lens on disability thus shows us how radio was connected to new modes of compulsory able-bodiedness and functioned as a cultural technology of both inclusion and exclusion for persons with disabilities.

This study also has implications for the theorization of media, disability, governmentality, and biopower, adding to our understanding of the subtle and diverse ways that media policies became, in Foucault's words, "techniques for achieving the subjugation of bodies and the control of populations."[48] In this, it helps to remember the ways in which broadcasting does not neatly fit into typical categories of biopolitical technologies. The development of modern forms of governmentality are, according to Foucault, about "render[ing] the populace visible to power and, hence, to regulation," yet radio introduced new forms of public participation in which the majority of the populace could remain *invisible*.[49] Governmentality is about managing bodies, yet radio was widely seen as *dis*embodied, and in contrast to prisons, clinics, and schools, did not directly regulate bodies in space nor require bodies to submit themselves to surveillance. Given those differences, the discourse of the shut-in helped construct radio as a biopolitical technology (despite its invisible listenership) by separating speaking from listening bodies; justifying the state's control over who may speak; advancing an understanding of radio that reinforced biopolitically inflected ideologies of capitalism, modernity, and nationalism; and functioning as a node for the exercise of compulsory able-bodiedness. In radio's absence of traditionally visible, confessing bodies, the imagined body of the all-inclusive "shut-in" became a useful mechanism of governmentality, allowing a symbolics of disability and able-bodiedness to guide the policymaking that transferred control of radio from unruly amateurs to disciplined delegates of the state, and then helped secure the place of corporate power and national culture within that sphere.

If instruments of governmentality, as Ouellette and Hay discuss, "[operate] as a network, distributed across various spheres of authority and expertise," and if broadcasting "has become instrumental to the networks that now link the public, private, and personal programs and techniques for administering welfare,"[50] then the shut-in helps us better understand the ways in which that process unfolded. Radio in the 1920s had not yet been brought fully under the control of authorities and experts to become a technology of cultural citizenship. The shut-in, as a privileged stakeholder in radio, connected the publicness of radio speech, the privateness of radio listening, and the health and welfare of the populace. The trope helped justify the creation of an easily supervised ideological system that had the corollary effect of socially normalizing the abnormal bodies that, at that key historical juncture, were especially troubling the governmental regulation of the population. Put another way, the trope of the shut-in helped manage the new configurations of bodies and speech that broadcasting introduced. At the same time, institutions that still needed bodies to regulate—churches, schools, workplaces—could draw on the trope of the shut-in to help enforce the performance of able-bodiedness upon which their logic depended.

The consequences for people with disabilities themselves were mixed. As a technological quick fix to the social "problem" of non-normative bodies, radio displaced calls for greater access, accommodation, and equality, and the discourse of the shut-in reinforced disabling stereotypes that justified the perpetuation of segregation and discrimination. Nonetheless, in constructing broadcasting as a technology that gave the lives of persons with disabilities more perceived value—a perception strongly endorsed by many shut-ins themselves—the discourse of the shut-in provided an alternative narrative to the eugenicist claim that abnormal bodies could never be incorporated into the healthy modern nation. For playing even a small part in undermining eugenics at its peak and representing people with disabilities as worthy of greater social inclusion, the discourse of the shut-in in the 1920s was itself, for all the complicatedness of its contributions, a blessed boon.

NOTES

This chapter is a heavily revised version of an essay that first appeared as Bill Kirkpatrick, "'A Blessed Boon': Radio, Disability, Governmentality, and the Discourse of the 'Shut-In,' 1920–1930," *Critical Studies in Media Communication* 29, no. 3 (2012), 165–84. I especially thank Anna Rumbough for her contributions to this revision.

1 Quin Ryan, "Inside the Loudspeaker," *Chicago Daily Tribune*, March 10, 1929, J11.

2 "Another 'other,'" as Catherine Kudlick put it ("Disability History").

3 Tremain, *Foucault and the Government of Disability*, 5–6.

4 "Broadcast Miscellany," *Radio Broadcast* 7, no. 6 (October 1925): 758.

5 Despite countless farm women, the "farmer" trope was consistently gendered male, while the shut-in's gender was more ambiguous, in part due to the feminization of disability that Rosemarie Garland-Thomson and others have discussed. See Garland-Thomson, *Extraordinary Bodies*, 28; for more on the gendering of disability see Scott and Bates, this volume. The shut-ins' seclusion in the private sphere further implied an underlying feminization above and beyond that which attached to their disability.

6 David Sarnoff, "Radio and the Farmer" (Address at the University of Missouri, January 7, 1924), in *Looking Ahead: The Papers of David Sarnoff* (New York: McGraw-Hill, 1968), 53.

7 "Deaf Ears Hear Again," *Radio Broadcast* 3, no. 5 (September 1923): 362–63; P. J. Risdon, "Radio for the Deaf," *Radio Broadcast* 2, no. 1 (November 1922): 63–64. See also Fuqua, *Prescription TV* (especially chapter 1), on the deployment of radio by hospitals and the medical industry.

8 "Helen Keller Gets Music by Radio," *New York Times*, February 10, 1924, S6.

9 Ibid.

10 See also Ellen Samuels's essay on *Iron Man 3*, this volume.

11 A. J. DeLong, "What Radio Is Doing for Me," *Radio Broadcast* 1, no. 5 (September 1922): 452.

12 Quoted in Taylor, "Music and the Rise of Radio," 433.

13 Quoted in ibid.

14 See Kirkpatrick, "Localism in American Media Policy," for more on how the public was gradually excluded from a meaningful role in U.S. media regulation.

15 "The Practical Side of Radio," *Fort Worth Star-Telegram*, July 27, 1922, 10.

16 Ernest Pierce, "What Is the Future of Radio?," *Leavenworth Post*, May 21, 1922, n.p.

17 "Opposes Jazz Airs on Sunday Radio," *New York Times*, March 14, 1927, 19.

18 Longmore, "Conspicuous Contribution," 136.

19 See, for example, Hilmes, *Radio Voices*.

20 Goggin and Newell, "Foucault on the Phone," 264.

21 Margaret Hastings, "The Arctic Listens," *Radio Digest* 29, no. 6 (January 1933): 49.

22 A useful analogy here is to the popularity of efforts to "Americanize" immigrants so as to reduce not just the threat of communist infiltration, but also cultural diversity of all kinds. In other words, radio's imputed ability to unify the nation by flattening linguistic and cultural diversity took many forms, of which the shut-in was but one.

23 Ada D. Harrison to Herbert Hoover, January 20, 1926, FRC Correspondence: Radio Division General Records, 1910–34 (RG173), FCC Office of Executive Director, General Correspondence 1926–47. National Archives and Records Administration, College Park, Md., Box 139, Folder 1732. Emphasis in original.

24 "Conductor Tells Why Radio Won Him From Concert Halls," *New York Times*, May 1, 1927, XX19.

25 Ibid.

26 Quin Ryan, "Inside the Loudspeaker," *Chicago Daily Tribune*, August 30, 1925, C14.

27 See, for example, Boyer, *Urban Masses*.

28 Longmore and Goldberger, "The League of the Physically Handicapped."

29 Quoted in Taylor, "Music and the Rise of Radio," 433.

30 Sally Joy Brown, "White City Chutes to Run Especially for Sally's Party," *Chicago Daily Tribune*, August 8, 1927, 21.

31 Sally Joy Brown, "A Friend in Need," *Chicago Daily Tribune*, August 16, 1925, E4.

32 Schweik, *The Ugly Laws*.

33 Longmore and Goldberger, "The League of the Physically Handicapped."

34 Quoted in Longmore and Goldberger, "The League of the Physically Handicapped," 894; see also Schweik, *The Ugly Laws*, 1–2.

35 See Schweik, *The Ugly Laws*.

36 Baynton, *Defectives in the Land*.

37 Longmore and Goldberger, "The League of the Physically Handicapped," 895–6.

38 See, for example, Pernick, *The Black Stork*; Schweik, *The Ugly Laws*, 120.

39 Goggin and Newell, "Foucault on the Phone," 263.

40 William C. Bagley, "Radio in the Schools," *Elementary School Journal* 31, no. 4 (December 1930): 256–58.

41 McRuer, "Compulsory Able-Bodiedness."

42 Kafer, "Compulsory Bodies," 80.

43 I thank Anna Rumbough for this insight about alternative meanings to "ideal abnormal."

44 "Rector on Radio Religion," *New York Times*, February 19, 1923, 5.

45 "Prominent Preachers Tell Value of Radio to Religion," *New York Times*, December 21, 1924, XX13.

46 "Religion Too Easy, Dr. Davis Asserts," *New York Times*, June 29, 1925, 18.

47 As in a 1938 NBC guide to programming standards: "Material which depends upon physical imperfections of deformities such as blindness, deafness, or lameness, for humorous effect is not acceptable. Physical infirmities are far from ludicrous to those afflicted, therefore radio must seek other sources for its humor." National Broadcasting Company, "Basic Broadcasting Policies," 1938, Box 93, Fldr. 43, National Broadcasting Company Files, 1921–1942. Wisconsin Historical Society, Madison, WI.

48 Foucault, *The History of Sexuality, Volume 1*, 140.

49 Bennett, "The Political Rationality of the Museum," 186.

50 Ouellette and Hay, *Better Living through Reality TV*, 9.

Afterwords

15

Afterword I

Disability in Disability Media Studies

RACHEL ADAMS

Notable disability studies scholar Rachel Adams reviews the conversation staged in this volume and identifies several features of the collection that point the way toward a disability media studies: the fruitful interplay between textual and non-textual approaches, the modeling of new forms of intersectionality, and the value of considering the specificity of media forms through the lens of disability. DMS, she argues, could benefit from more attention to earlier media forms and non-Anglophone media.

While preparing to write this afterword, I happened to see a remarkable exhibit at the Metropolitan Museum of Art. It featured the work of Matthias Buchinger, an Enlightenment-era artist who excelled at micrography, which involves the use of minutely printed letters to create intricate designs and patterns. I marveled at his finely wrought portrait of Queen Anne of Britain surrounded by an elaborate pattern of leaves, flowers, and curlicues. My astonishment grew when I looked more closely, using one of the magnifying glasses provided by the museum, and realized that the curls of her hair are made up of miniscule words spelling out three chapters from the Book of Kings. I was equally stunned by a coat of arms featuring a tiny chalice composed of an inscription of the Lord's Prayer; a self-portrait in which the artist's locks are made up of seven Psalms and the Lord's Prayer; and a two-inch-square portrait of King George I, whose face, hair, and neck are traced out in microscopic words.

These images are stunning in their own right. They are all the more so, given that Buchinger stood just 29 inches tall and was born with no legs or hands. In addition to being an artist, Buchinger was a magician and performer who entertained audiences with tricks, shooting, swordplay, and bowling. Modestly billed as "the greatest German living," he was married four times (outliving three wives) and fathered fourteen children.

Matthias Buchinger's life and art is a testament to the astonishing variability, creativity, and resilience of the human body. His story is also about the use of media to transform an artist into a celebrity, as well as the role of disability in the creation and circulation of a stage persona. Buchinger's fame was built and perpetuated via the dissemination of newspaper stories, advertisements, broadsides, pamphlets, and souvenir prints. These artifacts provide a record of his accomplishments, but they also document his evolution into a celebrity whose disability played a part in, but did not eclipse, his public persona. As such, Buchinger can offer a prehistory of the intersections of media and disability explored by this volume.

But Buchinger's story is also about present-day media technologies. His work came to hang in the Metropolitan Museum because it was collected by celebrity magician Ricky Jay. A passionate and knowledgeable collector, Jay had previously played up the more sensational aspects of Buchinger's story in a feature on him in *Jay's Journal of Anomalies*, a publication that also includes articles on such marvels as trained fleas, "A Compendium of Giant Children," and the public spectacle of nose amputation. Jay's collaboration with the Met solidified the seriousness of Buchinger's art, as well as Jay's status as a collector. In the book he wrote to accompany the exhibit, *Matthias Buchinger: "The Greatest German Living,"* Jay intersperses the story of Buchinger's life and art with that of his adventures as he sought to acquire Buchinger's work.[1] The latter story, which spans half a century, concerns Jay's use of modern communication technologies—telephone, photocopy, email, internet—to track down, authenticate, and study Buchinger's art. *Matthias Buchinger* thus entwines an account of how the media of one era created a celebrity with that of how the media of another kept his memory and work alive via another celebrity, whose fame and accomplishment were enabled, in large part, by modern media such as television and film. In both eras, disability enhances, but does not determine, the interest of the story.

Many of the topics explored by this volume resonate with the conjoined stories of Jay and Buchinger, from the celebrity of Lady Gaga to the kinship between comics and micrography (both visual art forms that create meaning from words and text) to hip-hop performers' creation of distinctive vocal signatures, questions about performance and spectatorship raised by televised freak shows, and the historical evolution that led from the public visibility of a figure like Buchinger to the isolated anonymity of the shut-in radio listener. But there are also limits to this comparison since *Disability Media Studies* is clearly concerned with the technologies that arise in the modern era and, thus, the *differences* between the creation and circulation of a disabled celebrity in the eighteenth century and the present are equally informative.

The essays in *Disability Media Studies* offer a series of case studies that are each interesting in their own right, but it also undertakes the more ambitious project of defining the methods and questions that constitute a new area of inquiry at the intersection of the key terms in its title. As editors Elizabeth Ellcessor and Bill Kirkpatrick explain in their introduction, "disability media studies" bridges two fields that each have something to gain from being put into conversation. Disability studies, which has tended to focus on textual analysis, stands to benefit from a more expansive and precise understanding of the technologies and industries that produce and have been shaped by modern conceptions of disability. And media studies is enhanced by a better understanding of how different types of embodiment have informed and been formed by technology, as well as greater attention to the way physical experience structures the form and content of media. Among its many contributions, *Disability Media Studies* is notable for the variety and breadth of the approaches taken in the volume; for modeling promising intersections of identities and methods; and for specifying how the meaning and value of different media are informed by their technological, formal, and thematic properties.

The prominence of the humanities within disability studies has meant that much scholarship within the field has been devoted to interpreting the significance of narrative and visual images (what Hagood calls a "sociotextual approach"). *Disability Media Studies* contains a number of excellent examples of this kind of work, including Shoshana Magnet and Amanda Watson on temporality and disability in graphic narratives, Robert McRuer on queerness and disability in the film *Any Day Now*, Tasha Oren on representations of autism in film and television narratives about Temple Grandin, Ellen Samuels on PTSD in the *Iron Man* films, D. Travers Scott and Meagan Bates on TV commercials for antidepressants, Katie Ellis and Gerard Goggin on news coverage of the Oscar Pistorius trial, and Julie Elman on disability in TV afterschool specials. These essays reveal the unexpected insights and alliances that emerge when media narratives are examined through the lens of disability.

Other essays go beyond, or offer alternatives to, textual analysis. For example, Mack Hagood is concerned with "biomediation," the role of non-narrative media in the diagnosis and treatment of tinnitus, an auditory disorder that has received little public attention and, as a result, lacks both adequate research and a support community. His analysis shows how technology can bring into being and thus target the symptoms of impairment, as well as how media might be enlisted to create disabled identity. Another alternative is modeled by Elizabeth Ellcessor, whose study of the web series *My Gimpy Life* engages with questions about media access and participation. Ellcessor opens up a discussion of "cultural accessibility" by considering the show's use of a Kickstarter campaign. As Ellcessor defines it, "cultural accessibility" is about giving people with disabilities access to production, enabling active engagement in the creation of material, technological, and cultural options that fulfill the needs of a wide range of bodies and minds. As such, cultural accessibility may serve as a pathway to civic participation and the growth of political alliances. Yet a third alternative is offered by Bill Kirkpatrick, whose essay focuses on the role of media policy in shaping understandings of civic engagement in the 1920s. In Kirkpatrick's reading, the disabled body—specifically the figure of the "shut-in" radio listener—was key to the formation of attitudes toward and government policy about early radio. During a crucial decade, the shut-in was used to demonstrate how technology could work to manage the health and well-being of a population and to justify the need for high-power commercial broadcasting. In this fascinating case, technology functioned to enable, but also to contain, the lives of people with disabilities that confined them to their homes.

A second valuable contribution made by this volume is to model new forms of intersectionality. Many essays offer insights about the more familiar intersections of disability identity with gender, sexuality, race, and class. Of particular interest are Robert McRuer's reading of *Any Day*

Now as a film that probes the intersection of queer and disabled identities at key moments in recent history, Lori Kido Lopez's consideration of how race and disability intersect in the spectacular bodies portrayed on the TV series *Freakshow*, and Alex S. Porco's account of how black rappers exploit disability to create distinctive verbal signatures. Others suggest promising intersections of approach and method. For example, in his essay on the diagnosis and treatment of tinnitus Hagood considers the potential to expand disability studies through the intersection of science and technology studies with media studies. In her essay on *My Gimpy Life*, Ellcessor studies how fandom intersects with funding and production of web media. And Elman's essay on afterschool specials considers the intersections of youth activism, sexual revolution, and debates about the role of TV in developing the ideal citizen.

A third contribution made by the essays in this volume is that they give serious consideration to the specificity of various media, the way differences in format, audience, and access may influence the production, circulation, and reception of media forms. In their analysis of narratives by Miriam Engelberg and Allie Brosh, Magnet and Watson argue that comics—because of the way they unfold on the page—are uniquely positioned to represent the passage of time and, as a result, to offer critical insight about the temporalities of disability. Lopez is sensitive to the differences between live confrontations with disability at freak shows of an earlier era, and the bodies portrayed in televised freak shows. Is there an ethical way to watch freak bodies on TV, Lopez asks, given the viewer's remove from the subjects on-screen? In her study of films about Temple Grandin, Oren explores why autism might be productively represented in cinema, a medium whose audiovisual properties are ideally suited to depict another person's interiority but also to stop us short, reminding audiences of the ways that the minds of others are unknowable. Films about Grandin ask the viewer to recalibrate their understanding of subjectivity as they contemplate the limits of empathic viewership. In focusing on the Kickstarter campaign for *My Gimpy Life*, Ellcessor considers the possibilities and limitations for people with disabilities to play a role in shaping and being shaped by the show's contents. And Kirkpatrick's study of the shut-in examines how the properties of radio were enlisted to create an idealized citizen-listener who was at once docile and educable.

Together, the essays in this volume offer incisive readings of a diverse set of media representations and technologies, but also a series of reflections on the methods and subjects that will shape further work at the intersection of disability and media studies. The editors make no claim to be exhaustive or systematic, and the heterogeneity of approaches and topics is one of the real strengths of this collection. Gaps in coverage make way for, rather than attempt to foreclose, the possibilities of future scholarship.

The case of Matthias Buchinger points to some promising opportunities to extend the terrain covered by *Disability Media Studies*. One is historical. The essays included in this volume cover a span of roughly one hundred years, from early radio broadcasting to such contemporary media as sound mixing, diagnostic devices, and web TV. In doing so, they implicitly define "media" as the product of mass communications and medical technologies that emerged at the beginning of the last century. However, Buchinger's story suggests another way of thinking about media that would have a much longer history. It would be interesting to see future work that extends further back to seek out lines of connection (and rupture) between contemporary media and more traditional forms like newspaper, books, and print advertising. What did media look like in a pre-electronic age, and how did disability get shaped and play a shaping role in its production and circulation? Promising avenues for further scholarship include the role of advertising, news, and other forms of mass communication in creating the great freak celebrities of the past, shaping medical knowledge, and perpetuating intersections of disability with ideas about race, gender, and national identity. It is also possible to imagine essays that look to the future to consider how media technologies like Google Glass or virtual reality might change the meaning and consequences of disability, while also being shaped by the needs of disabled designers and consumers.

The story of Buchinger—who was born in Germany and whose career extended throughout Northern Europe—points to a second area that remains underdeveloped within this collection: the role of media outside the Anglophone world. With the exception of Ellis and Goggin's essay on Oscar Pistorius and Toby Miller's on media refuse in Mexico, the volume is almost exclusively focused on the United States. Miller adds an important cautionary note about the lasting impact of waste created in the production and disposal of electronics. He thus reveals the dirty foot-print of our allegedly virtual media. Still, his essay perpetuates a view of the world in which Anglophone cultures produce the lion's share of media content while other populations are either passive consumers or victimized producers of media devices. In this, it continues in the vein of much disability studies scholarship, which has tended to concentrate on the United States and Britain and to derive its theoretical and politi-cal assumptions from those contexts. Julie Livingston's *Debility and the Moral Imagination in Botswana*, and, more recently, Nirmala Erevelles's *Disability and Difference in Global Contexts: Enabling a Transformative Body Politic*, Michele Friedner's *Valuing Deaf Worlds in Urban India*, and Don Kulick and Jens Rydström's *Loneliness and Its Opposite: Sex, Dis-ability, and the Ethics of Engagement* are notable exceptions that reveal the considerable insight to be gained by looking beyond the Anglophone west.[2] This book lays a groundwork that will allow other scholars to ex-plore a disability media studies in such contexts as the Bollywood film industry, Spanish-language broadcasting, Japanese anime, and Nordic noir; the use of 3D printing to make prosthetic limbs and adaptive fur-niture in developing countries; or the role of diagnostic technologies like ultrasound and prenatal genetic testing in non-western countries.

It would be fitting for Ricky Jay to conclude his book on Matthias Bu-chinger with the artist's death, but that isn't exactly where the book ends. Instead, a chapter appropriately titled "Greatly Exaggerated" relates the various hoaxes and rumors of Buchinger's death that circulated for some seventeen years before the artist's confirmed demise. The book's after-word tells the story of one final document, a letter written by Buchinger that fell into Jay's hands only after *Matthias Buchinger* had gone into pro-duction, in which the artist enumerates his skills and accomplishments to a potential patron. These provide Jay with "a written confirmation of early speculations" about Buchinger's many talents.

Letters, authored by but circulating in the absence of the bodies that produce them, are among the earliest forms of media, far predating the examples discussed in this volume. However, like the cases introduced by *Disability Media Studies*, Buchinger's writing bears the traces of, but is not defined or limited by, the disabled body. In this sense Buchinger helps us to clarify the collective wisdom of this volume: its vision of how bodies and minds that depart from the norm—so often seen only in terms of lack and inability—may inspire the work of creating, rethinking, and connecting with others, and the way that media technologies have done their part to produce and constrain those connections.

NOTES

1 Ricky Jay, *Matthias Buchinger: "The Greatest German Living"* (Los Angeles: Siglio, 2016).

2 Julie Livingston, *Debility and the Moral Imagination in Botswana* (Bloomington: Indiana University Press, 2005); Nirmala Erevelles, *Disability and Difference in Global Contexts: Enabling a Transformative Body Politic* (New York: Palgrave, 2011); Friedner, *Valuing Deaf Worlds in Urban India*; Don Kulick and Jens Rydström, *Loneliness and Its Opposite: Sex, Disability, and the Ethics of Engagement* (Chicago: University of Chicago Press, 2015).

16

Afterword II

Dismediation—Three Proposals, Six Tactics

MARA MILLS AND JONATHAN STERNE

Mara Mills and Jonathan Sterne, leading scholars of media technologies who have long incorporated disability into their analyses, propose "dismediation" as one avenue for the cross-pollination of disability and media studies. Referencing current scholarship in both fields, and engaging with a rich tradition of critical media studies, they argue that dismediation understands disability and media as mutually constitutive, while urging the ongoing interrogation and revision of media systems.

Disability and media are co-constituted. Yet disability studies and media studies, with their different focal points, often find themselves at cross-purposes. Popular culture seems to be "awash in representations of disability," as the editors write in the introduction to *Disability Media Studies*, but most of those representations are metaphorical, stereotypical, or spectacular. Toby Miller in this volume points out that recurring characters with disabilities in U.S. television dramas amounted to a mere 0.9% in 2015–2016. By now it is well understood that media compound and even generate disability, through stigmatizing popular representations and through means such as architectural prohibitions, toxic electronic waste, or technologies that establish bodily norms.[1] In the academy, media scholars have historically referenced disability in symbolic, clichéd, or otherwise uninterrogated terms. They continue to rely on concepts whose ableist genealogies have been forgotten. For this reason, disability theorists insist upon the disabling effects of *media studies* itself. Figures of disability—prosthesis, "crippling," schizophrenia—recur in canonical media theories, from Plato to Friedrich Kittler. Writing in the field is decorated with asides and object lessons about disability, as well as disparaging references to blindness and deafness as metaphors for ignorance and asociality. This situation has led Sharon Mitchell and David Snyder to argue that "disability underwrites the cultural study of technology writ large."[2]

Disability theorists, meanwhile, have emphasized the kinds of stories told about disability *in* media texts rather than the operations and institutions of media. Founding scholarship in disability studies, especially by those with literary training, predominantly investigated the cultural semiotics of written texts and the visual arts.[3] As the contributions to this anthology demonstrate, the new generation of media scholars taking up the challenge of disability studies has largely continued to analyze textual and visual representation, albeit in the wider array of television, movies, music videos, advertisements, and comics. We reiterate the calls—in the introduction and the chapters by Miller and Mack Hagood—for an even broader approach to "media" in disability media studies.

We agree with the editors that no grand synthesis of disability studies and media studies is necessary. But there are further opportunities for conversation and cross-pollination. Below, we outline a few propositions for thinking in terms of *dismedia*, that is, disability as a constituting dimension of media, and media as a constituting dimension of disability. We suggest dismediation as a critical counterpart to "remediation" and its cousins (premediation, demediation), specifically to theorize media change and technical design from a disability studies perspective.[4] Dismediation centers disability and refuses universal models of media and communication. It begins from a presumption of communicative and medial *difference* and *variety* rather than seeing media as either the tools to repair a damaged or diminished condition of human communication, or themselves the cause of a fall from prior perfection. Dismediation resists rehabilitation and standardization, but without recourse to the easy celebration of glitch, error, noise, jamming, or hacking that often wields "disablement" as the most convenient Other to the smooth functioning of contemporary corporatized media. Like José Esteban Muñoz's "disidentification," which hovers between the embrace and refusal of identity, dismediation appropriates media technologies and takes some measure of impairment to be a given, rather than an incontrovertible obstacle or a revolution.[5] Dismediation recognizes that impairments scale to disabilities unevenly within particular media systems, influenced by industrial and cultural settings. It embraces alienated or partial communication, reluctant technology adoption, targeted rather than wholesale rejection of mediation. Against the contemporary backdrop of "universal communication," it allows for minor and separatist media.

We understand media not as a comprehensive term for all dimensions of mediation and relationality, but rather as "socially realized structures of communication," to use Lisa Gitelman's phrase.[6] In other words, all technologies may mediate to some degree (for those who work with theories of mediation), but not all technologies are media. With this definition in mind, we call for more work on verbal, sonic, architectural, and tactile modes of communication; more attention to the material phases of media, including manufacture, design, infrastructure, distribution, pricing, adoption, domestication, repair, and disposal; attention to trans-local and trans-national inequalities of affordability and availability; a take-up of insights from science and technology studies by scholars who investigate media; and a material-semiotic approach to each layer of electronic media, from algorithms and hardware to their outputs. Mediation is not one kind of thing: it is contextually determined and structured through power relations. Dismediation demands that we radically expand the methods, sites, and contexts through which disability and media are understood. An attention to dismediation requires real interdisciplinary inquiry—curiosity around questions of engineering, chemistry, biology, political economy, policy, and ecology alongside more traditional interests in culture, whether they come from interpretive, historiographic, ethnographic, or phenomenological orientations. These interdisciplinary engagements may well be fraught and conflicted—as Hagood's chapter shows us—but they are an essential step in pluralizing the understandings of media and mediation within disability studies.

A theory of dismediation also strikes a delicate balance with regard to the epistemic authority of experience. It acknowledges the centrality and significance of the experience of disability, while also taking on board critiques of the transparency of experience, and subjects' availability to themselves, as epistemic fundaments for writing and researching disability. An understanding of dismediation requires that we also crip our own experiences. Testimony is necessary but necessarily insufficient. This might entail sacrificing or modifying media pleasures that require waste and exploitation, especially given that the gadgets and applications tied to these pleasures are often sold using concepts like "mobility" and "participation"—concepts widely problematized in the disability studies literature. It might entail risking and accepting slow and broken communication, instead of holding to an ideal of perfect transparency between subjects we imagine to be homologous to one another. It would mean accepting impairments in ourselves as well as others, claiming our limits as well as our abilities. And it would entail authors claiming disability at key theoretical junctures to disrupt compulsory able-bodiedness, while granting that dimensions of our own experience will always remain opaque to us.

Dismediation takes disability as method, not simply as content for media studies.[7] If, as Mel Chen explains, the underlying theme of disability studies is "redefining given conditions of bodily and mental life," dismediation foregrounds the conditions of communication. In the spirit of dismediation, we scrutinize the ways disability has been deployed as a routine, program, or resource in the history of technology. We work toward digital justice, which may take the forms of cripped or minor media or of mainstream access. We start from the premise of difference, even as we resist population-based disparities in the industrial or military production of impairment.

For a disability media studies that includes dismediation, we offer three propositions and six tactics:

1. Identify and Rethink Media Theories That Are Held Up by Narrative Prostheses

David Mitchell and Sharon Snyder criticize scholars such as Donna Haraway, Katherine Hayles, and Paul Virilio for using disability in the mode of "narrative prosthesis." Through this rhetorical technology, disability becomes merely a "crutch" or aid to representation. As a narrative prosthesis for media theorists, disability might serve as a titillation, a symbol of alienation, or a metaphor for breakdown and transformation. A canonical example from the tradition will outline the problem.

In his essay on "The Gadget Lover" in *Understanding Media*, Marshall McLuhan constructs an elaborate, ableist fantasy of the nervous system that corresponds to no accepted theory of physiology: "The principle of self-amputation as an immediate relief of strain on the central nervous system applies very readily to the origin of the media of communication from speech to computer. Physiologically, the central nervous system, that electric network that coordinates the various media of our senses, plays the chief role. Whatever threatens its function must be contained, localized, or cut off, even to the total removal of the offending organ."[8] While this frankly ridiculous passage is rarely cited in its entirety, a quick internet search of references to McLuhan's ideas of extension and amputation finds they are still in common use. Friedrich Kittler may be correct that early technical media were developed "by and for" deaf and blind users, but he ultimately reduces the significance of this point to passive illustration: "cripples and handicaps," he says, "lie like corpses along the technical paths to the present."[9] Titillation indeed.

So too for R. Murray Schafer's idea of "schizophonia," which is still widely cited as a description of the putative "effects" of sound reproduction in modern culture: "The Greek prefix *schizo* means split, separated; and *phone* is Greek for voice. *Schizophonia* refers to the split between an original sound and its electroacoustical transmission of reproduction. . . . I coined the term schizophonia in *The New Soundscape* intending it to be a nervous word. Related to schizophrenia, I wanted it to convey the same sense of aberration and drama."[10] Schafer's conception of sound reproduction as the violation of a previously whole, nontechnologized subject ignores centuries of prior media history, as well as the histories of the specific technologies he wrote about. Like McLuhan's nervous system, Schafer's schizophonia holds as its reference a selfsame, undamaged, idealized human body defined by its struggle against disability, debility, and difference.

These conceptualizations of media are erroneous at the descriptive and theoretical levels. Their ableist phenomenologies bear no resemblance to actual documented experiences of amputation and schizophrenia; they don't even fit with medical models of ability and disability. They are mostly rooted in these authors' fantasies *about* people with disabilities. To Georgina Kleege's hypothetical blind man,[11] we might want to add the hypothetical undamaged subject that exists prior to its encounter with media. A concept of dismedia inserts disability into critiques of the metaphysics of presence.

Those of us interested in media theory can leverage the critiques of a unified, whole, idealized body to turn universalist media theories on their head. We can combine the historicization and critique of norms in disability with the study of norming in science, technology, and medicine, all of which depend on representational technologies that render abstract human qualities as measurable quantities. In other words, we are arguing to bring together the analysis of norms and norming among writers like Lennard Davis, Rosemarie Garland-Thomson, and Susan Wendell with writers like Georges Canguilhem, Michel Foucault, and more recent work that focuses specifically on the representational dimensions of scientific instruments by writers like Jimena Canales, Robert Brain, and Alexandra Hui.[12] Doing so will reveal a human body that was never perfect; that always had its dependencies; whose variability is irreducible; and whose form is always partly but never completely technical. It will also reveal communication as something fraught, supplemented, and interdependent in all of its many forms. Treating media history as something other than a fall from wholeness frees us to understand our present in terms of possibilities for greater equality and variety. The same can be said for understandings of human bodies and subjects that leave wholeness behind.

All of this sounds nice, but it will take work—a lot of it. Media scholars' continued invocation of McLuhan, Schaffer, Kittler, Virilio, and Hayles on these very topics shows the depth and extensiveness of the problem. We will need new stories about media, new histories, but also new theories that do not rely on disability as their, well, crutch.

2. Document the Actual Centrality of Disability to Media, Engaging Closely with Disability Theories and Histories

In the words of Tobin Siebers, "the disabled body changes the process of representation itself,"[13] producing new techniques and technologies for communication. Yet this process is not captured by the loose theory of media-as-prosthesis, which has failed to account for the affordances of embodied difference; the politics of technical appropriation; the possibilities of design *for* disability (from minor media communities to "cripping" with technology); and the contradictions that lie within new media keywords such as "access," "extension," and "independence."

We also need to rethink our central concepts of the public, publicity, and the public sphere. In *The Ugly Laws*, Susan Schweik shows how the disappearance of disability from outdoor public life in the United States resulted from a patchwork of local laws that turned disability stigma into policy.[14] It became possible to physically police people with disabilities out of public spaces. It is perhaps a cliché of media studies and science and technology studies that technologies govern social relations (more or less effectively) as delegates for their designers or users. But we have only begun to explore that idea in terms of its consequences for disability, and we have only begun to understand how concepts of ability and disability shape widely held understandings of shared social life, political consensus, and civic action so central to our understandings of so-called liberal democracies.

We have both argued, in different ways, that there is no state of nature for the senses that is available without media, and that every media form is built around different ideas of the natures of human subjects and bodies. We have shown how ideas of disability shaped the emergence of modern sound media and how modern sound media shaped ideas of ability and disability. Jonathan's first book, *The Audible Past*, locates the origins of sound reproduction in nineteenth-century sound culture, with its peculiar conceptions of hearing, speech, and deafness. He considered Alexander Graham Bell's ear phonautograph—a device Bell credited with giving him "the idea for the telephone"—as a technology designed to eradicate cultural vestiges of deafness.[15] Similarly, Mara has shown how the quest for miniaturization in electronics was intimately tied to deaf stigma, aiming to hide the existence and workings of hearing aids. More broadly, her first book, *On the Phone*, shows how the modern concepts of "impairment" and "hearing loss," as well as the contributions of deaf and hard-of-hearing people, were central to the development of telecommunications technologies and signal processing in the twentieth century.[16] Both *On the Phone* and Jonathan's second book, *MP3*, show how telecommunications in turn impacted our current conceptions of hearing and its limits.[17]

But it goes further: histories of closed captioning, audio description, and subtitling demonstrate that users with disabilities are often at the forefront of innovation in media systems that make them more useful for everyone. Today, closed captioning is employed by a wide range of publics: we find it everywhere from sound-optional Facebook videos to television screens in gyms and airports. And yet, as Greg Downey has shown, broadcasters initially resisted closed captioning because of its connection to D/deaf and hard-of-hearing people; minoritized, the technology was viewed as an expense and an inconvenience. Instead, closed captioning has greatly increased the flexibility of audiovisual media for a wide swath of users in a host of situations. Current work on the internet and accessibility by Katie Ellis, Mike Kent, Helen Kennedy, Elizabeth Ellcessor, and others also shows the degree to which users in disability communities are at the forefront of adding flexibility and usefulness to media technologies, even as much of the new media discourse around the politics of access often leaves disability aside. This is a place where disability theory and media theory can have direct and significant impact on policy and activism.[18] The politics and economics of technology transfer also require scrutiny. As Mara has argued, disability "gains" are often appropriated without compensation or attribution, and incorporated into larger inaccessible systems—a mode of extraction she calls "technology removal."[19]

3. Document the Centrality of Media to Disability, Engaging Closely with Media Theories and Histories

The vast majority of disability scholarship on the topic of media, outside media studies, has focused on the ways *representation* produces disability. But the central insight of media studies, to paraphrase John Durham Peters, is that representations can never be analyzed apart from their means. In other words, not only do media produce disability through their textual representations *of* disability, they produce disability through their very operations, their institutional existences, and their policy and juridical dimensions. Certain disabilities—compulsive machine gambling, ink allergies and other print disabilities, some forms of photosensitive epilepsy—exist as a direct consequence of media technologies.[20]

Media also themselves become metaphors for both reason and its various others. Today, computational metaphors fly back and forth across the porous disciplinary borders of biology, computer science (and especially machine learning), and psychology. But one can also see it in the figuration and experience of various forms of mental illness. The work of Amit Pinchevsky and John Durham Peters is especially instructive here, as they have documented the ways in which schizophrenia and autism have been described and even experienced as media phenomena, from eroding the differences between impersonality and personal address in broadcast to the representation of autism as a communication disorder, and its inverse—the celebration of autism in some new media business environments. The very meanings and experiences of these conditions are defined through media and communication.[21] And as Tasha Oren's chapter in this volume shows, even representations of autism shift in relation to the changing cultural and institutional status of autism more broadly. Mental illness and media are thus the ultimate mangle: conceptions and experience of one almost always imply ideas about the other.

Beyond these broad juxtapositions of disability studies and media studies, as the fields currently exist, we offer the following tactics for dismediation:

1. Think Comparatively about Disability—as Concept and Experience—with Regard to History and Geography

Basic terms vary across contexts and even within languages: witness the differences of opinion on "people with disabilities" versus "disabled people" as descriptors, depending on whether one is working within the US or UK English-language context. In *Debility and the Moral Imagination in Botswana*, Julie Livingston discusses the Setswana word *bogole*, which does not line up neatly with the English word *disability*; instead, it encompasses impairment, illness, and senescence.[22] As an example of historical change, hard-of-hearing Germans called themselves *harthörig* in the eighteenth century and *schwerhörig* in the nineteenth. "Hard" in the former case meant tough, firm, or unyielding, whereas the later term refers to difficulty—implying a shift from anatomy to behavior and function. What counts as disability, and how it is experienced, are every bit as context-dependent as is terminology.

2. Think Transnationally about Disability as It Results from Global Supply Chains, War, and International Laws or Standards

From Donna Haraway's "Cyborg Manifesto" to Jack Qiu's *Goodbye iSlave: A Manifesto for Digital Abolition*, theorists of electronics have highlighted the North-South inequalities fueled by global media systems, with money, prestige, and knowledge disproportionately accumulating on one side, labor and waste on the other.[23] In his contribution to this collection, Toby Miller's analysis of "effluent citizenship" foregrounds disability within that ongoing discussion. Along the same lines, disability media studies might draw on insights from postcolonial theory, war and media studies, and the environmental justice movement to understand present-day disparities in incidences of disability (and the international attention they earn). The history and impact of international standards for thousands of human traits and functions, compiled in classification systems such as the ICD-10,[24] remain woefully understudied despite rampant theoretical interest in norms and medicalization. Aimee Medeiros has pointed out, as one example, that the World Health Organization employed—for three decades—pediatric growth charts based on a small study of bottle-fed babies in Ohio, with massive consequences for diagnoses of disability and malnourishment around the world.[25]

3. Allow That Technologies and Media Representations Are Actors—Socially Situated, but Sometimes Constraining Human Action or Generating Impairment at Immense Scales

This is the classic argument in Langdon Winner's "Do Artifacts Have Politics?" essay, which continues to guide research on the values embedded in technical designs—and their downstream impacts. Miller asks us to consider "how the media cause disability" in the case of electronics production and disposal. We can also consider how their presence in everyday interaction shape relations of ability and disability. For instance, Meryl Alper's *Giving Voice*, on autism and speech, considers the centrality of iPads and text-to-speech in structuring the relationships within families that have members on the spectrum. It is also the first full-length study of the iPad and touch tablets more generally, thereby placing disability at the center of an emerging media form. While there is a large body of work on technologies and power relations in several fields—feminist studies, cultural studies, science and technology studies, actor-network theory—relatively little of the canonical work directly confronts questions of ability and disability, despite common preoccupations with thinking about agency beyond the human.[26]

4. Consider the Occasions When Disability Becomes a Source of Value and Not Just a Source of Stigma, for Industries as Well as for People Who Identify as Disabled

In *Valuing Deaf Worlds in Urban India*, Michele Friedner tracks the ways deafness accrues social and economic value at businesses that employ disabled workers for reasons that include advertising benefits, affective labor, and reduced pay.[27] Graham Pullin's work has shown that disability itself can be fertile ground for basic research in design, as well as solving problems widely shared by people with disabilities and normate people. Similarly, while experiences of racial and sexual difference have been widely understood to be central to the history of a range of musics from jazz to electronica, we are only now beginning to understand how much disability has also shaped the history of music, for instance in the use of various disabilities as signs of "genius" and creative agency ranging from Beethoven's or Christine Sun Kim's deafness, to the blindness of Ray Charles and Stevie Wonder, to Syd Barrett's mental illness, or in the performance styles of particular musicians and artists, as documented by scholars like Jessica Holmes and George McKay.[28]

5. Diversify the Keywords and Matters of Concern for Disability Media Studies, Adding to Current Research on Access and Representation

Elizabeth Ellcessor has shown, in this volume and elsewhere, how attention to *access* in some media-theoretical and activist contexts has redefined the term away from the accessibility concerns central to disability politics. As a keyword, *access* has met with criticism from the digital justice and disability studies communities alike, for emphasizing a technical fix rather than training, production, ownership, or broader socio-economic change. We have already shown how *public* also needs to be rethought. Lisa Cartwright and Brian Goldfarb have explored the radical plasticity of sensing subjects, challenging ableist conceptions of the senses that still undergird most theories of media.[29] Other keywords in media studies, from *identity* to *commodity* to *environment*, will need similar rethinking.

6. Approach the Intersection of Media and Disability with a Wider Range of Theoretical Perspectives

Such perspectives should include affect studies, new realism, queer theory, and decolonial theory, as well as the contributions of artists and activists to our understandings of the intersections of media and disability—to name a few.[30] Rosemarie Garland-Thomson's work on staring and Anne Cvetkovich's work on depression are two examples, carried forward in this volume in Lopez's theorization of ethical television viewership and in Magnet and Watson's engagement with comics and temporalities of disability. The various strands of new materialism have thus far been especially resistant to disability as a concept, wrongly reducing it to ideation and identity. Given that materiality is such a central concept in media studies, perhaps a cripped materiality could be the next major breakthrough across our two fields.

NOTES

1 See in this volume, for example, Toby Miller's chapter on toxic waste, Mack Hagood's and Bill Kirkpatrick's chapters on normalization, and several chapters on stigmatizing representations.

2 David T. Mitchell and Sharon L. Snyder, *The Body and Physical Difference: Discourses of Disability* (Ann Arbor: University of Michigan Press, 1997), 8.

3 What Mack Hagood calls the *sociotextual approach* includes the discursive analysis of visual "texts" in such works as Siebers, *Disability Aesthetics*; Garland-Thomson, *Extraordinary Bodies*; Sharon Snyder and David Mitchell, "Body Genres and Disability Sensations," in *Cultural Locations of Disability* (Chicago: University of Chicago Press, 2005).

4 See Jay David Bolter and Richard Grusin, *Remediation: Understanding New Media* (Cambridge, MA: MIT Press, 1999); Richard Grusin, *Premediation: Affect and Mediality after 9/11* (New York: Palgrave, 2010); Garrett Stewart, "Bookwork as Demediation," *Critical Inquiry* 36, no. 3 (Spring 2010): 410–57.

5 José Esteban Muñoz, *Disidentifications: Queers of Color and the Performance of Politics* (Minneapolis: University of Minnesota Press, 1999).

6 Lisa Gitelman, *Always Already New: Media, History, and the Data of Culture* (Cambridge, MA: MIT Press, 2006), 7.

7 Here we draw inspiration from Wendy Hui Kyong Chun, "Race and/as Technology: Or How to Do Things to Race," *Camera Obscura* 24 (2009): 7–35.

8 Marshall McLuhan, *Understanding Media: The Extensions of Man* (New York: McGraw-Hill, 1964), 43.

9 Friedrich Kittler, *Optical Media* (New York: Polity, 2010), 120.

10 R. Murray Schafer, *The Soundscape: Our Sonic Environment and the Tuning of the World* (Rochester, VT: Destiny Books, 1994), 90, 91.

11 Georgina Kleege, "Blindness and Visual Culture: An Eyewitness Account," in *Disability Studies Reader*, 4th ed., ed. Lennard Davis (New York: Routledge, 2013), 447–55.

12 Jimena Canales, *A Tenth of a Second: A History* (Chicago: University of Chicago Press, 2009); Alexandra Hui, *The Psychophysical Ear: Musical Experiments, Experimental Sounds, 1840–1910* (Cambridge, MA: MIT Press, 2012); Robert Brain, *The Pulse of Modernism: Physiological Aesthetics in Fin-de-Siècle Europe* (Seattle: University of Washington Press, 2015).

13 Siebers, *Disability Aesthetics*, 54.

14 Schweik, *The Ugly Laws*.

15 Sterne, *The Audible Past*.

16 Mills, *On the Phone*.

17 Sterne, *MP3*.

18 Downey, *Closed Captioning*; Ellcessor, *Restricted Access*; Ellis and Kent, *Disability and New Media*; Helen Kennedy, *Net Work: Ethics and Values in Web Design* (New York: Palgrave MacMillan, 2012), especially the chapters on the ethics of web accessibility and users with intellectual disabilities.

19 Mills, *On the Phone*.

20 See Natasha Dow Schüll, *Addiction by Design: Machine Gambling in Las Vegas* (Princeton, NJ: Princeton University Press, 2013).

21 Amit Pinchevski, "Bartleby's Autism: Wandering along Incommunicability," *Cultural Critique* 78 (Spring 2011): 27–59; John Durham Peters, "Broadcasting and Schizophrenia," *Media, Culture & Society* 32, no. 1 (January 2010): 123–40; Amit Pinchevski and John Durham Peters, "Autism and New Media: Disability between Technology and Society," *New Media & Society* (2015), http://us.sagepub.com. See also Scott and Bates's chapter on anxiety (and depression) in this volume.

22 Julie Livingston, *Debility and the Moral Imagination in Botswana* (Bloomington: Indiana University Press, 2005).

23 Donna Haraway, "The Cyborg Manifesto," in *Cyborgs, Simians, and Women* (New York: Routledge, 1991); Jack Linchuan Qiu, *Goodbye iSlave: A Manifesto for Digital Abolition* (Urbana: University of Illinois Press, 2016).

24 World Health Organization, International Statistical Classification of Diseases and Related Health Problems, 10th ed. (1990), www.who.int.

25 Aimee Medeiros, "Size Matters: The History of Growth Charts in Pediatrics," *UCLA Library*, November 6, 2015, www.library.ucla.edu.

26 Langdon Winner, *The Whale and the Reactor: A Search for Limits in the Age of High Technology* (Chicago: University of Chicago Press, 1986); Harlan Hahn, "Disability and the Urban Environment: A Perspective on Los Angeles," *Environment and Planning D: Society and Space* 4 (1986): 279–88; Michelle Murphy, *Seizing the Means of Reproduction: Entanglements of Feminism, Health, and Technoscience* (Durham, NC: Duke University Press, 2012); Akhil Gupta, *Red Tape: Bureaucracy,*

Structural Violence, and Poverty in India (Durham, NC: Duke University Press, 2012); Alper, *Giving Voice*. In addition to Winner's work, readers unfamiliar with the work on technology and agency should consult Madeleine Akrich, "The De- Scription of Technical Objects," in *Shaping Technology, Building Society: Studies in Sociotechnical Change*, ed. Wiebe E. Bijker and John Law (Cambridge, MA: MIT Press, 1992), 205–24; Bruno Latour, *Aramis, or the Love of Technology* (Cambridge, MA: Harvard University Press, 1996); Jennifer Daryl Slack and J. Macgregor Wise, *Culture and Technology: A Primer*, 2nd ed. (New York: Peter Lang, 2014).

27 Friedner, *Valuing Deaf Worlds in Urban India*.

28 Jessica Holmes, "Singing beyond Hearing," *Journal of the American Musicological Society* 69, no. 2 (2016): 542–48; George McKay, *Shakin' All Over: Popular Music and Disability* (Ann Arbor: University of Michigan Press, 2013). See also Alex Porco's chapter in this volume.

29 Ellcessor, *Restricted Access*; Lisa Cartwright and Brian Goldfarb, "On the Subject of Neural and Sensory Prosthesis," in *The Prosthetic Impulse: From a Posthuman Present to a Biocultural Future*, ed. Marquard Smith and Joanne Morra, 125–54 (Cambridge, MA: MIT Press, 2006).

30 Garland-Thomson, *Staring*; Cvetkovich, *Depression*.

BIBLIOGRAPHY

Abbas, Ackbar, and John Nguyet Erni, eds. *Internationalizing Cultural Studies: An Anthology*. Malden, MA: Wiley-Blackwell, 2004.

Adams, Rachel. *Sideshow U.S.A.: Freaks and the American Cultural Imagination*. Chicago: University of Chicago Press, 2001.

Admon-Rick, Gaby. "Impaired Encoding: Calculating, Ordering, and the 'Disability Percentages' Classification System." *Science, Technology & Human Values* 39, no. 1 (2014): 105–29.

Aguilera, Raymond J. "Disability and Delight: Staring at the Devotee Community." *Sexuality & Disability* 18, no. 4 (2000): 255–61.

Ainspan, Nathan D., and Walter E. Penk, eds. *Returning Wars' Wounded, Injured, and Ill: A Reference Handbook*. Westport, CT: Praeger, 2008.

Alaniz, José. *Death, Disability, and the Superhero: The Silver Age and Beyond*. Jackson: University Press of Mississippi, 2014.

Alexander, Kern, and M. David Alexander. *American Public School Law*, 6th ed. St. Paul, MN: Wadsworth, 2005.

Allen, Robert C. *Horrible Prettiness: Burlesque and American Culture*. Chapel Hill: University of North Carolina Press, 1991.

Alper, Meryl. *Digital Youth with Disabilities*. Cambridge, MA: MIT Press, 2014.

———. *Giving Voice: Mobile Communication, Disability, and Inequality*. Cambridge, MA: MIT Press, 2017.

Andrejevic, Mark. "Exploiting YouTube: Contradictions of User-Generated Labor." In *The YouTube Reader*, edited by Pelle Snickars and Patrick Vonderau, 406–23. Stockholm: National Library of Sweden, 2009.

Angeloni, Silvia. "Integrated Disability Management: An Interdisciplinary and Holistic Approach." *SAGE Open* (2013): 1–15.

Anzaldúa, Gloria. *Borderlands/La Frontera*. San Francisco: Aunt Lute Books, 1987.

Armstrong, Thomas. *Neurodiversity: Discovering the Extraordinary Gifts of Autism, ADHD, Dyslexia, and Other Brain Differences*. Boston: Da Capo Press, 2010.

Asberg, Cecilia, and Ericka Johnson. "Viagra Selfhood: Pharmaceutical Advertising and the Visual Formation of Swedish Masculinity." *Health Care Analysis: Journal of Health Philosophy and Policy* 17, no. 2 (June 2009): 144–57.

Asch, Adrienne, and Michelle Fine, eds. *Women with Disabilities: Essays in Psychology, Culture, and Politics*. Philadelphia: Temple University Press, 1998.

Aslama, Minna, and Mervi Pantti. "Talking Alone: Reality TV, Emotions and Authenticity." *European Journal of Cultural Studies* 9, no. 2 (May 1, 2006): 167–84.

Avon, Antoinette. "Watching Films, Learning Language, Experiencing Culture: An Account of Deaf Culture through History and Popular Films." *Journal of Popular Culture* 39, no. 2 (2006): 185–204.

Bagley, William C. "Radio in the Schools." *Elementary School Journal* 31, no. 4 (December 1930): 256–58.

Baglia, Jay. *The Viagra Ad Venture: Masculinity, Media, and the Performance of Sexual Health*. New York: Peter Lang, 2005.

Bailey, Moya. "'The Illest': Disability as Metaphor in Hip Hop Music." In *Blackness and Disability: Critical Examinations and Cultural Interventions*, edited by Christopher Bell, 141–47. Berlin: Lit Verlag, 2011.

Baker, Anthony D. "Recognizing Jake: Contending with Formulaic and Spectacularized Representations of Autism in Film." In *Autism and Representation*, edited by Mark Osteen, 229–43. New York: Routledge, 2008.

Baker, Houston. *Blues, Ideology, and African-American Literature: A Vernacular Theory*. Chicago: University of Chicago Press, 1984.

Baker, Rodney R. "Benefits for Veterans: A Historical Context and Overview of the Current Situation." In *Returning Wars' Wounded, Injured, and Ill: A Reference Handbook*, edited by Nathan D. Ainspan and Walter E. Penk, 1–12. Westport, CT: Praeger, 2008.

Banet-Weiser, Sarah. "Branding the Post-Feminist Self: Girls' Video Production and YouTube." In *Mediated Girlhood: New Explorations of Girls' Media Culture*, edited by Mary Celeste Kearney, 277–94. New York: Peter Lang, 2011.

Baram, Michael. "Globalization and Workplace Hazards in Developing Nations." *Safety Science* 47, no. 6 (2009): 756–66.

Barker, Clare, and Stuart Murray. "Disabling Postcolonialism: Global Disability Cultures and Democratic Criticism." *Journal of Literary & Cultural Disability Studies* 4, no. 3 (2010): 219–36.

Barnartt, Sharon, and Barbara Altman, eds. *Disability and Intersecting Statuses*. Bingley, UK: Emerald Group Publishing, 2013.

Barnes, Colin. "Disabling Imagery and the Media: An Exploration of the Principles for Media Representations of Disabled People." London: British Council of Organisations of Disabled People, 1992.

Barnhurst, Kevin G. "Visibility as Paradox: Representation and Simultaneous Contrast." In *Media Queered: Visibility and Its Discontents*, edited by Kevin G. Barnhurst, 1–22. New York: Peter Lang, 2007.

Baron-Cohen, Simon. "Empathy—Freudian Origins and 21st Century Neuroscience." *Psychologist* 19, no. 9 (September 2006): 536–37.

———. *The Essential Difference: The Truth about the Male and Female Brain*. New York: Basic Books, 2003.

Barrett, Lindon. *Blackness and Value: Seeing Double*. New York: Cambridge University Press, 1999.

Barsade, Sigal G., Andrew J. Ward, Jean D. F. Turner, and Jeffrey A. Sonnenfeld. "To Your Heart's Content: An Affective Diversity Model in Top Management Teams." *Administrative Science Quarterly* 45, no. 4 (2000): 802–36.

Barthes, Roland. "The Grain of the Voice." In *Image, Music, Text*, 179–89. Translated by Stephen Heath. New York: Noonday, 1988.

———. *Mythologies*. Translated by Annette Lavers. New York: Hill and Wang, 1972.

Bartholomew, Robert E., and Simon Wessely. "Protean Nature of Mass Sociogenic Illness from Possessed Nuns to Chemical and Biological Terrorism Fears." *British Journal of Psychiatry* 180, no. 4 (April 1, 2002): 300–6.

Barton, Sarah. "Disability and Television: Notes from the Field." *Journal of Popular Television* 3, no. 2 (2015): 261–67.

Baym, Nancy. *Personal Connections in the Digital Age*. Cambridge, UK: Polity, 2010.

Beard, George. "Neurasthenia, or Nervous Exhaustion." *Boston Medical and Surgical Journal* 80, no. 13 (April 29, 1869): 217–21.

Bechdel, Alison. *The Essential Dykes to Watch Out For*. Boston: Houghton Mifflin Harcourt, 2008.

Bell, Susan E. "Premenstrual Syndrome and Medicalization of Menopause: A Sociological Perspective." In *Premenstrual Syndrome: Ethical and Legal Implications in a Biomedical Perspective*, edited by Benson Ginsburg and Bonnie Frank Carter, 151–73. Boston, MA: Springer, 2013 (reprint of 1987 1st ed.).

Beltrán, Mary, Jane Chi-Hyun Park, Henry Puente, Sharon Ross, and John Downing. "Pressurizing the Media Industry: Achievements and Limitations." In *Representing "Race": Racisms, Ethnicity, and Media*, edited by John Downing and Charles Husband, 160–74. London: Sage, 2005.

Bennett, Tony. "The Political Rationality of the Museum." In *Critical Cultural Policy Studies: A Reader*, edited by Justin Lewis and Toby Miller, 180–87. Malden, MA: Blackwell, 2003.

Berlant, Lauren. *Queen of America Goes to Washington City: Essays on Sex and Citizenship*. Durham, NC: Duke University Press, 1997.

Bernstein, Charles. "Introduction." In *Close Listening: Poetry and the Performed Word*, edited by Charles Bernstein, 3–26. New York: Oxford University Press, 1998.

Bersani, Leo. *Homos*. Cambridge, MA: Harvard University Press, 1995.

Bertling, Christoph, and Thomas Schierl. "Disabled Sport and Its Relation to Contemporary Cultures of Presence and Aesthetics." *Sport in History* 28, no. 1 (March 1, 2008): 39–50.

Bespalov, Anton Y., Marcel M. van Gaalen, and Gerhard Gross. "Antidepressant Treatment in Anxiety Disorders." In *Behavioral Neurobiology of Anxiety and Its Treatment*, edited by Murray B. Stein and Thomas Steckler, 361–90. Current Topics in Behavioral Neurosciences 2. Heidelberg: Springer 2009.

Blaskiewicz, Robert. "The Big Pharma Conspiracy Theory." *Medical Writing* 22, no. 4 (2013): 259–61.

Blos, P. "The Second Individuation Process of Adolescence." *Psychoanalytic Study of the Child* 22 (1967): 162–86.

Boddy, William. *Fifties Television: The Industry and Its Critics*. Champaign: University of Illinois Press, 1992.

Bodroghkozy, Aniko. *Groove Tube: Sixties Television and the Youth Rebellion*. Durham, NC: Duke University Press, 2001.

Bogdan, Robert. *Freak Show: Presenting Human Oddities for Amusement and Profit.* Chicago: University of Chicago Press, 1990.

Bonilla-Silva, Eduardo. *Racism without Racists: Color-Blind Racism and the Persistence of Racial Inequality in America*, 3rd ed. Lanham, MD: Rowman & Littlefield, 2009.

Booher, Amanda K. "Defining Pistorius." *Disability Studies Quarterly* 31, no. 3 (July 18, 2011). http://dsq-sds.org.

Booth, Paul. "Reifying the Fan: Inspector Spacetime as Fan Practice." *Popular Communication* 11, no. 2 (2013): 146–59.

Bourdieu, Pierre. *The Field of Cultural Production.* Translated by Randal Johnson. New York: Columbia University Press, 1993.

boyd, danah. *It's Complicated: The Social Lives of Networked Teens.* New Haven, CT: Yale University Press, 2014.

Boyer, Paul S. *Urban Masses and Moral Order in America, 1820–1920.* Cambridge, MA: Harvard University Press, 1978.

Brabazon, Tara. *Playing on the Periphery: Sport, Identity and Memory.* London: Routledge, 2006.

Brabham, Daren C. "Crowdsourcing as a Model for Problem Solving: An Introduction and Cases." *Convergence: The International Journal of Research into New Media Technologies* 14, no. 1 (February 1, 2008): 75–90.

Brennan, Tim. "Off the Gangsta Tip: A Rap Appreciation, or Forgetting about Los Angeles." *Critical Inquiry* 20, no. 4 (Summer 1994): 663–93.

Brewster, Bill, and Frank Broughton. *Last Night a DJ Saved My Life: The History of the Disc Jockey.* New York: Grove Press, 1999.

Brophy, Sarah, and Janice Hladki. "Connective Tissue: Summoning the Spectator to Visual Autobiography." In *Embodied Politics in Visual Autobiography*, edited by Sarah Brophy and Janice Hladki, 244–68. Toronto: University of Toronto Press, 2014.

———. "Visual Autobiography in the Frame: Critical Embodiment and Cultural Pedagogy." In *Embodied Politics in Visual Autobiography*, edited by Sarah Brophy and Janice Hladki, 3–30. Toronto: University of Toronto Press, 2014.

Brosh, Allie. *Hyperbole and a Half: Unfortunate Situations, Flawed Coping Mechanisms, Mayhem, and Other Things That Happened.* New York: Touchstone Books, 2013.

Brown, Brené. *Daring Greatly: How the Courage to Be Vulnerable Transforms the Way We Live, Love, Parent, and Lead.* New York: Gotham, 2012.

Brown, Wendy. *Regulating Aversion: Tolerance in the Age of Identity and Empire.* Princeton, NJ: Princeton University Press, 2008.

Burgess, Jean. "All Your Chocolate Rain Are Belong to Us?" In *Video Vortex Reader: Responses to YouTube*, edited by Geert Lovink and Sabine Niederer, 101–10. Amsterdam: Institute of Network Cultures, 2008.

Burkett, Brendan, Mike McNamee, and Wolfgang Potthast. "Shifting Boundaries in Sports Technology and Disability: Equal Rights or Unfair Advantage in the Case of Oscar Pistorius." *Disability & Society* 26, no. 5 (2011): 643–54.

Burnham, John. *Accident Prone: A History of Technology, Psychology, and Misfits of the Machine Age.* Chicago: University of Chicago Press, 2010.

Butler, Judith. *Gender Trouble: Feminism and the Subversion of Identity*. New York: Routledge, 1999.

Butler, Sandra, and Barbara Rosenblum. *Cancer in Two Voices*. Duluth, MN: Spinsters Ink Books, 1996.

Caldwell, John Thornton. *Production Culture: Industrial Reflexivity and Critical Practice in Film and Television*. Durham, NC: Duke University Press, 2008.

Callahan, John. *Don't Worry, He Won't Get Far on Foot*. New York: Vintage, 1990.

Calvino, Italo. *The Road to San Giovanni*. Translated by Tim Parks. New York: Vintage International, 1994.

Campbell, Fiona Kumari. *Contours of Ableism: The Production of Disability and Abledness*. New York: Palgrave Macmillan, 2009.

Carlson, Laurie Ann. "Wired for Interdependency: Push Girls and Cyborg Sexuality." *Feminist Media Studies* 13, no. 4 (September 1, 2013): 754–59.

Carpentier, Nico. *Media and Participation*. New York: Intellect Ltd., 2011.

Carrillo, Jorge, and Robert Zárate. "The Evolution of Maquiladora Best Practices: 1965–2008." *Journal of Business Ethics* 88, no. 2 (2009): 335–48.

Cartwright, Lisa. *Screening the Body: Tracing Medicine's Visual Culture*. Minneapolis: University of Minnesota Press, 1995.

Cavanagh, Allison. "Ladies of the *Times*: Elite Women's Voices at the Turn of the Twentieth Century." *Journalism Studies* (May 2016). www.tandfonline.com.

Centre for Reflection and Action on Labor Issues. *Labor Rights in a Time of Crisis: Third Report on Working Conditions in the Mexican Electronics Industry*. 2009. http://goodelectronics.org.

Centro Interdiciplinario para Prevención de la Contaminación. *Programa de difusión y capacitación sobre la elaboración de planes de manejo de residuos electrónicos: Reporte final*. Instituto Nacional de Ecología, 2012. www.inecc.gob.mx.

Centro de Reflexión y Acción Laboral. *El precio de la flexibilidad: Experiencias de trabajadores en la industria electrónica en México: Sexto informe sobre condiciones laborales en la industria electrónica en México*. 2015. www.cerealgdl.org.

Certeau, Michel de. *The Practice of Everyday Life*. Translated by Steven F. Rendall. Berkeley: University of California Press, 2011.

Chang, Heewon. "Re-examining the Rhetoric of the 'Cultural Border.'" Paper presented at the American Anthropological Association, Philadelphia, PA, December 1998.

Chang, Jeff. *Can't Stop Won't Stop: A History of the Hip-Hop Generation*. New York: St. Martin's Press, 2005.

Chapman, Chris. "Colonialism, Disability, and Possible Lives: The Residential Treatment of Children Whose Parents Survived Indian Residential Schools." *Journal of Progressive Human Services* 23, no. 2 (May 1, 2012): 127–58.

Charlton, James I. *Nothing about Us without Us: Disability Oppression and Empowerment*. Berkeley: University of California Press, 2000.

Chin, Bertha, Bethan Jones, Myles McNutt, and Luke Pebler. "Dialogue: Veronica Mars Kickstarter and Crowd Funding." *Transformative Works and Cultures* 15 (2014). http://journal.transformativeworks.org.

Christian, Aymar Jean. "Fandom as Industrial Response: Producing Identity in an Independent Web Series." *Transformative Works and Cultures* 8 (2011). http://journal. transformativeworks.org.

Chute, Hillary L. *Graphic Women: Life Narrative and Contemporary Comics.* New York: Columbia University Press, 2010.

Chute, Hillary, and Marianne DeKoven. "Graphic Narrative." *Modern Fiction Studies* 52, no. 4 (2006): 767–82.

Clare, Eli. *Exile and Pride: Disability, Queerness, and Liberation.* Cambridge, MA: South End Press, 1999.

Cleve, John Vickrey van, and Barry A. Crouch. *A Place of Their Own: Creating the Deaf Community in America.* Washington, DC: Gallaudet University Press, 1989.

Clowse, Barbara Barksdale. *Brainpower for the Cold War: The Sputnik Crisis and the National Defense Education Act of 1958.* Westport, CT: Greenwood, 1981.

Cohen, Ed. *A Body Worth Defending: Immunity, Biopolitics, and the Apotheosis of the Modern Body.* Durham, NC: Duke University Press, 2009.

Cole, C. L. "Oscar Pistorius's Aftermath." *Journal of Sport & Social Issues* 33, no. 1 (February 1, 2009): 3–4.

Coleman, Brian. *Check the Technique: Liner Notes for Hip-Hop Junkies.* New York: Villard, 2007.

Collins-Dogrul, Julie. "Governing Transnational Social Problems: Public Health Politics on the US-Mexico Border." *Global Networks* 12, no. 1 (2012): 109–28.

Connell, Raewyn W. *Southern Theory: Social Science and the Global Dynamics of Knowledge.* Cambridge and Malden, MA: Polity, 2007.

Connor, Steven. *Dumbstruck: A Cultural History of Ventriloquism.* New York: Oxford University Press, 2000.

Conrad, Peter. *The Medicalization of Society: On the Transformation of Human Conditions into Treatable Disorders.* Baltimore: Johns Hopkins University Press, 2008.

Coopman, Stephanie J. "Disability on the Net." *American Communication Journal* 3, no. 3 (June 2000). http://works.bepress.com.

Corbin, Alain. *The Foul and the Fragrant: Order and the French Social Imagination.* Cambridge, MA: Harvard University Press, 1986.

Corker, Mairian, and Tom Shakespeare. *Disability/Postmodernity: Embodying Disability Theory.* London: Bloomsbury Publishing, 2002.

Couser, G. Thomas, and Lennard J. Davis. "Disability, Life Narrative, and Representation." In *The Disability Studies Reader*, 2nd ed., edited by Lennard J. Davis, 399–401. New York: Routledge, 2006.

Cowie, Jefferson. *Capital Moves: RCA's Seventy-Year Quest for Cheap Labor.* New York: New Press, 2001.

Cummings, William. "Orientalism's Corporeal Dimension: Tattooed Bodies and Eighteenth-Century Oceans." *Journal of Colonialism and Colonial History* 4, no. 2 (2003): 19–20.

Cvetkovich, Ann. *Depression: A Public Feeling.* Durham, NC: Duke University Press, 2012.

D'Acci, Julie. "Cultural Studies, Television Studies, and the Crisis in the Humanities." In *Television after TV: Essays on a Medium in Transition*, edited by Lynn Spigel and Jan Olsson, 418–45. Durham, NC: Duke University Press, 2004.

Dávila, Arlene. *Latinos, Inc.: The Marketing and Making of a People*. Berkeley: University of California Press, 2001.

Davis, Lennard J. "Constructing Normalcy." In *The Disability Studies Reader*, 3rd ed., edited by Lennard J. Davis, 3–19. New York: Routledge, 2010.

———. "Depression and Disability." Public talk, Clemson University, Clemson, SC, November 19, 2013.

———. *Enforcing Normalcy: Disability, Deafness, and the Body*. London and New York: Verso, 1995.

———. "J'accuse!: Cultural Imperialism—Ableist Style." *Social Alternatives* 18 (1999): 36–41.

De Silva, J. P. *La televisión ha muerto*. Barcelona: Editorial Gedisa, 2000.

DiPaolo, Marc. *War, Politics and Superheroes: Ethics and Propaganda in Comics and Film*. Jefferson, NC: McFarland, 2011.

Donohue, J. "A History of Drug Advertising: The Evolving Roles of Consumers and Consumer Protection." *Milbank Quarterly* 84, no. 4 (2006): 659–99.

Douglas, Mary. *Purity and Danger: An Analysis of Concepts of Pollution and Taboo*. New York: Routledge Classics, 1966.

Douglas, Susan. *Listening In: Radio and the American Imagination*. New York: Times Books, 1999.

Downey, Gregory J. *Closed Captioning: Subtitling, Stenography, and the Digital Convergence of Text with Television*. Baltimore: Johns Hopkins University Press, 2008.

Dreisbach, Shaun. "Why Are Anxiety Disorders among Women on the Rise?" *NBC News*, October 15, 2010. www.nbcnews.com.

Duan, Huabo, T. Reed Miller, Jeremy Gregory, and Randolph Kirchain. *Quantitative Characterization of Domestic and Transboundary Flows of Used Electronics: Analysis of Generation, Collection, and Export in the United States*. Material Systems Laboratory, Massachusetts Institute of Technology. 2013. www.step-initiative.org.

Dubriwny, Tasha N. "Television News Coverage of Postpartum Disorders and the Politics of Medicalization." *Feminist Media Studies* 10, no. 3 (September 1, 2010): 285–303.

du Gay, Paul, Stuart Hall, Linda Janes, Hugh Mackay, and Keith Negus. *Doing Cultural Studies: The Story of the Sony Walkman*. Thousand Oaks, CA: Sage, 1997.

Duggan, Lisa. "The New Homonormativity: The Sexual Politics of Neoliberalism." In *Materializing Democracy: Toward a Revitalized Cultural Politics*, edited by Russ Castronovo and Dana D. Nelson, 175–94. Durham, NC: Duke University Press, 2002.

Dunbar-Hester, Christina. *Low Power to the People: Pirates, Protest, and Politics in FM Radio Activism*. Cambridge, MA: MIT Press, 2014.

Durbach, Nadja. *Spectacle of Deformity: Freak Shows and Modern British Culture*. Berkeley: University of California Press, 2009.

Dworzynski, Katharina, Angelica Ronald, Patrick Bolton, and Francesca Happé. "How Different Are Girls and Boys above and below the Diagnostic Threshold for Autism

Spectrum Disorders?" *Journal of the American Academy of Child and Adolescent Psychiatry* 51, no. 8 (August 2012): 788–97.

Dyer, Richard. *Heavenly Bodies: Film Stars and Society*, 2nd ed. New York: Routledge, 2004.

———. *The Matter of Images: Essays on Representation*. London: Routledge, 2002.

———. *Stars*. London: British Film Institute, 1998.

Eagleton, Terry. *The Meaning of Life: A Very Short Introduction*. Oxford: Oxford University Press, 2007.

Edelman, Lee. *No Future: Queer Theory and the Death Drive*. Durham, NC: Duke University Press, 2004.

Edwards, S. D. "Should Oscar Pistorius Be Excluded from the 2008 Olympic Games?" *Sport, Ethics and Philosophy* 2, no. 2 (August 1, 2008): 112–25.

Ellcessor, Elizabeth. "Bridging Disability Divides." *Information, Communication & Society* 13, no. 3 (April 2010): 289–308.

———. "Captions On, Off, on TV, Online: Accessibility and Search Engine Optimization in Online Closed Captioning." *Television & New Media* 13, no. 4 (2012): 329–52.

———. "Constructing Social Media's Indie Auteurs: Management of the Celebrity Self in the Case of Felicia Day." In *Making Media Work: Cultures of Management in the Entertainment Industries*, edited by Derek Johnson, Derek Kompare, and Avi Santo, 188–209. New York: New York University Press, 2014.

———. *Restricted Access: Media, Disability, and the Politics of Participation*. New York: New York University Press, 2016.

———. "Tweeting @feliciaday: Online Social Media, Convergence and Subcultural Stardom of Felicia Day." *Cinema Journal* 51, no. 2 (Winter 2012): 46–66.

Ellcessor, Elizabeth, and Sean C. Duncan. "Forming The Guild: Star Power and Rethinking Projective Identity in Affinity Spaces." *International Journal of Game-Based Learning* 1, no. 2 (2011): 82–95.

Elliott, Deni. "Disability and the Media: The Ethics of the Matter." In *The Disabled, the Media, and the Information Age*, edited by Jack Adolph Nelson, 73–80. Greenwood Publishing Group, 1994.

Ellis, Katie. "Cripples, Bastards and Broken Things: Disability in *Game of Thrones*." *M/C Journal* 17, no. 5 (October 25, 2014). www.journal.mediaculture.org.au.

———. "The Voice Australia (2012): Disability, Social Media and Collective Intelligence." *Continuum* 28, no. 4 (July 4, 2014): 482–94.

Ellis, Katie, and Gerard Goggin. *Disability and the Media*. Basingstoke, UK: Palgrave Macmillan, 2015.

Ellis, Katie, and Mike Kent. *Disability and New Media*. New York: Routledge, 2010.

Ellison, Ralph. *Shadow and Act*. New York: Vintage, 1995.

Elman, Amy R. "Mainstreaming Immobility: Disability Pornography and Its Challenge to Two Movements." In *Sourcebook on Violence against Women*, edited by Claire M. Renzetti, Jeffrey L. Edleson, and Raquel K. Bergen, 193–207. Thousand Oaks, CA: Sage, 2001.

Engelberg, Miriam. *Cancer Made Me a Shallower Person: A Memoir in Comics*. New York: Harper Perennial, 2006.

Estrada-Ayub, Jesús A., and Ramzy Kahhat. "Decision Factors for E-Waste in Northern Mexico: To Waste or Trade." *Resources, Conservation and Recycling* 86 (2014): 93–106.

Ewen, Elizabeth, and Stuart Ewen. *Typecasting: On the Arts and Sciences of Human Inequality.* New York: Seven Stories Press, 2009.

Fawaz, Ramzi. "'Where No X-Man Has Gone Before!' Mutant Superheroes and the Cultural Politics of Popular Fantasy in Postwar America." *American Literature* 83, no. 2 (June 1, 2011): 355–88.

Ferri, Beth A., and Jessica Bacon. "Beyond Inclusion: Disability Studies in Early Childhood Teacher Education." In *Promoting Social Justice for Young Children*, edited by Beatrice S. Fennimore and A. Lin Goodwin, 137–46. New York: Springer, 2011.

Ferus-Comelo, Anibel. "Mission Impossible?: Raising Labor Standards in the ICT Sector." *Labor Studies Journal* 33, no. 2 (2008): 141–62.

Fies, Brian. *Mom's Cancer.* New York: Abrams ComicArts, 2011.

Fish, Stanley Eugene. *Is There a Text in This Class?* Cambridge, MA: Harvard University Press, 1980.

Fiske, John. *Understanding Popular Culture.* Boston: Unwin Hyman, 1989.

Foley, Douglas E. *The Heartland Chronicles.* Philadelphia: University of Pennsylvania Press, 1995.

Forman, Murray. "'Represent': Race, Space and Place in Rap Music." *Popular Music* 19, no. 1 (2000): 65–90.

Foss, Chris, Jonathan W. Gray, and Zach Whalen, eds. *Disability in Comic Books and Graphic Narratives.* New York: Palgrave Macmillan, 2016.

Foucault, Michel. *Abnormal: Lectures at the Collège de France, 1974–1975*, edited by Valerio Marchetti and Antonella Salomoni. Translated by Graham Burchell. New York: Picador, 2003.

———. *The Birth of the Clinic: An Archaeology of Medical Perception.* Translated by Alan Sheridan. New York: Vintage, 1994.

———. *The History of Sexuality, Volume 1: An Introduction.* Translated by Robert Hurley. New York: Vintage, 1978.

———. *Psychiatric Power: Lectures at the Collège de France, 1973–74*, edited by Jacques Lagrange. Translated by Graham Burchell. Basingstoke, UK: Palgrave Macmillan, 2006.

———. *Technologies of the Self: A Seminar with Michel Foucault*, edited by Luther H. Martin, Huck Gutman, and Patrick H. Hutton. Amherst: University of Massachusetts Press, 1988.

Fouché, Rayvon. "Say It Loud, I'm Black and I'm Proud: African Americans, American Artifactual Culture, and Black Vernacular Technological Creativity." *American Quarterly* 58, no. 3 (September 1, 2006): 639–61.

Friedner, Michele. *Valuing Deaf Worlds in Urban India.* New Brunswick, NJ: Rutgers University Press, 2015.

Fuqua, Joy V. *Prescription TV: Therapeutic Discourse in the Hospital and at Home.* Durham, NC: Duke University Press, 2012.

Galbraith, Robert. *Career of Evil*. London: Sphere, 2016.

García, Connie, and Amelia Simpson. "Community-Based Organizing for Labor Rights, Health, and the Environment." In *Challenging the Chip: Labor Rights and Environmental Justice in the Global Electronics Industry*, edited by Ted Smith, David A. Sonnenfeld, and David Naguib Pellow, 150–60. Philadelphia: Temple University Press, 2006.

Garland-Thomson, Rosemarie. "Disability and Representation." *PMLA* 120, no. 2 (March 2005): 522–27.

———. *Extraordinary Bodies: Figuring Physical Disability in American Culture and Literature*. New York: Columbia University Press, 1997.

———. "Feminist Disability Studies." *Signs: Journal of Women in Culture & Society* 30, no. 2 (2005): 1557–87.

———. "Introduction: From Wonder to Error—A Genology of Freak Discourse in Modernity." In *Freakery: Cultural Spectacles of the Extraordinary Body*, edited by Rosemarie Garland-Thomson, 1–19. New York: New York University Press, 1996.

———. "Seeing the Disabled: Visual Rhetorics of Disability in Popular Photography." In *The New Disability History: American Perspectives*, edited by Paul K. Longmore and Lauri Umansky, 355–74. New York: New York University Press, 2001.

———. *Staring: How We Look*. Oxford and New York: Oxford University Press, 2009.

Gates, Henry Louis, Jr. *The Signifying Monkey: A Theory of African-American Literary Criticism*. New York: Oxford University Press, 1988.

Geers, Jeff. "'The Great Machine Doesn't Wear a Cape!': American Cultural Anxiety and the Post-9/11 Superhero." In *Comic Books and American Cultural History: An Anthology*, edited by Matthew Pustz, 250–62. New York: Bloomsbury Academic, 2012.

Gerber, David A. "The 'Careers' of People Exhibited in Freak Shows: The Problem of Volition and Valorization." In *Freakery: Cultural Spectacles of the Extraordinary Body*, edited by Rosemarie Garland-Thomson, 38–54. New York: New York University Press, 1996.

———. "Heroes and Misfits: The Troubled Social Reintegration of Disabled Veterans in 'The Best Years of Our Lives.'" In *Disabled Veterans in History*, enlarged and rev. ed., edited by David A. Gerber, 70–95. Ann Arbor: University of Michigan Press, 2012.

———. "Introduction: Finding Disabled Veterans in History." In *Disabled Veterans in History*, enlarged and rev. ed., edited by David A. Gerber, 1–51. Ann Arbor: University of Michigan Press, 2012.

Gerber, Elizabeth M., Michael Muller, Rick Wash, Lilly C. Irani, Amanda Williams, and Elizabeth F. Churchill. "Crowdfunding: An Emerging Field of Research." In *Proceedings of the Extended Abstracts of the 32nd Annual ACM Conference on Human Factors in Computing Systems*, 1093–98. New York: ACM, 2014.

Ghosh, Bishnupriya. *Global Icons: Apertures to the Popular*. Durham, NC: Duke University Press Books, 2011.

Gill, Rosalind. "'Life Is a Pitch': Managing the Self in New Media Work." In *Managing Media Work*, edited by Mark Deuze, 249–62. Thousand Oaks, CA: Sage, 2010.

Gillespie, Tarleton. "The Relevance of Algorithms." In *Media Technologies: Essays on Communication, Materiality, and Society*, edited by Tarleton Gillespie, Pablo J. Boczkowski, and Kirsten A. Foot, 167–94. Cambridge, MA: MIT Press, 2014.

Gillespie, Tarleton, Pablo J. Boczkowski, and Kirsten A. Foot, eds. *Media Technologies: Essays on Communication, Materiality, and Society*. Cambridge, MA: MIT Press, 2014.

Gilligan, Carol. "In a Different Voice: Women's Conceptualizations of Self and Morality." *Harvard Educational Review* 47 (1977): 481–517.

Gilman, Sander L. *Difference and Pathology: Stereotypes of Sexuality, Race, and Madness*. Ithaca, NY: Cornell University Press, 1985.

Gitlin, Todd. *Inside Prime Time*. New York: Pantheon, 1983.

Glassner, Barry. *The Culture of Fear: Why Americans Are Afraid of the Wrong Things*. New York: Basic Books, 2000.

Gledhill, Christine, ed. *Stardom: Industry of Desire*. London: Routledge, 1991.

Goffman, Erving. *Stigma: Notes on the Management of Spoiled Identity*. Englewood Cliffs, NJ: Prentice-Hall, 1963.

Goggin, Gerard. *Cell Phone Culture: Mobile Technology in Everyday Life*. London: Routledge, 2006.

Goggin, Gerard, and Mark McLelland, eds. *Internationalizing Internet Studies: Beyond Anglophone Paradigms*. New York: Routledge, 2008.

Goggin, Gerard, and Christopher Newell. *Digital Disability: The Social Construction of Disability in New Media*. Critical Media Studies. Lanham, MD: Rowman & Littlefield, 2003.

———. "Foucault on the Phone: Disability and the Mobility of Government." In *Foucault and the Government of Disability*, edited by Shelley Tremain, 261–77. Ann Arbor: University of Michigan Press, 2005.

Goodley, Dan. *Disability Studies: An Interdisciplinary Introduction*. Thousand Oaks, CA: Sage, 2010.

Gordon, Avery F. *Ghostly Matters: Haunting and the Sociological Imagination*, 2nd ed. Minneapolis: University of Minnesota Press, 2008.

Gray, Herman. *Watching Race: Television and the Struggle for "Blackness."* Minneapolis: University of Minnesota Press, 1995.

Gray, Jonathan, Cornel Sandvoss, and C. Lee Harrington, eds. *Fandom: Identities and Communities in a Mediated World*. New York: New York University Press, 2007.

Gray, Mary L. *Out in the Country: Youth, Media, and Queer Visibility in Rural America*. New York: New York University Press, 2009.

Grech, Shaun, and Karen Soldatic, eds. *Disability in the Global South: The Critical Handbook*. New York: Springer, 2015.

Gross, Larry. *Up from Invisibility: Lesbians, Gay Men, and the Media in America*. New York: Columbia University Press, 2001.

Grossberg, Lawrence. *Cultural Studies in the Future Tense*. Durham, NC: Duke University Press, 2010.

Gumpert, Gary, and Robert Cathcart. "A Theory of Mediation." In *Mediation, Information, and Communication*, edited by Brent David Ruben and Leah A. Lievrouw, 21–36. New Brunswick, NJ: Transaction Publishers, 1990.

Hacking, Ian. "Kinds of People: Moving Targets." *Proceedings of the British Academy* 151 (2007): 285–318.

Halberstam, J. Jack. *Gaga Feminism: Sex, Gender, and the End of Normal*. Boston: Beacon Press, 2012.

———. *In a Queer Time and Place: Transgender Bodies, Subcultural Lives*. New York: New York University Press, 2005.

Hall, Stuart. "Cultural Studies: Two Paradigms." *Media, Culture & Society* 2 (1980): 57–72.

———. "Encoding/Decoding." In *Critical Visions in Film Theory*, edited by Timothy Corrigan, Patricia White, and Meta Mazaj, 77–87. Boston: Bedford-St. Martins, 2011.

———. "For Allon White: Metaphors of Transformation." In *Stuart Hall: Critical Dialogues in Cultural Studies*, edited by David Morley and Kuan-Hsing Chen, 286–305. London: Routledge, 1996.

Haller, Beth. *Representing Disability in an Ableist World: Essays on Mass Media*. Louisville, KY: Avocado Press, 2010.

Haller, Beth A., and Sue Ralph. "Are Disability Images in Advertising Becoming Bold and Daring? An Analysis of Prominent Themes in US and UK Campaigns." *Disability Studies Quarterly* 26, no. 3 (June 15, 2006). http://dsq-sds.org.

Havens, Timothy, Amanda D. Lotz, and Serra Tinic. "Critical Media Industry Studies: A Research Approach." *Communication, Culture & Critique* 2, no. 2 (2009): 234–53.

Häyry, Matti. "Neuroethical Theories." *Cambridge Quarterly of Healthcare Ethics* 19, no. 2 (April 2010): 165–78. doi:10.1017/S0963180109990430.

Hendricks, Ann M., and Jomana H. Amara. "Current Veteran Demographics and Implications for Veterans' Health Care." In *Returning Wars' Wounded, Injured, and Ill: A Reference Handbook*, edited by Nathan D. Ainspan and Walter E. Penk, 13–29. Westport, CT: Praeger, 2008.

Herring, Scott. *Another Country: Queer Anti-Urbanism*. New York: New York University Press, 2010.

Hevey, David. "The Enfreakment of Photography." In *The Disability Studies Reader*, 3rd ed., edited by Lennard J. Davis, 507–21. New York: Routledge, 2010.

Higgins, Paul C., and Jeffrey E. Nash, eds. *Understanding Deafness Socially: Continuities in Research and Theory*. Springfield, IL: Charles C Thomas Publisher, 1987.

Hills, Matt. *Fan Cultures*. London: Routledge, 2002.

Hilmes, Michele. *Radio Voices: American Broadcasting, 1922–1952*. Minneapolis: University of Minnesota Press, 1997.

Hinck, Ashley. "Theorizing a Public Engagement Keystone: Seeing Fandom's Integral Connection to Civic Engagement through the Case of the Harry Potter Alliance." *Transformative Works and Cultures* 10 (2012). http://journal.transformativeworks. org.

Hladki, Janice. "'Nothing Big. Nothing Small': Allyson Mitchell's Video Autobiography." *ARIEL: A Review of International English Literature* 39, nos. 1–2 (January 1, 2008).

Hoffmeister, Robert. "Border Crossings by Hearing Children of Deaf Parents: The Lost History of Codas." In *Open Your Eyes: Deaf Studies Talking*, edited by H-Dirksen L. Bauman, 189–215. Minneapolis: University of Minnesota Press, 2008.

Holt, Jennifer, and Alisa Perren. *Media Industries: History, Theory, and Method*. Malden, MA: Wiley-Blackwell, 2009.

Hoornweg, Daniel, and Perinaz Bhada-Tata. *What a Waste: Global Review of Solid Waste Management*. Washington, DC: World Bank, 2012.

Hott, Lawrence R. "Creating the History through Deaf Eyes Documentary." *Sign Language Studies* 7, no. 2 (2007): 135–40.

Hui, Julie S., Michael D. Greenberg, and Elizabeth M. Gerber. "Understanding the Role of Community in Crowdfunding Work." In *Proceedings of the 17th ACM Conference on Computer Supported Cooperative Work & Social Computing*, 62–74. New York: ACM, 2014.

Hutchins, Brett, and David Rowe, eds. *Digital Media Sport: Technology, Power and Culture in the Network Society*. New York: Routledge, 2013.

———. *Sport beyond Television: The Internet, Digital Media and the Rise of Networked Media Sport*. New York: Routledge, 2012.

Hyde-Clarke, Nathalie, ed. *The Citizen in Communication: Re-Visiting Traditional, New and Community Media Practices in South Africa*. Claremont, S. Africa: Juta Legal and Academic Publishers, 2010.

Ihlebæk, K. A., and A. H. Krumsvik. "Editorial Power and Public Participation in Online Newspapers." *Journalism* 16, no. 4 (2015): 470–87.

Irvine, Janice M. *Talk about Sex: The Battles over Sex Education in the United States*. Berkeley: University of California Press, 2004.

Jaarsma, Pier, and Stellan Welin. "Autism as a Natural Human Variation: Reflections on the Claims of the Neurodiversity Movement," *Health Care Analysis* 20, no. 1 (2011): 20–30.

Jacott, Marisa, Cyrus Reed, and Mark Winfield. *The Generation and Management of Hazardous Wastes and Transboundary Hazardous Waste Shipments between Mexico, Canada and the United States since NAFTA: A 2004 Update*. Austin: Texas Center for Policy Studies, 2004.

Jaeger, Paul T. *Disability and the Internet: Confronting a Digital Divide*. Boulder, CO: Lynne Rienner Publishers, 2012.

Jameson, Frederic. "The Vanishing Mediator; or, Max Weber as Storyteller" (1973). In *Ideologies of Theory*. Minneapolis: University of Minnesota Press, 1988.

Jankowski, Katherine. *Deaf Empowerment: Emergence, Struggle, and Rhetoric*. Washington, DC: Gallaudet University Press, 1997.

———. "A Metaphorical Analysis of Conflict at the Gallaudet Protest." Unpublished seminar paper. University of Maryland, 1990.

Jarvis, Simon. "For a Poetics of Verse." *PMLA* 125, no. 4 (2010): 931–35.

Jastreboff, Pawel J., and Jonathan W. P. Hazell. *Tinnitus Retraining Therapy: Implementing the Neurophysiological Model*. Cambridge, UK, and New York: Cambridge University Press, 2008.

Jeffares, Stephen. *Interpreting Hashtag Politics: Policy Ideas in an Era of Social Media.* Basingstoke, UK, and New York: Palgrave Macmillan, 2014.

Jenkins, Henry. "'Cultural Acupuncture': Fan Activism and the Harry Potter Alliance." *Transformative Works and Cultures* 10 (2012). http://journal.transformativeworks. org.

———. *Textual Poachers: Television Fans and Participatory Culture.* New York: Routledge, 1992.

Jenkins, Henry, Sam Ford, and Joshua Green. *Spreadable Media: Creating Value and Meaning in a Networked Culture.* New York: New York University Press, 2013.

Jenson, Joli. "Fandom as Pathology: The Consequences of Characterization." In *The Adoring Audience: Fan Culture and Popular Media,* edited by Lisa A. Lewis, 9–29. New York: Routledge, 1992.

Jespersen, Ejgil, and Mike J. McNamee, eds. *Ethics, Dis/ability and Sports.* Routledge, 2013 (reprint of 2009 1st ed.).

Johnson, Derek. *Media Franchising: Creative License and Collaboration in the Culture Industry.* New York: New York University Press, 2013.

Johnson, Jeffrey K. *Super-History: Comic Book Superheroes and American Society, 1938 to the Present.* Jefferson, NC: McFarland, 2012.

Johnson, Richard. "What Is Cultural Studies Anyway?" *Social Text* 16 (December 1, 1986): 38–80.

Johnson, Victoria E. *Heartland TV: Prime Time Television and the Struggle for U.S. Identity.* New York: New York University Press, 2008.

Jones, Tiffany Fawn. *Psychiatry, Mental Institutions, and the Mad in Apartheid South Africa.* New York: Routledge, 2012.

Kafer, Alison. "Compulsory Bodies: Reflections on Heterosexuality and Able-Bodiedness." *Journal of Women's History* 15, no. 3 (Autumn 2003): 77–89.

———. *Feminist, Queer, Crip.* Bloomington: Indiana University Press, 2013.

Kalm, Sara. "Emancipation or Exploitation? A Study of Women Workers in Mexico's Maquiladora Industry." *Statsvetenskaplig Tidskrift* 104, no. 3 (2001): 225–58.

Katzman, Martin A. "Aripiprazole: A Clinical Review of Its Use for the Treatment of Anxiety Disorders and Anxiety as a Comorbidity in Mental Illness." *Journal of Affective Disorders* 128, suppl. 1 (January 2011): S11–20.

Kelley, Robin D. G. *Yo' Mama's Disfunktional!: Fighting the Culture Wars in Urban America.* Boston: Beacon Press, 1997.

Kember, Sarah, and Joanna Zylinska. *Life after New Media: Mediation as a Vital Process.* Cambridge, MA: MIT Press, 2014 (reprint of 2012 1st ed.).

Kim, Eunjung. *Curative Violence: Rehabilitating Disability, Gender, and Sexuality in Modern Korea.* Durham, NC: Duke University Press, 2017.

King, Samantha. *Pink Ribbons, Inc.: Breast Cancer and the Politics of Philanthropy.* Minneapolis: University of Minnesota Press, 2008.

Kirkpatrick, Bill. "'A Blessed Boon': Radio, Disability, Governmentality, and the Discourse of the 'Shut-In,' 1920–1930." *Critical Studies in Media Communication* 29, no. 3 (2012): 165–84.

———. "Localism in American Media Policy, 1920–1934: Reconsidering a 'Bedrock Concept.'" *Radio Journal* 4, nos. 1–3 (2006): 87–110.

Kociemba, David. "'This Isn't Something I Can Fake': Reactions to *Glee*'s Representations of Disability." *Transformative Works and Cultures* 5 (2010). http://journal. transformativeworks.org.

Kohlberg, Lawrence. "Stage and Sequence: The Cognitive Developmental Approach to Socialization." In *Handbook of Socialization Theory and Research*, edited by David Goslin, 347–80. Chicago: Rand McNally, 1969.

Kolářová, Kateřina. "The Inarticulate Post-Socialist Crip: On the Cruel Optimism of Neoliberal Transformations in the Czech Republic." *Journal of Literary & Cultural Disability Studies* 8, no. 3 (2014): 263–80.

Kudlick, Catherine J. "Disability History: Why We Need Another 'Other.'" *American Historical Review* 108, no. 3 (June 2003). www.historycooperative.org.

Kuppers, Petra. *Disability and Contemporary Performance: Bodies on Edge*. New York: Routledge, 2003.

———. *Disability Culture and Community Performance: Find a Strange and Twisted Shape*. New York: Palgrave Macmillan, 2011.

Kuppers, Petra, Neil Marcus, and Lisa Steichmann. *Cripple Poetics*. Ypsilanti, MI: Homofactus Press, 2008.

Kuusisto, Stephen. "A Roundtable on Disability Blogging." *Disability Studies Quarterly* 27, nos. 1–2 (Winter/Spring 2007). http://dsq-sds.org.

Laqueur, Thomas. *Making Sex: Body and Gender from the Greeks to Freud*. Cambridge, MA: Harvard University Press, 1992 (reprint of 1990 1st ed.).

Leaver, Tama. "Joss Whedon, *Dr. Horrible*, and the Future of Web Media." *Popular Communication* 11, no. 2 (April 2013): 160–73.

LeFrançois, Brenda A., Robert J. Menzies, and Geoffrey Reaume, eds. *Mad Matters: A Critical Reader in Canadian Mad Studies*. Toronto: Brown Bear Press, 2013.

Leigh, Irene. *A Lens on Deaf Identities*. Oxford and New York: Oxford University Press, 2009.

Lenze, E. J., B. H. Mulsant, M. K. Shear, G. S. Alexopoulos, E. Frank, and C. F. Reynolds. "Comorbidity of Depression and Anxiety Disorders in Later Life." *Depression and Anxiety* 14, no. 2 (2001): 86–93.

Lero, Donna, Carolyn Pletsch, and Margo Hilbrecht. "Introduction to the Special Issue on Disability and Work: Toward Re-Conceptualizing the 'Burden' of Disability." *Disability Studies Quarterly* 32, no. 3 (February 7, 2012). http://dsq-sds.org.

Levine, Elana. *Wallowing in Sex: The New Sexual Culture of 1970s American Television*. Durham, NC: Duke University Press, 2007.

Lewinsohn, P. M., I. H. Gotlib, M. Lewinsohn, J. R. Seeley, and N. B. Allen. "Gender Differences in Anxiety Disorders and Anxiety Symptoms in Adolescents." *Journal of Abnormal Psychology* 107, no. 1 (February 1998): 109–17.

Lewis, David A. "The Militarism of American Superheroes after 9/11." In *Comic Books and American Cultural History: An Anthology*, edited by Matthew Pustz, 223–36. London and New York: Bloomsbury Academic, 2012.

Lewis, Justin, and Toby Miller, eds. *Critical Cultural Policy Studies: A Reader*. Malden, MA: Blackwell, 2003.

Lexchin, Joel. "Bigger and Better: How Pfizer Redefined Erectile Dysfunction." *PLoS Medicine* 3, no. 4 (April 11, 2006): 429–32.

Liddiard, Kirsty. "Liking for Like's Sake: The Commodification of Disability on Facebook." *Journal of Developmental Disabilities* 20, no. 3 (2014): 94–101.

Lillard, Angeline S., and Jennifer Peterson. "The Immediate Impact of Different Types of Television on Young Children's Executive Function." *Pediatrics* 128, no. 4 (2011): 644–49.

Linton, Simi. *Claiming Disability: Knowledge and Identity*. New York: New York University Press, 1998.

Lipari, Lisbeth. "Listening Otherwise: The Voice of Ethics." *International Journal of Listening* 23, no. 1 (2009): 44–59.

Lisi, Deborah. "Found Voices: Women, Disability and Cultural Transformation." *Women & Therapy* 14, nos. 3–4 (February 17, 1994): 195–209.

Longmore, Paul K. "Conspicuous Contribution and American Dilemmas: Telethon Rituals of Cleansing and Renewal." In *The Body and Physical Difference: Discourses of Disability*, edited by David T. Mitchell and Sharon L. Snyder, 134–58. Ann Arbor: University of Michigan Press, 1997.

———. "'Heaven's Special Child': The Making of Poster Children." In *The Disability Studies Reader*, 4th ed., edited by Lennard J. Davis, 34–41. New York: Routledge, 2013.

Longmore, Paul K., and David Goldberger. "The League of the Physically Handicapped and the Great Depression: A Case Study in the New Disability History." *Journal of American History* 87, no. 3 (December 2000): 888–922.

Lorde, Audre. *The Cancer Journals*. Argyle, NY: Spinsters Ink, 1980.

Love, Heather. "Queer ____ This." In *After Sex?: On Writing Since Queer Theory*, edited by Janet Halley and Andrew Parker, 180–91. Durham, NC: Duke University Press, 2011.

Lowe, Lisa. *Immigrant Acts: On Asian American Cultural Politics*. Durham, NC: Duke University Press, 1996.

Luker, Kristin. *When Sex Goes to School: Warring Views on Sex—and Sex Education—Since the Sixties*. New York: W. W. Norton, 2006.

Lupton, Deborah. *The Imperative of Health: Public Health and the Regulated Body*. Thousand Oaks, CA: Sage, 1995.

Lush, Rebecca M. "The Appropriation of the Madonna Aesthetic." In *The Performance Identities of Lady Gaga: Critical Essays*, edited by Richard J. Gray II, 173–87. Jefferson, NC: McFarland, 2012.

Lutz, Tom. *American Nervousness, 1903: An Anecdotal History*. Ithaca, NY: Cornell University Press, 1991.

Lynch, Dennis A. "Rhetorics of Proximity: Empathy in Temple Grandin and Cornel West." *Rhetoric Society Quarterly* 28, no. 1 (Winter 1998): 5–23.

Mackenzie, Sir Morell. *The Hygiene of the Vocal Organs: A Practical Handbook for Singers and Speakers*, 2nd ed. New York: MacMillan and Co., 1886.

Magee, Michael. *Emancipating Pragmatism: Emerson, Jazz, and Experimental Writing*. Tuscaloosa: University of Alabama Press, 2004.

Mahler, Margaret, Fred Pine, and Anni Bergman. *The Psychological Birth of the Human Infant: Symbiosis and Individuation*. New York: Basic Books, 1975.

Maines, Rachel P. *The Technology of Orgasm: "Hysteria," the Vibrator, and Women's Sexual Satisfaction*. Baltimore: Johns Hopkins University Press, 2001.

Mairs, Nancy. "Sex and Death and the Crippled Body: A Meditation." In *Disability Studies: Enabling the Humanities*, edited by Sharon L Snyder, Brenda Jo Brueggemann, and Rosemarie Garland-Thomson, 156–70. New York: Modern Language Association of America, 2002.

Marchetto, Marisa Acocella. *Cancer Vixen: A True Story*. New York: Pantheon, 2009 (reprint of 2006 1st ed.).

Marello, Marta, and Ann Helwege. *Solid Waste Management and Social Inclusion of Waste Pickers: Opportunities and Challenges*. Global Economic Governance Initiative Paper 7. 2014. www.bu.edu.

Marino, Olinca, and Enrique Rosas. *ICTs and Environmental Sustainability: Mapping National Policy Contexts—Mexico Baseline Study*. Association for Progressive Communications and LaNeta. 2012. www.apc.org.

Martin, Emily. *Flexible Bodies: The Role of Immunity in American Culture from the Days of Polio to the Age of AIDS*. New York: Beacon Press, 1995.

Marwick, Alice Emily. *Status Update: Celebrity, Publicity, and Branding in the Social Media Age*. New Haven, CT: Yale University Press, 2013.

Mauldin, Laura. "Precarious Plasticity: Neuropolitics, Cochlear Implants, and the Redefinition of Deafness." *Science, Technology, & Human Values* 39, no. 1 (January 1, 2014): 130–53.

Mauss, Marcel. *Sociology and Psychology: Essays*. Translated by Ben Brewster. Boston and Toronto: Routledge and Kegan Paul, 1979.

Mavhungu, Johanna, and Hayes Mawindi Mabweazara. "The South African Mainstream Press in the Online Environment: Successes, Opportunities, and Challenges." In *Online Journalism in Africa: Trends, Practices and Emerging Cultures*, edited by Hayes Mawindi Mabweazara, Okoth Fred Mudhai, and Jason Whittaker, 34–48. New York: Routledge, 2013.

Maxwell, Richard, and Toby Miller. *Greening the Media*. Oxford: Oxford University Press, 2012.

McCaffery, Steve. *Prior to Meaning: The Protosemantic and Poetics*. Evanston, IL: Northwestern University Press, 2001.

McDougall, Kathleen. "'Ag Shame' and Superheroes: Stereotype and the Signification of Disability." In *Disability and Social Change: A South African Agenda*, edited by Brian Watermeyer, 387–400. Cape Town: HSRC Press, 2006.

McGavin, Laura. "'Why Should Our Bodies End at the Skin?': Cancer Pathography, Comics, and Embodiment." In *Embodied Politics in Visual Autobiography*, edited by Sarah Brophy and Janice Hladki, 189–208. Toronto: University of Toronto Press, 2014.

McRobbie, Angela. *The Aftermath of Feminism: Gender, Culture and Social Change*. Los Angeles and London: Sage, 2009.

McRuer, Robert. "Compulsory Able-Bodiedness and Queer/Disabled Existence." In *The Disability Studies Reader*, 2nd ed., edited by Lennard J. Davis, 88–99. New York: Routledge, 2006.

———. *Crip Theory: Cultural Signs of Queerness and Disability*. New York: New York University Press, 2006.

Medina, Martin. *The World's Scavengers: Salvaging for Sustainable Consumption and Production*. Lanham, MD: AltaMira, 2007.

Medovoi, Leerom. *Rebels: Youth and the Cold War Origins of Identity*. Durham, NC: Duke University Press, 2005.

Mendoza, Jorge Eduardo. "The Effect of the Chinese Economy on Mexican Maquiladora Employment." *International Trade Journal* 24, no. 1 (2010): 52–83.

Meynen, Gerben, and Guy Widdershoven. "Emotionality and Competence: Changing Emotions versus Dealing with Emotions." *AJOB Neuroscience* 2, no. 3 (2011): 64–66.

Miller, Toby. *Cultural Citizenship: Cosmopolitanism, Consumerism, and Television in a Neoliberal Age*. Philadelphia: Temple University Press, 2007.

———. "Media Effects and Cultural Studies: A Contentious Relationship." In *The Sage Handbook of Media Processes and Effects*, edited by Robin L. Nabi and Mary Beth Oliver, 131–43. Thousand Oaks, CA: Sage, 2009.

———, ed. *The Routledge Companion to Global Popular Culture*. New York: Routledge, 2014.

———. *Technologies of Truth: Cultural Citizenship and the Popular Media*. Minneapolis: University of Minnesota Press, 1998.

Mills, Mara. "Deafening: Noise and the Engineering of Communication in the Telephone System." *Grey Room* 43 (2011): 118–43.

———. *On the Phone: Deafness and Communication Engineering*. Durham, NC: Duke University Press, forthcoming.

Missika, Jean-Louis. *La fin de la télévision*. Paris: Seuil, 2006.

Mitchell, David T., and Sharon L. Snyder. *The Biopolitics of Disability: Neoliberalism, Ablenationalism, and Peripheral Embodiment*. Ann Arbor: University of Michigan Press, 2015.

———. *Narrative Prosthesis: Disability and the Dependencies of Discourse*. Ann Arbor: University of Michigan Press, 2001.

———. "Representation and Its Discontents: The Uneasy Home of Disability in Literature and Film." In *Handbook of Disability Studies*, edited by Gary L. Albrecht, Katherine Delores Seelman, and Michael Bury, 195–218. Thousand Oaks, CA: Sage, 2001.

Mogk, Marja Evelyn. *Different Bodies: Essays on Disability in Film and Television*. Jefferson, NC: McFarland, 2013.

Mol, Annemarie. "Ontological Politics. A Word and Some Questions." In *Actor Network Theory and After*, edited by John Law and John Hassard, 74–89. Oxford: Blackwell, 1999.

Moran, Jeffrey P. *Teaching Sex: The Shaping of Adolescence in the 20th Century.* Boston: Harvard University Press, 2002.

Morley, David. *Family Television: Cultural Power and Domestic Leisure.* London: Routledge, 1986.

Moser, Ingunn. "Disability and the Promises of Technology: Technology, Subjectivity and Embodiment within an Order of the Normal." *Information, Communication & Society* 9, no. 3 (2006): 373–95.

Moser, Ingunn, and John Law. "'Making Voices': New Media Technologies, Disabilities, and Articulation." In *Digital Media Revisited*, edited by Gunnar Liestøl, Andrew Morrison, and Terje Rasmussen, 491–520. Cambridge, MA: MIT Press, 2003.

Moten, Fred. "Rock the Party, Fuck the Smackdown." In *Hughson's Tavern*, 23. Providence, RI: Leon Works, 2007.

Mukherjee, Sanjukta (with Central Department for Development Studies, Tribhuvan University). *Child Ragpickers in Nepal: A Report on the 2002–2003 Baseline Survey.* Bangkok: International Labor Organization, 2003.

Mulvey, Laura. "Visual Pleasure and Narrative Cinema." *Screen* 16, no. 3 (September 21, 1975): 6–18.

Mumme, Stephen P., and Kimberly Collins. "The La Paz Agreement 30 Years On." *Journal of Environment & Development* 23, no. 3 (2014): 303–30.

Muñoz, José Esteban. *Cruising Utopia: The Then and There of Queer Futurity.* New York: New York University Press, 2009.

Murphy, Kevin P., Jason Ruiz, and David Serlin, eds. "Editors' Introduction." *Radical History Review* 100 (2008): 1–9.

Murray, Stuart. *Representing Autism: Culture, Narrative, Fascination.* Liverpool: Liverpool University Press, 2008.

Murray, Susan. "I Know What You Did Last Summer: Sarah Michelle Gellar and Crossover Teen Stardom." In *Undead TV: Essays on Buffy the Vampire Slayer*, edited by Elana Levine and Lisa Parks, 42–55. Durham, NC: Duke University Press, 2007.

Nash, Ilana. "Hysterical Scream or Rebel Yell? The Politics of Teen-Idol Fandom." In *Disco Divas: Women and Popular Culture in the 1970s*, edited by Sherrie A. Inness, 133–50. Philadelphia: University of Pennsylvania Press, 2003.

Norden, Martin F. *The Cinema of Isolation: A History of Physical Disability in the Movies.* New Brunswick, NJ: Rutgers University Press, 1994.

Nordenstreng, Kaarle, and Daya Thussu, eds. *Mapping BRICS Media.* London and New York: Routledge, 2015.

Norman, Moss E., and Fiona Moola. "'Bladerunner or Boundary Runner'?: Oscar Pistorius, Cyborg Transgressions and Strategies of Containment." *Sport in Society* 14, no. 9 (2011): 1265–79.

O'Brien, Sharon. *The Family Silver: A Memoir of Depression and Inheritance.* Chicago: University of Chicago Press, 2004.

O'Connor, Erin. *Raw Material: Producing Pathology in Victorian Culture.* Durham, NC: Duke University Press, 2000.

Omi, Michael, and Howard Winant. *Racial Formation in the United States: From the 1960s to the 1990s*, 2nd ed. New York: Routledge, 1994.

Ormel, Johan, Tineke Oldehinkel, Els Brilman, and Wim van den Brink. "Outcome of Depression and Anxiety in Primary Care: A Three-Wave 3 1/2-Year Study of Psychopathology and Disability." *Archives of General Psychiatry* 50, no. 10 (1993): 759–66.

Osucha, Eden. "Exceptional Subjects: Disability, Biopower, Law." Paper presented at the Seventh Annual Cultural Studies Association, Kansas City, MO, April 2009.

O'Toole, Corbett Joan. "Disclosing Our Relationships to Disabilities: An Invitation for Disability Studies Scholars." *Disability Studies Quarterly* 33, no. 2 (2013). http://dsq-sds.org.

Ott, Katherine. "The Sum of Its Parts: An Introduction to the Modern History of Prosthetics." In *Artificial Parts, Practical Lives: Modern Histories of Prosthetics*, edited by Katherine Ott, David H. Serlin, and Stephen Mihm, 1–42. New York: New York University Press, 2002.

Ott, Katherine, David H. Serlin, and Stephen Mihm, eds. *Artificial Parts, Practical Lives: Modern Histories of Prosthetics*. New York: New York University Press, 2002.

Ouellette, Laurie, and James Hay. *Better Living through Reality TV: Television and Post-Welfare Citizenship*. Malden, MA: Blackwell, 2008.

Ovid. *Metamorphoses*. Translated by A. S. Kline. 2000. Ovid Collection at the University of Virginia. http://ovid.lib.virginia.edu.

Padden, Carol A., and Tom L. Humphries. *Deaf in America: Voices from a Culture*. Cambridge, MA: Harvard University Press, 1988.

———. *Inside Deaf Culture*. Cambridge, MA: Harvard University Press, 2006.

Pálsson, Gísli, and Paul Rabinow. "The Icelandic Genome Debate." *Trends in Biotechnology* 19, no. 5 (2001): 166–71.

Panchasi, Roxanne. "Reconstructions: Prosthetics and the Rehabilitation of the Male Body in World War I France." *differences* 7, no. 3 (1995): 109–40.

Patinkin, Mark. *Up and Running: The Inspiring True Story of a Boy's Struggle to Survive and Triumph*. New York: Center Street, 2005.

Patsavas, Alyson. "Recovering a Cripistemology of Pain: Leaky Bodies, Connective Tissue, and Feeling Discourse." *Journal of Literary & Cultural Disability Studies* 8, no. 2 (2014): 203–18.

Pedersen, Sarah. "What's in a Name? The Revealing Use of Noms-de-Plume in Women's Correspondence to Daily Newspapers in Edwardian Scotland." *Media History* 10, no. 3 (2004): 175–85.

Peers, Danielle. "(Dis)empowering Paralympic Histories: Absent Athletes and Disabling Discourses." *Disability & Society* 24, no. 5 (2009): 653–65.

Pekar, Harvey, and Joyce Brabner. *Our Cancer Year*. New York: Running Press, 1994.

Perez-Maldonado, Ivan N., Rogelio Costilla Salazar, César A. Ilizaliturri-Hernandez, Guillermo Espinosa-Reyes, Francisco J. Perez-Vazquez, and Juan C. Fernandez-Macias. "Assessment of the Polychlorinated Biphenyls (PCBs) Levels in Soil Samples Near an Electric Capacitor Manufacturing Industry in Morelos, Mexico."

Journal of Environmental Science and Health, Part A: Toxic/Hazardous Substances and Environmental Engineering 49, no. 11 (2014): 1244–50.

Perlman, Allison. *Public Interests: Media Advocacy and Struggles over U.S. Television.* London: Routledge, 2016.

———. "Reforming the Wasteland: Television, Reform, and Social Movements, 1950–2004." Ph.D. dissertation, University of Texas at Austin, 2007.

Pernick, Martin S. *The Black Stork: Eugenics and the Death of "Defective" Babies in American Medicine and Motion Pictures Since 1915.* New York and Oxford: Oxford University Press, 1996.

Pezzoli, Keith, Justine Kozo, Karen Ferran, Wilma Wooten, Gudelia Rangel Gomez, and Wael K. Al-Delaimy. "One Bioregion/One Health: An Integrative Narrative for Transboundary Planning along the US-Mexico Border." *Global Society* 28, no. 4 (2014): 419–40.

Pfeiffer, David. "The Philosophical Foundations of Disability Studies." *Disability Studies Quarterly* 22, no. 2 (April 15, 2002). http://dsq-sds.org.

Phillips, Marilynn J. "Damaged Goods: Oral Narratives of the Experience of Disability in American Culture." *Social Science & Medicine* 30, no. 8 (1990): 849–57.

Pick, Marcelle. "Depression, Mood and Anxiety Disorders." *Women to Women*, 2011. www.womentowomen.com.

Pistorius, Oscar. *Blade Runner: My Story.* London: Random House, 2009.

Pittion-Vouyovitch, S., M. Debouverie, F. Guillemin, N. Vandenberghe, R. Anxionnat, and H. Vespignani. "Fatigue in Multiple Sclerosis Is Related to Disability, Depression and Quality of Life." *Journal of the Neurological Sciences* 243, nos. 1–2 (April 15, 2006): 39–45.

Plantinga, Carl. "The Scene of Empathy and the Human Face on Film." In *Passionate Views: Film, Cognition, and Emotion*, edited by Carl Plantinga and Greg M. Smith, 239–56. Baltimore: John Hopkins University Press, 1999.

Pough, Gwendolyn. *Check It While I Wreck It: Black Womanhood, Hip-Hop Culture, and the Public Sphere.* Boston: Northeastern University Press, 2004.

Premalatha, M., Tabassum-Abbasi, Tasneem Abbasi, and S. A. Abbasi. "The Generation, Impact, and Management of E-Waste: State of the Art." *Critical Reviews in Environmental Science and Technology* 44, no. 14 (2014): 1577–678.

Price, Margaret. *Mad at School.* Ann Arbor: University of Michigan Press, 2010.

Puar, Jasbir. *Terrorist Assemblages: Homonationalism in Queer Times.* Durham, NC: Duke University Press, 2007.

Qian, Zhenchao. "Breaking the Last Taboo: Interracial Marriage in America." *Contexts* 4, no. 4 (November 1, 2005): 33–37.

Quinlan, Margaret, and Benjamin Bates. "Dances and Discourses of (Dis)Ability: Heather Mills's Embodiment of Disability on *Dancing with the Stars*." *Text and Performance Quarterly* 28, nos. 1–2 (January 1, 2008): 64–80.

Quinn, Kelly, and Renee M. Powers. "Revisiting the Concept of 'Sharing' for Digital Spaces: An Analysis of Reader Comments to Online News." *Information, Communication & Society* 19, no. 4 (2016): 442–60.

Rajiva, Mythili. "Trauma and the Girl." In *Becoming Girl: Collective Biography and the Production of Girlhood*, edited by Marnina Gonick and Susanne Gannon, 137–59. Toronto: Canadian Scholars' Press, 2014.

Ransom, Lillie, and Beth Haller. "Accessing New Deaf Representations on TV: A Case Study of Marlee Matlin on 'The L Word.'" National Communication Association. San Diego, CA, 2009. http://media-and-disability.blogspot.com.

Ray, Manas Ranjan, Gopeshwar Mukherjee, Sanghita Roychowdhury, and Twisha Lahiri. "Respiratory and General Health Impairments of Ragpickers in India: A Study in Delhi." *International Archives of Occupational and Environmental Health* 77, no. 8 (2004): 595–98.

Reygadas, Luis. *Ensamblando culturas: Diversidad y conflicto en la globalización de la industria*. Barcelona: Editorial Gedisa, 2002.

Rich, Adrienne Cecile. *Blood, Bread, and Poetry: Selected Prose, 1979–1985*. New York: W. W. Norton, 1994.

Riley, Charles A. *Disability and the Media: Prescriptions for Change*. Lapham, NH: UPNE, 2005.

Robertson, Lindsay A., Helena M. McAnally, and Robert J. Hancox. "Childhood and Adolescent Television Viewing and Antisocial Behavior in Early Adulthood." *Pediatrics* 131, no. 3 (2013): 439–46.

Rodan, Debbie, Katie Ellis, and Pia Lebeck. *Disability, Obesity and Ageing: Popular Media Identifications*. Farnham, UK: Ashgate, 2014.

Romagnoli, Alex S., and Gian S. Pagnucci. *Enter the Superheroes: American Values, Culture, and the Canon of Superhero Literature*. Lanham, MD: Scarecrow, 2013.

Rose, Hilary, and Steven Rose. "The Changing Face of Human Nature." *Daedalus* 138, no. 3 (2009): 7–20.

Rose, Tricia. *Black Noise: Rap Music and Black Culture in Contemporary America*. Hanover, NH: Wesleyan University Press, 1994.

———. "Black Texts/Black Contexts." In *Black Popular Culture*, edited by Gina Dent, 223–27. Seattle: Bay Press, 1992.

Rushton, Jack. *It's Good to Be Alive*. Springville, UT: Cedar Fort, 2010.

Rutherford, Susan D. "The Culture of American Deaf People." *Sign Language Studies* 59 (1988): 129–47.

RZA. *The Wu-Tang Manual*. New York: Penguin/Riverhead, 2005.

Samuels, Ellen. "Examining Millie and Christine McKoy: Where Enslavement and Enfreakment Meet." *Signs* 37, no. 1 (2011): 53–81.

———. "My Body, My Closet: Invisible Disability and the Limits of Coming-Out Discourse." *GLQ: A Journal of Lesbian and Gay Studies* 9, no. 1 (2003): 233–55.

Sandahl, Carrie. "Queering the Crip or Cripping the Queer?: Intersections of Queer and Crip Identities in Solo Autobiographical Performance." *GLQ: A Journal of Lesbian and Gay Studies* 9, no. 1 (2003): 25–56.

Sanford, Matthew. *Waking: A Memoir of Trauma and Transcendence*. Emmaus, PA: Rodale Books, 2006.

Savarese, Ralph James. *Reasonable People*, annotated ed. New York: Other Press, 2007.

Savran, David. *Taking It Like a Man: White Masculinity, Masochism, and Contemporary American Culture*. Princeton, NJ: Princeton University Press, 1998.

Scarry, Elaine. *The Body in Pain: The Making and Unmaking of the World*. New York: Oxford University Press, 1987.

Schatan, Claudia, and Liliana Castilleja. "The Maquiladora Electronics Industry on Mexico's Northern Boundary and the Environment." *International Environmental Agreements* 7, no. 2 (2007): 109–35.

Scheper-Hughes, Nancy. "The House Gun: White Writing, White Fears and Black Justice." *Anthropology Today* 30, no. 6 (December 1, 2014): 8–12.

Schuchman, John S. *Hollywood Speaks: Deafness and the Film Entertainment Industry*. Urbana: University of Illinois Press, 1988.

Schweik, Susan. *The Ugly Laws: Disability in Public*. New York: New York University Press, 2009.

Scott, Allan, Alan Davidson, and Karen Palmer. "Antidepressant Drugs in the Treatment of Anxiety Disorders." *Advances in Psychiatric Treatment* 7 (2001): 275–82.

Scott, D. Travers. "Ergonomic Diagrams, Medical Perception, and the Technological Subject." Paper presented at the International Communication Association, Singapore, June 24, 2010.

Scully, Pamela, and Clifton Crais. "Race and Erasure: Sara Baartman and Hendrik Cesars in Cape Town and London." *Journal of British Studies* 47, no. 2 (April 2008): 301–23.

Seedat, Mohamed, Ashley Van Niekerk, Rachel Jewkes, Shahnaaz Suffla, and Kopano Ratele. "Violence and Injuries in South Africa: Prioritising an Agenda for Prevention." *Lancet* 374, no. 9694 (September 2009): 1011–22.

Segal, Judy Z. "Breast Cancer Narratives as Public Rhetoric: Genre Itself and the Maintenance of Ignorance." *Linguistics and the Human Sciences* 3 (November 21, 2009): 3–23.

Sen, Amartya. *Development as Freedom*. New York: Alfred A. Knopf, 2000.

———. *The Idea of Justice*. Cambridge, MA: Harvard University Press, 2009.

Serlin, David. "Introduction: Toward a Visual Culture of Public Health: From Broadside to Youtube." In *Imagining Illness: Public Health and Visual Culture*, edited by David Serlin, xi–xxviii. Minneapolis: University of Minnesota Press, 2011.

———. *Replaceable You: Engineering the Body in Postwar America*. Chicago: University of Chicago Press, 2004.

Shakespeare, Tom. "Cultural Representation of Disabled People: Dustbins for Disavowal?" *Disability & Society* 9, no. 3 (1994): 283.

———. "The Social Model of Disability." In *The Disability Studies Reader*, 4th ed., edited by Lennard J. Davis, 214–21. New York: Routledge, 2013.

Shakespeare, Tom, Kath Gillespie-Sells, and Dominic Davies. *The Sexual Politics of Disability: Untold Desires*. London: Cassell, 1996.

Sharma, Sarah. *In the Meantime: Temporality and Cultural Politics*. Durham, NC: Duke University Press, 2014.

Sherry, Mark. "(Post)colonizing Disability." *Wagadu* 4 (2007): 10–20.

Shimizu, Celine. *The Hypersexuality of Race: Performing Asian/American Women on Screen and Scene*. Durham, NC: Duke University Press, 2007.

———. *Straitjacket Sexualities: Unbinding Asian American Manhoods in the Movies*. Stanford, CA: Stanford University Press, 2012.

Shklovsky, Viktor. "Art as Technique." In *Russian Formalist Criticism: Four Essays*, edited by Lee T. Lemon and Marion J. Reiss, 3–24. Lincoln: University of Nebraska Press, 1965.

Shohat, Ella, and Robert Stam. *Unthinking Eurocentrism: Multiculturalism and the Media*. London: Routledge, 1994.

Shome, Raka. "Post-colonial Reflections on the 'Internationalization' of Cultural Studies." In *Cultural Studies of Transnationalism*, edited by Handel Kashope Wright and Meaghan Morris, 6–31. London: Routledge, 2013 (reprint of 2012 1st ed.).

Showalter, Elaine. *The Female Malady: Women, Madness and English Culture, 1830–1980*. London: Virago Press, 1987.

Siebers, Tobin. *Disability Aesthetics*. Ann Arbor: University of Michigan Press, 2010.

———. *Disability Theory*. Ann Arbor: University of Michigan Press, 2008.

Silva, Carla Filomena, and P. David Howe. "The (In)validity of Supercrip Representation of Paralympian Athletes." *Journal of Sport & Social Issues* 36, no. 2 (May 1, 2012): 174–94.

Silva, Marcelo Cozzensa da, Anaclaudia Gastal Fassa, and David Kriebel. "Minor Psychiatric Disorders among Brazilian Ragpickers: A Cross-Sectional Study." *Environmental Health* 5, no. 17 (2006). www.ncbi.nlm.nih.gov.

Silva, Marcelo Cozzensa da, Anaclaudia Gastal Fassa, C. E. Siquiera, and David Kriebel. "World at Work: Brazilian Ragpickers." *Occupational and Environmental Medicine* 62, no. 10 (2005): 736–40.

Simpson, Amelia. "Warren County's Legacy for Mexico's Border Maquiladoras." *Golden Gate University Environmental Law Journal* 1 (2007): 153–74.

Slack, Jennifer Daryl. "The Theory and Method of Articulation in Cultural Studies." In *Stuart Hall: Critical Dialogues in Cultural Studies*, edited by David Morley and Kuan-Hsing Chen, 112–27. London and New York: Routledge, 1996.

Small, David. *Stitches: A Memoir*. New York: W. W. Norton, 2009.

Smit, Christopher R. "Body Vandalism: Lady Gaga, Disability, and Popular Culture." *Review of Disability Studies* 10, nos. 1–2 (2014): 28–39.

Smith, Lauren Reichart. "The Blade Runner: The Discourses Surrounding Oscar Pistorius in the 2012 Olympics and Paralympics." *Communication & Sport* (January 14, 2014). http://com.sagepub.com.

Smith, Ted. "Why We Are 'Challenging the Chip': The Challenges of Sustainability in Electronics." *International Review of Information Ethics* 11 (2009): 9–15.

Smitherman, Geneva. *Talkin and Testifyin: The Language of Black America*. Boston: Houghton Mifflin, 1977.

Soldatic, Karen, and Shaun Grech. "Transnationalising Disability Studies: Rights, Justice and Impairment." *Disability Studies Quarterly* 34, no. 2 (March 18, 2014). http://dsq-sds.org.

Soldatic, Karen, and Helen Meekosha, eds. *The Global Politics of Impairment and Disability: Processes and Embodiments.* New York: Routledge, 2014.

Sontag, Susan. *Illness as Metaphor.* New York: Vintage Books, 1979.

———. *Regarding the Pain of Others.* New York: Macmillan, 2003.

Spigel, Lynn. *Make Room for TV: Television and the Family Ideal in Postwar America.* Chicago: University of Chicago Press, 1992.

Squier, Susan M. "So Long as They Grow Out of It: Comics, the Discourse of Developmental Normalcy, and Disability." *Journal of Medical Humanities* 29, no. 2 (June 2008): 71–88.

Stadler, Jane. "Media and Disability." In *Disability and Social Change: A South African Agenda,* edited by Brian Watermeyer, Leslie Swartz, Theresa Lorenzo, Marguerite Schneider, and Mark Priestley, 374–86. Cape Town: Human Sciences Research Council, 2007.

Sterne, Jonathan. *The Audible Past: Cultural Origins of Sound Reproduction.* Durham, NC: Duke University Press, 2003.

———. "Bourdieu, Technique, and Technology." *Cultural Studies* 17, nos. 3–4 (2003): 367–89.

———. *MP3: The Meaning of a Format.* Durham, NC: Duke University Press, 2012.

Stiker, Henri-Jacques. *A History of Disability.* Ann Arbor: University of Michigan Press, 1999.

Stoever-Ackerman, Jennifer. "Research Project." Cornell University Society for the Humanities. Cornell University, 2012.

Stras, Laurie. "The Organ of the Soul: Voice, Damage, and Affect." In *Sounding Off: Theorizing Disability in Music,* edited by Neil Lerner and Joseph N. Straus, 173–84. New York: Routledge, 2006.

Straus, Joseph N. *Extraordinary Measures: Disability in Music.* New York: Oxford University Press, 2011.

Streeter, Thomas. *Selling the Air: A Critique of the Policy of Commercial Broadcasting in the United States.* Chicago: University of Chicago Press, 1996.

Striphas, Ted. *The Late Age of Print: Everyday Book Culture from Consumerism to Control.* New York: Columbia University Press, 2011 (reprint of 2009 1st ed.).

Stryker, Susan. "Transgender History, Homonormativity, and Disciplinarity." *Radical History Review* 100 (Winter 2008): 145–57.

Swartz, Leslie. "Oscar Pistorius and the Melancholy of Intersectionality." *Disability & Society* 28, no. 8 (2013): 1157–61.

Swartz, Leslie, and Brian Watermeyer. "Cyborg Anxiety: Oscar Pistorius and the Boundaries of What It Means to Be Human." *Disability & Society* 23 (2008): 187–90.

Switaj, Elizabeth Kate. "Lady Gaga's Bodies: Buying and Selling *The Fame Monster.*" In *The Performance Identities of Lady Gaga: Critical Essays,* edited by Richard J. Gray II, 33–51. Jefferson, NC: McFarland, 2012.

Taylor, Timothy D. "Music and the Rise of Radio in 1920s America: Technological Imperialism, Socialization, and the Transformation of Intimacy." *Historical Journal of Film, Radio & Television* 22, no. 4 (October 2002): 425–43.

Thacker, Eugene. "Biomedia." In *Critical Terms for Media Studies*, edited by W. J. T. Mitchell and Mark B. N. Hansen, 117–30. Chicago: University of Chicago Press, 2010.

Thomas, Carol. "Disability and Impairment." In *Disabling Barriers-Enabling Environments*, edited by John Swain, Sally French, Colin Barnes, and Carol Thomas, 21–27. London: Sage, 2013.

———. *Sociologies of Disability and Illness: Contested Ideas in Disability Studies and Medical Sociology*. Basingstoke, UK: Palgrave Macmillan, 2007.

Tiffany, Daniel. *Infidel Poetics: Riddles, Nightlife, Substance*. Chicago: University of Chicago Press, 2009.

Titchkosky, Tanya. *The Question of Access: Disability, Space, Meaning*. Toronto: University of Toronto Press, 2011.

Tongson, Karen. *Relocations: Queer Suburban Imaginaries*. New York: New York University Press, 2011.

Torrusio, Ann T. "The Fame Monster: The Monstrous Construction of Lady Gaga." In *The Performance Identities of Lady Gaga: Critical Essays*, edited by Richard J. Gray II, 160–71. Jefferson, NC: McFarland, 2012.

Treichler, Paula A. "AIDS, Gender, and Biomedical Discourse: Current Contests for Meaning." In *AIDS: The Burdens of History*, edited by Elizabeth Fee and Daniel M. Fox, 190–266. Berkeley: University of California Press, 1988.

Tremain, Shelley. *Foucault and the Government of Disability*. Ann Arbor: University of Michigan Press, 2005.

———. "Foucault, Governmentality, and Critical Disability Theory: An Introduction." In *Foucault and the Government of Disability*, edited by Shelley Tremain, 1–26. Ann Arbor: University of Michigan Press, 2005.

Turner, Bryan S. *The Body and Society: Explorations in Social Theory*, 3rd ed. Los Angeles: Sage, 2008.

United Nations. Convention on the Rights of Persons with Disabilities. 2006. www.un.org.

Urrea, Luis Alberto. *By the Lake of Sleeping Children: The Secret Life of the Mexican Border*. New York: Anchor, 1996.

van Dijck, José. "Medical Documentary: Conjoined Twins as a Mediated Spectacle." *Media, Culture & Society* 24, no. 4 (July 2002): 537–56.

Wailoo, Keith. *Drawing Blood: Technology and Disease Identity in Twentieth-Century America*. Baltimore: Johns Hopkins University Press, 1999.

Wasserman, Herman. *Popular Media, Democracy and Development in Africa*. New York: Routledge, 2011.

Watermeyer, Brian. "Is It Possible to Create a Politically Engaged, Contextual Psychology of Disability?" *Disability & Society*, 27, no. 2 (2012): 161–74.

Watermeyer, Brian, Leslie Swartz, Theresa Lorenzo, Marguerite Schneider, and Mark Priestley, eds. *Disability and Social Change: A South African Agenda*. Cape Town: Human Sciences Research Council, 2007.

Watson, Amanda Danielle, Heather Hillsburg, and Lori Chambers. "Identity Politics and Global Citizenship in Elite Athletics: Comparing Caster Semenya and Oscar Pistorius." *Journal of Global Citizenship & Equity Education* 4, no. 1 (October 13, 2014). http://journals.sfu.ca.

Watters, Ethan. *Crazy Like Us: The Globalization of the American Psyche*. New York: Free Press, 2011 (reprint of 2010 1st ed.).

Weeber, Joy E. "What Could I Know of Racism?" *Journal of Counseling & Development* 77, no. 1 (January 1, 1999): 20–23.

Wendell, Susan. "Toward a Feminist Theory of Disability." In *The Disability Studies Reader*, 2nd ed., edited by Lennard J. Davis, 243–56. New York: Routledge, 2006.

Weheliye, Alexander G. "'Feenin': Posthuman Voices in Contemporary Black Popular Music." *Social Text* 20, no. 2 (Summer 2002): 21–47.

Wheeler, Stephanie K. "Legacies of Colonialism: Toward a Borderland Dialogue between Indigenous and Disability Rhetorics." *Disability Studies Quarterly* 34, no. 3 (June 16, 2014). http://dsq-sds.org.

White, Patrick. "How the Blind Became Heterosexual." *GLQ: A Journal of Lesbian and Gay Studies* 9, nos. 1–2 (2003): 133–47.

Williams, Linda. *Hard Core: Power, Pleasure, and the "Frenzy of the Visible."* Berkeley: University of California Press, 1989.

Williamson, Vanessa, and Erin Mulhall. *Invisible Wounds: Psychological and Neurological Injuries Confront a New Generation of Veterans*. New York: Iraq and Afghanistan Veterans of America, 2009.

Wilson, David, Costas Velis, and Chris Cheeseman. "Role of Informal Sector Recycling in Waste Management in Developing Countries." *Habitat International* 30 (2006): 797–808.

Wolcott, Harry F. "Propriospect and the Acquisition of Culture," *Anthropology & Education Quarterly* 22, no. 3 (September 1, 1991): 251–73.

Wright, Bradford W. *Comic Book Nation: The Transformation of Youth Culture in America*. Baltimore: Johns Hopkins University Press, 2001.

Yosso, Tara, William Smith, Miguel Ceja, and Daniel Solórzano. "Critical Race Theory, Racial Microaggressions, and Campus Racial Climate for Latina/o Undergraduates." *Harvard Educational Review* 79, no. 4 (Winter 2009): 659–91.

Rachel Adams is Professor of English and Comparative Literature at Columbia University. Her work includes the memoir *Raising Henry: A Memoir of Motherhood, Disability, and Discovery* (2013), as well as *Continental Divides: Remapping the Cultures of North America* (2009) and *Sideshow U.S.A.: Freaks and the American Cultural Imagination* (2001).

Meagan Bates holds an MA in Communication, Technology, and Society from Clemson University, where she was a research assistant and co-author on a study of the health impact of BP's Deepwater Horizon incident on local communities. She currently works in marketing and PR in the area of health communication at Levick in Washington, DC.

Krystal Cleary is a Ph.D. candidate in Gender Studies at Indiana University. Her research interests include critical disability studies, feminist and queer theory, and popular culture. Her dissertation work considers how the legacy of the freak show is being restaged and revised in contemporary media texts.

Elizabeth Ellcessor is Assistant Professor in Media Studies at the University of Virginia. She is the author of *Restricted Access: Media, Disability, and the Politics of Participation* (New York University Press, 2016), and her work has been published in *Cinema Journal*, *New Media & Society*, and *Television and New Media*.

Katie Ellis is Associate Professor in the School of Media, Culture and Creative Arts at Curtin University where her work focuses on disability, digital televisions and smartphones. She has written widely on disability and the media, including *Disability and New Media* (2011, co-authored with Mike Kent), *Disability and Popular Culture: Focusing Passion, Cre-*

ating Community and Expressing Defiance (2015), and, with Gerard Goggin, *Disability and the Media* (2015). Her co-edited collection with Mike Kent *Disability and Social Media: Global Perspectives* was published in 2016.

Julie Passanante Elman is Assistant Professor of Women's and Gender Studies at the University of Missouri. She is the author of *Chronic Youth: Disability, Sexuality, and US Media Cultures of Rehabilitation* (New York University Press, 2014). Elman's work has also appeared in the *Journal of Bioethical Inquiry, Journal of Literary and Cultural Disability Studies*, and *Television & New Media*.

Gerard Goggin is the inaugural Professor of Media and Communications at the University of Sydney, where his work focuses on the social, cultural, and political aspects of digital technologies, especially the Internet and mobile phones and media. He has published 13 books, including *Disability in Australia* (2004) and *Digital Disability: The Social Construction of Disability in New Media* (2002), which he co-authored with Christopher Newell; *Disability and the Media* (2015; with Katie Ellis); and the co-edited volumes, *Routledge Companion to Disability and Media* (2018) and *Normality & Disability: Intersections Among Norms, Laws and Culture* (2018).

Mack Hagood is Robert H. and Nancy J. Blayney Professor of Comparative Media Studies at Miami University, Ohio. He does ethnographic research in digital media, sound technologies, and popular music, focusing on how people use audio media to control their spatial surroundings, social interactions, and sense of self. His work has been published in *American Quarterly, Cinema Journal*, and *Popular Communication*.

Bill Kirkpatrick is Associate Professor of Media Studies in the Communication Department at Denison University in Granville, Ohio. His work on media history and policy has appeared in *Critical Studies in Media Communication, Television & New Media, Radio Journal, Journal of the Society of American Music, Communication and Critical/Cultural Studies*, and several anthologies. He is currently completing a book on the intersections of disability and early radio.

Lori Kido Lopez is Associate Professor of Communication Arts at the University of Wisconsin–Madison. Her research examines how minority groups such as women, racial minorities, and queer communities use media in the fight for social justice. She is the author of *Asian American Media Activism: Fighting for Cultural Citizenship* (New York University Press, 2016), and her work has been published in *The International Journal of Cultural Studies* and *New Media & Society*.

Shoshana Magnet is Associate Professor in the Institute of Feminist and Gender Studies at the University of Ottawa. She is the author of *When Biometrics Fail: Gender, Race, and the Technology of Identity* (2011) and has published in *Qualitative Inquiry, New Media & Society, Communication Review*, and many other journals.

Robert McRuer is Professor of English at George Washington University. His books include *Crip Theory: Cultural Signs of Queerness and Disability* (New York University Press, 2006), *The Queer Renaissance: Contemporary American Literature and the Reinvention of Lesbian and Gay Identities* (New York University Press, 1997), and an anthology, *Sex and Disability*, co-edited with Anna Mollow (2012).

Toby Miller is Emeritus Distinguished Professor, University of California, Riverside; Sir Walter Murdoch Professor of Cultural Policy Studies, Murdoch University; Profesor Invitado, Escuela de Comunicación Social, Universidad del Norte; Professor of Journalism, Media and Cultural Studies, Cardiff University/Prifysgol Caerdydd; and Director of the Institute for Media and Creative Industries, Loughborough University London. The author and editor of over 40 books, his work has been translated into Spanish, Chinese, Portuguese, Japanese, Turkish, German, Italian, Farsi, and Swedish. His most recent volumes are *The Sage Handbook of Television Studies* (edited with Manuel Alvarado, Milly Buonanno, and Herman Gray, 2015), *The Routledge Companion to Global Popular Culture* (edited, 2015), *Greening the Media* (with Richard Maxwell, 2012), and *Blow Up the Humanities* (2012).

Mara Mills is Associate Professor of Media, Culture and Communication at New York University. Her work exploring the intersections of disability and technology has appeared in *Grey Room*, *Social Text*, the *IEEE Annals of the History of Computing*, and many other journals. Her first book, *On the Phone: Deafness and Communication Engineering*, is forthcoming from Duke University Press. She is currently working on a history of "reading formats" beyond print, such as audiobooks and text-to-braille reading machines.

Tasha Oren is Associate Professor of English and Media Studies and teaches in the Media, Cinema, and Digital Studies Program at the University of Wisconsin—Milwaukee. She is the author of *Demon in the Box: Jews, Arabs, Politics, and Culture* (Rutgers University Press, 2004) and co-editor of *Global Currents: Media and Technology Now* (Rutgers University Press 2004), *East Main Street: Asian American Popular Culture* (New York University Press, 2005), *Global Formats: Understanding Television Across Borders* (Routledge, 2012), and *Global Asian American Popular Culture* (New York University Press, 2016). She is completing a book on food culture and media, *FoodTV* (Routledge, forthcoming) and, with Andrea Press, editing the forthcoming *Routledge Handbook of Contemporary Feminism*.

Alex S. Porco is Assistant Professor of English at the University of North Carolina Wilmington. His research and teaching focus on hip-hop music and culture, twentieth-century poetry and poetics, and the history of the avant-garde. He is the editor of the critical edition of Jerrold Levy and Richard Negro's *Poems by Gerard Legro* (Toronto: BookThug, 2016).

Ellen Samuels is Associate Professor in English and Gender and Women's Studies at the University of Wisconsin–Madison. Her research interests include American literature, cultural studies, body theory, and feminist/queer theory. Her book, *Fantasies of Identification: Disability, Gender, Race*, was published by New York University Press in 2014.

D. Travers Scott is Associate Professor of Communication at Clemson University. His work on cultural studies of technology, sexuality, and gender has appeared in publications such as *American Quarterly, Journal of Communication Inquiry, Feminist Media Studies*, and *Communication and Critical/Cultural Studies*. Dealing with similar themes, his popular writing includes two novels, a story collection, and numerous articles and essays over the past 25 years.

Jonathan Sterne is Professor and James McGill Chair in Culture and Technology at McGill University. His books include *MP3: The Meaning of a Format* (2012) and *The Audible Past: Cultural Origins of Sound Reproduction* (2003). Beyond the work on sound and music, he has published over fifty articles and book chapters that cover a wide range of topics in media history, new media, cultural theory, and disability studies. Visit his website at http://sterneworks.org.

Amanda Watson is currently Lecturer in Sociology at Simon Fraser University, Vancouver. She writes regularly for the *Ottawa Citizen* and other publications. Her dissertation was on the history of breastfeeding promotion in Canada.

INDEX